A SHORT HISTORY OF MODERN ARABIC LITERATURE

A Short History of Modern Arabic Literature

M. M. BADAWI

CLARENDON PRESS · OXFORD
1993

Oxford University Press, Walton Street, Oxford OX2 6DP
Oxford New York Toronto
Delhi Bombay Calcutta Madras Karachi
Petaling Jaya Singapore Hong Kong Tokyo
Nairobi Dar es Salaam Cape Town
Melbourne Auckland
and associated companies in
Berlin Ibadan

Oxford is a trade mark of Oxford University Press

Published in the United States
by Oxford University Press, New York

British Library Cataloguing in Publication Data
Data available
ISBN 0-19-826542-5

Library of Congress Cataloging in Publication Data
Badawī, Muḥammad Muṣṭafá.
A short history of modern Arabic literature / M. M. Badawi.
Includes bibliographical references and index.
1. Arabic literature—1801—History and criticism. I. Title.
PJ7538.B265 1993
892'.709005—dc20
ISBN 0-19-826542-5

Photoset by Rowland Phototypesetting Limited
Bury St Edmunds, Suffolk
Printed in Great Britain by
Bookcraft (Bath) Ltd
Midsomer Norton, Avon

FOR MIEKE

PREFACE

DESPITE the fact that the Nobel Prize for literature was awarded to the Egyptian novelist Naguib Mahfouz (Najīb Maḥfūẓ) in 1988, modern Arabic literature is hardly known outside a narrow circle of academic specialists. There is no book in English, or in any major European language for that matter, that attempts to give a concise, clear, and authoritative survey of the whole of modern Arabic literature. There are indeed monographs on certain aspects of the subject, on genres, or individual authors, or specific issues, or the literature of particular regions of the modern Arab world. But there is no one volume that provides a unified treatment of the whole of modern Arabic literature with a view to helping the general intelligent English reader as well as the student to form a clear picture of the literary achievements of the modern Arabs.

There is, of course, J. A. Haywood's *Modern Arabic Literature 1800–1970*, which came out in 1971, but in all fairness it cannot really be said that this book does justice to its subject. It is ill-informed, full of factual errors, narrow in scope, bizarre in its organization and emphasis, and generally lacking in enthusiasm. Despite its good intentions the book has, not surprisingly, conspicuously failed to arouse much interest in modern Arabic literature. Very different indeed is Professor Pierre Cachia's recent volume *An Overview of Modern Arabic Literature* (1990), which contains many deep insights and thought-provoking observations and is written in a lively and elegant style. But excellent as it is, *An Overview* is mainly a collection of articles published in various journals over a long period of time. Because they were originally addressed to different audiences the articles inevitably form a mixed bag: some can be followed only by the Arabic specialist, while others are far too general and brief to satisfy the needs of the reader who wishes to acquire an adequate knowledge of the subject. Professor Cachia's book is not the survey that is so badly needed at present, which is a comprehensive critical account of creative writing by Arab men and women since the mid-nineteenth century in their attempt to adapt the imported forms of the novel, short story, and drama as well as the indigenous poetic and prose tradition to meet the requirements of the modern world as a result of the general drive for modernization in the Arab world.

To attempt to write such a survey, however, is a daunting undertaking. Arabic literature today is no longer confined to the traditional centres of Arabic culture; it is produced all over the Arab world which stretches from Morocco on the shores of the Atlantic to the Gulf States of Kuwait and United Arab Emirates, and from Syria in the north-east of the Mediterranean to the Sudan near the heart of Africa. To discuss or even to keep abreast of all the poetry and prose published in this vast Arabic-speaking area is wellnigh impossible. A recent bibliography of Syrian novels alone, published between 1970 and 1989, compiled for the *Journal of Arabic Literature* lists nearly 200 novels over a period of nineteen years. And the Syrian novel has a much shorter history than the Egyptian. Because of the enormous output of modern Arabic literature and the limited size of this book, it was imperative to be rigorously selective over authors and books to be discussed. Otherwise the discussion might have turned into a mere roll-call of names and titles that would mean little or nothing to the reader. Together with intrinsic merit, the criteria for selection included the representativeness of the authors or regions concerned. Because of lack of space many interesting works do not even get a mention, let alone a brief treatment. This also explains why Francophone North African literature was excluded, apart from the obvious fact that it is not strictly speaking *Arabic* literature.

Furthermore, because only a tiny fraction of Arabic literature is available in an English translation, as is seen from a glance at the Bibliography, it was felt necessary to provide brief summaries of plots of novels or plays, even though space was at a premium. Nevertheless, room had to be found for a limited amount of verse quotations, designed to give the reader some taste of the original poetry. In several places I have naturally drawn upon my earlier and more extensive treatment of some aspects of the subject.

Modern Arabic literature is very much alive and flourishing. New authors keep appearing, established ones change their course, striking new, interesting paths. To mention but one example, the distinguished Egyptian short-story writer Bahā' Ṭāhir has lately turned to the novel, producing a number of remarkable works during the last few years. Yet it has not been possible to discuss them in this brief survey. A halt had to be called somewhere.

Clearly no history and certainly no short history of a living culture can fully cover the last minute developments. It is only to be hoped that this book will, in the course of time, be supplemented by others that will attempt to bring the story up to date.

I should like to express my gratitude to the Committee responsible for The Rockefeller Foundation's Study and Conference Center in Bellagio for kindly inviting me for a residency to work on the final stages of this book. I should also like to thank my friend Dr Sabry Hafez for his valuable advice and for kindly lending me some of the texts not available in this country.

M. M. BADAWI

St Antony's College
Oxford

CONTENTS

NOTE ON TRANSLITERATION AND TRANSLATIONS

For ease of reading diacritical marks and marks indicating vowel lengthening are used on the first occurrence only of personal, place, or technical names. On subsequent mentions the same spelling is used but the marks are simply omitted. In the Index, however, the fully transliterated forms of all names is given.

All translations from Arabic used in this book are the author's own work.

Introduction

A New Conception of Arabic Literature

MODERN Arabic literature is the literature, written in Arabic, of the modern Arab world and this is generally assumed to begin with the French campaign in Egypt in 1798. The date is significant, for it marks the dramatic opening of the Arab world, which was then part of the Ottoman Empire, to the West, ultimately with momentous consequences in its political, economic, social, and cultural development. Out of the fruitful meeting of the indigenous Arabic literary tradition and the cultural forces of the West modern Arabic literature was born. It was a slow and gradual process, hedged round with doubts and uncertainties, and characterized by as much conservative opposition and reluctance as pioneering enthusiasm and radical fervour. For various reasons it began to make itself felt in Egypt and Syria (which then included Lebanon) from which it spread slowly to the rest of the Arab world.

The Arabs had started their steady decline early in the sixteenth century with the rise to power of the Ottoman Turks who imposed their rule over virtually the whole of the Arab world until early in the twentieth century, beginning with Syria and Egypt, which they conquered in 1516 and 1517 respectively. With the weakening of the Ottoman Empire in the eighteenth century, the subject peoples suffered from an increasingly heavy burden of taxation, oppression by corrupt officials and tax farmers, insecurity caused by the local rulers' bloody struggles for power, as well as periodic raids by bedouin tribesmen. Yet they continued to form an integrated society with commonly held views and assumptions about this world and the next. They may have resented much of the ill-treatment they received at the hands of their Turkish rulers and their subordinates, the rapacious and bloodthirsty warring Mameluke Beys. Nevertheless, in the days prior to nationalism the Arabs felt strongly that they all constituted the Muslim *Ummah*, the Community of Believers, and that as defenders of the *Sharīʿa*, the sacred law of Islam, the Ottoman rulers had the right to be obeyed. Moreover, they lived in seemingly total cultural isolation from the West, smugly convinced of the superiority of the Muslim civilization.

Although historians of Arabic literature may have exaggerated the decline there is no doubt that the Ottoman period is characterized by the virtual absence of originality and loss of vigour. By the time we reach the eighteenth century we find that prose writers and poets had become equally enamoured of an excessively ornate, artificial type of style, known as *badīʿ*, in which more attention is given to manner than to matter. Their work generally lacked seriousness, while those who cared for the content of their writing, such as historians, tended to employ an undistinguished prose which did not possess much literary merit. In creative writing the themes were circumscribed: *maqāma*s (short narrative pieces written in a highly ornate mixture of rhyming prose and verse, in which the protagonist was often an eloquent rogue living by his wits), *maqāma*-like prose epistles, pious verses in praise of the Prophet, popular sufi or ascetic poems, empty panegyrics addressed to local notables, celebrations of trivial social occasions, and numerous cold and conventional love poems. With very few exceptions indeed, such as some of the poetry of the Egyptian Ḥasan Badrī al-Ḥijāzī (d. 1718) and the Syrian ʿAbd al-Ghanī al-Nābulsī (d. 1731), the imagery poets used was stock in trade and the language cliché-ridden: in short, it was a literature of an exhausted, inward-looking culture, albeit complacent and perfectly self-satisfied.

Out of this complacency Arabic culture was rudely awakened when Bonaparte invaded Egypt in 1798. The shock suffered by the inhabitants was recorded by the distinguished Egyptian historian ʿAbd al-Raḥmān al-Jabartī (1756–1825) in his eyewitness account in his chronicle *'Ajā'ib al-āthār fī'l tarājim wa'l-akhbār*. The easy victory achieved by the French forces over the Mameluke army brought home to the population the enormous superiority, efficiency, and military might of the West. Bonaparte brought with him a team of French experts, scientists, and scholars who undertook a painstakingly thorough survey of Egypt and its resources: they conducted scientific experiments in the *Institut d'Egypte*, founded for that purpose, and published their findings in a newly established French-language periodical. He also brought with him from the Vatican an Arabic language press, the very first Arabic printing press to enter Egypt, for the publication of French proclamations in Arabic. The Egyptians admired the efficiency and organization of the French. Educated men such as al-Jabartī and Ḥasan al-ʿAṭṭār, the teacher of the pioneer of modern Arab thought, Rifāʿa Rāfiʿ al-Ṭahṭāwī, who had the chance to visit the *Institut*, were impressed by its library and fascinated by some of the scientific experiments they were shown and they were intrigued by the manners and ways of the French, such as their dramatic entertainments. On the other hand, they felt humiliated at being ruled by infidels, whose revolutionary doctrines the Ottoman government had thoroughly condemned. They were critical of the behaviour of the French troops and of what they regarded as the immorality of French women, alarmed at the dangerous example the latter had set to some of their own Muslim women. Moreover, in response to the blockade imposed upon them by the Anglo-Ottoman fleets in the Mediterranean, the French forces of occupation had to resort to such harsh measures of taxation that the Egyptian people, led by the ancient theological university of al-Azhar, rebelled. The rebellion was ruthlessly put down by the French troops, some of whom committed scandalous atrocities.

Although the French occupation lasted only three years, its significance for Egypt (and the rest of the Arab world) cannot be exaggerated. It brought to an end the isolation of the Arab world from the West, signalling the beginning of a process of Western expansion and colonization, which eventually resulted in almost the entire Arab world falling under the domination of Western powers, notably France and Britain. The bloody and unequal encounter with the West, which varied in ferocity and violence from one Arab country to another, and according to whether the colonizer was France, Britain, or Italy, had such a profound and traumatic effect upon the Arab imagination that to this day the East–West opposition has remained one of the leading motifs in Arabic literature. In their search for identity, modern Arab writers have for many generations tried to define themselves in relation to the other, the other being almost invariably the European.

Likewise, the nationalist struggle for independence became a permanent, indeed at times obsessive, preoccupation for writers for many years: the end of the mandate in Iraq came only in 1932, the Anglo-Egyptian treaty which gave Egypt her relative independence was concluded in 1936, the mandate for Syria and Lebanon came to an end in 1941. In 1946 Transjordan attained her independence,

Libya in 1951, Sudan, Tunisia and Morocco in 1956, Kuwait in 1961, while Algeria achieved hers after a prolonged and bloody struggle as late as 1962. In 1948 the mandate for Palestine came to an end and the state of Israel was established. Even after the Arab states formally attained their independence, they remained within the spheres of influence of Western powers for a long time, in fact until Jamāl ʿAbd al-Nāṣir (Colonel Nasser) appeared on the scene after the Egyptian army revolution of 1952, which in its turn helped to push Arabic literature in other directions.

The whole course of modern Arabic literature might have been entirely different if it had not been for one indirect result of the French campaign, namely the emergence of Muhammad Ali. Muhammad Ali was an Albanian officer who came to Egypt with the Ottoman forces to help drive out the French and who, in the confusion that followed the latter's departure, managed through a combination of sheer genius, machiavellian intrigues, and utter ruthlessness to become in 1805 the ruler of Egypt (1805–48), creating a dynasty which ruled the country until its last descendant King Farouk was forced to abdicate by the revolutionary junta led by Nasser. Inspired by the example of the Ottoman Sultan Selim III, the ambitious Muhammad Ali launched a comprehensive programme of military reform along the lines of the superior and well-organized Western armies of which he had first-hand experience. He imported not only Western technicians and military advisors, but also Western forms of education and sent local Arabs on educational missions to the West (mainly to France), to learn the secret of its military supremacy. In 1816 he started a process of superimposing upon the country a Western type of educational system which had very little in common with the traditional religious Azhar system. He set up a number of modern technological and military schools in which modern sciences and European languages were taught. The members of his educational missions in Europe were all regarded and treated as army officers, being trained in modern technology. Nevertheless, in the long run it was difficult for these young men to keep interest in Western technology entirely separate from interest in some of the cultural values underlying that technology. Furthermore, the setting up of a new secular system of education, different from the traditional theocentric one, a system which produced men intended to occupy important posts in the government, was bound to result eventually in the weakening of the authority of traditional values. Arab Muslim society therefore ceased to be the 'closed' culture it had been for so long.

Because Muhammad Ali needed books and manuals for his modern schools and the army, he ordered an Arabic printing press. This press, later to be known as the Government Press, was to play an important cultural role in the Arab Muslim world: it printed translations of European works, at first scientific and technological, but later on literary translations as well as Arabic classics, which became more widely available than they used to be when they were accessible only in the form of expensive manuscripts copied out by hand. Likewise, the Press printed the very first periodical in 1828, an official gazette, *al-Waqāʾiʿ al-Miṣriyya.* This marked the birth of journalism, which was to become a potent factor in the development of not only modern Arab thought, society, and politics, but also of modern Arabic literature. Together with translations of scientific works, journalism helped gradually to change the style of Arabic prose, ridding it of excessive rhetorical devices, making it a simpler and fitter vehicle for conveying ideas as well as for sustained narrative.

The editing of the official gazette was assigned to the distinguished Rifāʿa Rāfiʿ al-Ṭahṭāwī (1801–73). An Azharite by training he was sent to France in 1826 on the recommendation of his teacher Shaykh Ḥasan al-ʿAṭṭār as an Imam to the large batch of mission students, but he spent his five years in Paris learning French and studying various aspects of French culture. After his return to Egypt he published in 1834 his observations and impressions of his trip in *Takhlīṣ al-ibrīz ilā talkhīṣ bārīz*, in which, as well as in his numerous other writings, he expressed his admiration for the rationality and the good organization of social and political institutions, the civic virtues such as the love of the fatherland (*al-waṭan*), of the West, qualities which he advocated as necessary for the betterment of Islamic society in Egypt. Al-Tahtawi was also appointed director of one of the important modern schools founded by Muhammad Ali in 1835, the Cairo School of Languages for the teaching of Italian, French, and English, which produced a number of distinguished translators and writers. A Translation Bureau was set up in 1841, marking the beginning of a significant translation movement, which at first was limited to technological and military books, but in the course of time included literary and historical writings.

Muhammad Ali's various projects resulted in a remarkable rise in the number of European experts residing in Egypt, and hence in the spread of European schools as well as missionary activity. His liberal attitude towards Europeans made the decade of Egyptian occupation of Syria (1831–40) one of crucial importance in its cultural history: for it led to a dramatic increase in French, British, and American missionary and educational activities. These culminated in the Americans founding a College in 1847 which became the American College in 1866, later to be named the American University of Beirut, the Jesuits transferring their College (the University of St Joseph) to Beirut in 1874. Missionary schools for girls were also opened. The graduates of these Western institutions were naturally more receptive to Western ideas with the result that they played a pioneering role in Westernization. Coming after the earlier generation of Nāṣīf al-Yāzijī (1800–71), who was among the first Christian writers to develop a keen and serious interest in Arabic language and literature, these younger Christians were eager to experiment in new literary forms, such as drama and the novel, hitherto unknown in the Arabic literary heritage. Whole families, such as those of al-Yaziji, al-Bustānī, al-Naqqāsh, became associated with these new forms, together with translations and adaptations as well as serious journalism of a general cultural and literary type. Salīm al-Bustānī began publishing his novels serially in his Beirut periodical *al-Jinān* in 1870. Yaʿqūb Ṣarrūf and Fāris Nimr founded their epoch-making cultural periodical *al-Muqtaṭaf* in Beirut in 1876, which gave the Arab reader much information about Western thought, science, and technology (in 1885 it was transferred to Egypt where it continued to appear until 1952). The prolific Jurjī Zaydān, among his various activities in Cairo, published the monthly cultural periodical *al-Hilāl*, (1892) in which his numerous novels first came out and which still appears to this day.

As a result of the religious conflicts and disturbances in Syria in the wake of the enforced evacuation of the Egyptian troops, which culminated in the massacre of 1860 and the harsh rule of the Ottomans, many Syrians left their country; some went to America and were eventually to make a significant contribution to Arabic writing, known as the literature of *al-Mahjar* (the Emigrants or Expatriates). Others went to Egypt, lured by the reports of the munificence of Khedive Ismail (1863–79). Khedive Ismail had been educated in France, and despite his foolish extravagance which ultimately led to British occupation in 1882, he showed remarkable interest in promoting culture. Unlike his grandfather Muhammed Ali, who cared only for the technological type of school immediately relevant to the needs of his army, Ismail was genuinely interested in popular education (including the education of girls) which was organized by his able Minister of Education ʿAlī Mubārak, an engineer who was himself a product of the new secular school system. By the 1860s Arabic had replaced Turkish as the official language of Egypt. Ismail also allowed a large number of Christian missions to establish schools, where many Egyptian children, girls as well as boys, received their education in a European language, mainly French. In 1872 he established Dār al-ʿUlūm (a teachers' training college), which aimed at combining traditional Islamic Arabic culture with Western learning. He founded learned societies, a museum, an observatory, and patronized exploration, scholarly research, and the arts. In 1870 he set up Dār al-Kutub (The National Library). He founded the Opera House in Cairo, which was opened in 1869 with a performance of *Rigoletto*, as part of the extravagant celebrations of the opening of the Suez Canal. He encouraged (for a while) the first Egyptian dramatist Yaʿqūb Ṣannūʿ, on whom he allegedly conferred the honorific title 'The Egyptian Molière', as well as visiting theatrical troupes from Syria. He gave financial aid to Buṭrus al-Bustānī (1819–83) to enable him to work on his Arabic encyclopaedia. Ismail was intent on making Egypt, as it were, part of Europe. European methods of administration and finance were followed and legal codes were translated. Even European dress was adopted by Egyptian civil servants and members of the professions. Under his rule many of the major topographical changes in Cairo took place, some in imitation of Baron Hausmann's Paris; over a hundred European schools were opened, the number of Europeans residing in Egypt rose from a few thousand in 1860 to over a hundred thousand in 1876. In short, the course of Westernization was assured, even though for some time it remained skin deep.

Westernization, however, was problematic in a Muslim country. The key issue which preoccupied the minds of most Arab intellectuals was how to Westernize or modernize while remaining Muslims. The problem, of course, did not arise in the case of Christian Arabs, some of whom adopted an anti-clerical stance, like Fāris al-Shidyāq (1804–87), or even advocated secularization, like Shiblī Shumayyil (1860–1917) and Faraḥ Anṭūn (1874–1922), who believed in the need to separate secular and religious powers. As Albert Hourani rightly observed, for the first generation of modern thinkers (up to 1870), that of al-Tahtawi of Egypt and Khayr al-Dīn of Tunisia (1810–89), Europe stood for material progress and science rather than political power and aggressive imperialist expansion of which later generations were made painfully aware. Their problem was how to reconcile reason and the rationalism of the French Enlightenment with *Shariʿa*, the divine law of Islam. For the subsequent generation the situation had changed radically. It was no longer a question of Islam trying to copy or catch up with the West, but one of survival, of fighting against external danger. The main problem for Muslim thinkers, such as the Messianic and controversial Jamāl al-Dīn al-Afghānī (1839–97), who lived in Egypt from 1871 until his expulsion in 1879 by Khedive Tawfiq for fear of his revolutionary views, and al-Afghani's most influential disciple Muḥammad ʿAbduh (1849–1905), was how to reinterpret Islam so as to derive strength from it in meeting the needs of living in the modern world. Afghani preached the need to revitalize Islam, by opposing the autocratic government of Muslim despots and limiting absolute rule through constitutions, as well as the need to unite the Muslims so that they could fight against European intervention. Muhammad ʿAbduh's position, which was more moderate than Afghani's, was one of eclecticism with a strong rationalist Muʿtazilite component. He held that Islam was never opposed to science or rational enquiry, and that a distinction must be drawn between the permanent core of Islam, namely its simple doctrines and its inessential elements which may be changed according to individual judgement. One of ʿAbduh's many devoted followers was the Islamic reformer and modernizer Qāsim Amīn (1865–1908), who in his books *Taḥrīr al-Marʾa* (*The Emancipation of Woman*, 1899) and *al-Marʾa al-Jadīda* (*The New Woman*, 1901) argued, against much conservative opposition in Egypt, that the emancipation of women, which was essential to the revival of Muslims, is in no way against Islamic doctrine.

In the course of the twentieth century many changes took place. These included the growth of nationalist feeling, be it religious, territorial, ethnic, or linguistic, the emergence of, and subsequent disillusionment with, political parties, the failure of the liberal democratic experiment in Egypt, conducted, as it was, against the unfavourable background of an interfering foreign imperial power, and a ruling autocratic monarchy. Furthermore, there was the deterioration of the economic situation as a result first of the Depression, then of the inflation brought about by World War II, the alarming rate of population growth, the gaping gulf separating the urban and rural poor from the greedy and often corrupt rich, and the emergence of the lumpenproletariat as a result of the mass migration of destitute peasants to the few overcrowded cities in search of employment. Seeking a solution to their pressing and intractable problems, many people were driven to the Islamic fundamentalist position of the Muslim Brotherhood movement started in 1928 by Ḥasan al-Bannā (d. 1949), a follower of ʿAbduh's Syrian disciple and biographer Rashīd Riḍā, while others turned to an equally extreme leftist position, held by largely underground communist activists. After the war the loss of Palestine and the creation of Israel in 1948 enforced both Islamic fundamentalism and Arab nationalism of the secular variety, and indirectly led to the Egyptian army revolution of 1952, which, under the spreading influence of Nasserism, was followed by a series of army coups in other newly independent Arab states. New regimes arose, whose ideals were often a mixture of Arab nationalism and socialism.

Among the important changes mention must be made of the significant growth of the middle classes which led to some monarchies and feudal or semi-feudal ruling houses being ousted by members of the middle or lower middle class, usually army officers, who assumed power and ruled, often dictatorially, in the name of the people. This was accompanied by the spread of education and the decrease of illiteracy, and the rise in importance of the position of women, especially in socialist regimes. The constant pursuit of the ideal of Arab unity, prompted by the awareness of the Israeli threat, has been frustrated by interminable inter-state strife. This in turn has been fed by the differences and contradictions between the political systems of these states, which polarized as they were caught up in the cold war between Soviet Russia and America, who since the 1950s have gradually replaced Britain and France as the dominant foreign forces in the region. Other developments include not only the sufferings of the Palestinian diaspora and of the victims of the prolonged Arab–Israeli conflict as well as the tragic Lebanese civil war, but also the dramatic rise in the importance of the role of oil in the economy, the position of some of the states in the region, and the subsequent migration of labour from the poor to the richer Arab states. Added to that is the phenomenon of the exiled and self-exiled intellectuals fleeing from hostile authoritarian governments. All these developments are reflected in the literature of the time.

However, for literature to reflect such developments, a radical change had to take place in the conception of what literature was and the function of the writer. The medieval view which had dominated until well into the nineteenth century and which regarded writing as either morally and spiritually edifying or else entertaining through mastery of language and verbal skill, gradually gave way to the attitude that literature should reflect and indeed change social reality. The patron prince or ruler who encouraged poets to flock to his court to sing of his achievements and immortalize his name in memorable *qaṣīdas* (formal sonorous odes) was being replaced by a middle-class reading public, educated in secular and not theocentric schools. As a result of the introduction of printing, they had access to printed books instead of relying on a few hand-copied manuscripts and were wooed not through oral recitation or declamation, but on the pages of newspapers and magazines. In a society where the degree of illiteracy was extremely high, the size of the reading public was initially very small, but their number grew rapidly with the spread of popular education. Gone therefore was the poet craftsman who offered his panegyrical verse to the highest bidder; in his place came the 'inspired' poet, the man of feeling who valued sincerity above any other quality, or the campaigner who had strong views about wider issues, particularly the ills of his society. The traditional prose writer, the author of *adab (belles lettres)*, who sought to entertain the privileged learned minority by drawing, but not too heavily, on diverse aspects of knowledge, or who embroidered his epistles to fellow writers or his *maqāma*s with all kinds of figures of speech *(badīʿ)*, in the most artificial manner imaginable, gave way to the concerned essayist or journalist burning with reforming zeal in matters intellectual, religious, social, and political, no less than in language and literature. Whatever the attitude to the mimetic view of literature nowadays in the era of Post-structuralism and Deconstruction, it is the emergence of literature as a *mimesis*, as an imitation of life, that has signalled the arrival of modern Arabic literature on the scene. Instead of the ideal types provided in traditional medieval literature, presented in the most elaborate language ('what oft was thought but ne'er so well express'd'), concrete observable reality has become the subject matter of writers, particularly in the newly imported forms of drama and fiction.

The history of modern Arabic literature may be divided into three main periods: the first from 1834 to 1914, which may be termed the 'Age of Translations and Adaptations' as well as 'Neo-classicism'; the second is the inter-war period, which may be described as the 'Age of Romanticism and Nationalism'; the third is from the end of World War II to the present: it embraces a wide variety of schools, approaches, and styles but may conveniently be called the 'Age of Conflicting Ideologies'.

The year 1834 is an important landmark, because it marks the publication of al-Tahtawi's account of his trip to France, *Takhlīṣ al-Ibrīz*, which contains specimens of his translations of French verse, thus signalling the very beginning of the process of introduction to, and assimilation of, Western literature. In his account, al-Tahtawi also tells us that during his mission in Paris he read works by Racine, Voltaire, Rousseau, and Montesquieu, amongst other things, and he studied the art of translation, '*Fann al-tarjama*'. Equally 1914 is an appropriate date to end this first period, for around that date significant works appeared in which Arab authors seemed to go beyond the stage of translation or adaptation, revealing their mastery or near-mastery of the imported literary forms, for example Muḥammad Ḥusayn Haykal's novel *Zaynab* and Ibrāhīm Ramzī's comedy *Dukhūl al-Ḥammām* (*Admission to the Baths*) and his historical drama *Abṭāl al-Manṣūra* (*The Heroes of Mansura*).

As has been mentioned above, this early period witnessed the emergence of the Arabic printing press which not only made the Arabic classics to which authors turned for inspiration in an attempt to assert their identity in the face of external danger more widely available, but also produced an increasing number of governmental, and more importantly for our purpose, non-governmental periodicals of a general cultural nature. Early translations, adaptations, and imitations of Western fiction were thus published which catered for a new type of reader, the product of missionary institutions in Syria or Ismail's new, more secular type of school, a reader who was not deeply grounded in the Arabic classics but who sought entertainment in a simpler and more direct Arabic style than that provided in the traditional *maqama*. The newspapers provided a forum for political activists, and religious and social reformers, resulting in the birth and development of the modern essay from the rather crude informative attempts at providing information or instruction in official or semi-governmental periodicals made by the pioneer generation of al-Tahtawi to the more powerful and impassioned work of politically committed Egyptian and Syrian essayists, mostly the disciples of al-Afghani, who published their articles in, for example, *al-Ahrām*. Under the influence of Muhammad ʿAbduh they sought to express their views in a less ornate style, a sinewy prose, relatively free from the artificialities of *badīʿ*. They include Adīb Isḥāq, Salīm al-Naqqāsh, ʿAbdallah Nadīm, Muḥammad ʿUthmān Jalāl, Muhammad ʿAbduh himself, Ibrāhīm al-Muwayliḥī and ʿAbd al-Raḥmān al-Kawākibī. Their work was further developed under British occupation by ʿAlī Yūsuf in the conservative *al-Muʾayyad*, Muṣṭafā Kāmil in *al-Liwāʾ*, the organ of the Nationalist Party, particularly Aḥmad Luṭfī al-Sayyid (1872–1963) in *al-Jarīda*, the mouthpiece of the *Ummah* Party which represented the more liberal Arab intellectuals and stood for intelligent Westernization, rationality, and a scientific attitude in education and social reform. Lutfi al-Sayyid's thoughful essays, in which he stated his responsible and enlightened secular, liberal, and patriotic position, earned him the title of *Ustādh al-jīl* (the master/mentor of the generation) and through *al-Jarida* many of the leading writers and essayists found their way to the public: ʿAbd al-Raḥmān Shukrī, ʿAbd al-ʿAzīz al-Bishrī, Ibrahim Ramzi, Muḥammad al-Sibāʿī, ʿAbd al-Ḥamīd Ḥamdī, Muhammad Husayn Haykal, Ṭāhā Ḥusayn, al-Mazīnī, al-ʿAqqād, Muṣṭafā ʿAbd al-Rāziq, Salāma Mūsā, as well as women essayists like Labība Hāshim, Nabawiyya Mūsā, and Malak Ḥifnī Nāsif. In the hands of some of these writers, particularly al-Mazini and Taha Husayn it can be said that the essay had attained its most elegant form.

During this period a close connection between journalism and serious literature was established to the extent that we find not only *qaṣīda*s by the major poets and short stories, but whole novels such as those by Jurji Zaydan appearing (serially) in the papers or magazines. In fact this connection was strengthened in later periods: leading novelists and even literary critics (such as Taha Husayn) first published their works in newspapers. Even today Najīb Maḥfūẓ's novels first appear in instalments in *al-Ahram*, and the literary page of a newspaper is still regarded as one of its distinguishing features and a valuable asset. No doubt this is also due to the fact that it has been extremely difficult for a modern Arab writer to live on the royalties of his books alone, hence the need to have another regular job, which often tends to be journalism.

It is not surprising that the period between the two world wars was the Age of Romanticism and Nationalism. The First World War resulted in the dissolution of the Ottoman Empire and the placing of its remaining Arab provinces under British and French mandate. Egypt, already under British occupation was declared a Protectorate in 1914. The strength of nationalist feeling erupted in a series of major revolts first in Egypt (1919), where the conflagration was nationwide and the events acquired an enormous significance in the national consciousness, then in Iraq (1920), and Syria (1925). The search for specifically Egyptian literature and for an Egyptian identity was a slogan of many authors in Egypt, especially a group of young men associated with what became known as *al-madrasa al-ḥadītha* (The New School), such as Maḥmūd Ṭāhir Lāshīn and the Taymūr brothers (Muḥammad and Maḥmūd), who later distinguished themselves both in fiction and in drama. Related to this is the call for the use of the Egyptian colloquial at least in dialogue. The emphasis on the Pharaonic past of Egypt by writers such as Haykal and Tawfīq al-Ḥakīm is paralleled by the need to relate to the Phoenician civilization expressed by Saʿīd ʿAql in Lebanon.

The desire to achieve progress and modernity (which meant Westernization) was keenly felt and this entailed a critical and at times rejectionist stance to traditional values. In the wake of the abolition of the caliphate in Istanbul in 1924 by Kemal Atatürk (1881–1938), two famous debates took place as a result of the publication of two revolutionary books: ʿAlī ʿAbd al-Rāziq's *al-Islām wa Uṣūl al-Ḥukm* (*Islam and the Principles of Government*), which appeared in 1925, and in which he argued that the caliphate is not an integral part of Islam, and Taha Husayn's *Fī'l Shiʿr al-Jāhilī* (*On Pre-Islamic Poetry*), published in 1926, which cast doubt on the authenticity of pre-Islamic poetry and the historical veracity of certain allusions in the Koran. The former caused its author to be expelled from the body of ulema while the latter cost Taha Husayn his job and brought about calls for his trial and imprisonment.

In literary criticism several iconoclastic works appeared such as *al-Dīwān* by the Egyptians alʿAqqād and al-Māzinī in 1921, the Mahjari Mikhā'īl Nuʿayma's *al-Ghirbāl (The Sieve)* in 1923, and the Tunisian al-Shābbī's *al-Khayāl al-Shiʿrī ʿind al-ʿArab* (*The Arab Poetic Imagination*) in 1929. Other considerations apart, it was quite natural for Arab writers, particularly poets, to turn for their inspiration to European Romanticism which was a literature of revolt. Unlike Classicism which, with its stress on polish and good form, is an expression of a fairly stable culture in which there is common agreement on fundamental issues, Romanticism is a product of a society which is at odds with itself and in which the individual questions the relevance of traditional values. Since the traditional Arab conception of literature shares many of the fundamental assumptions of European Classicism (such as the ideal of clarity and rationality in poetry and more particularly in literary criticism, the relatively low place assigned to imagination, the view of form as something external to be joined to content, the heavy reliance on rhetoric, neat balance, and antithesis, and the strict adherence to decorum), it was understandable that when the desire to break with their past and enter the modern world was genuinely felt, Arab poets found in European Romanticism, which was professedly anti-classical, the assumptions and ideals which seemed to them to fulfil adequately their own needs. However, the Arab Romantics, whether in the Arab East or in the Americas, were not simply imitating Western postures. The heightened sense of individuality, the agonizing feeling of social and cultural change, the political malaise, the occasional awareness of loss of direction and of being strangers in an unfamiliar universe, were in one way or another facts of Arab existence for some time. Furthermore, the Arab Romantics were by no means dreamers inhabiting an ivory tower: many were politically committed nationalists, and they were keenly aware of the ills of their society.

After the Second World War Arabic literature, indeed the whole of the Arab world, entered a new phase. Romanticism was discredited, political commitment increased, and competition grew fierce between clashing loyalties and ideologies, against a background of internal and external changes. In the aftermath of the war Britain and France ceased to be the dominant foreign powers in the area, their roles were gradually assumed, albeit in a different form, by America and the Soviet Union which, unlike Britain and France were not simply two rival superpowers with imperialist ambitions, but also stood for opposite ideologies. This no doubt contributed to the polarization of the Arab states and of intellectuals within the same state. But what proved to be the most important single external development for the Arab world was the creation of Israel in 1948. The series of Arab–Israeli wars which ensued generally ended in frustration and bitter disappointment, and thus helped to determine the Arabs' attitude to the outside world. Israel's impact upon Arabic literature, both prose and poetry, has been overwhelming.

The Second World War accelerated the process of independence of Arab states and the League of the Arab States was formed in 1945. Some of the energy of resistance against the external enemy was therefore directed at the enemy within: war was waged on the privileged communities and the feudal rich who had collaborated with the foreign occupier, or the ruling élites who, in the opinion of the people, were guilty of corruption and mismanagement. These were glaringly evident in the disastrous defeat of the Arab armies in the first Arab–Israeli war of 1948, some of whom were fighting with defective arms supplied to them by their own government. In Egypt the disillusionment with the short-lived democratic experiment and with the performance of political parties coincided with the rapid growth of an educated urban middle-class suffering from the result of inflation caused by the war and the inevitable profiteering that ensued. The gap between the rich and the poor, particularly the destitute masses who migrated from the countryside in search of a meagre living in overcrowded cities, became wider than ever, thus giving rise to popular movements and mass demonstrations in which students (and workers) figured prominently. With the failure of the liberal democratic experiment the populace looked for salvation either to the extreme Right (Muslim Brotherhood) or the extreme Left (Marxism).

The need for literature to promote socialist values was reiterated by the radical Egyptian thinker Salāma Mūsā (1887–1958), who fell under the influence of the Fabian Society and who continued the tradition of the early Lebanese secularizers such as Shibli Shumayyil. As early as 1929 he published his progressive review *al-Majalla al-Jadīda*, which advocated the adoption of a scientific attitude to life and society and demanded that literature should be written for the people about the problems of the people, and in a language that the people could understand. Salama Musa's ideas found a response among many distinguished critics and writers, such as Luwīs ʿAwaḍ (1915–90) and Najib Mahfuz. Leftist magazines appeared in other parts of the Arab world, for example *al-Ṭalīʿa* in 1935 in Damascus and *al-Ṭarīq* in 1941 in Beirut. Marxist ideas were propagated by 'Umar Fākhūrī in Damascus and Ra'īf Khūrī (1912–67) in Lebanon. During the war years young Arab intellectuals became increasingly interested in Marxist philosophy as favourable information about the Soviet regime became more available in the cultural centres of the Middle East. In 1945 the influential Egyptian critic Muḥammad Mandūr (1907–65) gave up his academic career to engage in active leftist politics, and after the 1952 revolution became editor of the Arabic Soviet cultural periodical *al-Sharq*, supporting the cause of socialist realism, at least in a moderate form. A stream of novels of angry social protest began to pour out in 1944: these were heavily documented works which describe in great detail the misery and deprivation of Egyptian urban life, adding social injustice and class struggle to national independence as political themes. The pursuit of social realism in fiction is not confined to the younger generation of ʿĀdil Kāmil and Najib Mahfuz, but can be found in the work of the older generation of Yaḥyā Ḥaqqī and Taha Husayn in Egypt.

The early 1950s witnessed the eruption in Cairo and Beirut of noisy debates about commitment in literature, in which leading critics and writers, young and old alike, took part. The Arabic word for commitment, *iltizām*, became an essential part of the vocabulary of literary criticism soon after its first appearance on the literary scene around 1950. Its meaning was diffuse, to be sure: sometimes it meant the adoption of a Marxist stand, at other times an existentialist position, but at all times it denoted at least a certain measure of nationalism, Arab or otherwise. In other words, it emphasized the need for a writer to have a message. This need was explicitly expressed in the manifesto-like editorial note to the first volume of Suhayl Idrīs's Beirut monthly periodical *al-Ādāb* (January 1953), which, more than any other, helped to determine the course of modern Arabic literature by the publication both of creative work and of criticism and evaluation of contemporary literature. In August 1954 one contributor to the *Ādāb* wrote that 'the idea of committed literature dominates the Arab world now'. The reaction against Romanticism was understandably prompted by a growing painful awareness of the harsh political and social realities of the Arab world, an awareness that was later reinforced by subsequent developments ranging from the horrors of the Arab–Israeli wars, the plight of the Palestinians, oppressive Arab regimes, and the Iran–Iraq war, to inter-Arab strife and the civil war in the Lebanon.

The early success of the 1952 Egyptian army revolution and the rise of Nasserism gave a boost to Arab nationalism and created for a while a mood of euphoria and optimism. One expression of this nationalistic pride and self-confidence was the hectic search for autonomous or indigenous Arab art forms, such as the specifically Arab or Egyptian or Moroccan theatre, which swept all over the Arab countries. Optimism, however, turned into bitterness when the dream of Arab unity was shattered, civil liberties were crushed by totalitarian regimes, and the Arabs were disastrously defeated by the Israelis in 1967. Despite the disillusionment and set-backs the search continues in some quarters for cultural autonomy, for independent narrative and dramatic art forms, for authentic Arab, or more specifically, Islamic, values. This is undertaken even by those who themselves received Western intellectual training and therefore employ Western categories in their search, and yet who reject the West, a rejection which may in some measure be explained by the generally unsympathetic, if not at times downright hostile, attitude adopted to the Arabs in their various conflicts by the Western powers. Indeed the limited Arab victory of 1973, achieved by the destruction of the Bar Lev line and the crossing of the Suez Canal, may have restored some Arab dignity, but it coincided with the rise of Islamic fundamentalism, which may be related to this search for total cultural independence by more moderate Arab or Muslim intellectuals. Yet it is a mark of the complexity of the current Arab cultural scene that at the same time several Arab intellectuals have not been immune to the allure of the latest Western critical fashions of Structuralism, Post-structuralism and Deconstruction.

It hardly seems necessary to point out that the dates suggested here for the three periods of development of modern Arabic literature do not constitute sharp lines of demarcation, and that there is considerable overlapping between the periods. Furthermore, not all the Arab states have developed at the same rate: for instance, the states of North Africa and the Arabian Peninsula began to make their distinct contribution to the mainstream of modern Arabic literature only some time after the Second World War. However, it is to be hoped that these dates will serve as useful pointers or signposts along our journey.

Part One

Poetry

I

Neo-Classical and Romantic

FROM ancient times the power of the word, as best exemplified in poetry, has been proverbial among the Arabs. In the tribal society of pre-Islamic Arabia the emergence of a poet, we are told by one often-quoted authority, was regarded by the members of a tribe as a momentous and joyful happening, for through his eloquence the tribe's honour would be defended, its enemies vilified, and its heroic deeds blazoned throughout the land. Under Islam the poet's social and political status may have suffered, but the importance of his work remained undiminished. The early Arabs used to describe poetry as 'the register of the Arabs', implying that it was in their poetry that the salient events of their history, their battles of long ago, their values, and their mores were consecrated and preserved. Equally, every Muslim Arab ruler of note, almost until modern times, made sure that his court attracted distinguished poets who, in their panegyrical odes, would celebrate his achievements and render his name immortal.

The Arab's sensitivity to his language, with the attendant pride he took in it, a pride subsequently reinforced by the Muslim belief that the Arabic Koran is literally the word of God, has had two opposite results. On the one hand, it provided encouragement, including material reward, to poets across the ages: until relatively recently every educated Arab tried his hand at composing verses. On the other hand, it tended to create in the Arab, where poetry was concerned, a feeling of self-sufficiency which, in the course of time, turned into smugness and debilitating cultural isolation. In their golden age early medieval Arab authors translated from the superior Greek and Persian cultures with which they came into contact, particularly from the former. These translations included works of philosophy, mathematics, science, and medicine, but seldom if at all any poetry, so convinced were they of the superiority of the Arabic poetic tradition. The twin indigenous broad poetic forms or kinds, namely the formal ode (*qaṣīda*) and the shorter occasional poem or fragment (*qiṭʿa*)—both a public sort of poetry, presupposing an audience and meant to be declaimed loudly because of their pronounced rhetorical and musical features—continued to be the ideal which Arab poets pursued from the seventh century to the beginning of the twentieth century. There were indeed several diverse and subtle innovations, but they occurred within the framework of the two ancient forms.

I

The pre-Islamic tribal formal ode is a polythematic poem of some length, in truth more like a ritual celebrating the values of the tribe, mainly physical courage and endless hospitality, and asserting life impulses in the hostile physical environment of the desert, which imposes a nomadic way of life. Generally the poet begins with an elegiac amatory preamble, occasioned by the parting or the memory of parting with the beloved, or the sight of the ruins or traces of her desert encampment, and laments the passage of time, death, and decay. He then seeks consolation by embarking on a journey on his camel's back, in which he describes in loving detail various aspects of desert life, both social and physical, particularly desert animals, and he concludes his poem positively with self-praise or praise of the tribe or a patron, a comforting moralization or even a natural description. The Muslim courtly ode, on the other hand, which may be called the 'secondary qasida', to distinguish it from the 'primary', which is the pre-Islamic, was a product of a different sensibility and spirit. It did not possess the same ritualistic function, but was more 'literary' and tended to emphasize the element of panegyric at the expense of other themes. Under Islam the occasional poem gradually, with the development of civilization, acquired intellectual subtlety, an emotional complexity, and a sophisticated ironic tone: the untrodden paths of the soul, the uncharted regions of the mind began to be explored in the idealized love poem, the wine poem, and mystical verse.

For various reasons, literary, cultural, and sociological, the conventions of early Arabic poetry, its poetic diction, its predominant desert imagery, motifs and topoi, its traditional division of types (*aghrāḍ*) into panegyric, lampoon, self-praise, elegy, amatory, descriptive, and gnomic verse were followed by most poets, sometimes with a surprising degree of irrelevance to their own conditions in time and place. Furthermore, apart from a few minor exceptions, the prosody and versification of early Arabic poetry remained unchanged: the well-known sixteen metres with their elaborate structure of feet, the division of a line into two hemistichs of equal metrical value, the absence of rhymeless verse, the use of monorhyme in the serious poems and of rhyming couplets for less weighty themes, for which *rajaz*, a vaguely iambic-like metre (generally accorded a lower status), was usually employed. The most significant of the exceptions was the emergence in Muslim Spain in the eleventh century of a complex type of strophic or stanzaic verse (*muwashshaḥāt*).

Because of the common belief that the store of ideas or themes is exceedingly limited, poets became inordinately interested in style and form. Partly as a result of that there developed in the ninth century, under the influence of philosophical or theological thinking, the highly ornate rhetorical style known as *badīʿ*, which soon attained wide popularity, leaving its mark on most later poets. The word *badīʿ* literally means 'new', but it was used to refer to this highly figurative and argumentative way of writing—somewhat similar to the English 'Metaphysical' style—in which 'modern' poets of the time tried to assert their originality in the face of the upholders of the 'ancients' (pre-Islamic models). The poets' obsessive concern with the minutae of style led to the dominance of the conception of the poet not as a seer or spokesman of the tribe (as he had been viewed in pre-Islamic Arabia), but as a craftsman, a jeweller whose medium was words. *Badīʿ* itself lost its original connection with philosophical thinking and became yet another convention which poets felt they had to follow.

There is no doubt that in the long run these conventions exercised a stranglehold on the development of Arabic poetry for a long stretch of time. This is particularly true of what is generally regarded as the period of decadence, beginning with the Ottoman conquest of Syria and Egypt early in the sixteenth century, although signs of weakness, artificiality, general fatigue, and loss of energy are to be found in poetry written much earlier. When we reach the eighteenth century we find that with very few exceptions, such as ʿAbd al-Ghanī al-Nābulsī in some of his mystical verse, poets were gripped by a passion for verbal jugglery and motivated primarily by a desire to display their linguistic skill and their ability to manipulate words to produce acrobatic effects. For instance, they wrote verses in which every word alliterates, or in which a word begins with the same letter as that with which the preceding one ends, or in which every word or every letter, or every other letter is dotted. They showed an essential lack of seriousness in their pursuit of *badīʿ*, empty figures of speech for their own sake, and in the large amount of verse which they composed on trivial social occasions. Their vision is seldom fresh, as their traditional verses, be they panegyric, mystical, devotional and didactic or amatory, bacchic or descriptive, abound in conventional imagery: in amatory verse, for example, the beloved is always likened to a gazelle, her swaying figure to a willow branch, her face to a full moon; her lips are like red beads, her teeth like pearls, her cheeks like roses, and her breasts like pomegranates. Her languid eyes send forth fatal darts which pierce the hearts of men, but she is coy and unwilling and the poet is desperately forlorn, and so on.

It is this cumbersome weight of convention which modern Arabic poetry has had to contend with to arrive at its present position. The very richness of this unbroken tradition was the most serious obstacle in the way of those Arabs who were responding to the exigencies of modern life as well as to the Western literary influences which began to make themselves felt in the nineteenth century. They were becoming increasingly aware that the medieval poetic conventions, which had once served Arabic poetry well, had long outlived their usefulness, for they had degenerated to largely meaningless clichés, thereby becoming absurdly irrelevant to modern life and modern sensibility. The struggle of the modern poet, which proved to be painfully long and tortuous, was therefore precisely the struggle to break free from these conventions, while at the same time retaining a sufficient link with the poetry of the past to render modern Arabic poetry at once both modern and Arab. From the nineteenth century onwards the outlook of many Arabs underwent a dramatic change as a result of the spread of modern secular education, the movement of translation, the development of nationalism in reaction to growing Western imperialism, the wide use of printing, the rise of journalism, and the resultant simplification of the language of writing. A growing middle-class reading public eventually replaced the traditional patron prince, ruler, or notable, thereby making the predominantly panegyric traditional ode even more irrelevant.

II

The modern revival of poetry was a slow process. For a long time after their initial contact with the West, Arab poets continued to pursue the same path as in the eighteenth century. The same imitativeness and lack of originality, the same preoccupation with verbal jugglery, the same preference for hyperbole are to be found in equal measure in the works of the celebrated poets of the first half of the nineteenth century, such as the Egyptians Sheikh Ḥasan al-ʿAṭṭār, al-Sayyid ʿAlī Darwīsh, the Syrians Buṭrus Karāma and Sheikh Amīn al-Jundī, as well as the Lebanese Hāj ʿUmar al-Unsī. The subjects these poets attempted consisted largely of empty panegyrics addressed to local rulers and officials, commemorations of social events in poems ending in chronograms or trivial social occasions, and mutual congratulations and greetings couched in grossly exaggerated, inflated and high-falutin terms. The Arabic is stilted and the style generally turgid and devoid of feeling. The imagery is conventional and lacking in original perception. We meet with the same armoury of epithets and similes time and time again.

It is in the second part of the nineteenth century that we can detect signs of the poetic revival, most notably in the work of the Egyptian Maḥmūd Sāmī al-Bārūdī (1839–1904), who can be described as the true precursor of this revival, although mention must also be made of the Lebanese Nāṣīf al-Yāzijī (1800–71). The work of both these poets is marked by a conscious return to the classicism of early medieval poetry, especially that of the Abbasid period (750–1258). Yaziji's contribution is rather a negative one: it does not lie in his originality or creative imagination, but in his purifying the language of poetry of much of the artificiality and the absurd hyperbole of the past centuries of decadence, by his attempt to recapture the tautness and the forceful rhetoric of the Abbasid poets, particularly al-Mutanabbī whose poetry he edited. Yet there is nothing in Yaziji's poetry that suggests even remotely that it was written in the nineteenth century. Despite his marked skill Yaziji must be regarded as basically an imitative poet, drawing upon the traditional imagery of the desert. On the whole his work strikes the reader as too bookish and divorced from the poet's own concrete living experience. Al-Barudi, on the other hand, managed to combine a return to the purity of diction and the classicism of the Abbasids, an anthology of whose poetry he had compiled, with the ability to express his own individual experience often, though by no means always, in terms of the environment in which he actually lived. At his best he wrote poetry which is free from artificiality and which is a direct and forceful expression of an earnest mind and an impressive personality. Thanks to him Arabic poetry was brought once more to bear upon the serious business of life. Barudi did not prostitute his poetic talent: as he tells us in the important introduction to his *Dīwān* (Collected Verse) he wrote poetry only from an inner impulse: when, overwhelmed by the sense of tradition and the feeling of *ars longa vita brevis*, he once decided to give up writing, he failed to carry out his resolution because he was unable to go against his own nature. Hence the immediate relevance of his poetry to himself and to his age.

Given the cultural context of the nineteenth century, al-Barudi wrote in the classical Arabic poetic idiom, the only idiom available to him. Indeed he could not have done otherwise even if he had been exposed to Western literature. Later in the century when the Egyptian Aḥmad Shawqī (1868–1932) dared to suggest that an Arab poet might benefit from his knowledge of French poetry he was severely rebuked by Muḥammad al-Muwayliḥī, who himself was not averse to innovation in *prose* as is shown in his *Ḥadīth ʿIsā ibn Hishām*, a landmark in the history of modern Arabic fiction. Apart from other considerations, the return to the past glory of Arabic poetry was an expression of the Arabs' desire for self-assertion in a world dangerously threatened by powerful alien forces. In this connection it is not surprising that until the beginning of the Second World War the poets who enjoyed the greatest popularity in the Arab world were neo-classical poets: followers of al-Barudi, for instance, the Egyptians Ahmad Shawqi and Ḥāfiẓ Ibrāhīm (1871–1932), the Iraqis Jamīl Ṣidqī al-Zahāwī (1863–1936), and Maʿrūf al-Ruṣāfī (1875–1945), and to a lesser extent among the younger generation the Iraqi Muḥammad Mahdī al-Jawāhirī (b. 1900) and the Syrian Badawī al-Jabal (b. 1907). They were perhaps the last significant survivors of the neo-classical school.

The neo-classical poets accepted as their norm the old Arabic ode, *qasida*, with its monorhyme and monometer, its heavy reliance upon rhetoric and declamation, and the sonority of its music. They even attempted in some of their work to reproduce the imagery, themes, and even the structure of pre-Islamic or early Islamic *qasida*, often with results that strike us now as not a little comical. Al-Barudi, for instance, is capable of writing poems that give us a picture, at a third or fourth remove, of love, war, and desert life in a tribal or heroic society, which have absolutely nothing to do with the nineteenth-century Egyptian poet. Similarly, but to a somewhat lesser extent, Shawqi begins a poem occasioned, among other things, by the problem of food shortages in Egypt after World War I, by weeping over the deserted ruins of the encampment of his beloved. He opens another dealing with a burning political question at the time, namely Lord Milner's proposals affecting the future of Egypt's independence, with a *nasīb*, a love prelude of no less than seventeen lines couched in purely conventional phraseology, where women are referred to as wild cows and gazelles, their slim figures as willow branches, but their heavy buttocks as sand hillocks, their eyes as narcissi, and so on. Likewise, Hafiz Ibrahim chooses to begin a poem inspired by the opening of an orphanage with a detailed description of a railway journey, just as the pre-Islamic poet might describe his journey on camelback, and the internal combustion engine is conceived by him in terms of the desert beast of burden. Shawqi, too, describes his journey by steamer in terms of desert imagery: the surging waves piling upon one another are like 'rocks' in a desert and the movement of ships rising and falling on the crest of waves is likened to that of camels in a caravan. Not only did poets write panegyrics, sometimes in the old grand style, but they also often compared themselves to classical poets: Shawqi, in praising his patron, likened himself to the ninth-century poet Abū Tammām praising the Caliph al-Muʿtaṣim; al-Barudi before him had, in his long poem on the Prophet, compared himself to Ḥassān ibn Thābit, the poet who eulogized Muhammad. Moreover, poets wrote *muʿāraḍāt*, poems that by following the rhyme and meter of earlier works were meant to vie with the original models or at least invite comparison with them, in the way, but not quite with the same degree of originality as Pope, for instance, imitated Horace, or Johnson Juvenal. However, we must never forget that the old Arabic ode, *qasida*, was not simply regarded as a sacrosanct ideal by the neo-classicists, but was actually made to accommodate the modern poet's political, social, and indeed psychological needs.

Here is al-Barudi writing about his experience in prison, after the failure of the ʿUrābī revolution in which he had played a key role:

> Wasted by grief, worn out by lack of sleep,
> I am blinded by curtains of care.
> Neither will the dark night pass
> Nor is the bright morning to be expected.
> There is no companion to listen to my complaint,
> No news to come, no figure to pass my way.
> Here I am between the walls and behind a door securely bolted,
> Which creaks as soon as the gaoler begins to open it.
> Pacing up and down he is outside,
> But at the slightest sound I make he halts.
> Whenever I turn to do a thing darkness says to me:
> Stop, do not move.
> I grope my way, looking for what I want,
> But neither do I find the object of my search,
> Nor does my soul find its repose.
> Darkness without a single star
> Broken only by the fire of my breath.
>
> So be patient, my soul, till you attain your desire,
> For good patience is the key to success.
> We are indeed no more than breaths which are spent,
> And man is a prisoner of Fate, wherever he may be.

The poet's feelings of grief, anxiety, isolation, loneliness, and tragic disappointment are rendered with just sufficient concrete details to make the situation reasonably well realized. Yet in the Arabic version we find most of the rhetorical features of classical poetry: the use of antithesis, parallelism, paronomasia or word play, hyperbole, and even the traditional generalities of moralizing verse at the end, as well as Koranic allusions. But the individuality of the poet's experience and the generalization of the conclusion are organically related. The idea of man being a prisoner of fate is suggested by the poet actually being a prisoner at the time. By generalizing his own personal situation, by making his own fate the fate of all mankind the poet is in fact fortifying himself to face his own predicament. He is using the classical poetic idiom and convention to give expression to his own personal experience.

The neo-classical poets were not constantly engaged in servile imitation. They did imitate *creatively* when they were inspired, and when this happened the result was not lacking in subtlety. While giving expression to their experiences they managed to place their work securely within the larger poetic tradition, making full use of what is now known as inter-textuality, and the old classical idiom was then used as a kind of shorthand, a set of culturally charged symbols. Apart from his cunning use of the potentialities of the Arabic language and his extraordinary gift for what Coleridge once described as 'the sense of musical delight', part of the wide appeal that a poet like Shawqi had for the reader steeped in the classical Arabic poetic tradition is doubtless due to this fact.

Within the formal and stylistic limitations of the *qasida* the neo-classical poets managed to give adequate expression to their modern problems and preoccupations. At their hands the role of the poet was considerably changed. The poet as the craftsman who was prepared to sell his wares to the highest bidder, or who vied with his fellow craftsmen in verbal acrobatics and display of stylistic ingenuities, as was indeed the case before the modern revival, was gradually but unmistakably replaced by the poet as the spokesman of his community. It is true, of course, that in the history of Arabic poetry this was by no means a new function: but it was a function long lost, and by recovering it Arabic poetry, after centuries of intellectual frivolity, was once more made relevant to life. Since the problems and preoccupations of twentieth-century Arab society were obviously not the same as those of, say, a pre-Islamic tribe, it cannot be said that the most successful of neo-classical poems are in any meaningful sense a mere copy or pale reflection of classical poems. The distinguished Egyptian writer Yaḥyā Ḥaqqī clearly realized this when, in an interesting essay on Shawqi's elegies written for the Cairo periodical *al-Majalla* in 1968, he said: 'Shawqi is a modern extension of the tribal poet in his golden age.' This role of spokesman of the community was not, of course, confined to Shawqi, although because of his greater poetic gifts he obviously excelled in it and took great pride in it. He said, for instance: 'My poetry was the song in the joys of the east, and the comfort in its sorrows.' At the fall of Islamic Macedonia (1912) Shawqi wrote a poem opening with these somewhat archaic lines, where the crescent moon is used as the obvious symbol of Islam:

> Farewell, sister of Andalusia,
> Islam and the caliphate have fallen from thee
> The crescent moon has gone down from thy sky.

Would that the heavens had folded up
And darkness enveloped all the globe.

In 'Tutankhamon and Parliament' Shawqi imagines an Egyptian Pharaoh rising from the tomb only to be shocked by the lowly state of his country under foreign domination:

Travelling forty centuries all told
Until he came to his land, only to behold
England, her army and her Lord,
Her sword drawn to defend her Indian lands,
Straddling the Sudan, building her dam,
And fixing her flag beyond the canal.

Stricken with grief the Pharaoh cried
Would that the walls of the tomb had never opened
And sleep had never parted from my eyes!
Arise, poet Binta'ur, tell what disaster has occurred?
Egypt, my daughter has no more respect for her lord,
Outside my grave she has let her jazz band play,
Has let the lions rove freely among her fawns.

All the neo-classicists, in one way or another, played the role of community spokesmen with such frequency and seriousness that they had a lasting effect upon the later development of Arabic poetry: modern Arabic poetry has never been entirely free from social or political commitment. But the resounding phrase, the oratorical tone, the rhetorical magniloquence and grand style, the pronounced and almost incantatory rhythm, and the clinching rhyme of the *qasida* style rendered it a perfect form for this 'public' type of poetry. Poems of this type have been likened to leading articles: they may indeed have fulfilled similar functions for a while, but they do much more besides, and at its best this is journalism of the very highest order, the order of Dean Swift's 'A Modest Proposal' or similar tracts. Because it is poetry that relies heavily upon the peculiar formal features of the language, unlike journalism (and, of course, unlike much later poetry), it is bound to lose a great deal in translation, but it is most doubtful if the anger and devastating irony of poems like Shawqi's *Wadāʿ al-Lord Cromer* (Bidding Farewell to Lord Cromer), or Hafiz Ibrahim's *Ḥādithat Danshiwāy* (The Danshiway Incident), or *Muẓāharat al-Sayyidāt al-Miṣriyyāt* (Egyptian Women's Demonstration) could have been better or more forcefully expressed in any other form. Hafiz Ibrahim writes a mock heroic poem of considerable irony, with echoes of Abbasid poetry, on the British army's handling of a demonstration of Egyptian women protesting against the arrest and exile of the nationalist leader Saʿd Zaghlūl in 1919:

The ladies came out in protest. I watched their rally.
They assumed black garments as their banner,
They looked like stars shining bright in the midst of darkness,
Marching down the road, making for Saʿd's house,
Revealing their feelings, in an orderly procession,
When lo, an army approached, with galloping horses,
And soldiers pointed their swords at the women's necks,
Guns and rifles, points and swords, a circle of horses and horsemen
  formed around them.
That day the women were armed with roses and sweet basil,
The two armies clashed for hours: by the end the babies' hair would
  have turned grey.
Then the women faltered, for women have not much stamina,
Defeated, they scattered in disarray, back to their homes,
So let the proud army rejoice in its victory and gloat over their defeat.
Could it have been that amongst those women the British had thought
  there were German soldiers wearing veils,
A host led by Hindenburg in disguise,
So the army feared their strength and was alarmed at their cunning?

Or take al-Rusafi's remarkable short poem *al-Ḥurriyya fī Siyāsat al-Mustaʿmirīn* (Freedom under Imperialist Policy), in which the poet comments on the intention of the Western powers to divide up the Arab world after World War I. Under tyranny, the poet complains, because of the threat of force, all values are completely reversed: the only people who prosper are those who willingly forgo their reason, understanding, speech and the sense of hearing, to say nothing of the desire for happiness or justice, in short those who willingly give up their very humanity. Full of bitter sarcasm, barely suppressed anger, and self-laceration, and gathering force until it rises to a powerful crescendo, this seething political poem would not have been the same without the monometer and monorhyme of the *qasida* form which help create a feeling of inevitability, of mechanical and almost imbecile repetition to accord with the idea of the completely dehumanized automaton one is reduced to under a system that robs one of all dignity. In this manner we are prepared for the climax of the poem, the final couple of lines in which the idea of rejoicing, which the poet asks his people to indulge in at the impending dismemberment of their country, is expressed as a grotesque version, or ghastly travesty of mystical fervour and spiritual ecstasy during a dervish dance.

Similarly, the expressiveness and violence of imagery in al-Jawahiri's poems like, for instance, *Aṭbiq Dujā* (Descend, Darkness) or *Tanwīmat al-Jiyāʿ* (Lullaby for the Hungry) would have lost much of their effect if it had not been for the tension created by the restraining exigencies of the *qasida* form. Al-Jawahiri was perhaps the political poet *par excellence*. His work is unique in that the form is obviously classical and the diction at times archaic, yet the degree and kind of political consciousness and the fervour of the revolutionary impulse are thoroughly modern. Listen to him giving vent to his grief and anger in his elegy on his brother, who was brutally killed during a demonstration held in Baghdad to protest against the Portsmouth Treaty in 1947:

> It is not mere fancy what I say, my brother,
> For he who has to take revenge is always awake: he does not dream.
> But inspired by my patient endurance,
> (What the future hides can sometimes be revealed),
> I see the heavens with no stars, lit up in red blood
> And a rope, rising like a ladder, on which to climb from the earth,
> Whoever reaches out to cut it has his hand chopped off
> By a figure emerging from the huge corpses around him, where the glory is even more huge.
> And I see a hand stretching beyond the veil, writing on the horizon
> A generation gone and a generation come
> And before them rose an enkindled flame.

Al-Jawahiri's often explosive and repulsive imagery has an almost physical impact on the listener, the poet's anger at social injustice, political corruption, and the degradation of man becomes infectious and reaches a degree of intensity at times terrifying. This is amply illustrated in the first part of his poem 'Descend, Darkness' which by its repetition and diction has the effect of magical incantations or curses:

> Descend, darkness and fog, and clouds without rain,
> Burning smoke of conscience and torture, descend,
> Woe and destruction, descend upon those who their own destruction defend!

Punishment and retaliation upon the makers of their own tombs
Descend, croaking of ravens, and let your echoes be greeted by the hooting of owls. Ruin, descend.
Descend upon those sluggards of whose laziness even flies complain,
From too much cringing of their necks they cannot tell the colour of the sky.
Their heads trampled underfoot as often as dust is.
Descend upon those starving goats that are still taken to be milked,
Upon those misshapen creatures whose life even dogs would not stoop to,
In whose limbs you can see the marks of a predator's claw or tooth,
A festering wound whose flowing pus indignity has turned into the fragrance of musk.
Descend, night, upon those worms flung far from the endless wastes,
Upon those faces that are like unreal images,
Whose features are dumb, revealing neither question nor response,
Whose eyes roll senselessly in their heads, whose certainties are only the illusions of a mirage.

Because the neo-classical poets used the language of statement at its highest potency, and were masters of rhetoric and the art of persuasion, their political and social poetry, which took the form of direct address to the reader, was on the whole more successful than their short narrative poems (favoured by al-Zahawi and al-Rusafi), which related stories designed to point an obvious moral connected with a political or social problem.

Although the neo-classical form and style are eminently suited for public themes where the poet is constantly aware of the presence of an audience to exhort or instruct, or to derive comfort and reassurance from (and it is no accident that it was poetry that was recited or declaimed at public gatherings and that its effect is greatest when read *aloud*), the figure of the poet in communion with his own thoughts was not entirely absent from neo-classicism. For instance, in *Sajīn* and *al-Hilāl* (The Crescent Moon) al-Barudi and Shawqi respectively were able to express something of their inner thoughts and feelings within the framework of convention, in fact, by putting the conventions themselves to their own personal use. S. K. Jayyusi in Volume I of her *Trends and Movements in Modern Arabic Poetry* (see section 3A of the Bibliography) has admirably pointed out how Badawī al-Jabal expresses his innermost thoughts and deep feelings, his 'private agony and ecstasy' in poems with a mystical dimension, in which he draws upon certain elements, particularly imagery and motifs, from the Sufi (mystical) tradition in medieval Arabic poetry.

Yet, despite the fact that in a man like al-Zahawi self-preoccupation can sometimes turn into an irritating feeling of self-pity, on the whole, neo-classical poetry, as is to be expected, is characterized by its impersonality. One of the best examples of this impersonal art is Shawqi's poem *Maṣā'ir al-Ayyām* (The Destiny of Days) in which, with great irony, calm contemplation, and detachment the poet describes in alternate moods of humour and deep seriousness, a class of schoolchildren and meditates on their diverse individual futures, both pitiful and great, tracing them until they are all lost in the wastes of time. Finally, it must not be forgotten that, despite the fact that the neo-classicists generally sought many of their ideals and models in the Arab past, in the course of time they were not averse to importing the new Western literary genre of drama: Shawqi's verse dramas were not a solitary phenomenon; they found their successors in the plays of ʿAzīz Abāẓa among others—even though it must be admitted that neither Shawqi nor Abaza thought of using anything other than the traditional metrical forms in his dramatic verse.

III

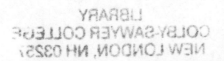

Although the revolt against neo-classicism goes back as far as the turn of the century, if not earlier still, for our present purpose it is convenient to start with a major figure like Khalīl Muṭrān (1872–1949), who both in theory and in much of his practice showed his dissatisfaction with the classical conventions, and set out to write what he regarded as 'modern' poetry (*ʿaṣrī*). Mutran, a product of Lebanese missionary education who emigrated to Egypt at the age of 20, had a thorough knowledge of French literature, and his reaction to the limitations of classicism was an expression of a much wider movement towards Westernization. Mutran was a highly conscious artist who introduced into Arabic poetry a number of attitudes and assumptions which were fully incorporated into the poetic thinking of later generations, to the extent that he, more than anybody else, can be regarded as the true father of the new or modern school of poetry. The most important of these assumptions is firstly that of the unity of the poem: he systematically and deliberately sought to achieve unity of structure. In so doing he ran counter to the mistaken but commonly held belief, popularized by medieval Arabic literary critics, that the classical Arabic poem consisted of single independent lines loosely strung together. Later on, the alleged absence of structural unity from most of Shawqi's poems became a target for the severely adverse criticism of the younger generation of poets like ʿAbbās Maḥmūd al-ʿAqqād.

Second, there is the belief in the primacy of meaning, expressed in Mutran's description of himself in the famous Preface written in 1908 to the first volume of his Collected Poems as not being 'a slave to his verse or to the necessities of rhyme or metre'. While not neglecting the language of his poetry or even the traditional metres and rhymes, Mutran is hardly ever guilty of mere verbiage, of pursuing high-sounding words or figures of speech for their own sake. This has resulted in the poet rising above the rhetorical temptations which are almost inherent in the very nature of most traditional Arabic poetry from the late Abbasid period onwards, and to which the neo-classicists certainly succumbed. In his serious output, particularly in the first volume of his *Diwan*, the tone of Mutran's poetry is much more subdued and less declamatory than that of the poetry of either Shawqi or Hafiz. The followers of Mutran went a step further and sought an even greater freedom and independence in their desire for self-expression. Inspired by their master, who claimed (in the same Preface) that he had written to relieve his soul in solitude, they gave an even freer expression to their personal emotions.

Third, Mutran regarded what he called the 'uncommonness of the imagination and the strangeness of the subject' as essential qualities that he tried to realize in his poetry. These qualities, which represent significant departures in the history of Arabic poetry, are very far from the tendency to keep to the conventional themes, the conventional poetic diction, and therefore the conventional poetic vision of the neo-classicists. We are now close to the originality and creative imagination that were the watchwords of the European Romantics. There is, in fact, an interesting parallelism between Mutran's insistence on 'uncommonness of imagination and the strangeness of subject, together with essential truthfulness, minuteness and accuracy of description' and the avowed intentions of the authors of the *Lyrical Ballads* (although it is exceedingly unlikely that Mutran was *directly* influenced by Wordsworth and Coleridge).

Mutran wrote a number of highly subjective poems, such as the well-known *al-Masā'* (Evening) and *al-Asad al-Bākī* (The Lion in Tears), which reveal a deep and intense emotion very different from the generally controlled and impersonal character of neo-classical poetry. In fact, the sensibility expressed in these poems is something quite new in Arabic poetry. For instance, in 'Evening' we have the lonely figure of the poet in the presence of nature: the poet primarily as an introspective, thinking, and feeling being communing with himself. It is essentially a romantic sensibility which finds a deep spiritual affinity between external nature and the mind of man and feels the entire universe to be bound together by love:

Invisible atoms coming together
Revealing themselves in visible forms,
Seeds are hugged by the earth
Which makes of them gardens in bloom.
And yonder stars, are they not pearls
Afloat on teeming seas?
Scattered, yet strung together in orderly constellations,
Love binding them to one another,
And each perpetually seeking its like?

Here again Mutran had a great influence upon many of the younger generation of poets (especially his acknowledged Egyptian disciples Aḥmad Zakī Abū Shādī and Ibrāhīm Nājī), who developed further this romantic attitude to nature. Furthermore, unlike the neo-classicists, who favoured the explicitly stated moral, Mutran had a distinct preference for the oblique type of poetry, for the narrative poem or dramatic monologue (which he seems to have introduced into modern Arabic poetry) like, for example, his love poems *Ḥikāyat ʿĀshiqayn* (Tale of Two Lovers), *Finjān Qahwa* (A Cup of Coffee). His best-known narrative and dramatic poems, whether based upon historical events or incidents from contemporary life, contain an indirect political or moral commentary. For example, *Buzurjumihr* and *Fatāt al-Jabal al-Aswad* (The Maid from Montenegro), both written just after the turn of the century, attack Turkish tyranny and embody an oblique passionate plea for freedom. *Al-Janīn al-Shahīd* (The Martyred Foetus), written at the same time, attacks social and moral ills such as the suffering of the poor and the immorality of the city, and ends with a powerful dramatic monologue expressing the thoughts and feelings of a poor young unmarried mother about to abort herself to save her child from a life of shame and misery.

Mutran's introspection and self-preoccupation have not prevented him completely from writing direct political poetry of deep passion. Here, for instance, is his angry reaction to Sir Eldon Gorst's curbing the freedom of the Egyptian press in 1909:

Disperse her best men by land and sea
Slaughter her free men one by one,
The good shall be good till the end of time,
And so the evil shall evil remain.
Smash all the pens, would that prevent
Hands from chiselling on stone?
Cut off the hands, would that restrain
Eyes from staring in anger?
Put out the eyes, would that prevail
Against the fieriness of breath?
Stop then the breath, for that would be
The utmost you could do to us
And for that we would offer our thanks.

Yet despite Mutran's originality and greater lyricism and his freedom in handling stanzaic forms—in 1907 he even attempted to write *vers libre* which he called *shiʿr manthūr*—there is much in his use of the language which harks back to the Abbasids; his constant polishing of his style, his dominant self-control, his occasional archaism and difficult vocabulary render his poetry somewhat deficient in the type and degree of spontaneity necessary to make him a thoroughgoing romantic. There is often a tension between the old form and new content, which may justify our calling him pre-Romantic. In this respect Mutran resembles the Dīwān group of poets, the Egyptians ʿAbd al-Raḥmān Shukrī (1886–1958), ʿAbbās Maḥmūd al-ʿAqqād (1889–1964), and Ibrāhīm ʿAbd al-Qādir al-Māzinī (1890–1949), who, in spite of the important role they played in the development of Arabic poetry, were less gifted poets than Mutran.

Heavily influenced by much nineteenth-century English (and to a lesser extent German) literature, the Dīwān poets set out as early as the first decade of the century to demolish in their polemic criticism the neo-classicism of Shawqi and Hafiz and to advocate both in their criticism and in their poetry a more personal type of poetry which accords with the spirit of the age. Their revolt was contemporaneous with that of Mutran, but apparently, and despite many partisan allegations to the contrary, independent of his. Their most violent onslaught on the literary establishment, however, namely the two volumes of criticism entitled *al-Dīwān* which were written jointly by al-ʿAqqad and al-Mazini, was published in 1921 when the three of them no longer formed a group. The immediate relevance of *al-Diwan* to our purpose lies in that, despite its obvious extremism and partisanship, it eventually succeeded in preparing the reading public, especially the younger generation, for the acceptance of a new type of poetry, different from the neo-classical. Although neo-classicism proved to be hard to kill, and Shawqi's prestige remained unaffected for a long time, from this point on no truly major figure, with the possible exception of one or two poets like the Iraqi al-Jawahiri, sought to write in the traditional neo-classical style. And it is no wonder that a radical revolutionary like Mīkhā'īl Nuʿayma (1889–1988), who lived in the USA at the time, hailed the appearance of *al-Diwan* with such rapturous enthusiasm in his equally, if not even more, iconoclastic volume *al-Ghirbāl* (*The Sieve*), published in 1923.

Like Mutran, the Diwan group believed in the unity of a poem, although their conception of it is more sophisticated and organic. They all held an exalted opinion of poetry: according to them the poet is not a mere craftsman or even a higher type of journalist, recording the happenings in his society. He is a man with a deep emotional experience and a personal attitude or philosophy; he should, therefore, rise above writing imitative panegyrics to rulers, or verses on trivial social occasions, and, instead, strive to write literature that is universal, Egyptian, and Arabic at one and the same time. The poetry the group advocated is primarily of a subjective nature, the product not of cold and mechanical imitation but of direct experience, for sincerity is of prime importance. The influence of the Western Romantic poets and critics they read is abundantly clear both in their theorizing and in their actual practice. Their best poetry was of a dominantly introspective kind, its prevalent tone one of sorrow and melancholy. They attempted to write, with varying degrees of success, about ordinary scenes from everyday life in Egypt, about nature, starlit and moonlit night, local birds (al-ʿAqqad's preference for concrete, real experience to literary convention or imitation is shown in his choice of the Egyptian bird, the curlew, instead of the nightingale, which, he claimed, was not known in Egypt). They had a common attitude to the Arabic language: like Mutran, they tried to avoid sheer verbiage and the use of archaic and far-fetched words which made it necessary for the neo-classicists, or their editors, to provide with their poems glosses to explain the meaning of difficult vocabulary. But, unlike the Mahjar poets (the Syrian Arab poets who emigrated to America at the turn of the century), they were meticulous about their Arabic, proud of the achievement of the Arabs, especially the Abbasids of whom they were extremely fond. Except for Shukri, their intention outstripped their poetic ability. Their knowledge of Western literature did not seem to have been fully assimilated, but remained at variance with their more spontaneous traditional responses to and experience of Egyptian life around them—a source of anxiety and tension.

Al-Mazini's poetry is interesting chiefly as a record of the malaise of the time, the painful awareness of living in an age of cultural change, when values were in a state of flux. He wrote poems on themes such as the faded rose, dead flowers, 'life is but a dream', reflections in solitude. These poems have an atmosphere of romantic sadness; in them the poet complains, in the manner of Shelley, of the world, of life, and of time. They are after all mostly poems of adolescence. Al-ʿAqqad's truly successful poems are very few, considering the bulk of his output; they are descriptions of romantic scenery or poems dealing with childhood themes, like, for example, his moving elegy on the death of a little girl, which is strongly reminiscent of Wordsworth's 'Lucy' poems. As he developed, however, a strong element of intellectuality began to enter his poetry, unfortunately to its detriment. Much of his poetry is taken up with meditations on love, or objects of nature, from birds to flowers, especially the rose. Like Shawqi, he also wrote descriptive poems on the remains of ancient Egyptian civilization, as well as political exhortations to the Egyptian people in which he could be almost as direct as Shawqi, and his language just as much a language of statement. Far more than the other two, Shukri, a complex and enigmatic personality, is primarily a subjective and meditative poet, much of whose poetry reminds one of Edward Young's 'Night Thoughts'. Shukri's fascinating semi-autobiographical prose work *Kitāb al-Iʿtirāf* (*Book of Confessions*), written in 1916, is a book of remarkable frankness, full of profound self-analysis and acute observations on art and man, life and death. It not only depicts the malaise of the Egyptian intellectual at the beginning of the century, but also shows Shukri to be a man suffering from hypersensitivity which borders on the pathological. Happiness and great sensitivity, we are told at the outset, are mutually exclusive, for a man of feeling is inevitably a man of suffering. The recurring themes of Shukri's poetry are those of hopeless unrequited love, the human soul confronted with the mysteries of life and death, the spiritual impact of nature, the morbid preoccupation with decay and dissolution. His scepticism was at times almost absolute, embracing not only man and his social and moral values, not only the here, but also the hereafter. But he was no cynic; his poetry is imbued with a strong feeling of pity as is clear, for instance, in his dramatic monologue *al-Mujrim* (The Murderer). Like the other two, he wrote about love and death, and the Unknown *(Ila'l-Majhūl)*, a word that became very potent indeed in romantic vocabulary.

It is now clear how much the image of the poet that emerges from this differs from that of the craftsman or spokesman of society. Put crudely, the shift is from the 'public' figure to that of the introspective individual, the introvert, the man of feeling. The image is perhaps further defined by a poem by Shukri called *al-Shāʿir wa Ṣūrat al-Kamāl* (The Poet and the Image of Perfection): it depicts a poet who, in the pursuit of the ideal (which is ultimately Perfect Beauty—the creation of his imagination), is lured to his destruction. Clearly it is a variation on the theme of Keats's 'La Belle Dame sans Merci': we are now not very far from the world of Romanticism, where imagination is regarded as a tool of insight into a higher order of reality—a reality, however, which may render those who have glimpsed it incapable of coping with this mundane world.

Yet, despite the profound influence of English Romantic poetry on him, Shukri's style remains in many respects traditional: the vocabulary is still quite difficult, requiring a glossary at times, and the verse does not flow smoothly enough for the particular themes it tries to express. Occasionally he uses conventional love and desert imagery and has an unmistakable tendency to express himself in generalizations, sentiments, and moral precepts in the manner of traditional gnomic verse. Although he can attain a high degree of lyricism, as in his well-known *Ṭā'ir al-Firdaws* (The Bird of Paradise), he not infrequently descends to the level of what is largely poetry of mere statement, even in a poem dealing with a specifically

Romantic theme as *al-Mathal al-Aʿlā* (The Ideal), which extols the infinite inner world of dreams and the imagination, preferring it to the drab and limited external reality.

IV

The tension between form and content, between language and sensibility, which we noticed in the work of Mutran and the Diwan group, disappears altogether from the works of the Romantic poets, whether they belong to the expatriate Mahjar, or come from the Arab world itself. The full flowering of the Mahjar Romantic poetry occurred a few years earlier, and it had considerable influence on many poets in the Arab world but, as in the case of new poetry after World War II, to try to establish exactly who started what is very difficult and indeed futile, since the desire for change and the 'romantic' impulse had been in the air for some time and soon swept over almost the entire Arab world.

As is to be expected the Arab Romantics did not revolt against their immediate predecessors, the poets we have been considering. There were squabbles between them at times, but no real conflict of principles. They were after all an extension or a further development of the attitudes and assumptions of Mutran and the Diwan group. In fact, the transition from the one group to the other was smooth and almost imperceptible. We have seen how Nuʿayma approved of the attack on Shawqi's neo-classicism launched by al-ʿAqqad, of whom the Mahjari Jibrān Khalīl Jibrān (Gibran) entertained a high opinion.

But the revolt of some of the Romantics against classicism was even more extreme than that of the authors of *al-Diwan*. The Romantic rebels tended to reject almost the entire Arabic poetic heritage in favour of the European, with which they compared it to its great disadvantage. The more important and extreme documents in this connection are Nuʿayma's *al-Ghirbāl* (*The Sieve*) (see above) and *al-Khayāl al-Shiʿrī ʿind al-ʿArab* (*The Arab Poetic Imagination*) published in 1929 by the Tunisian Abu'l-Qāsim al-Shābbī (1909–34). Nuʿayma's book is well known, but the significance of al-Shabbi's, which is seldom discussed in any detail, has not been sufficiently realized until quite recently. Al-Shabbi's essay, based on a lecture he gave to his shocked Tunisian audience, is certainly an impressive performance, coming as it did from a young man of twenty, with no knowledge of a single European language. Admittedly, it suffers from the headiness of youth and its proclivity for making sweeping generalizations, supported by, probably unconsciously, highly selected evidence. On the other hand, it lacks neither courage nor integrity. After a general discussion of imagination, the essay deals in separate chapters with the poetic imagination in relation to Arab mythology, Arab attitudes to nature, to women, and to narrative literature, then ends with a brief discussion of Arabic literature in general and (typically for the time) the Arab spirit or the Arab mind.

Like the thoroughgoing romantic he is, al-Shabbi is keenly aware of the importance of imagination, which he considers to be as essential to man in apprehending and interpreting reality as the air he breathes, and, of course, he sees the relation between it and metaphorical language. Al-Shabbi finds Arab mythology deficient in poetic imagination, compared with the Greek, Roman, or Scandinavian. In his essay he reviews the treatment of nature in Arabic poetry, both pre-Islamic and Islamic, compares it with the European treatment as revealed in two examples from Goethe and (inevitably) Lamartine, and finally concludes that 'Arab poets have not expressed such deep poetic feeling because their attitude to nature lacked reverence for its sublime life: they only looked at it as they looked at a beautifully ornamented garment or pretty embroidery'. Likewise, al-Shabbi dismisses summarily the Arab attitude to woman, which he finds superficial and limited to the world of the senses:

> The attitude of Arabic literature to woman is base and ignoble . . . It only sees in woman a body to be desired and one of the basest pleasures in life to be enjoyed. As for that noble view which combines love and reverence, fondness and worship, as for that deep spiritual attitude which we find in the Aryan poets, it is totally or almost totally absent from Arabic literature.

Then he asks: 'Have you heard anyone among them [the Arab poets] talk about woman, who is the altar of love in this universe, in the way a devout worshipper talks about the house of God?' and compares the Arab view with the idealized image expressed by Jibrān (1883–1931) in *al-Ajniḥa al-Mutakassira* (*The Broken Wings*). Al-Shabbi goes on to point out the total irrelevance of Arabic literature:

> Arabic literature no longer suits our present spirit, temperament, inclinations or aspirations in life . . . [It] was not created for us, children of

these times, but for hearts that are now silenced by death . . . We must never look upon Arabic literature as an ideal which we have to follow or whose spirit, style, and ideas we have to imitate, but we must consider it simply as one of those ancient literatures which we admire and respect and no more . . . We have now come to desire life. But we must first realize that we are hungry and naked and that that huge and abundant wealth bequeathed to us by the Arabs cannot satisfy or fulfil our need and hunger.

The reasons why al-Shabbi considers Arabic literature irrelevant are significant: 'Everything the Arab mind has produced in all the periods of its history', he writes, 'is monotonous and utterly lacking in poetic imagination', superficial, and 'does not penetrate into the reality of things'. The two chief characteristics of the Arab spirit are oratory and materialism. Materialism stops at the level of the senses while oratory and keen sensibility generally do not go together. The effect of these two tendencies of the Arab spirit is that 'the Arabs did not view the poet as we now do, namely as the prophet or messenger who brings life to the children of the world, lost in the paths of time; they did not distinguish between him and the orator who defended his tribe and protected its honour with his tongue.' The only difference between many Arabic poems and public speeches lies in their use of metre and rhyme. Among the effects of oratory are the use of rhetoric, the unity of the single line, and the abundance of synonyms. Arab critics too did not form a proper conception of literature, they failed to see that 'it is the voice of life, which gives hope and consolation to mankind and accompanies them on their weary, monotonous and harsh journey in the deserts of time'.

It is not my intention, of course, to refute here al-Shabbi's false or inaccurate critical ideas, which were derived mainly from al-ʿAqqad, who was influenced by Herbert Spencer, Ernest Renan, and Tito Vignoli. However, I have quoted from this remarkably iconoclastic work partly to show the extent of the Romantic rebellion in certain cases, and partly because the words in which the author expresses his view on literature, poetry and mythology, on nature, love, and women, seem to me to provide an admirably faithful description of the attitude to these topics, revealed in his own poetry and indeed in much of the best work of the Arab Romantic poets. Together with al-Shabbi's views we ought perhaps to cite one or two passages from the earlier work, Mikha'il

Nuʿayma's *al-Ghirbal*, which seems to have had some influence on al-Shabbi. Keenly aware of the shortcomings of the classical Arabic tradition, Nuʿayma, in a piece entitled 'Let Us Translate', strongly advises Arab authors to concentrate upon translating the literary masterpieces of the world as a necessary step to put Arabic literature on the map of world literature. (Incidentally, the part played by translations from Western Romantic poetry in the development of modern Arabic Romantic poetry is vital and has been studied in some detail by Muhammad Abdul-Hai (see Bibliography, section 3A.) This is how Nuʿayma defines the poet in *al-Ghirbal*:

What is a Poet? A Poet is a prophet, a philosopher, a painter, a musician, and a priest in one. He is a prophet because he can see with his spiritual eye what cannot be seen by other mortals. A painter because he is capable of moulding what he can see and hear in beautiful forms of verbal imagery, a musician because he can hear harmony where we can find only discordant noise . . . Lastly a poet is a priest because he serves the goddess of Truth and Beauty.

Jibran wrote that 'the poet is an angel sent down by the gods to teach men divine things'. Perhaps the self-image of the Arab poet at this stage is best expressed by ʿAlī Maḥmūd Ṭāhā (1902–49) in his poem *Mīlād Shāʿir* (A Poet is Born), which he opens thus:

He descended on earth like a ray of celestial light, bearing the wand of a magician and the heart of a prophet.
A spark of the iridescent spirit has dwelt in the folds of a human frame, inspiring his heart and tongue with every elevated thought from the world of wisdom and light.

The romanticizing is now complete: instead of being a skilful craftsman or spokesman of the community, with which he is completely identified, the poet is now placed above his community and regarded as being a thing of the spirit, a magician, a mighty philosopher, a 'seer' and a prophet all in one. It is interesting to see how many poems about the poet or the suffering of the poet, and how many elegies on actual poets written during the third or fourth decades of this century embody this essentially Romantic conception.

Romanticism was to spread very fast indeed in Arabic poetry, shaping the works of an unusually large number of gifted poets who were active particularly during the inter-war period. To choose but a few outstanding names: Aḥmad Zakī Abū Shādī

(1892–1955), Ibrāhīm Nājī (1898–1953), and ʿAlī Maḥmūd Ṭāhā in Egypt, Ilyās Abū Shabaka (1903–47) in Lebanon, ʿUmar Abū Rīsha (b. 1910) in Syria, al-Shabbī in Tunisia, and Yūsuf Bashīr al-Tijānī (1912–37) in the Sudan; in the USA: Jibrān, Nasīb ʿArīḍa (1887–1946), Mikhā'īl Nuʿayma, and Īliyā Abū Māḍī (1889–1957); and in South America: Rashīd al-Khūrī (1887–1984), Ilyās Faraḥāt (1893–1977), and Fawzī al-Maʿlūf (1899–1930). Their works are marked by a great lyricism and spontaneity, simple and evocative language, subjective feelings, a sense of mystery and wonder, reverence for nature and life in general, in short, a keen sense of individuality, a deeper self-awareness coupled with more freedom in handling stanzaic forms. Their achievement is so great and manifold that it would be absurd to try to give an idea of it in a couple of paragraphs: each of these poets in fact deserves a serious full-length study. The following remarks are therefore made with this strong reservation in mind. For the sake of convenience only I shall deal with the Mahjar poets as a group—although they include many distinguished poets of notable individuality and one, Iliya Abu Madi, who is perhaps the greatest of the Arab Romantics.

The part played by the Mahjar poets in spreading romantic attitudes was enormous. Both historically and culturally these poets, who left for America in search of political freedom or wealth, were an extension of Lebanese and Syrian poetry. They were enterprising individualists, all of them Christians brought up in missionary schools. The better-educated ones amongst them were imbued with modernist and anti-traditional ideas, and in America they had more freedom for literary experimentation than those of their compatriots who chose to settle in Egypt, thereby exposing themselves to the moderating influences of traditional Arab culture. They seemed to have been influenced by the latter-day romanticism and transcendentalism of American literature, namely Thoreau and Emerson (although some, who had received higher education in Russia, such as Nuʿayma and ʿArida, were influenced by Russian romanticism, for example Tyutchev), and were on the whole much more anti-traditionalist than those who emigrated to South America. An interesting feature that all the Arab Americans had in common was that they suffered from a sense of exile, a lack of belonging. In a country where the language of their literature and traditions was not spoken they felt their cultural existence to be threatened, and this drove them to form associations and societies and to set up their own Arabic literary reviews. Their work is permeated by a feeling of homesickness, no doubt intensified by their awareness of being outsiders. This feeling often underlies their yearning to return to nature and to simple rural life, and is closely related to their idealization of their homeland, to the opposition they set up between the spirituality of the East and the materialism of the West, an idea repeated *ad nauseam* in the work of all these poets. Some of the romantic features, which we find in their work, like the sense of isolation and the heightened feeling of individualism, are therefore not mere imitations of certain postures in Western Romantic poetry. They are based upon the real facts of their concrete situation in an alien community or culture.

It can safely be said that the whole generation of Romantic Arab poets who reached their maturity in the inter-war period fell under the spell of the Mahjar poets, especially those of the USA, who exercised a liberating influence upon modern Arabic poetry. The Mahjar poets contributed toward the introduction of a new conception of poetry, which added, as it were, a spiritual dimension to it. They turned away from rhetoric and declamation in search of a quieter and more subdued tone of voice, concentrating on the more subjective experience of man in relation to nature and ultimate questions. They introduced biblical themes and images into their poetry and had a distinct preference for short metres and stanzaic forms and even tried poetic prose and prose poetry (Amīn al-Rīḥānī and Jibran). Indeed, the extremist views of some of them were often rejected in the Arab world, their tendency to turn their back on the Arab cultural past was violently attacked, and their language sometimes severely criticized for not being sufficiently correct. Nevertheless, their role in shaping modern Arab sensibility cannot be exaggerated. Apart from their seminal influence, their actual poetic achievements are remarkable, for example the work of Nuʿayma, Nasib ʿArida, and particularly Abu Madi, the great poet of 'moods', who gave memorable expression to intense feelings of joy and sorrow. In his best poems Abu Madi's meditations on the mystery of life and death arise naturally from a concrete situation vividly and poignantly portrayed in a narrative or dramatic context as, for instance, in his poem *al-Masāʾ* (Evening). The sight of a girl resting her cheek on her hand and looking sad at 'the dying of the light' and the approach of night, inspires the poet to write a poem in a masterfully controlled stanzaic form about the human predicament, comparable to Gerard Manley Hopkins's 'Spring and Fall'. Abu Madi ends his poem with this exhortation:

> Dead is the light of day, the morning's child; ask not how it has died.
> Thinking about life only increases life's sorrows,
> So leave aside your dejection and grief,
> Regain your girlish merriment
> In the morning your face was like the morning, radiant with joy:
> Cheerful and bright:
> Let it be also so at night.

In the Arab world itself the contribution of the Romantic poets was immense. The person who played the largest role in spreading Romantic poetry, although as a poet he was easily surpassed by many others, was Abu Shadi, a man of astonishing versatility, and an acknowledged disciple of Mutran. In this he was assisted by Naji, another ardent admirer of Mutran. Thanks largely to the efforts of these two remarkable physicians, and of the young men who gathered around them in the Apollo Society of which Abu Shadi was the founder and Naji the vice-president (and through its magazine *Apollo* (1932–1934)), the spirit of Romanticism which had already begun to make itself felt in Mahjar poetry swiftly spread and dominated much of the poetry written in the 1930s and 1940s in most Arabic-speaking countries. Abu Shadi's prodigious output was most uneven; unlike Mutran he was often too prosaic and diffuse, but he continued to experiment both with form and content until his death. He wrote narrative poems, dramatic poems, lyrics, especially love lyrics of great charm, symplicity, and pathos, descriptive poems about paintings and Greek mythology, nature poems, especially poems inspired by the sea. Naji was certainly one of the most interesting love poets in modern Arabic: his poetry covers the gamut of the emotion of love, ranging from the passionate adoration of the beloved, in which both the physical and spiritual meet in a manner that brings to mind John Donne's poem 'The Ecstasy', to pure romantic despair in which the woman is ethereally idealized and placed beyond the reach of ordinary mortals in the tradition of *ʿudhrī* or courtly love.

Despite the feverish tone of his writings, Abu Shabaka seems to have developed his obsession with sensual pleasures into a conscious pose. In the midst of his celebrating the pleasures of the flesh he was agonizingly aware of the expense of spirit which they entail. In *Ghalwā'*, published in 1945, he wrote:

Unless you suffer, and dip your pen
Into the very depths of your sorrow
Your rhymes will remain mere glittering ornaments,
Dry bones in a marble tomb.

And in 'The Altar of Lust' he is pathetically torn between desire and fear of temptation at night, between the attraction and revulsion of sex:

The colours and shades of your lovely pale face
On which the flame flickers with desire
Strike terror in my soul.

Influenced by Baudelaire, his volume *Afāʿī 'l-Firdaws* (*The Serpents of Paradise*), first published in 1938, created his image as that of the Arab *poète maudit*. A master of Romantic rhetoric, he wrote in a fiery style, full of images of violence about sensual themes derived from the Bible. Although he thought of himself as a prophet, misunderstood and alienated from his society, he attained great serenity in his later poetry; in fact, his poetry shows a remarkable development in his attitude to love and women: instead of being a symbol of lust and damnation woman becomes a noble angel of mercy.

Unlike the earlier Abu Shabaka there was nothing in the least theatrical about al-Shabbi, with his exquisite sensibility and his idealization of women. His poetry is characterized by his heroic attitude to human suffering, his celebration of the forces of life, his sense of the holiness and sanctity of nature and love, the rich profusion of his imagery, his mastery of rhythm, and the haunting simplicity of his language. At his hands the Romantic use of language attained its greatest power of suggestion—a power which was to be developed in a Symbolist direction by the Lebanese Saʿīd ʿAql, author of the chief Symbolist experiment in modern Arabic poetry. Two years before his death, as his health was deteriorating, al-Shabbi wrote in 'A storm in the Dark' the following lines:

If I had time in the clutch of my hand
I would disperse the days to the wind like grains of sand
And I would say to the wind, 'Wind take them away,
And scatter them among distant hills,
Or rather, in the mountain passes of death, a world
Where no light dances, no shade.'

If I had this world in the clutch of my hand
I would hurl it into the fire, the fire of Hell,
For what is this world? What are these men?
This sky and those stars?
Fire is a more fitting place
For slaves to sorrow, this stage of death and this nest of cares.
I say to the past that is gone
Folded away in death and eternal night
I say to the present of men that still is
And to the future not yet born:
'Absurd is what this world of yours is
And lost in a darkness without end.'

Yet a year later al-Shabbi was capable of adopting a heroic attitude to human suffering as we see in the following poem 'Hymn of the Mighty or Thus Sang Prometheus':

I shall live in spite of sickness and enemies
Like the eagle on the highest summit,
Looking at the bright sun, mocking
The cloud, the rain and the storms.
I shall not look down at the gloomy shadow,
I shall not peer into the bottom of the dark pit
I shall roam in the world of feeling,
Dreaming and singing, for such is the poet's bliss.
Listening to life's music and inspiration
Melting the world's soul in my creation,
Heeding the divine voice which breathes life
Through the dead echoes in my heart.

And I shall say to Fate which pits itself
Against my hopes with every blow,
'The bright flame in my blood shall not be quenched
By sorrow's waves or tempests of misfortune,
Buffet my heart as hard as you can
It shall stay steadfast as a solid rock.'

Towards the end of his life al-Shabbi welcomed death as the only means to end his suffering. But his address to death is in no way an expression of total defeat. As is clear from his imagery, particularly his light imagery, he regarded death as a means of attaining a fuller and more significant life. This we find in one of his last poems, if not his very last, entitled 'The New Morning', which is certainly one of the most haunting poems in modern Arabic. The final image in this poem, of the poet unfurling the sails of his lonely boat on a strange and vast sea, welcoming the hazards of the unknown, appears as a perfect and moving symbol of frail but heroic man.

There are indeed mystical elements in some of al-Shabbi's poetry, but it is al-Tijani who enriched Arabic Romantic poetry by his moving accounts of his mystical experiences. His Blake-like awareness of the sanctity of life, of the holiness of the minutest creature, is expressed in his poem 'A Mystic's Passion':

> Inside all that is in the universe the Lord moves.
> This minute ant is an echo of Him
> He dwells in its belly and in His soil it lives
> And when it gives up its soul God is there ready
> To catch it in His hands.
> It does not die, for in it God lives if only you could see Him.

Like Gerard Manley Hopkins he never ceased to be surprised that so much beauty has been created by God for the enjoyment of man. In 'Dawn in the Desert' he asks: 'Lord, is it possible that all that beauty, splendour and magic are here for the sake of this one mortal?' Different from al-Shabbi and al-Tajani is ʿUmar Abu Risha, whose poetry reveals a vehement passion, a fiery imagination, vivid and at times violent imagery, a preoccupation with the themes of change and ravaging effect of time, an ability to write angry political poems of a high degree of complexity, such as his well-known poem *al-Nisr* (The Eagle).

But, although by no means the greatest of the Arab Romantics, ʿAli Mahmud Taha deserves a special mention in this context on account of the part he (unconsciously) played in hastening the downfall of the Romantic ideal. He was a cunning artist who, like Shawqi, was gifted with a highly developed sense of music. His first volume of verse, published in 1934 and significantly entitled *al-Mallāḥ al-Tāʾih* (*The Lost Mariner*), was characteristically dedicated to 'those enamoured of longing for the Unknown, those lost on the sea of life, those who haunt the deserted shore', words that in fact set the keynote to the contents of the entire volume. The poems are variations on the themes of nostalgia and mysterious longings for strange and undefined objects, the strong emotive appeal of the Unknown, vague metaphysical doubt as to the end and meaning of existence, the feeling of loss of direction. Despite their relative superficiality of thought, the poems reveal a consistently hedonistic attitude to life which Taha managed to maintain until the end of his life, but perhaps best expressed in his collection *Layālī al-Mallāḥ al-Tā'ih* (*Nights of the Lost Mariner*), published in 1940. In Taha's work Europe plays a role in some ways similar to that of the exotic and sensuous East in Western Romantic poetry: as Jayyusi put it in volume II of *Trends and Movements* (See Bibliography Section 3A): 'the charms of the west with its seemingly liberal enjoyment of life, the freedom it allowed to the individual provided a great Romantic appeal to the Arab youth of the forties'. Quite rightly she sees that Taha's popularity was partly due to the fact that it provided one of the greatest outlets for the emotionally and sexually suppressed youth of the Middle East. Many of the women whose beauty he celebrated are European, his mistresses tend to be fair, with golden hair. He chose as romantic settings for his poems Venice, Capri, Como, or Lugano. He wrote about the wine of the Rhine, the effect of the music of Wagner, and the waltzes of Johann Strauss. In his 'Question and Answer' (from his late collection 'The Return of Longing') he sums up his work:

> My life is a tale which began with a wine cup
> And a fair woman. For both I made my song.

The modern Arab student or the critic familiar with Western Romantic poetry may find little of profundity in Taha's imagery and choice of themes, but it must be admitted that in Arabic literature by Taha's time such themes or images had not yet become as commonplace as they are now. In fact, it was Taha himself who, by his exceedingly skilful use of them in his highly musical verse, encouraged a whole generation of younger men among his admirers to imitate them, thereby rendering such themes and images the mere stock-in-trade of facile Romantic poetry. It was Taha's followers, therefore, who were largely responsible for their demotion. Yet it must be remembered that without Taha the modernists Nizār Qabbānī and Badr Shākir al-Sayyāb would not have been possible.

The heyday of Arab Romanticism was the period between the two world wars, a period of political turmoil and great cultural and sociological change. The seemingly unending struggle for independence from the colonial powers was matched only by internal political party strife, intensified by the worsening economic situation, partly as a result of the world Depression. The hectic search for cultural identity took many forms, one of which was the call for further Westernization. The emergence of an urban middle class as a potential political, social, and cultural force of considerable importance was accompanied by an increase in secularization. Poets wrote about their subjective feelings, their unfulfilled desires, their vague longings and their sense of mystery and wonder in the presence of nature, poems marked by their highly lyrical evocative language, and a greater freedom in handling stanzaic forms. The heightened sense of individuality revealed in their deeper self-awareness and their feelings of loss of direction were by no means mere imitations of certain postures in Western Romanticism, but were an indirect expression of their agonizing awareness of social and cultural change and of the political malaise of the time. Despite its rarefied atmosphere, Romantic Arabic poetry was in fact intimately, though subtly related to its contemporary Arab world.

2

The Modernists

THE modernity of Romantic Arabic poetry was not regarded as sufficient by the generation that emerged after the Second World War. There were several reasons for this apart from the obvious one relating to the generation gap. By the 1940s Arab Romanticism had developed its own conventional vocabulary, imagery, motifs, and attitudes, and had acquired its own poetic diction, which was regarded as no less of an obstacle to genuine self-expression than the poetic diction of neo-classicism. Romanticism was thought too vague, too escapist and too full of beauty and daydreams, too sugary and sentimental to express the social and political reality of the Arab world, which was growing increasingly harsh during and immediately after the Second World War. Whatever the truth of these accusations, not surprisingly the centre of interest of Romantic Arabic poetry was, on the whole, the individual rather than society, and its vision of society tended to be expressed in somewhat idealized terms, in a language more suited to the communication of subtle subjective feelings and moods rather than conveying the shock and immediacy of external reality.

The horrors and degradation of urban life were intensified by the war with its attendant inflation, racketeering, growing lumpenproletariat as a result of mass migration of agricultural workers to cities in search of a living, the fast widening chasm separating the rich from the poor, increasing corruption, and the appalling absence of social justice. Because Russia was an ally, Russian literature and the Soviet regime were given some publicity in the Arab world as part of the war propaganda effort, with the result that young Arab intellectuals, especially in Egypt, became increasingly interested in Marxist thought. The two events that impressed themselves on the minds and imaginations of creative writers were the Palestine tragedy of 1948, which exposed the fundamental weakness and corruption of Arab governments, and the 1952 Egyptian army revolution under the leadership of Colonel Nasser, which was an indirect result of this exposure, overthrowing the monarchy in Egypt and providing the inspiration and the model for similar revolutions or army coups in other Arab countries, staged professedly in the name of the masses. Such events made it difficult for poets to continue to dream about a world of beauty and love, instead of following the general call for political commitment. Many Arab poets who had begun their career as romantics (such as the Iraqis ʿAbd al-Wahhāb al-Bayātī and Sayyab) were therefore driven by the internal situation to rebel against Romanticism. In 1946 the Marxist Egyptian poet Kamāl ʿAbd al-Ḥalīm (b. 1926) attacked the Romantic poet who derived his inspiration from nature and the world of imagination in a poem entitled 'To an Errant Poet':

> When you sing you turn to the stars, to the flowers and birds,
> The God of wine has blessed you. So you sing nonsense and seek the wine jug.
> But fold your wings in the sky of fancy, that you may drop down amidst us and become one of us,
> Leave aside the beauty of imagination, enter the cave of the millions and tell our story to the world;
> Art is but a tear and a flame—fancy and wandering are no art.

Salāma Mūsā (1887–1958), the radical Egyptian thinker, published his progressive review *al-Majalla al-Jadīda* in 1929–30 and between 1934 and 1942, and later collected his socialist articles in books which had the significant titles *Literature for the People* and *Censored Articles*. Among his followers were distinguished writers like Muḥammad Mufīd al-Shūbāshī, Luwīs ʿAwaḍ (1914–90) and at one time Najib Mahfuz. In 1947 Luwis ʿAwad published his *Plutoland and Other Poems* (later to be suppressed by the Censor), to which he wrote a revolutionary introduction stressing the need to overthrow the traditional metrical forms and write the poetry of the people. In 1951 al-Shubashi wrote a well-known article in the leading Cairo periodical *al-Thaqāfa* entitled 'The Erring Literature', dismissing the whole of Romantic literature as 'adolescent', attacking the shortcomings of the ivory-tower literature, which either derived its inspirations from the Arab past or imitated Western Romantic models, and calling for socialist realism and the writers' commitment. From 1944 onwards a stream of Egyptian novels of angry social protest began to pour out, emphasizing the themes of social injustice and class struggle.

In 1945 the great Egyptian literary critic Muḥammad Mandūr (1907–65) gave up his academic post to devote himself to leftist politics and he later became editor of the Arabic-language Soviet periodical *al-Sharq*. Leftist reviews appeared in other Arab capitals: *al-Ṭalīʿa* (1935–48) in Damascus and *al-Ṭarīq* (1941) in Beirut. In Syria ʿUmar Fākhūrī attacked the literature of the ivory tower while in the Lebanon Ra'īf Khūrī (1912–67) consistently advocated a Marxist view of literature. In the Arab world the early 1950s witnessed a noisy debate about *iltizām* (commitment), which for many years was to be a key term in Arab critical vocabulary. The word, no doubt a translation of Sartre's *engagement* (his articles on *Qu'est-ce que la littérature* came out in book form in 1948), was popularized by the most influential post-war Arabic literary monthly periodical, the Lebanese *al-Ādāb*, edited by the Lebanese writer Suhayl Idrīs. The manifesto-like editorial note to the first issue in January 1953 was a trumpet call for committed literature. In the following year a controversy erupted in Cairo newspapers about the issue of commitment in which the younger Marxist writers Maḥmūd Amīn al-ʿĀlim and ʿAbd al-ʿAẓīm Anīs were ranged against Taha Husayn and al-ʿAqqad; in 1955 they published their articles in book form in Beirut under the title *On Egyptian Culture*, with an introduction by the distinguished Marxist literary critic Ḥusayn Muruwwa, who himself produced his own book of Marxist criticism *Literary Issues* the following year.

The book by al-ʿAlim and Anis enjoyed an enormous popularity among the young in the Arab world as it obviously expressed the dominant mood of the time. In fact from the middle of the 1950s onwards 'commitment' seemed to become the rule rather than the exception. Many young poets who began writing in a romantic vein were soon attracted to social or socialist realism. Poets with Marxist leanings, particularly the Iraqis ʿAbd al-Wahhab al-Bayati and Badr Shakir al-Sayyab, had a large following in the Arab world, especially as their names were linked with the new freer verse form, even though that form was not confined to Marxist poets. The influence of social realism can be seen in the work of most of the younger poets such as the Iraqis Kāẓim Jawād and Buland al-Ḥaydarī, the Egyptians Ṣalāḥ ʿAbd al-Ṣabūr, Aḥmad ʿAbd al-Muʿṭī Ḥijāzī, and Muḥammad Miftāḥ al-Faytūrī. Even the Syrian Nizar Qabbani no longer confined his poetry to his former favourite subjects love and women, but began to write poems of frank and biting social criticism such as 'Bread, Hashish and Moon'. Bayati continued to espouse Marxism while Sayyab recanted later in life, launching an intemperate attack on Marxist commitment in 1961. ʿAbd al-Sabur (and to some extent al-Fayturi) became increasingly interested in mysticism. However, those who opposed Marxism were not entirely free from commitment to some cause or ideal. Adūnīs (ʿAlī Aḥmad Saʿīd) at some point supported Syrian nationalism, Khalīl Ḥāwī was a fervent champion of Arab nationalism, while Yūsuf al-Khāl, like Saʿid ʿAql before him, was an adherent to Lebanese nationalism.

Besides commitment, whether to Marxism or Arab nationalism, one of the factors that contributed to the demise of Romanticism was the Arab poet's increasing knowledge of Western post-Romantic poetry, of Symbolism and Modernism, and in particular the work of T. S. Eliot. The latter exercised a strangely powerful influence upon the development of modern Arabic poetry, after Luwis ʿAwad in 1946 had introduced him to readers in a long article in Taha Husayn's distinguished literary periodical *al-Kātib al-Miṣrī*. In the late 1950s and during the 1960s his poems were translated, and his literary views were the subject of constant and often heated discussion in endless essays and debates in literary journals in Cairo and Beirut. Eliot's influence reveals itself not only in the structure and style, the use of myth and allusion in Iraqi, Lebanese, and Egyptian poetry but his attacks on the English Romantic poets also contributed towards the Arab poets' rejection of their own Romantic poetry. The interest taken in Eliot was in fact an expression of a much wider concern with modern Western poetry in general, to be seen especially in the group of symbolist and surrealist poets (led by the Lebanese Yusuf al-Khal and the Syrian Adunis) connected with the Beirut avant-garde poetry magazine *Shiʿr* which was founded in 1957, and was itself a powerful means of propagating modernist anti-romantic attitudes. Although they generally opposed social realism and Marxism this group shared with the Marxists their dislike of Romanticism which some of them described as 'a disease'.

However, rejection of Romantic themes and style was by no means the only manifestation of the revolt of the so-called 'New' poetry against the past. Formally at least its revolt was more extreme than any other revolt in the whole history of Arabic poetry. It has rejected many of the basic conventions of Arabic verse. Put superficially, a printed page of 'New' poetry looks different from what Arabic verses always looked like until the late 1940s: the *bayt*, i.e. the line that consisted of two hemistichs of equal length or metrical value, has disappeared and been replaced by lines of unequal length. For a long time poets had been searching for new metrical forms that they felt would allow them a greater freedom of self-expression and enable them to achieve a tighter organic unity in their work, as well as extending the scope of Arabic poetry to make possible the writing of verse drama that was truly dramatic and not rhetorical, like the plays of Shawqi and his followers, or lyrical, like those of Saʿid ʿAql. Recently the story of this long quest and hectic experimentation with verse has been thoroughly studied by more than one scholar (see in particular the studies by S. Moreh and S. K. Jayyusi cited in section 3A of the Bibliography). The new form that has gradually found acceptance throughout almost the entire Arab world is that connected with the names of the Iraqi poets Badr Shakir al-Sayyab and Nāzik al-Malā'ika, who used it in 1947. It relies upon the use of the single foot *(tafʿīla)* as the basic unit, instead of a fixed number of feet or a combination of certain different feet per line. Which of the two Iraqi poets was the originator of this new form was for a while a matter of some dispute, but the fact is that *al-Shiʿr al-ḥurr* (free verse) as this new form was called, was a culmination of a long series of prosodic experiments that had begun early in the century but was accelerated by the generation of poets born in the 1920s, and had already been used in Egypt by Muḥammad Farīd Abū Ḥadīd and ʿAlī Aḥmad Bākathīr. The new form, used with or without rhyme, was strongly opposed by the literary establishment, even ironically enough by a former rebel like al-ʿAqqad, who refused to recognize it as poetry.

An even more extreme form used by some poets does without the principle of prosody altogether: it is the prose poem *Qaṣīdat al-nathr*, which one moderate poet prophesied with some truth might be the form of the future. *Qasidat al-nathr*, the prose poem or *poème en prose*, should be distinguished from *al-shiʿr al-manthūr* (*vers libre*), which under the influence of Western poetry, in particular that of Walt Whitman, was used by Amin al-Rihani (1826–1940) and more successfully by Jibran and Mayy Ziyāda (1886–1941). *Vers libre* does not adhere to any of the traditional metres or follow any regular pattern, but relies upon euphony, rhythm, imagery, and occasionally rhyme. It was used extensively in translations from Western poetry (especially in the 1930s) and subsequently by highly westernized poets such as the Egyptian Munīr Ramzī (1924–45) and the Lebanese Albert Adīb, particularly the surrealists Jūrj Ḥunayn (1914–73) in Egypt, Urkhān Muyassar (1914–65), and ʿAlī Nāṣir in Syria. Amongst the most distinguished users of *vers libre* in the post-war period are the Palestinian Jabrā Ibrāhīm Jabrā (b. 1926), Tawfīq Ṣāyigh (1923–71), and the Syrian Muḥammad al-Māghūṭ (b. 1934), perhaps the greatest poet of them all.

Like *al-shiʿr al-manthur, qasidat al-nathr* observes neither metre nor rhyme, but employs to the full internal harmony, euphony, and imagery. However, it differs from *al-shiʿr al-manthur* in that it appears on the page as prose and is generally divided not into lines, but short paragraphs and relies more heavily on its daring verbal constructions. This form was originally connected with the names of the Lebanese Unsī al-Ḥājj (b. 1937), who wrote exclusively in it, and of Adunis and Yusuf al-Khal, who both made occasional use of it. In 1960, in his introduction to *Lan* (*Shall Not*), his first collection of poems in this form, Hajj describes the prose poem as 'the highest point in language to which the poet has so far aspired' and claims that the only form in which the liberated Arab poet can fully express his modern attitudes is the free form of the prose poem and that the author of the prose poem 'has great need to invent his language continuously'. Hajj's introduction brings out in the strongest terms the revolutionary thinking underlying the prose-poem experiment.

Leaving formal considerations aside, we find that the first generation of the 'New' or modernist poets vary considerably in the degree of their revolt against convention. Some, like al-Mala'ika were basically an extension of Romantic sensibility; despite her use of 'New' techniques al-Mala'ika is a conservative at heart as is clear from her book *Qaḍāya al-Shiʿr al-Muʿāṣir* (*Problems of Contemporary Poetry*). At the opposite extreme we find the thoroughgoing revolutionaries of the *Shiʿr* group, who wished to cut themselves off from Arabic literary conventions and align themselves with the cause of contemporary Western poetry. This is true of, for instance, Adunis to some extent, but more particularly Unsi al-Hajj. They were so vocal in their vehement rejection of Arab traditional values that they came to be known in the Arab world as 'poets of rejection' *(shuʿarāʾ al-rafḍ).* Those who fell under French symbolist and surrealist influence, such as Adunis, formed a view of poetry with metaphysical and mystical dimensions. Others in whom the influence of modern English poetry (particularly that of Eliot) is apparent, like Khalīl Ḥāwī, al-Sayyab, and al-Khal, resorted to the use of asides, interior monologue, mythology, allusions to popular songs and beliefs, and occasional use of colloquialisms. The two influences, however, are not kept separate in the writings of these poets: each group has learned something from the techniques of the other. And perhaps the most important features of the 'New' poetry is its syntax and its peculiar use of imagery: it is this feature that links it to contemporary Western poetry. The modern Arab poet, whether he is a Marxist or an existentialist, deliberately avoids the language of statement: in this he has learned from the experience of Romanticism, which exploits the evocative power of words, but has gone a step further in resorting to an oblique style, to imagery as a means of objectifying his emotional experience. In thinking in imagery, as it were, he has sometimes transcended logic, and it is often the absence of logical relationships and of all explicit connections that makes the syntax of this poetry as difficult as in the case of the most obscure Western poetry.

Perhaps the most committed of the post-war generation of modernist poets is the Iraqi ʿAbd al-Wahhab al-Bayati (b. 1926). A graduate of the Baghdad Teachers' Training College, because of his communist beliefs, he was for many years driven to a life of exile both in Arab countries and Eastern Europe and Russia. Since his reinstatement he has for many years been Iraq's cultural attaché in Madrid. He read Mayakovsky, Nazim Hikmet, Paul Eluard, Aragon, Lorca, and Neruda, all of whom left their mark on his poetry. He has published a very large number of volumes of verse as well as a prose work in which he gives an account of his poetic experience, together with his reflections on poetry. His early work was markedly romantic in style, but by the time his second volume entitled *Abārīq Muhashshama* (*Broken Pitchers*) was published in 1954, he had been able to find his true voice. In one of his best-known poems 'The Village Market', which begins with the following lines:

> The sun, the lean donkeys, the flies,
> A soldier's old pair of boots
> Being passed from hand to hand

While a peasant stares into space
Thinking 'In the New Year, for sure,
My hands will fill with coins
And then I can buy those boots'

Bayati inaugurated a fashion of writing poems about the countryside in which the poor peasant is idealized, while every grim detail of his miserable life is all too realistically portrayed, in sharp contrast to the 'romantic' image of the village popular in the work of an earlier generation. Similarly, in the same volume, Bayati portrays the city as a menacing place, in which fear stalks the streets, crimes are daily committed and the wretchedness of the sick and starving masses is increased severalfold, as we find in the poem entitled 'Night, the City and Tuberculosis':

The depths of the city
In silence still give birth to the living
Spew the dead onto warm dusty pavements
In the arms of the tubercular night
. . . .
Spitting out the wretched in their thousands
In its cafés, its dark accursed streets
And on its yellow ugly trees fear is born

'Broken Pitchers' expresses the poet's boundless hope for the emancipation of the proletariat:

God and the radiant sky! The slaves feel their chains
'Tomorrow you must build your cities close to erupting Vesuvius,
You must not be satisfied with anything beneath the stars,
Let violent hope and deep joy set your hearts on fire.'
Whoever sells his eagles dies of starvation.
Those who ape men stand at the new crossroads
One-eyed and confused.
'Night will come to the bat, though it is daybreak now
The sheep forgets the face of its aged shepherd
The son turns against the father, the tear-soaked loaf
Of bread tastes of ashes. In the dwarf's head
There is a glass eye that denies the free light.'
Widows follow those who ape men beneath the sky
There is neither a future for them nor a grave.
God and the radiant sky! The slaves feel their chains.
'A new spring has gushed forth in our dead life
Let the dead bury the dead.
Let the deluge sweep before it those ugly pitchers, strike the drums

And let the gates be opened for spring and the bright sun.'

The images of the 'one-eyed' and those who 'ape men' (like dwarves), fly swatters, spiders' webs, history's rubbish heap, and the green moon are among the recurrent motifs in Bayati's poetry, but the strident, loud Mayakovskyian tone of the poem he is not always able to maintain. When he writes about the plight of Palestinian refugees the dominant mood is one of grief and sorrow. In the course of time the tone becomes less aggressive, but the political position remains consistent. He welcomes the Iraqi Revolution of 1958 in a jubilant poem of the utmost simplicity, and in 1965 in a poem addressed to President Nasser, full of enthusiasm for the Arab socialist ideal, he writes in a fairly direct style:

O generation of defeat, this revolution
Will wipe out your shame, dislodge the rock
Peel off your crust, and in the barren wastes
Of your life cause a flower to bloom.

Proportionate to his enthusiasm was his bitter disappointment at the shock of the Arab defeat of 1967, which he treats in his 'Lament for the June Sun' written in 1968—a poem marked by its bitter self-criticism and self-condemnation, typical of the breast-beating and soul-searching which the Arab intellectuals experienced in the wake of the Six Day War.

In the cafés of the East we have been ground
By the war of words,
Minced by wooden swords,
Lies and horsemen of the air.
We did not kill a camel or even a sand grouse
We did not try the game of death

. . . .

In the cafés of the East we swat flies
We wear the masks of the living in history's rubbish heap,
Aping men.
We dared not ask the one-eyed charlatan, the anti-Christ,
Why did you escape?
We are the generation of free death
Recipient of alms. (Translated by Desmond Stewart)

In Bayati's later poetry the symbolist style grows in density and his imagery becomes more surrealistic. His early facile enthusiasm and strident tone are replaced by a quieter voice, enriched and deepened by disillusionment and an increased awareness of the tragic complexities of life. To the early symbols and allusions he adds a wide variety of personages, historical and fictitious from both East and West, such as the classical Arab poets Ṭarfa, Abū Firās of Ḥamdān, Mutanabbī, Maʿarrī, the Persian poet and mathematician Khayyām, the Sufi martyr Ḥallāj, Alexander the Great, Hamlet, Sindbad, Ché Guevara, Picasso, Nazim Hikmet, Albert Camus. The symbols include cities and rivers, for example the Koranic many-columned city of Iram, Damascus, Naisapur, Granada, Madrid, Cordova, Euphrates. In 1970 he wrote in the collection *Inscriptions in Clay*:

What did the song say?
Birds are dying on the pavements of the night,
The long-awaited prophet
Is still asleep in his cave, and rain is falling
Upon the walls of old dilapidated houses,
Upon the roofs of the pregnant city and the notices of estate agents.
While in the street I walk holding a corpse
Hiding my face from God and you.

Mystical and surrealistic elements become increasingly dominant features of Bayati's style, thus occasionally risking unintelligibility. A more moderate example is the following excerpt from a poem with the significant title 'The Nightmare' from the collection *Qaṣāʾid Ḥubb ʿalā Bawwābāt al-ʿAlām al-Sabʿ (Love Poems on the Seven Gates of the World)*, published in 1971:

At the gate of hell stood Picasso, and the guitar player from Madrid
Raised the curtain for the ravished theatre queens,
Restored to the clown his virginity,
Hid weapons and seeds in the earth until another resurrection.
He died in a café in exile, his eyes turned towards his distant land,
Gazing through clouds of smoke and the newspaper.
His hand tracing in the air
A mysterious sign pointing to the weapons and seeds.
The guitar player from Madrid dies
In order that he may be born again,
Under the suns of other cities and in different masks,
And search for the Kingdom of rhythm and colour,
And for its essence which activates a poem,
Live through the revolutions of the ages of Faith and Rebirth,
Waiting, fighting, migrating with the seasons,

Returning to mother earth with those wearing a crown of torturing light,
The dissenters and the builders of creative cities
On the bottom of the sea of rhythm and colour.

It seems likely that the later development in Bayati's style owes as much to the work of Marxists like Mayakovsky, Aragon, Eluard, and Neruda, which was either futuristic, or surrealistic, or opaquely symbolist, as to the growing influence of Adunis' poetry, which contains a mystical element and seeks to destroy logical connections, relies heavily on surrealistic imagery, and resorts to the use of masks. Fortunately not all Bayati's poetry is impenetrably obscure: on the contrary there are several poems, such as 'Love Under the Rain', which are of a considerably more direct appeal.

Like Bayati, Badr Shakir al-Sayyab (1926–64), one of the two or three greatest poets of his generation, was a graduate of the Baghdad Teachers' Training College. He too suffered persecution and exile for his political views, but unlike Bayati, was not eventually reinstated because of his early death as a result of a painful incurable disease. Deeply influenced by modern English poetry, Eliot and Edith Sitwell in particular, he also translated Ezra Pound, Stephen Spender, C. Day Lewis, and (through the medium of English) Lorca, Neruda, Rimbaud, Prévert, and Aragon. Like Bayati, al-Sayyab began as a romantic poet, a follower of Taha and Abu-Shabaka, as is clear from his first collection *Azhār Dhābila* (*Withered Flowers*), strangely enough written in 1947 when he was a communist. However, there are already signs of change in his second volume *Asāṭīr* (*Myths*), published in 1950. In the preface he drew attention to his metrical experiments inspired by his readings in English poetry, to the relative obscurity of some poems in which he drew upon his Unconscious, and to his belief in the social and political function of poetry. In at least two poems 'In the Ancient Market Place' and 'An Ancient Song' he goes beyond the general limitations of the Romantic experience, creating atmosphere by exploiting the poetic potentialities of realistic detail, unconventional imagery and a daring use of language close to that in symbolist poetry.

After *Myths* al-Sayyab turned to socially and politically committed poetry. The long poem is a form which had a great fascination for him: he wrote three such poems, 'The Grave Digger', in 1952, and in 1954 'The Blind Prostitute' and 'Arms and the Children', all of which he republished in his volume *Unshūdat al-Maṭar* (*Hymn to Rain*), which contains some of his best and most mature poems. 'The Grave Digger' describes the evil of making a living out of death and destruction, while the theme of 'The Blind Prostitute' is the iniquitous social and political conditions which drive a poor woman to prostitution. As for 'Arms and the Children' it is based on the obvious contrast between the innocence of childhood and the wickedness of the arms trade. But despite his many gifts, such as his extraordinary power of evolving imagery and recording vivid sensations, al-Sayyab was unable to write a long poem that is free from structural weaknesses or uncluttered by a farrago of mythological allusions both Greek and biblical, such as Cain, Gog and Magog, Oedipus, Medusa, and Aphrodite.

It is in the relatively shorter poems which he began to write around 1953, poems such as 'A Stranger on the Gulf' and 'Hymn to Rain', that al-Sayyab attained the full height of his creativity. In such poems he managed to fuse together in the heat of the imaginative act the most disparate elements of his experience, with the result that it is impossible to disentangle the individual predicament of the suffering poet from the commitment to a social or national ideal. In them we find an emotional complex of elements related to the man who since early childhood has been yearning for a mother's love and who has therefore been nostalgically looking back to the happy days of his early childhood in his native village (Jaykūr) with its river (Buwayb), its shells and its palm trees. This is the emotionally starved young man who seems to be constantly suffering from unrequited love, the committed Marxist dismissed from his job as a schoolteacher and hunted by the police in an authoritarian state, forced into exile for long periods of time in Iran and Kuwait (where he earned his keep by washing up dishes and doing domestic chores). Take, for instance, 'Hymn to Rain'. The poem describes al-Sayyab's feelings as he watches rain falling on the Arabian Gulf in Kuwait, where he is a political exile. The mood alternates between nostalgia for the poet's childhood and homesickness for his country, between grief over the present situation in Iraq and hope for the future. Rain is life-giving and results in flowers and crops, but in Iraq it brings only hunger for the people. However, despite the prevailing sadness of the poem it does not end on a pessimistic note:

> I can almost hear the palm trees drinking rain
> In Iraq, the villages groan, and exiles

With oars and sails struggling against the gusts
And thunders of the Gulf, chanting:
Rain. Rain.
Famine in Iraq.
At harvest time corn is scattered,
To feed ravens and locusts
In the fields a mill
Rotates, grinding grain and rock
With people around.
Rain. Rain.
Not a year has passed without famine in Iraq.
Rain. Rain.
In every drop of rain
A red or yellow flower bud
Every tear drop of the hungry and naked
Every blood drop of the enslaved
Is a smile awaiting new lips
Or a roseate nipple in the mouth of a newborn
In the youthful world of tomorrow, giver of life
Rain. Rain.
Iraq will grow green with the rainfall!

The word rain (in Arabic it is the almost onomatopoeic *maṭar*) is repeated several times like a refrain at the end of each section of the poem with a hypnotic effect, creating an almost magical atmosphere in which the poet is confident that his prayer for life-giving rain (i.e. political salvation) for the whole of his country will be answered. It is interesting that the last section of the poem contains no more than these words:

And the rain pours down.

'Hymn to Rain' is marked by the complexity of its themes, its tight organization, its rapid succession of images all of which are strictly functional and not merely decorative, its cunning use of obliquities and symbols, including the archetypal 'rain' and fertility myth, as well as its subtle internal music and the incantatory effect of its language. The same successful interweaving of the personal and the public is achieved in other powerful poems, such as 'The River and Death' and 'City without Rain.'

Al-Sayyab wrote some of the most nightmarishly horrifying comments on the bloody events in Qasim's Iraq, as, for instance, in 'The City of Sindbad', where we read:

The Tartars have come, their knives dripping with blood
Our sun is blood and our food
Is blood served on platters.
They have set fire to Muhammad the orphan
And the night is alight with the blaze
Hot blood gushing forth from his feet,
His hands and his eyes

. . . .

A horseman rode in the streets
Murdering women
And dyeing cradles in blood

. . . .

It seems that Babel, the ancient walled city, is back again
With its high domes of iron, its ringing bells
Mournful as a graveyard,
The sky above it the courtyard of a slaughterhouse,
Its hanging gardens planted with heads
Cut off with sharp axes, and crows
Pecking at their eyes.

Al-Sayyab became gradually more introspective and subjective and less absorbed in political or public themes as a result of the illness which began to affect him in 1961. In the 1962 collection *al-Maʿbad al-Gharīq (The Sunken Temple)* there is a marked interest in death, in the Persephone myth, in figures from the poet's past such as his cousin Wafiqa (who died while giving birth to a child and on whom he projected the persons of his mother and mistress): Wafiqa's gardens are identified with Persephone's in the underworld of Pluto. The volume contains a prayer to God in which the poet asks Him to put an end to his suffering. In his subsequent poetry he writes about his experience of disease and approaching death. He is constantly raging against the dying of the light, although at times he is pathetically trying to learn to accept death. The mood changes from self-pity and self-delusion and false hope to resignation to God's will, to homesickness for Iraq and nostalgia for the past. Using a simpler style, less cluttered by mythological references, al-Sayyab adopted the persona of Job through whom he expressed his trials and tribulations and his attitude towards his Maker. Yet, towards the end of his life and as the realization of the hopelessness of his condition became apparent, far from being resigned, al-Sayyab was in an almost continuous state of hectic and feverish poetic activity, so much so that poetry seemed to be the only means by which he felt he could still hold on to life, just as his excessively erotic imagery was an expression of a desperate attempt to prove to his paralyzed and impotent body that he was still alive. The abundant poetry he produced had an almost demonic quality: he wrote as if he were possessed. It teems with vivid impressions and primary sensations and at its best it is an eloquent and moving record of the terror of death, of man's helplessness when he is reduced to a physical wreck bound to a hospital bed.

Like Bayati, the Egyptian Ṣalāḥ ʿAbd al-Ṣabūr (1931–81) wrote realistic poetry about the village which reveals the degree of his social commitment. In a poem which gives his first volume of verse its title *People in My Country* (*al-Nāsu fī Bilādī*) and which was first published in al-Ādāb in 1954, he says:

> People in my country are predatory like hawks,
> Their singing is like the winter wind blowing through the trees,
> Their laughter like the hissing of wood-consuming fire.
> When they walk their feet wish to sink into the earth,
> They murder and steal, they belch when they drink
> And yet they are human
> When they have a handful of money they are good
> And they believe in Fate.

The poet proceeds to give a picture of a pious old uncle sitting at the entrance of his village, whiling away the hours of dusk, surrounded by men all listening intently to the tale he tells them, 'the fruit of life's experience', a painful simple tale that made them sob, bend their heads and gaze into the stillness 'into the deep waves of terror', and set them wondering about the end of man's toil in this life and the inscrutable ways of the Lord, who sends His Messenger of Death to apprehend the soul of a rich man who had built castles and 'owned forty rooms filled with glittering gold', and send it rolling down into the depths of Hell. This is how the poem ends:

> Yesterday I revisited my village . . . Uncle Mustafa had died,
> And his head had been laid in the dust.
> He never owned castles (his hut had been built with unburned brick)
> Behind his old coffin there walked
> Those who, like him, possessed only one old linen gown.
> They mentioned neither God nor the Angel of Death, nor the
> mysterious words,
> For it was a year of hunger.
> At the mouth of the grave stood my friend Khalil,

The grandson of uncle Mustafa,
Lifting his muscular arm to the sky
And a look of scorn surging in his eyes
For it was a year of hunger

Unlike Bayati, in his subsequent volumes *Aqūlu lakum* (*I Say unto You*, 1961), *Aḥlām al-Fāris al-Qadīm (Dreams of the Ancient Knight*, 1964) and *Ta'ammulāt fī Zaman Jarīḥ* (*Meditations on a Wounded Age*, 1971), ʿAbd al-Sabur turned from the poetry of commitment to the socialist ideal, shown in his first volume, to an increasingly personal vision which alternates between mild mysticism and melancholy meditations on death and even despair at times. For instance, he says in 'Song for the Winter':

This year's winter tells me that I shall die alone
One such winter
This evening tells me that I shall die alone
One such evening
That my past years have been lived in vain
That I inhabit the open air, with no roof over my head.
This year's winter tells me that inside me
My soul is shaking with cold
That my heart has been dead since the autumn
That it withered with the withering of the first leaves
And dropped to the ground with the first drop of rain
Receding deeper into the stony ground with every cold night.

The poet's overpowering pessimism is obvious, especially in the poem 'Memoirs of the Sufi Bishr al-Ḥāfī', where the world is felt to be infected and diseased beyond all cure and where man does not look a pretty sight in the eyes of the Lord. The gloom was unrelieved in his later poetry, and was no doubt accentuated by the Arab defeat in 1967, which encouraged a withdrawal from painful external reality, and is not confined to poetry, but can also be noticed in other aspects of Arabic literature.

In the collection 'Meditations on a Wounded Age' the poet experiences a recurring nightmare in which he is shot, disembowelled, and made to hang as an exhibit in a museum. He amuses himself by pretending to dismember and reshape the passers-by and by conceiving equally violent ideas, as, for instance, in 'Conversations in a Café'. The volume paints the picture of a sad world in which unhappy man finds in rather joyless sex a temporary escape from disillusionment and misery as in, for example,

'Female'. Gone is the angry and vehement rebellious impulse of the earlier work: here are no false heroic gestures, but only the quiet heroism of modern man, crushed and defeated by overwhelming forces, but determined to go on against great odds. To Jayyusi, in her *Modern Arabic Poetry—An Anthology* (see section 3A of the Bibliography), ʿAbd al-Sabur 'seemed to embrace modernity more than any other poet of the period' and unlike 'the grand sweep of [Palestinian] Resistance verse and of such poets as Adunis, ʿAbd al-Sabur's more subdued rhythms remind the reader of the condition of men and women around him who are the victims of a social and political order that tyrannizes and wastes their lives'. She comments on his 'almost ascetic avoidance of ornament and over-stylization' and his 'profound break from inherited rhetoric, style and diction' and his 'modern consciousness of the world'. In *My Life in Poetry*, which was written in 1969 and records his later thoughts on the subjects, ʿAbd al-Sabur offers a deeply moral and spiritual conception of poetry which he regards as akin to mysticism and launches an attack on the conventional Marxist view, stressing the need for poetry to affirm values like truth, freedom and justice.

Another Egyptian poet, Aḥmad ʿAbd al-Muʿṭī Ḥijāzī (b. 1935) describes the loneliness, bewilderment, and anxiety, the feeling of loss and fear of anonymity experienced in the great and impersonal metropolis of Cairo by those simple souls drawn to it from the countryside in desperate search of a means of earning their livelihood. Here is an elegy on a village boy run over by a car in a Cairo street from his first collection, published in 1959, which bears the self-explanatory title *Madīna bilā Qalb* (*Heartless City*):

Death screamed in the square
Then silence descended lying like a shroud.
A green fly came from sad country tombs
And folded its wings on a boy
Who died in the city.

Not an eye wept.
Death screamed in the city,
The wheels screeched, then stopped.
Whose child is it? they asked,
But no one replied;
Only he knew the name.
'Poor child!' was uttered by a person in grief

Who was soon gone.
Eyes met, but no one replied.
In the big city people are mere numbers:
One boy came,
One boy died.
His heart had grown still;
His hand that had clutched the earth
As he parted with life is now relaxed,
His lidless eyes gazing in terror.
It was time for the wandering legs to rest.
They dumped the body in a white car
And a green fly hovered above the blood-stained spot.

Hijazi's two subsequent volumes *Lam Yabqa illa'l-Iʿtirāf* (*There Remains only Confession*) and *Marthiyyat al-ʿUmr al-Jamīl* (*Elegy on a Handsome Life*), published in 1965 and 1973 respectively, give ample expression to his commitment to Nasserism and Arab socialism. In his more recent poetry such as *Kā'ināt Mamlakat al-Layl* (*Creatures of the Night Kingdom*), which was published in 1978, Hijazi has shed his facile optimism and displays an admirable complexity and a great power of evolving vivid but surprising imagery, betraying the influence of surrealism, but without losing his commitment to the Palestine cause or to the Left, or giving up entirely his loud rhetorical tone in his overtly political poetry.

Like Hijazi in his early work, Muḥammad Miftāḥ al-Faytūrī (b. 1930), a Sudanese poet born and brought up in Egypt, wrote compassionately about the victims of city life as in his well-known poem 'Under the Rain', a little vignette showing both the bleeding carriage horses and the emaciated driver whipping them inhabiting a world in great need of mercy. Fayturi's first collection, *Aghānī Ifrīqiyā* (*Songs of Africa*), which appeared in 1955, contains poems denouncing colonialism and the exploitation of the black by the white written in a dense euphonious style, rich in imagery and remarkable for its vividness and vitality. The same theme of Black Africa is pursued in the subsequent volumes *ʿĀshiq min Ifrīqiyā* (*A Lover from Africa*), which came out in 1964, and *Udhkurīnī yā Ifrīqiyā* (*Remember me, Africa*), published in 1968. Like other poets, after the Arab defeat of 1967 Fayturi turned to mysticism in, for instance, *Maʿzūfa li Darwīsh Mutajawwil* (*Music for an Itinerant Derwish*), although his sufi poetry does not sound as convincing as some of his earlier political verse. Fayturi's later work, such as his *Statements of a Witness for the Prosecution*, does not represent any material advance, either technically or thematically, on his earlier poetry.

Much more popular in the Arab world than al-Fayturi is the Syrian Nizār Qabbānī (b. 1923), who in successive volumes wrote about love and women in a sensuous language of great simplicity and elegance. That he too was converted to socially and politically committed writing in 1955 is a measure of the extent to which commitment had spread. Starting with 'Bread, Hashish and Moon' Qabbani moved on to a more responsible and adult poetry in which he criticized Arab society in outspoken terms for living in day-dreams and in a world of pleasant sensations invoked by drugs. *ʿAlā Hāmish Daftar al-Naksa* (*In the Margin of the Book of Defeat*) expresses a more bitter and sweeping condemnation of Arab leadership after the Arabs' defeat in the Six Day War.

The Six Day War brought to the fore the work of Palestinian poets, who were and are among the most committed Arab poets. Many of them are Marxists, influenced by Bayati and al-Sayyab, who followed the new metrical form of the single *tafʿila*, as well as the techniques of their contemporaries, including the use of Greek, ancient Egyptian, Babylonian, Arab, Islamic, and Christian mythologies. For instance, Ulysses is the dispossessed wandering Arab, Penelope is Palestine, and Telemachus is the poet who opts to stay with his mother and work towards the return of Ulysses. Among the most significant of these Palestinian poets, generally referred to as the Poets of Resistance and Poets of the Occupied Homeland, are Maḥmūd Darwīsh (b. 1942), Samīḥ al-Qāsim (b. 1939), and Tawfīq Zayyād (b. 1932), the first being the most distinguished of them all, in fact arguably the greatest Arab poet of his generation. With the publication in 1966 of his third collection *ʿĀshiq min Filisṭīn* (*A Lover from Palestine*) Darwish established himself as one of the foremost poets in the entire Arab world and since then he has gone from strength to strength.

In 1970 Darwish left Israel to escape harassment by the Israeli authorities and joined the Palestinian diaspora in the Arab world. While the mature Darwish gained in complexity, as Jayyusi sensitively puts it in the Introduction to her *Modern Arabic Poetry—An Anthology*, his poetry 'never lost its basic tenderness and rapture, nor its capacity to recount the predicament of the Palestinian experience in telling images and statements' and it is 'saved from the spleen and gloom that emanate from his dominant themes by a shimmering lyrical flow, and tender appeal to the heart, a vibrant diction, and above all a metaphorical originality'. To that we may add Darwish's supreme technical skill, particularly his masterly use of rhyme and rhyme schemes in many of the long poems in his later collections.

The dominant mood of Darwish's poetry, as indeed of Palestinian poetry in general, is not one of defeat or despair, but of hope, of determination to continue the struggle. In *A Lover from Palestine*, published in 1966, he says in 'Roses and Dictionary':

> I must reject death
> Even though all my myths die

And in 'My Country':

> My country is not a bundle of tales
> Not a memory or a field of moons,
> It is not a story or a song:
> This earth is the skin on my bones
> Above its grass my heart hovers like a bee.

Nearly twenty years later in *Fewer Roses* he can still write in 'I am Able to Talk about Love':

> By the sheer force of defiance I shall live.

But Darwish in no way minimizes the difficulties involved, he is not guilty of facile optimism, since he is fully aware that the struggle is against great odds. In *Taḍīqu binā 'l-Arḍ* (The Earth Closes on Us), one of a series of poems consisting of ten rhyming lines published in 1984, he writes:

> The earth closes on us, pressing us into the last narrow passage; we have to tear off our limbs to pass.
> The earth squeezes us. Would that we were its corn, we would then live again after we die.
> Would that the earth were our mother; our mother would be merciful to us
> . . . .
> Where can we go after the last frontier? Where can the birds fly when they reach the last sky?
> Where can the plants lie to rest after the last breath of air is gone?
> We will write our names in crimson vapour
> Cut off the hand of our song and complete the song with our flesh.
> Here we will die: here in the last narrow passage. Somewhere here our blood will plant its olive trees.

In another of these poems, entitled 'Like other People We Travel' he says:

> Like other people we travel, but we return to nowhere.

Clearly addressing those worried by the Palestinian presence in Lebanon he writes in 'The Dust of Caravan' from the collection *Hiya Ughniya, Hiya Ughniya (It's only a Song)*, composed in 1984–5, and published in Beirut in 1986:

> We are for oblivion. We shall not stay here long,
> We shall beat no drum. We shall neither disturb you nor let you hear our dreams;
> We shall not sleep in your village for long, nor pick any rose from your garden.
> We shall not intrude in your prayers, shall not give cause for concern to the god who has fashioned you in his image and chosen you for his people;
> We shall not leave behind in your public places a drop of our blood,
> We shall be gone even before you awake from your sleep
> Before the entry of Chosroes or any other potentate.

While anticipating the worst he never loses his resolve: in the collection *Fewer Roses* he says with grim determination:

> A darker night will come . . . there will be fewer roses;
> The road will divide into more paths than we have seen; the valley will split open;
> The mountainside will collapse on us; a wound will assault us; our people will be dispersed;
> The murdered among us will kill each other to forget the look in their victims' eyes
>
> . . . .
>
> But I shall continue with my song in the same strain even though my roses are fewer.

In the light of the preceding survey it can safely be said that during the second half of the twentieth century a new and crucial phase in the pursuit of modernity in modern Arabic poetry set in. At no other period in the history of Arabic poetry has the call for modernity been louder or more persistent. Of course we can argue that until then Western poetic influence had been largely confined to that of the nineteenth century and earlier. There were several reasons for this, of which only two will be mentioned here. One is the fact, already indicated, that Arab poets, reacting against their own tradition, found some kinship in Western Romanticism with its emphasis on individuality, rebellion and the questioning of traditional values. The other is that Arab poets needed time to digest earlier phases of European poetry before being able to respond favourably to the avant-garde obscure and sophisticated verse produced in twentieth-century Europe. In the second half of the century young Arab poets could read with considerable enthusiasm the work of T. S. Eliot, Ezra Pound, W. B. Yeats, and Edith Sitwell as well as Paul Valéry, Louis Aragon, Saint-John Perse, Rilke, and Mayakovsky, some of which was beginning to be available in Arabic translation. Modernism, therefore, was one of the things that Arab poets absorbed when they fell under the spell of such major 'modernist' figures in twentieth-century Western poetry.

But surely more is needed to explain the degree of persistence with which at least some Arab poets endeavoured to be modern in the late 1950s and during the 1960s and 1970s. In the work of the leading poets of the time, especially those whose names became associated with the Lebanese poetry magazine *Shiʿr*, modernity or newness became a positive value in itself. They called themselves the New Poets and one of the early enthusiastic students of the movement, the critic Khālida Saʿīd, wife of the poet Adunis, wrote perceptively that the only thing that the New or Modern poets had in common was their intention to be modern. Countless articles and books have been written, very largely, though not exclusively, in defence of modernism (*al-ḥadātha*). The issue of modernism was sharpened, though it became somewhat distorted in the process, by the fact that the rebellion of the New Poets did not simply reject the themes and style of Romanticism, but took the more extreme form of rejecting basic conventions of Arabic versification. This was done to express the experience of modern man with more honesty and fewer restrictions than the exigencies of monorhyme and monometre would allow. Modernism therefore took an easily identifiable external form, which for a long time deflected the attention of many people from the true nature of what our poets sought, for the formal rebellion was by no means a mere matter of the external form of verse, but was intimately associated with a more general attitude towards traditional Arab society and culture.

The most articulate champion of modernism, one who has tirelessly continued to explain, define, and defend it almost *ad nauseam*, is the distinguished Syrian poet Adunis (ʿAlī Aḥmad Saʿīd, b. 1930). His influence on the subsequent development of contemporary Arabic poetry is probably greater than that of anybody else, including even the Marxist Iraqi al-Bayati. A graduate in philosophy from the Syrian University in 1954, Adunis engaged in political activity on behalf of the Syrian Nationalist Party, which landed him in gaol at one point, an event which drove him to leave Syria in 1956 and to settle in Beirut, acquiring Lebanese nationality. The year he spent studying at the Sorbonne at the expense of the French Government (1960) strengthened the French influence on his work.

Adunis is a prolific author who since 1950 has been publishing volumes of verse, the most significant of which are *Leaves in the Wind* (1958), *Songs of Mihyar the Damescene* (1961), *The Book of Metamorphosis and Migration to the Region of Day and Night* (1965), *The Stage and the Mirrors* (1968), *A Time between Ashes and Roses* (1970), *A Tomb for New York* (1971), *Singular in the Form of Plural* (1974), *Further Songs of Mihyar the Damascene* (1975), *The Book of Five Poems* (1980), and *The Book of Siege* (1985).

Inspired by French thinking, namely the ideas of René Clair, André Malraux, Rimbaud, and Baudelaire, in an essay first published in *Shiʿr* in 1959, and later reprinted in his book *Zaman al-Shiʿr* (*The Time for Poetry*), Adunis defined New Poetry as a 'vision', 'a leap beyond present concepts', 'a change in the order of things and in the way of looking at them'. Because it is a vision it is 'obscure, hesitant and illogical . . . It rises above formal requirements because it needs greater freedom, greater mystery and prophecy'. Yet Adunis's ideas about modernism are intimately bound up with his attitude to contemporary Arab society and culture. The modernist movement, he said, rested upon three principles: 'a radical rebellion against traditional mentality', 'a rejection of the old conception of poetry as something static and as no more than emotion and craftsmanship, and a rejection of the view that ancient Arabic poetry is a model to be imitated by all subsequent poetry, or that it is an autonomous and self-sufficient world independent of all the poetic heritage in other languages'. In order that the New Arab poet may liberate himself from static values in poetry and language it is necessary for him, therefore, to free himself also from static values in the whole of Arab culture. With Adunis it can be said that modernism in modern Arabic poetry has been achieved. In fact, Adunis's infatuation with the concept of 'modern' is such that on certain occasions the term ceases to have any temporal significance at all, and becomes an expression of a value judgement. Thus a medieval poet could be described as 'modern', if certain conditions were realized in his style and approach and vision of the world. Gone now is the feeling of complacency and self-sufficiency of the Arab poet. Even more radically than al-Shabbi does Adunis dismiss the Arabic past poetic tradition as the source of inspiration and emulation for the modern Arabic poet.

In fact, the poets' attitude to their past poetic heritage could be regarded as a reliable indicator of their degree of modernism. As is to be expected, different stages in the development of modern Arabic poetry were accompanied by related changes in the attitude to the past indigenous tradition. The forerunner of neo-classicism, al-Barudi, compiled a huge and influential anthology of Arabic poetry of the past which was largely confined to the poetry of the Abbasid era, the very poetry the neo-classicists regarded as their model. In their reappraisal of the Arabic tradition the pre-Romantics of the Diwan School favoured those Abbasid poets noted for their individuality or emotionalism, such as Ibn al-Rūmī, ʿAbbās al-Aḥnaf, and al-Maʿarrī. The Romantics favoured poetry which celebrated the world of the senses and intense emotion such as the poetry of love, wine, and mysticism. Unlike al-Shabbi, who is obviously an extreme case, they searched the tradition for precisely those qualities which they wished to realize in their own poetry. This is equally true of the modernists. The last and most celebrated example of reappraisal of the past heritage is furnished by Adunis who not only compiled his own idiosyncratic anthology of Arabic poetry of the past, but provided several studies of the Arabic poetic tradition, as well as a massive, searching, and provocative historical study of classical Islamic culture, *al-Thābit wa'l-Mutaḥawwil* (*The Constant and the Changing*), published in 1974, in which he emphasizes the value of the intellectual rebel or dissident, the prototype of the twentieth-century Arabic modernist.

In 1970 Adunis wrote: 'It is impossible to create a revolutionary Arab culture except by means of a revolutionary language'. The progress of Adunis the poet can fairly be described as the story of his attempt to create this revolutionary language: it is a journey from the poetry of direct social and political protest to that which suggests more than it states, and sees a deeper significance in phenomena, a hidden meaning behind the form, linking it to mysticism and surrealism. The revolutionary stand which he adopted in the 1950s, when together with Yusuf al-Khal he edited *Shiʿr* magazine, he came to regard as not sufficiently revolutionary in the 1960s, when he dissociated himself from the magazine. In his own avant-garde magazine *Mawāqif*, published in 1969, he claimed that his aim was not simply to establish the new *poem*, but a new *writing* altogether, which is an exploration of the Unknown, in which the emphasis is on total originality and creativity, and traditional distinctions between literary forms like poetry, drama, and narrative disappear. How far he has succeeded in this unrealistically ambitious objective of creating metapoetry and metalanguage is very doubtful. What is beyond doubt, however, is the enormous influence his 'surrealistic' style has had on younger poets throughout the Arab world.

Already in Adunis's quite early poetry, where the revolutionary content is clear, we find Arabic symbolist poetry of a very high order. Consider these two brief poems from his 1957 collection *Qaṣāʾid Ūlā* (*First Poems*), 'The Frontiers of Despair':

> On the frontiers of despair my house stands,
> Its walls like yellow foam,
> Hollow and disjointed like clouds,
> My house is lattice made of dough.
> It consists of holes.
>
> It is shaken by the wind until the wind grows tired,
> And is relieved by the gale.
> My house is deserted by the sun, despite its nearness;
> It is deserted even by sparrows.
>
> My house by its convulsions has been turned
> Into something invisible, transcendental,
> Fixed beyond the invisible world.
> In it I sleep and around me the world
> Lies asleep, with voice muted and choked.

and 'The Way':

> The lost stone is the colour of care,
> The colour of a phantom passing through the night,
> I wonder who it was
> That passed this way and was burned.
>
> My footsteps enjoy the red flame;
> They enjoy glory;
> The longer the way,

The greater their pride.

Whenever I ask my way, 'how much longer
Am I to endure this journeying by night?
When shall I see what I am yearning for,
Reach the end and find my rest?'
My way replies, 'Here I begin'.

In both poems the complexity of structure is such that the purely subjective and autobiographical elements of the experience (we know, for instance, that Adunis's father died in a fire) are completely fused with the impersonal comment. It is difficult to discard the symbol altogether once we have arrived at what we regard as the meaning, for the symbol itself has become an essential part of the meaning.

Despite the growing mysticism and inwardness in his work, Adunis is tragically concerned about the future of his society and of Arab culture. In *Songs of Mihyar The Damascene* (which contains some of his best poetry), the poet assumes the mask or persona of the medieval Arab outsider poet Mihyar to express his attitude towards political, social, and spiritual reality. Mihyar is identified with figures from biblical, Koranic, and Greek mythology, for example Noah, who survives the destruction of the world by the Flood to build another, better one, Shaddād ibn ʿĀd the creator of a magnificent world of great architectural splendour, or Ulysses, the eternal wanderer, symbol of restless man engaged in an endless quest. The poems are suffused by a mystical awareness of a deeper reality underlying the world of appearances, a twilight state of consciousness where man and God merge into one another, a pantheistic experience marked by its fluidity and dream-like quality. He can write a poem charged with mystical feeling like 'I Said to You':

I said to you I have listened to the seas
Reciting their poetry to me, I have listened
To the music that lies dormant in shells.
I said to you I have sung
At the devil's wedding, at the banquet of fables.
I said to you I have seen
In the rain of history, in the blaze of distance
A fairy and a mansion.

Because my sea journeys take place in my eye
I said to you I was able to see all

At the very first step I took.

He can also write 'You Have No Choice', which is a metaphysical as well as a cultural comment:

What? You will then have to destroy the face
Of the earth and form another.

What? You will then have no choice
Other than the path of fire
Other than the hell of denial—
When the earth becomes
A dumb guillotine or a god.

or 'The Little Times', which similarly operates on two levels:

Ours is the deceitful mirage and the sightless day
Ours is the guide's corpse
We are the generation of the Arc
The children of these little times

The faithful seas that chant the dirge of departure
Have brought us to this maze—

We are the generation of the long dispute
Between our ruins and God.

or the even more complex 'Homeland':

To the faces that harden behind a mask of gloom
I bow, and to streets where I left behind my tears,
To a father who died, green as a cloud
With a sail on his face, I bow,
And to a child that is sold
In order to pray and be a bootblack
(In our land we all pray and are bootblacks).
To a stone I inscribed with my hunger
Saying it was lightning and rain, drops rolling under my eyelids,
And to a house whose dust I carried with me in my loss
I bow—all these are my homeland, not Damascus.

Yet, although Adunis does not lose sight of his people and their plight, there is no doubt that he has been moving to a much more solipsistic universe and that his language has become increasingly obscure. Here are two brief poems from *The Book of Metamorphosis*, which may give the reader some idea of the original; first 'The Tree of Fire':

A Family of leaves
Sitting beside a water spring
Wound this earth of tears
Reading aloud to the water from the book of fire

My family did not wait for my coming
They went and now there is
Neither trace nor fire.

and 'From the Regions of Day and Night':

The wall becomes a tear and tear turns into laughter
The day grows old and yearns for death
Everything journeys under the banner of buds
  Buds of Resurrection and the grave
  Straw and rain
  Sowing and reaping
Everything is a black flower.

Adunis's voice is never the voice of utter despair. Even though the poet confidently prophesies in 1968 (in *The Stage and the Mirrors*) the rise of 'the sun that loves to destroy and annihilate', the annihilation is not final, but it is essential for the present order to die before another is born:

To our homeland that is dug like a grave into our life
Our homeland that is drugged and murdered
From our millennial slumber, our paralysed history,
A sun will come without worship
A sun that will kill the sand Sheikh and the locust.

A sun that loves to destroy and annihilate
Will rise from behind yonder bridge.

and in 1969 in 'This is My Name' (in *Time between Ashes and Roses*), he wrote what is probably a lament for Arab defeat:

I have said this broken jar
Is a defeated nation
That space is an eye disease
These eyes are holes
I have said madness
Is a star hidden in a tree
I shall see the face of the crow
In my country's features
I shall call this book a shroud
I shall call this city a corpse.

Elsewhere in the poem he says, 'We rave, I rave so that I may die well', and at one point he says in anguish:

> I try to spell and draw a star
> Fleeing from my country in my country
> I try to spell and draw a star
> In the wake of its defeated days
> O ashes of the word
> Is there a child in store for my history in your night?
> ONLY MADNESS REMAINS

It seems that here the poet evinces an extreme reaction to the Arab tragedy, for to bring about a rebirth everything has to be changed, absolutely everything, including the basic rules of logic and sanity. Hence the incomprehensible and illogical language of Adunis's poetry. It is a sad irony that a poet who is motivated by an overwhelming desire to change Arab reality and recreate Arab *society* should by the very means he adopts towards that end, namely the recreation of the Arabic language, simply end in such *solipsism*. Close to the end of *A Tomb for New York*, a work of impressive dimensions, in part a satire on the capitalist metropolis, which contains prose poetry revealing biblical influences in rhythm and sentence structure as well as echoes of Walt Whitman, Adunis asserts his total freedom from all rules: 'Thus I end all rules and for each moment I make up its rule. Thus I approach, but do not go, and when I go I do not return.'

Adunis's latest collection, *The Book of Siege*, written between June 1982 and June 1985, is a strange work indeed, containing poems based on the single foot, prose poetry as well as pure, discursive prose, all divided into separate chapters. Although in parts it describes effectively the horror and destruction of war and civil war in Lebanon, it suffers from exessive self-indulgence, extreme arbitrariness in the choice of imagery, a surrealistic mode of writing that results in the kind of obscurity which often defies understanding.

Of the many poets connected at some time or other with the magazine *Shiʿr*, space allows only two poets to be briefly discussed, both Lebanese: Yusuf al-Khal (1917–87) and Khalil Hawi (1925–82). Al-Khal, a graduate of the American University of Beirut in Philosophy and English Literature, was exposed to the work of Eliot and Pound during a brief spell in America. In Beirut he gathered around him a number of young poets, including Adunis, and set up in 1957 the poetry quarterly *Shiʿr*, which became the rallying ground for most of the avant-garde poets in the Arab world, playing a role similar to that of Abu Shadi's *Apollo* in the 1930s. Al-Khal also ran a publishing house which brought out a large number of volumes of verse by avant-garde poets such as Unsi al-Hajj (b. 1937), Shawqī Abī Shaqrā (b. 1935), Fu'ād Rifqa (b. 1930), ʿIṣām Maḥfūẓ (b. 1939), and Tawfiq Ṣāyigh (1923–71). Concurrently he owned a modern art gallery (Gallery One) in which he and many avant-garde writers and poets held their weekly literary salons on Thursdays. Although the publishing house collapsed through lack of funds the magazine *Shiʿr* continued to appear until 1964, then in 1967 was resurrected and kept alive for another three years.

Al-Khal began as an admirer and follower of the symbolist poet Saʿid ʿAql, but turned away from the rarefied atmosphere of ʿAql's cold craftsmanship after he became acquainted with modern English and American poetry. In 1958 he published an anthology of Arabic translations of works by Whitman, Emily Dickinson, H. D. Wallace Stevens, E. E. Cummings, William Carlos Williams, Auden, and Robert Lowell among others, and he also translated jointly with Adunis Eliot's *The Waste Land*. Al-Khal published two volumes in the New style: *al-Bi'r al-Mahjūra (The Forsaken Well)* in 1958 and *Qaṣā'id fī 'l-Arbaʿīn* (*Poems at the Age of Forty*) in 1960. Further poems appeared in *Selected Poems*, selected and introduced by Adunis, published around 1965.

The first poem in *The Forsaken Well*, significantly dedicated 'To Ezra Pound' shows clearly that al-Khal's poetic ideal is derived from contemporary English and American poetry. It also brings out al-Khal's conception of the poet as a Christ-like figure, in the sense that he not only brings life, but he also has to make the ultimate sacrifice to redeem his people, a conception which is enforced by other poems in the volume, such as 'The Poet', but especially in the poem that lends it its title. Like Tawfiq Sayigh's remarkable free verse, al-Khal's poetry is specifically Christian: the Christian image is more than a myth whose primary function is to organize the poems. What appears to him to be stagnant and dead poetry is a symptom of a dying culture: to breathe life into the poetry meant therefore the revival of Arab culture and society. 'The Forsaken Well' is a modern variation on the theme of crucifixion: the poet's friend Ibrāhīm, an ordinary and unassuming man, walks straight into the enemy fire in the hope that his self-sacrifice might remove evil and injustice and bring about peace and plenty on earth. Other men of cruder substance take Ibrahim to be mad, but not the poet, according to whom Ibrahim has shown us the need to turn to the well which we have forsaken, the inner spiritual depths within each of us. The water image in the poem is part of the contrast between water and desert, life and death, which is to be found as much in the work of al-Khal as in that of Adunis and al-Sayyab. Apart from its ancient ancestry in pre-Islamic poetry it has an ultimately religious and anthropological significance reinforced by the influence of Eliot's *The Waste Land*. The sea is another recurrent symbol in al-Khal's poetry, for example 'The Return' and 'The Call of the Sea': it stands for the spirit of adventure, the metaphysical quest essential to the rebirth of the Arabs.

Poems at the Age of Forty contains several poems of spiritual fulfilment rather than yearning, but the physical world is never absent. For instance 'A Poet's Wish' is about love, God, and poetry all at once. The flesh is not mortified: love between man and woman is sacramental and sanctified. 'Prayer at an Altar' celebrates sexual pleasure, but it is also a religious and devotional piece of writing, full of biblical overtones. Al-Khal's vision of the world, despite the many images of suffering in his poetry, is a hopeful Christian vision, but it is not one of facile optimism. On the contrary, as is clearly shown in 'The Departure' or in 'The Long Poem', he denounces, much in the manner of an Old Testament prophet, contemporary Arab society, its lack of authenticity, its stagnation, mediocrity, and false values. In a series of powerful images rendered in a style biblical in its rhythm and associations, he paints a horrifying and vivid picture of the world and ends with an alarming prophecy. Many of the poems in this collection are prose poems. Later in life al-Khal becomes increasingly dissatisfied with the limitations not only of the New metrical forms, but with the limitations of literary Arabic, that is the language of writing as different from the language of speech which he advocates as the proper medium for serious literature.

Like al-Khal and Tawfiq Sayigh, Khalil Hawi employs Christian symbols, although he claims that he does not use them for their doctrinal content, but for their universal significance as archetypal images. After graduating in philosophy and Arabic from the

American University of Beirut, he did an MA thesis on the question of reason and faith in al- Ghazālī and Averröes, then obtained a doctorate from Cambridge University on his thesis on Jibran, later to be published as *Kahlil Gibran, His Background, Character and Works* (see section 3A of the Bibliography). While studying in England he deepened his knowledge of English literature, as well as French. On his return he worked as an academic at the American University of Beirut and was a dominant literary presence in Beirut. In many ways Hawi can be regarded stylistically as a modern development of Ilyas Abu Shabaka: both poets were masters of rhetoric. Hawi was a perfectionist who did not publish a lot—only four volumes of verse: *The River of Ashes* (1957), *The Flute and the Wind* (1961), *The Threshing Floor of Hunger* (1965) and *The Wounded Thunder* (1979).

The River of Ashes opens with 'The Mariner and the Darwish', one of Hawi's best-known poems, dealing with the poet's choice between two ideals, science or reason and mysticism. The mariner, who stands for Western man (Ulysses/Faust/Huxley), or rather the poet who has followed him, is disenchanted with reason, science and inquiry, and the heroic humanist ideal, and goes hopefully to the ideal of mysticism only to find that mysticism is no more satisfactory than reason. At the end Hawi describes the disillusioned mariner thus:

Neither will heroic deeds save him
Nor the humility of prayer.

The dilemma is more than that of the poet's own personal salvation: the conflict between mysticism and science takes the form of a polarization of East versus West: the poet clearly stands for the modern Arab intellectual, as is shown by the rest of the poems in the volume, all thirteen of which are meant to be interdependent sections of one long poem. In the second poem, 'The Nights of Beirut', the poet is unable to face the monster of tedium having lost his belief in a forthcoming paradise: he cannot give meaning to his life either by the pursuit of wealth or physical pleasure. In 'The Coffin of the Drunkards', the poet goes to a brothel, in a futile attempt at self-escape, and rails at a prostitute in a manner reminiscent of Abu Shabaka. In the next few sections 'Without Address', 'Inside the Whale', 'Laughter and Children', 'Sodom', he virtually descends into hell to face his own spiritual death as well as that of his society. The section entitled 'The Magi in Europe' is a bitter satire on his people, containing these lines (so memorable in Arabic):

> We are from Beirut, alas, we were born
> With borrowed faces and with borrowed minds.
> Our thoughts are born whores in the market places
> Then spend their lives pretending to be virgins.

In the tenth section, 'After the Ice', a glimmer of hope begins to appear which grows brighter in the remaining sections, affording a contrast with the loss and despair of 'The Mariner and the Dervish' at the beginning. The recovery of the poet is enforced by the use of the hopeful myths of Tammuz and the Phoenix. In the final section, 'The Bridge', the poet prophesies boldly:

> They will cross the bridge nimbly in the morning
> A firm bridge wrought with my ribs
> From the caves and the marshes of the East
> To another East that is new.

Once more we encounter the conception of the poet as the Redeemer whose sacrifice will save his people, and who will take his society out of the stagnant marshes of the Arab East and lead them to the new East.

Hawi's next volume, *The Flute and the Wind*, is much less sombre, though more subjective and complex: it consists of four poems. In 'With the Fortune-Teller' the poet asserts his will, defying the words of the fortune-teller. 'The Flute and the Wind', which employs symbols somewhat arbitrarily, shows in sinewy verse of great originality the conflict between the poet's family obligations and academic duties and his love of freedom necessary for his poetry. We are reminded, however, that there is an intimate, though subtle connection between his poetic creativity and the creativity and birth of his society. The two last poems 'The Faces of Sindbad' and 'Sindbad on his Eighth Voyage' employ the persona of the character from *The Arabian Nights* as the poet's mouthpiece. Both poems are intensely subjective: the first depicts the effect of time and place on the poet, ending with his mature acceptance of time. The second even more triumphantly records the poet's journey within himself, throwing overboard his luggage consisting of old outworn preoccupations and useless inherited attitudes, one by one, until he stands all alone and naked. Sindbad returns from his eighth voyage 'a poet with glad tidings', a vision of Arab revival.

In sharp contrast to this triumphant mood is that of the next collection, *The Threshing Floor of Hunger*, published in 1965 after the break-up of the union between Syria and Egypt and the shattering of the dream of Arab unity in which Hawi was a fervent believer. In the opening poem, 'The Cave', the poet gives expression to his frustration and impatience because his prophetic vision has not been realized and may not even happen at all. It is a powerful and eloquent poetic statement of fruitless waiting, bordering on despair. But it is in the last poem, the long 'Lazarus 1962', that we find some of the most eloquent expression of disillusionment in Arabic poetry since the Second World War. Using as a scaffolding for his poem a modified version of the biblical story of Lazarus, Hawi records in poetry of great rhetorical effect his disenchantment with the dream of Arab revival, his painful awareness of how, when values die in the soul of the leader, the hero turns into a mere tyrant. Hawi never quite recovered from this pessimistic mood. Being a man of passionate intensity he took his own life two days after the Israeli invasion of Lebanon in June 1982.

Arabic modernism is no longer the shocking phenomenon that it appeared to be in the 1950s and 1960s: several of Adunis's assumptions, at least his early assumptions, are tacitly accepted by many of the younger generation of poets writing today. Even his belief in modernity as a timeless concept and as a value in itself seems to have gained wide currency, judging at least by the special issue of the Iraqi cultural magazine *Al-Aqlām* on Contemporary Poetry, published in October–November 1981, and edited by the poet Ṭarrād al-Kubaysī, and the two issues of the influential Cairo quarterly review *Fuṣūl*, devoted to the subject of *al-Ḥadātha* (modernism), which came out in April–June and July–September 1984, not to mention the countless conferences held periodically in various Arab capitals on modernism and modernity. It is true that not many serious poets were prepared to join Adunis in his later extremist attempt to create metapoetry and metalanguage and to write not simply what he, writing in *al-Māwaqif* on 15 June 1971, called 'the new *poem* but a new *writing* altogether, which is an exploration of the Unknown, in which the emphasis is on total originality and creativity, and traditional distinctions between literary forms like poetry, drama and narrative disappear'. Nor would many Arab intellectuals agree with Adunis's more recent reductionist views of East and West, his near absolute sharp opposition between the religion-bound East and the secular humanist West, and his conflicting views on the role of Islam in discouraging modernity in the sense of total uniqueness and autonomy in a work of art, views which he put forward in his two essays 'The Shock of Modernity' (1978) and 'Manifesto of Modernity' (1980).

Nevertheless, the predominantly surrealistic image, the highly allusive style, the somewhat self-indulgent arbitrary choice of word or idea are common features of much of the Arabic poetry written today. Prose poetry and the prose poem are no longer unusual phenomena. Furthermore, modernism has ceased to be confined to the major cultural centres of Lebanon, Syria, Egypt and Iraq where the avant-garde poetry movement was born. It has now spread to the entire Arab world: poets write in a modernist style (of varying degrees of complexity and sophistication of course) in Morocco (Muḥammad Bannīs, b. 1948), Tunisia (Muḥammad al-Ghuzzī, b. 1949), Sudan (Muḥammad ʿAbd al-Ḥayy, 1944–89), Jordan (Amjad Nāṣir, b. 1955), Bahrain (Qāsim Ḥaddād, b. 1948), Kuwait (Khalīfa al-Wugayyān, b. 1941), Oman (Sayf al-Raḥābī, b. 1956), Saudi Arabia (Ghāzī al-Gusaybī, b. 1940) and Yemen (ʿAbd al-Azīz al-Maqāliḥ b. 1939), just as they do in Egypt (Muḥammad ʿAfifi Maṭar b. 1935, Amal Dunqul, 1940–82), Iraq (ʿAbd al-Razzaq ʿAbd al-Wāḥid, b. 1933, Yūsuf al-Ṣā'igh, b. 1933, Ṣalāḥ Niyāzī, b. 1935, Yāsīn Ṭāhā Ḥāfiẓ b. 1938, Sāmī Mahdī, b. 1940, Ḥāmid Saʿīd, b. 1941, Ḥasab al-Shaykh Jaʿfar, b. 1942, Saʿdī Yūsuf, b. 1943), Lebanon (ʿAbbās Bayḍūn, b. 1939) Syria (Mamdūḥ ʿUdwān, b. 1941, Salīm Barakāt, b. 1951, Nūrī Jarrāḥ b. 1954), as well as the Palestinians (Muḥammad al-Asʿad, b. 1944, Khayrī Manṣūr, b. 1945, Aḥmad Daḥbūr, b. 1946), and Murīd Barghūthī, b. 1946).

The desire to change present Arab social, political, and cultural reality in order to bring it closer to the twentieth-century world, which in the last analysis underlies the modernism of Adunis and his generation, is still keenly felt by the younger poets of today. This is perhaps what distinguishes them from many 'modern' poets in the rest of the world, whose work is becoming increasingly available in Arabic translations and who therefore exercise some influence upon them. While they try very hard to write poetry of a universal appeal, using a post-Symbolist style of writing, common to most sophisticated poetry written throughout the world today, the Arab component, particularly the political component of their poetry, is still very large, even in the writings of the small dissident group of Egyptian poets who set out to attack the literary establishment and publish their poems in their own self-financed magazines *Iḍā'a 77* and *Aṣwāt*. This political interest does not seem to be getting any smaller, either, as long as such political misfortunes as the plight of the Palestinians, the Lebanese civil war and inter-Arab conflict as well as internal political oppression and abuse of individual freedom continue to be part of Arab experience.

There is, however, one notable change in the more recent poetry: the dominant image of the poet that emerges from the work of the more serious and less self-indulgent poets, even among the Palestinians locked as they are in their struggle for liberation and the Iraqis until recently at war with Iran, is no longer that of the hero, the saviour, or redeemer which we have seen in the work of the generation of what is now known in the Arab world as the Pioneers of Modernism. The tone of writing has become much quieter, less strident, and more reflective and subdued. It is closer to that of Tawfiq Sayigh, Salah ʿAbd al-Sabur and Muhammad al-Maghut than to Hawi, the early Bayati and Adunis. In painting a picture of the predicament of the modern Arab stripped of all melodramatic effects and false heroic gestures, of rhetorical flourishes and hyperbole, concentrating on man as a tragic but stoic victim and viewing him with a certain amount of irony, modern Arabic poetry can be seen as an expression of a truly modern sensibility.

Part Two

The Novel and the Short Story

3

The Pioneers

Of the literary forms which were borrowed from the West, the novel proved to be, despite the great technical difficulties it presented, or perhaps because of them, at once the most alluring and the most important in modern Arabic literature. Although initially regarded as morally suspect, to the extent that as late as the second decade of the twentieth century in Egypt a lawyer who was also a writer might prefer not to admit his authorship of a novel lest this should jeopardize his career in the legal profession, the novel, conceived as a pure work of the imagination with no explicit didactic end in view, is now considered a highly serious and respectable art, and successful novels and novelists are awarded the highest State prizes. In 1952 we find the distinguished Lebanese critic Mārūn ʿAbbūd writing in *Ruwwād al-Nahḍa al-Ḥadītha* (*Pioneers of the Modern Arabic Renaissance*) that, whereas in the past to be a poet used to be the greatest ambition of a literary man, nowadays the highest thing he aspires to is to be counted among novelists. Few writers today receive the universal respect accorded the great Egyptian novelist Najib Mahfuz throughout the Arab world. It is no accident that he is the first Arab author to be awarded the Nobel Prize for literature (in 1988).

As is well known, medieval classical Arabic literature, was not devoid of narrative writing. There were works which, like *Kitāb al-Aghānī* (*The Book of Songs*) by al-Iṣfahānī (d. 967), relate stories about famous poets and tales of love; others gave accounts of wars and battles. There was also religious narrative, such as *Qiṣaṣ al-Anbiyāʾ* (*The Stories of Prophets*) by the eleventh-century al-Kisāʾī or al-Thaʿālibī, elaborations on stories told in the Koran and elsewhere, as well as the more strictly literary type of narrative such as the *maqāma*s, works written in a euphuistic, ornate style in a mixture of rhyming prose and verse. The best-known examples of the latter describe the tricks of an eloquent picaresque-like protagonist who has to live by his wits, as we find in al-Hamadhānī

(968–1008), generally regarded as the inventor of the form, and his most illustrious follower al-Ḥarīrī (1054–1122). Other examples of literary narrative that could be cited are *Ḥikāyat Abī'l-Qāsim al-Baghdādī* (*The Tale of Abū Qāsim of Baghdad*) by the twelfth-century writer al-Azdī, the poet al-Maʿarrī's (973–1057) *Risālat al-Ghufrān* (*Epistle on Forgiveness*), or the philosophical romance *Ḥayy ibn Yaqẓān* by Ibn Ṭufayl (d. 1185), a kind of philosophical *Robinson Crusoe*. On the more popular level, and therefore until fairly recently utterly neglected by serious Arabic literary critics and historians of literature, there are, of course, the *Alf Layla wa Layla* (*A Thousand and One Nights/Arabian Nights*) and the medieval romances, tales of love and adventure about historical or semi-historical figures—ʿAntara, Abu Zayd al-Hilālī, or Baybars—which were recited at popular gatherings by professional reciters, to whom the simpler and less literate type of audience still flocked to listen in the first part of the twentieth century.

Of course, it cannot be claimed that any of these works, including the structurally fascinating *Arabian Nights*, contain even in a most rudimentary form the seed of a novel. Yet they all have certain narrative elements which could have served as the basis for novelistic development for the men who sought to infuse a new life into Arabic literature in the latter part of the nineteenth century. This, however, did not happen. With the exception of one man, Muḥammad al-Muwayliḥī, who, by making it more relevant to modern times, managed, not altogether deliberately, to bring the traditional *maqama* a step nearer to the novel, the authors of the first conscious attempts at writing novels in Arabic, both in Lebanon and in Egypt, whether they had any literary pretensions at all or were merely catering for the popular taste of the time, derived their models directly or indirectly from Western literature.

Although an Arabic translation of *Robinson Crusoe* (presumably by Buṭrus al-Bustānī) appeared quite early in the nineteenth century, it is in the 1860s and 1870s that the movement for translating Western novels (and short stories) into Arabic really began in Lebanon and Egypt. Significantly enough one of the earliest translators was the leader of modern Arab thought, the Egyptian Rifāʿa Rāfiʿ al-Ṭahṭāwī, who published his version of Fénélon's didactic novel *Télémaque* in Beirut in 1867 under a rhyming title, in accordance with traditional canons of taste: *Mawāqiʿ al-Aflāk fī Waqāʾiʿ Tilimāk*. In 1871 a translation of *Le Comte de Monte Cristo* by Alexandre

Dumas *père* by Bishāra Shadīd appeared in Cairo. Also in Cairo in the following year Muḥammad ʿUthmān Jalāl (1829–94), one of the distinguished graduates of the School of Languages and Translation run by al-Tahtawi, produced his interesting arabization of Bernadin de Saint-Pierre's *Paul et Virginie* under the rhyming title *al-Amānī wa'l Minna fī Ḥadīth Qabūl wa Ward Janna*. In 1875 Yūsuf Sarkīs published (in Beirut) his translation of Jules Verne's *Cinq Semaines en Ballon*, choosing for it the predictably rhyming title *al-Riḥla al-Jawwiyya fi'l-Markaba al-Hawā'iyya*. By the end of the first decade of the twentieth century more than a hundred novels and tales had been translated from the French alone. These were not always the best that French literature had to offer, but were a mixture of heterogeneous standards and types, ranging from sentimental stories of love and adventure to didactic novels, from historical romances to science fiction, crime, and detective stories. The authors included not only serious writers such as the romantics Chateaubriand and Hugo, but also more popular writers of sentimental novels such as Georges Ohnet, Henri Bordeaux, Comtesse Dash, Bernadin de Saint-Pierre, and Pierre Loti: or writers of novels of adventures, sensational events, and cloak-and-dagger plots, or of crime and detection, such as Eugene Sue, Ponsonde Terrail, Michel Zevago, and Maurice Leblanc. In the fields of historical romance and science fiction, respectively, the names of Alexandre Dumas (father and son) and Jules Verne head the list of translations. Some of the chief characters in these novels, such as Arsène Lupin, Rocambole, Pardaillan, and the Comte de Monte Cristo, became household names in Egypt early in this century.

For obvious reasons translations from the French were the first to appear and were more abundant than those from other literatures. However, in the course of time other translations followed, among the English writers translated or adapted being Sir Walter Scott, Conan Doyle, Wilkie Collins, and Disraeli (and later Dickens and Thackeray), in whose works translators were attracted by strongly marked elements of adventure, romance, and detection. The reading public for these translations was created largely by the rise and spread of journalism. From 1858 onwards scores of magazines and newspapers in Beirut and Cairo (and sometimes Alexandria) published serially translations of Western novels and short stories and later original works. Indeed in the course of time many magazines and periodicals specialized in the publication of fiction, mainly in

Cairo, such as *Muntakhabāt al-Riwāyāt* (1894), *Silsilat al-Riwāyāt* (1899), *al-Riwāyāt al-Shahriyya* (1902), *Musāmarāt al-Nadīm* (1903), *Musāmarāt al-Shaʿb* (1905), etc.

The reception that these translations had was understandably mixed. First, with the semi-educated they attained a level of popularity that was felt to be alarming by the educated minority, such as Fatḥī Zaghlūl, Louis Cheikho, and even Jurjī Zaydān (although it is to Sheikh Muḥammad ʿAbduh's credit that he pointed out as early as 1881, in an article in *al-Ahrām*, the potential value of translations of good Western novels, however vague and inadequate his conception of a novel might have been). It is not surprising that Arabic translations of Western novels were generally frowned upon by those who were seriously concerned about Arabic literature. Obviously the spread of the habit of reading them represented a further stage in the dangerous 'infiltration' of Western values into traditional Muslim society. In this connection it is not mere coincidence that most of those who at this stage either translated Western novels or followed their example were Christian Arabs, mainly from the Lebanon, where they had received some Western education. Secondly, the nature of most of the translated novels was such that their acceptance by traditionally minded people with a strongly marked moral outlook was rendered difficult, if not wellnigh impossible. If we examine the novels translated, we find that the vast majority were centred upon sensational events, love and adventure, crime and detection: in short, upon improbabilities and sentimental subjects. The medieval Arab view of literature, which was still dominant, was analogous to Horace's *utile et dulce*: it conceived of literature as having one, or both of two functions: to provide moral lessons, and to provide intellectual enjoyment by means of stylistic excellence or elaborate and ingenious verbal patterns. The first of these functions could not possibly have been served by such translations; as for the second, they were found, quite rightly, to be offensive. Bad as some of these novels were in the original as literature, they became much worse in translation, for they often appeared in distorted versions, in a poor and vulgarized form of Arabic which was enough to condemn them in the eyes of people trained in the classics of Arabic literature, where care for language and style sometimes reached the extent of attaching more importance to manner than to substance.

However, the Arabic translations of Western fiction were not without their use in the development of the Arabic novel. More and more people were growing familiar with the novel as a literary form, even though the examples they read did not help to introduce them to the best that was written in that form. Indeed it is a matter for debate whether the public at that stage of unfamiliarity with Western literature was capable of appreciating great Western novels. Stories of love and adventure, on the other hand, made no great claims on the reader: they had an immediate, almost universal, appeal. In fact, stripped of their veneer of Western culture, which provided their setting, the translated novels appeared to have much in common with popular romance literature such as that of ʿAntara and Abu Zayd al-Hilali. There were the same improbable situations, the same exaggerated responses, the same unlifelike and grossly simplified characters, the same tendency towards the forced unravelling of complications to secure if possible a happy ending in which virtue is rewarded and evil is not allowed to pass unpunished. Furthermore, although most translations were regarded by the orthodox-minded as harmful material, devoid of all literary merit, the fact that some distinguished authors with a great command of the Arabic language, such as the essayist Muṣṭafā Luṭfī al-Manfalūṭī (1876–1924) and the poet Ḥāfiẓ Ibrāhīm, were not averse to translating some Western fiction gradually helped to remove the stigma attached to the reading and writing of novels.

By creating a demand for the novel these translations encouraged many an Arab author to try his hand at writing novels. Although undistinguished, these early attempts paved the way for the rise of the serious novel, particularly as regards style and language. By using the simple and more straightforward language of journalism they helped to rid literary Arabic prose of its artificial features such as its rhymes (*sajʿ*), far-fetched conceits, and other laboured figures of speech, thereby rendering it in the course of time a more suitable medium for narrative.

The first experiments in the novel began almost at the same time as the translations. Their authors were Lebanese: among them Faransīs Marrāsh (1836–73), whose didactic novel *Ghābat al-Ḥaqq* (*Forest of Truth*) came out in 1865, and Salīm al-Bustānī (d. 1884), the eldest son of the distinguished author of the first modern Arabic encyclopaedia, Buṭrus al-Bustānī. Salim published serially in the periodical *al-Jinān* nine novels, historical and non-historical, the first of which, *al-Huyām fī Jinān al-Shām* (*Love in Syrian Gardens*), came out in 1870. It is a story of love and adventure, hairbreadth escapes, chivalry, journeying by land and sea, attacks by bandits and pirates, imprisonment, escape, and a happy ending in which lovers are married. The number of similar experiments in Arabic, published in Lebanon or Egypt over a long period of time, is legion. Whether their aim is explicitly didactic or mere entertainment, they tended to have a number of features in common. This is no less true of a novel such as *Dhāt al-Khidr* (*The Secluded Lady*), by Saʿīd al-Bustānī (d. 1901), which came out in 1884, than of *Fatāt Miṣr* (*The Maid of Egypt*), published nearly twenty years later in 1905 by the distinguished Lebanese editor of *al-Muqtaṭaf*, Dr Yaʿqūb Ṣarrūf. Like most of the translations already discussed, they have much in common with popular romances and even with folk-tales—and this despite the novelist's avowed lofty moral aim expressed in the preface to a work or his impressive learning in many fields. The novels tend to be marked by violence, melodramatic events, adventures, coincidence and gross improbabilities, the occasional appearance of the figure of the scheming old servant common to traditional folk-tales, simplified characters painted in black and white, and a complicated plot with a happy ending in which poetic justice is observed.

One particular feature of most of the novelistic writing of the time which deserves special comment is the introduction of Western characters or settings. This cannot be explained simply as the authors' blind imitation of Western models. Because of the prevalent conception of the novel as dealing primarily with love, authors found it difficult to treat love at any reasonable length within the context of traditional Arab life, which before the modern period was marked by the absence of social intercourse between men and women. Hence the need to bring in Western characters, or to transport local characters to Europe for the sake of the greater freedom of social intercourse this would provide. But since neither the authors, in most cases, nor the readers were familiar with the West this tendency had a harmful effect upon the writing: it resulted in a vague setting for the characters derived from second-hand knowledge and often imitated in general terms from popular Western novels. In fact, the most serious criticism that could be levelled at these early novels is the absence of a specifically Arab setting or specifically Arab characters. That their authors did not dare to come to grips with contemporary local life, be it Lebanese or Egyptian, delayed the appearance of the genuine novel in which real Arab characters arise organically from, and react naturally to, a real local environment. The first two works of fiction which go a long way towards fulfilling some of these requirements, and which have some literary merits, are Muhammad al-Muwaylihi's *Ḥadīth ʿIsā Ibn Hishām* (*The Story of Isa Ibn Hisham*), published in 1907, and Muḥammad Ḥusayn Haykal's *Zaynab*, which came out in 1913. The former is by no means a novel proper, nor was it intended to be, but as far as setting and character go it is a major contribution to modern Arabic fiction. As for the latter, it is the first fully fledged novel of literary merit in Arabic, in spite of the many serious shortcomings that are inevitable in all pioneering works.

Yet there were attempts made by some serious writers to surmount the difficulty of tackling contemporary life, not by resolving the problem but by running away from the present to a remote period of the past. The outstanding name linked with these attempts is that of Jurji Zaydan (1861–1914). But the writing of historical novels in Arabic flourished considerably in the last quarter of the nineteenth century. The use of themes derived from Arab history, which, incidentally is to be found also in Arabic drama of the period, was obviously an expression of nascent Arab nationalism in the face not only of the vastly superior contemporary civilization of the West, but also, particularly in the case of Syrian and Lebanese writers, in the face of the oppression of Ottoman rule.

The first to write historical novels seems to have been the Lebanese Salim al-Bustani, who published in his periodical *al-Jinan, Zenobia,* in 1871, *Budūr,* in 1872, the story of the Umayyad princess who helped her cousin ʿAbdul Raḥmān, later founder of the Umayyad dynasty in Spain, to escape the Abbasid massacre, and in 1874 *al-Huyām fī Futūḥ al-Shām* (*Love and the Conquest of Syria*) which deals with the Islamic conquest of Syria. Besides conveying historical information, these novels, which share many of the features of folk-romance literature, contain love themes, in which one pair of lovers (or more) meet with improbable adventures before they are ultimately reunited. Of greater significance are the novels which Zaydan published, nearly all serially, in his periodical, *al-Hilāl*: twenty-one novels, the first of which appeared in 1891 and the last in 1914. Except for one work, *Jihād al-Muḥibbīn* (*Lovers' Struggle*, published in 1894)—a sentimental domestic love-story set in the westernized Christian Syrian community in contemporary Egypt, they are all historical novels. It was an ambitious scheme in which he hoped to present the whole of Islamic history.

Although Zaydan was acquainted with the Western historical novel, his intention was primarily to teach history to the less serious reader who needed to have his interest sustained by means of extra-historical material: tales of love and adventure. Zaydan's method is uniform throughout. It is to choose a period of Arab history which involves a clash between two sets of forces, a turning point, a time of trouble and strife, which could provide easy opportunities for violent adventure. For instance in *ʿAdhrāʾ Quraysh* (*The Virgin of Quraysh*), *Ghādat Karbalāʾ* (*The Maid of Karbala*), and *al-Hajjāj ibn Yūsuf*, he chooses the period of political instability towards the end of ʿUthmān's reign and the early stage of Umayyad rule in the seventh century. In *Abū Muslim al-Khurāsānī* the period chosen is marked by the clash between the Arabs and Persians in the following century, while in *al-ʿAbbāsa* the clash is between Harun al-Rashid and the Barmakids at the beginning of the ninth. Against the background of these historical events, generally factually presented in the first two chapters, he sets his idealized lovers in whose path all manner of obstacles arise due either to unsympathetic parents or to unfavourable circumstances. The development of the love theme is the story of their obstacles and the lovers' attempts to overcome them until they reach their happy reunion in the end, for apart from a few exceptions, the end is always a happy one, often brought about by the author's heavy reliance upon chance and coincidence.

Zaydan's novels became exceedingly popular, and he directly or indirectly inspired others to follow in his footsteps. Among the many similar works written in this form in Lebanon or Egypt primarily to impart historical and factual information, we may mention by way of example Faraḥ Anṭūn's *New Jerusalem*, published in 1904, which deals with the Arab conquest of Jerusalem, and Yaʿqub Sarruf's *The Prince of Lebanon*, which appeared in 1907, and which revolves around the more recent history of the 1860 massacre in Lebanon.

That the efforts of a large number of Arab writers were first or dominantly directed towards the writing of historical fiction can be explained in a number of ways. First, the historical novel seems to pose fewer technical problems than the non-historical novel.

Because it does not attempt to represent immediate reality, the need for description of contemporary life, which demands acute powers of observation, or the even more difficult question of the language of dialogue, does not arise. Besides, the author of historical fiction could justify his creation both to himself and to his public on the grounds that his aim was not to amuse but to teach by acquainting his readers with a period of the past, and indirectly by providing the young with moral examples from history. The view that regards literature as a free and autonomous activity of the imagination is a somewhat late arrival in the modern Arab world. Al-Muwaylihi, the author of *Hadith ʿIsa Ibn Hisham*, was most apologetic about the use of imaginative narrative, and in the preface to his work he carefully pointed out that his aim was truth, which in his case obviously means moral truth. To provide historical information, therefore, in the guise of a novel could be regarded as a respectable activity, all the more so as in the Arabic literary tradition, historiography has always occupied a large and distinguished place.

The early attempts at writing historical fiction were, in fact, a curious combination of historiography and popular romance. Instead of reducing history to an artistic form, the early writers superimposed upon historical events the loose frame of the popular romance. There is no real resolution of the tension between historical truth and the exigencies of the novel. The latter, indeed, did not even begin to exist in the minds of the authors. Questions of plot and complex characterization simply did not arise. The dry facts of the annalist were given almost directly and around them, to sugar the pill as it were, were woven stories of love and adventure, improbable situations, and highly idealized characters lacking any psychological subtlety.

It can indeed be argued that, in a literature which has no novels, to begin by writing historical novels is perhaps a reversal of the natural, certainly of the historical, order of things. The historical novel is a later development in Western literature: it is after all the product of the Romantic movement. To write about his own society imposes certain limitations upon an author's unbridled imagination, a certain adherence to an observable norm, a discipline essential to the novelist's art. The exigencies of the novel, the need to provide a convincing setting, plausible action, and psychologically identifiable characters, seem to have arisen from the nature of the realistic novel, which deals with a contemporary situation. Once these exigencies were defined it was easy, at a later stage in the development of Western consciousness, to extrapolate them to a period of the past. The past had to be presented and interpreted with the same rigour with which contemporary reality had to be presented and interpreted. In other words, there were models to follow, models known to authors and readers alike. This situation, of course, did not obtain in Arabic literature, with the result that the historical novel did not offer a discipline in novelistic writing. Rather, it became an extension of the popular medieval romance, which is an altogether different genre of writing catering for different needs. Although the distinguished Egyptian novelist Najib Mahfuz began by writing historical fiction, the Arabic historical novel proved to be a dead end, and the really fruitful beginnings of the novel are to be sought elsewhere, namely in the serious imaginative writings which attempted to present contemporary Arab reality, in works such as *Hadith ʿIsa* and *Zaynab*.

Hadith ʿIsa Ibn Hisham was originally a series of articles published by the Egyptian Muhammad al-Muwaylihi (1858–1930) in his father's newspapers, *Miṣbāḥ al-Sharq*, between 1898 and 1902 under the title of *Fatra min al-Zaman* (*A Period of Time*). Muhammad al-Muwaylihi, like his father Ibrāhīm, was a politically active intellectual who fell under the influence of al-Afghani and Muhammad ʿAbduh, and because of his involvement with the unsuccessful ʿUrābī Revolution was dismissed from his Government post. He spent some time in Italy with his father, who had joined Khedive Ismail in his exile, then in France, where he helped al-Afghani to produce his well-known newspaper *al-ʿUrwa al-Wuthqā*. After a spell in Istanbul he returned to Egypt to collaborate with his father, editing *Misbah al-Sharq*, which soon became a leading organ of political and social criticism, noted for its virulent attacks on the British occupation. When in 1907 al-Muwaylihi republished his articles with some modifications, in book form, he decided to give them the title *Hadith ʿIsa Ibn Hisham*, the name by which they became known. The book attained considerable popularity, ran into several editions, later became a set text for schools, and more recently was the subject of a popular television series in Egypt.

In the preface to the fourth edition of his work al-Muwaylihi writes that 'although his story is cast in an imaginative form, it is, in fact, truth apparelled in the dress of imagination', his aim being to try 'to set forth the manners and ways of our time and to describe the faults which it is imperative for people of all classes to avoid as well as the virtues to which it is their duty to adhere'. In his choice of title, among other things, the author is careful to affirm his link with Arabic literature of the past: 'Isa Ibn Hisham, whom he impersonates, is the narrator in the *maqamas* of al-Hamadhani, the creator of the *maqama* form in the tenth century, and *hadith* means discourse, something nearer to the *maqama*. However, the preface points to an important difference between al-Muwaylihi and the authors of the traditional *maqama*. Although like him they, especially the later ones, had didactic ends in view, what they wanted to teach (and display) above all was language, linguistic and technical ability. The further we move from al-Hamadhani, who reflected the manners and society of his day, the more purely linguistic in emphasis the *maqama* becomes and form dominates content to the extent of the virtual extinction of the latter. Significantly enough, al-Muwaylihi, who possessed a keen awareness of social reality, went for his inspiration to al-Hamadhani rather than to the far more verbally minded al-Hariri, despite the latter's greater popularity.

Another important difference between al-Muwaylihi and his predecessors is that they were so anxious to reveal, and instruct in, linguistic skill that the subject they treated, the conventional trickeries and acts of deception, were at times far from being morally edifying. Al-Muwaylihi's aim, on the other hand, is fundamentally moral. A disciple of ʿAbduh and al-Afghani, he regarded himself primarily as a moralist and social reformer, a responsible journalist writing articles with an obvious social and political message. *Hadith ʿIsa* represents a serious shift of interest in the modern Arab writer's work: its author is primarily interested not in the language, but in the content of the *maqama*, although it must be emphasized what a master of Arabic style al-Muwaylihi is. This primacy of content over form or language marks a dramatic change in *maqama* literature, the significance of which cannot be overrated. It is this which in the last analysis makes *Hadith ʿIsa* an essentially modern work. Furthermore, since in the traditional *maqama* form and language are the primary consideration, this shift of interest could only lead to the destruction of the form of the *maqama* itself. Although begun as *maqama, Hadith ʿIsa* grew beyond its boundaries, thereby bursting through the form and developing into something which, because of certain narrative and descriptive features, stood half way between the *maqama* and the novel. Each episode or original article began with some *saj*ʿ (rhyming prose) but the *saj*ʿ was gradually lost as the narrative developed and a measure of continuity of narration was realized.

The transitional nature of the form of *Hadith ʿIsa* as a bridge connecting the traditional and the modern is, in a sense, a reflection of its main theme which is the change from the traditional to the modern modes of life and thought. In this respect, too *Hadith ʿIsa* occupies a crucial position in the subsequent development of Arabic literature, especially in the field of the novel and novella, for the theme of the impact of Western or modern culture upon Islam or the clash between Western and traditional Islamic values proved to be one of the chief themes in modern Arabic literature. Having lived in a period of transition, al-Muwaylihi bore witness to the great social and intellectual change that occurred in Arab society. In a similar way most subsequent writers of merit, especially Egyptian novelists, recorded their impressions of, and their attitude to, other phases of this change, writers such as Tawfīq al-Ḥakīm, Yaḥyā Ḥaqqī, Najib Mahfuz, ʿAbd al-Ḥakīm Qāsim, the Sudanese al-Ṭayyib Ṣāliḥ, and the Saudi Arabian ʿAbd al-Raḥmān Munīf. Al-Muwaylihi was not content with observing and recording social change: he tried both to define and to judge the direction in which contemporary society was moving.

The plan of *Hadith ʿIsa* is simple. The narrator ʿIsa, a writer by profession, dreams that while walking amidst the tombs of a Cairo cemetery one night, he feels the earth quaking and sees a grave opening, out of which arises the figure of a Pasha who, when alive, was in charge of the War Department under Muhammad Ali. In terror ʿIsa hastens away, but the Pasha orders him to stop and lend him his outer garment and accompany him to his mansion. Thus begins a companionship between the two which lasts throughout the book, a companionship which on ʿIsa's part is motivated first by fear, then by compassion, and lastly by a desire for learning. The experiences that the Pasha goes through, arising naturally from the gap of fifty years of which he was at first not aware, give the author an opportunity to compare and contrast past and present and comment on the respective values of each. The Pasha discovers that Cairo has changed almost beyond recognition: topographically, socially, legally, culturally, and morally. The immorality of the city, revealed in the spread of nightclubs, dancing, alcohol drinking and prostitution, together with other things, is attributed to the movement of Westernization towards which the author adopts a critical though by no means completely prejudiced attitude. Such themes are often introduced by means of concrete situations, a thing which lends *Hadith ʿIsa* its artistic quality and prevents it from being merely a treatise on moral or social reform. For instance, while the Pasha and ʿIsa are on their way to the former's mansion they are accosted by a muleteer who is intent on getting some money out of them, a situation which leads to an amusing incident in which the cunning muleteer calls the police. Thus the Pasha is involved with the police, and partly because of his temperament and his ignorance of the passage of time and the change of conditions, partly because of the inefficiency and corruption of the police, he finds himself on the wrong side of the law and in need of legal aid. Thus the long and tortuous story of his dealings with the police and the law courts begins.

Similarly his search for his property and his descendants leads to a description of certain aspects of upper-class life, especially that of the idle rich as well as the *Shariʿa* lawyer and court of law. His heartbreak at the realization that his property has gone and his grandchildren have disowned him, the harsh treatment he received at the hands of the police, the debts incurred in his attempt to extricate himself from the iron clutches of the law—all lead to the breakdown of his health, which brings in the subject of medicine and doctors both quack and genuine. This picaresque-like structure arising from events moving in one direction with some degree of interaction between the incidents or chapters is an advance on the separate nature of incidents in the *maqama*. In the course of this narrative the author managed to draw a number of memorable satirical sketches, for example the scene in the police station or the portrait or rather caricature of the *Shariʿa* lawyer, sketches pulsating with life and therefore among the most appealing in modern Arabic fiction. However, once the Pasha is cured of his illness the author seems to be at a loss to find a plausible motive for continuing the companionship. The Pasha's expressed desire to be shown a cross-section of Egyptian society is no more than an excuse for the author to comment on the manners and customs of contemporary Egypt. Hence the detailed sketch of the *ʿumdah*, the country squire, fascinated and baffled by the great city, whom the Pasha and ʿIsa see in the Azbakiyya gardens, and whose various amusing adventures occupy over one fourth of the book. Although it is not organically related to the plot this section certainly forms one of its most readable parts.

Although it is not, nor was it meant to be, a novel, al-Muwaylihi's work took Arabic literature a step further in the direction of the novel. His aim as a social and moral reformer kept him closer to contemporary social reality than those who professed to write novels. Although there is a certain measure of characterization which at times does not fail to produce an exquisitely comic effect, it is hardly enough to satisfy the requirements of a novel. Unlike the *maqamas* which dealt with a series of separate situations, *Hadith ʿIsa* presents an attempt at sustained narrative, of a picaresque-like nature; but the narrative is broken off half way through, with the result that the work lacks the most essential requirement of a novel, namely plot. It therefore remains a series of satirical and comical sketches of varying degrees of continuity, but concretely and convincingly set in contemporary Egypt.

Like al-Muwaylihi, the author of *Zaynab* was directly exposed to Western culture, but he viewed it much more sympathetically. Born to a well-to-do landed family in a little village in the Nile Delta, the scene of most of the action of the novel, Muhammad Husayn Haykal (1888–1956) received his early education in the village Koranic school, was subsequently sent to Cairo, where he studied at the modern 'secular' schools, and after graduating in law he went to Paris to obtain a doctorate in political economy in 1912. On his return to Egypt he practised law for a while, lectured at the Egyptian University, and became involved in journalism and politics, assuming in 1922 the duties of editor of *al-Siyāsa*, the influential newly established newspaper of the Liberal Constitution Party. As well as *Zaynab*, which appeared in 1913, he published in the early 1920s a two-volume work on the philosopher Rousseau, whose romanticism and social philosophy had a profound impact upon him, and some travel literature, political memoirs, and several collections of essays, mainly in literary criticism. His best-known collection of essays is *Thawrat al-Adab* (*The Literary Revolution*), published in 1933, in which he deals with the emergence of 'national' literature after the Urabi Revolution and discusses the vital questions of the language of literature, the relation between classical and modern Arabic, and between the written and spoken language, and argues that in modern literature language can be no more than a dress for ideas since content is of primary importance. Haykal also wrote a series of books on Islam and Islamic biographies such as the life of Muhammad (1935), of Abū Bakr (1942), and ʿUmar (1945). He published one other novel, *Hākadhā Khuliqat* (*That is How She was Made*), in 1950, late in his life.

Zaynab was published anonymously in 1913. In the Preface to the second edition of 1929, which bears his name, Haykal tells us that he began writing it in Paris in 1910, wrote parts of it in London and Geneva, and finished the work in Paris in 1911. When he returned to Egypt in 1912 he decided against publishing the novel in his name for fear that being known as a novelist might adversely affect his career as a lawyer. Haykal was particularly careful in his choice of words to describe both the work and its author in the first edition. He did not call it a 'novel', but 'scenes and characters from country life'. Likewise, he deliberately described the author as *Miṣrī Fallāḥ* (an Egyptian of peasant stock), to emphasize his Egyptianness, an obvious expression of his strong nationalist feelings. By choosing both the words 'peasant' and 'Egyptian', the author continues, he intended to show the world that the Egyptians and the peasants, who were generally despised by the ruling class in Egypt, were indeed worthy of respect. After the First World War, however, with the strengthening of the nationalist movement, Egyptianism, Haykal points out, became a respectable notion.

In the same Preface Haykal recognizes that *Zaynab* is a work of youth, having the qualities, both good and bad, of a youthful endeavour. Moreover, he is aware that the dominant note of the work is that of nostalgia for Egypt, which he felt while he was abroad. He also admits the deep influence which French literature generally exercised upon him. In it he says he found qualities other than what he saw in Arabic literature, notably economy and precision in expression and description, and a simplicity of language, the result of caring more for content than for means of expression. This may help to explain Haykal's deliberate choice of an easy flowing language, both in his narrative and in his description, and the absence from his style of all manner of artificialities like *sajʿ* and other forms of studied expression. Needless to say without such a straightforward and natural style no novel would be possible. In his pursuit of simplicity of language Haykal does not refrain from employing colloquialisms at times or even ungrammatical usage, to say nothing of his bold use of spoken Arabic in dialogue.

When we turn to the first edition of the novel we can detect in the author's brief 'Dedication' three of the motifs of the work: first, a romantic attitude to nature and to the Egyptian landscape, not surprising in an ardent admirer of Rousseau; second, a strong feeling of patriotism, the author taking pride in the fact that Egypt was the cradle of civilization; and third, a romantic predilection for sorrow, what can be described as the Werther motif, after the hero of Goethe's romance. We must remember that in *The Literary Revolution* Haykal describes Goethe's book as 'an immortal work'.

What is *Zaynab* about? In a sense it is about love and the place of love in Egyptian society, both among the peasant class and the middle class of landlords. Zaynab, the poor peasant girl, is representative of the former while Ḥāmid, the son of the village landlord, obviously stands for the latter. There are two separate plots, related only tenuously through the figure of Hamid. Hamid, who goes to school in Cairo, comes home to his village during the summer vacation, and sees the pretty village-girl Zaynab with whom he becomes infatuated. His feelings for her, however, are no more than the vague flirtations of an adolescent. Of a relatively more serious nature is his attachment to his cousin ʿAzīza, who went to school till the age of 12, when she was veiled and kept at home in a town in the Delta. Occasionally she accompanies her family on a visit to the village where she sees Hamid, but never without an escort. The youth, therefore, is driven to use the device of sending her clandestine passionate letters to which he receives rather coy but encouraging replies from her. One day, however, after her return to her town, he is shocked to receive a farewell note from her informing him that reluctantly she has had to accede to the wishes of her parents to marry her to a young man who has asked for her hand. Bitterly disappointed, Hamid tries in vain to find comfort in the company of peasant girls, resists with difficulty an overwhelming desire to possess the unwilling Zaynab, by now a married woman, and is driven by feelings of guilt to confess to a passing sufi Sheikh, held in great esteem in the village. He soon discovers that the sufi is an impostor, and disgusted at his own weakness and feeling utterly dejected and incapable of continuing to live with his parents, he decides to run away from the village and his parents, mysteriously disappears in Cairo, leaving behind a long letter telling them the whole course of his unsuccessful pursuit of love in the village and of his intention never to return until he finds his ideal woman.

Unlike Hamid's story, that of Zaynab is not left unfinished. Zaynab, who never took Hamid's flirtation seriously, being fully aware that the unbridgeable social gap between them would render the idea of their marriage unthinkable, falls in love with an intelligent, but poor peasant, Ibrāhīm, who works as a foreman supervising the work of the farm labourers of whom Zaynab was one, and her love is reciprocated. Her parents, however, have chosen for her Ḥasan, the son of a farmer who owns a small-holding. Unable to face her mother's misery and her father's shame if she goes against their wishes she has to sacrifice her own happiness. Although she remains faithful to her husband she cannot forget her desperate love for Ibrahim, who is drafted into the army and goes to serve in the Sudan. Despite the solicitous care lavished upon her by her remarkably kind husband Zaynab becomes exceedingly unhappy, contracts tuberculosis, and dies a tragically premature death, in a manner reminiscent of the *Dame aux Camélias*.

Despite the absence of any real causal link between them, the two plots are to some extent thematically related. Zaynab's love for Ibrahim is balanced against Hamid's love for ʿAziza. Both Zaynab and ʿAziza are forced by tyrannical social custom to marry persons other than those they love, in compliance with their parents' wishes. Hamid's quest for the ideal marriage, that is one based on love, leads him to go outside the world of the novel, and by implication outside Egyptian society, while the characters who remain inside this world contract unhappy marriages, which in the case of the sensitive end in disaster. It is this preoccupation with the question of marriage which gives the novel whatever unity it may have. It is ultimately what the novel is about. The author regards marriage as the crucial problem in Egyptian society: in fact, not satisfied with the novelistic technique of presenting two plots illustrating the opposition between love and the outworn marriage customs, he often preaches to the reader directly, much in the manner of an essayist, as is seen in Hamid's lengthy letter to his parents, which reveals the influence of Qāsim Amīn, who championed the cause of the emancipation of the Egyptian woman.

Far from being a mere work of entertainment or a love-story divorced from contemporary reality, *Zaynab*, therefore, is an embodiment of a frontal attack on one of the major problems of Egyptian society. All the characters are Egyptian, and the scene of action is almost entirely an Egyptian village. Haykal deals with numerous general problems, social, political, religious, and moral, like that of the veil, to which he attributes many social and moral evils such as prostitution. He attacks the lack of integrity in government officials, who were notorious for their bribery and corruption, and the tyranny of the Turkish and the British, the gross injustice in the system of military service, which allowed the rich to buy their way out of conscription, the pernicious influence of the lazy, greedy and ignorant sufi Sheikhs, who never practised the asceticism they preached. Besides these general problems common to the whole country, the novel deals with questions peculiar to villages and village life: the abject poverty of the peasant, his hard life, his constant toil, his enslavement to the soil, his eternal lack of means, his anxieties and lack of medical knowledge, the many debts that a small farmer incurs which leave him an easy prey to foreign money-lenders, who charge him exorbitant interest and end by expropriating all his possessions. All these matters, together with the gayer aspects of village life, the peasants' festivities, dancing, singing, and merry-making are vividly portrayed, with the result that the novel is rich in social details.

Yet, despite the density of its social texture *Zaynab* does not paint a truly realistic picture of the Egyptian village. For the novel is dominated by the Egyptian landscape, and whenever this is dealt with, and it is dealt with far too often, it is described in highly idealized terms. Here the author's romanticism is most apparent, for the sky, the stars, the moon, the fields and the running brooks, sunrise and sunset, summer evenings with the croaking of frogs and the chirping of crickets, seem to provide an invariable background to the action. The world of *Zaynab* is constantly bathed in moonlight; the author indulges in lyrical descriptions of landscape and skyscape, with the result that the narrative flow is clogged and impeded. The author's romanticism and idealization spill over into his handling of character. For the characters, though they are infinitely more developed and consistently drawn than anything that had appeared in earlier Egyptian fiction, are in fact no less idealized than the natural setting. Zaynab is a paragon of beauty, virtue, and sensitivity with nothing of the appearance of a farm labourer about her. Similarly Ibrahim, the man she loves, is an example of virtue, purity, and chivalry, and her husband, Hasan, is likened to ʿAntara and Abu Zayd al-Hilali, the heroes of the medieval romances. Undoubtedly there is an element of Rousseau's philosophy in this primitivistic picture of man near the state of nature, for Haykal's idealization is largely confined to the main peasant characters: there is not much idealization in the middle-class Hamid and ʿAziza, or in the minor characters, whether they are peasants like the husband who brutally beats up his wife, or educated townsfolk like the doctor who is called to help the dying Zaynab and who has all the time to indulge in a leisurely conversation with the *ʿUmdah*, but is in a hurry only when he examines the poor patient. On the whole Haykal's power of characterization is far less than his power of description. The only major character which has any degree of complexity is Hamid, who in some respects must be a self-portrait of the author and is often definitely used as his mouthpiece. His strange disappearance and withdrawal from the world of the novel is symptomatic of his feeling of being an outsider, of his uprootedness. He represents the lack of communication between the older generation living in villages and the younger, brought up in secular city schools: Hamid is aware of this chasm and feels guilty about it. The indeterminate end of this character is a reflection of a generation that is lost and torn.

From the preceding brief discussion it is clear that *Zaynab* constitutes a major step forward in the development of the Arabic novel. It has been called the first Egyptian novel, and quite rightly so, for here we have a sustained story narrated in a language that is natural and easy flowing, an imaginative interpretation of contemporary Egyptian life, based upon a serious and central social problem and having a plot that is not lacking in probability, characters which are fairly consistent, and a convincing, if idealized, setting. Despite its obvious defects, its unmistakable signs of primitive technique, and its excessive sentimentality, *Zaynab* has more than historical importance: it is still read with considerable pleasure today, unlike many works published in the early years of this century, such as Yaʿqub Sarruf's *Fatat Misr* (*The Maid of Egypt*), Nīqūlā Ḥaddād's *Ḥawwāʾ al-Jadīda* (*The New Eve*), or even Maḥmūd Ṭāhir Ḥaqqī's *ʿAdhrāʾ Dinshawāy* (*The Virgin of Dinshaway*) for which some have recently made large claims.

The influence of *Zaynab* upon subsequent novel-writing was great. Haykal's successful description of certain aspects of the Egyptian village drew the attention of writers to Egyptian country-life, from which they derived many of their themes. In his use of the colloquial Arabic in dialogue, Haykal had many followers and indeed raised one of the major problems in the Arabic novel. *Zaynab* set the pattern for many subsequent novels in the juxtaposition of country and city life, such as *ʿAwdat al-Rūḥ* (*Return of the Spirit*) (by Tawfiq al-Hakim), *Azhār al-Shawk* (*Thorn Flowers*) (by Muḥammad Farīd Abū Ḥadīd) and *al-Arḍ* (by ʿAbd al-Rahmān al-Sharqāwī). Hamid, the young man from a well-to-do family, returning from the city, where he studies, to his home in the village to spend his summer vacation, became the prototype for many figures in future novels. The most obvious descendant of Hamid is Muḥsin in *ʿAwdat al-Ruh*. These figures view life in the countryside not from the viewpoint of the local villager, as we shall find much later in ʿAbdul al-Ḥakīm Qāsim's *Ayyām al-Insān al-Sabʿa* (*The Seven Days of Man*), but from that of the city dweller in search of relaxation; hence the idealization (in varying degrees, of course) in their attitudes to the Egyptian countryside. In this respect it is right to regard Haykal as the father of the Egyptian novel. After *Zaynab*, Haykal did not return to the novel form until 1950, when he published *That is How She was Made*, in no way a significant contribution to the Arabic novel, which in the intervening forty-odd years had developed far beyond his scope and novelistic abilities. However, it is worth pointing out that in the last chapter of *That is How She was Made* the narrator, or rather the author, explicitly denies that novels should have any moral at all, claiming that it is enough that a novel should be interesting. This shows us how far the modern Arabic novel has travelled since the opening decades of the century. Obviously the novel has integrated itself into the main body of imaginative writing to the extent that the Arabic novelist of the 1950s no longer felt the need to insist that novels should justify themselves on moral or didactic grounds.

With *Zaynab* it can be said that the novel, as a serious genre of Arabic imaginative writing, was born. The period between its publication in 1913 and that of the next important work, Ibrāhīm ʿAbd al-Qādir al-Māzinī's *Ibrāhīm al-Kātib* (translated as *Ibrahim the Writer*) in 1931, did not witness the appearance of any major work of fiction, unless we regard as such Ṭāhā Ḥusayn's celebrated *al-Ayyām*. This first came out serially in the periodical *al-Hilāl* between 1926 and 1927, was subsequently published in book form in 1929, and appeared in an English translation as *An Egyptian Childhood* in 1932. Using the third person as narrator, Taha Husayn (1888–1973) relates the story of a blind boy growing up in a family of modest means in an Upper Egyptian village until he leaves for Cairo at the age of thirteen to pursue his religious education at the Azhar. In the course of this narrative the author gives a highly critical account of life in an Egyptian village, particularly the state of education and religion, harmful superstitions and popular mysticism, as well as lack of proper medical care. But despite the fact that it is one of the most attractive literary works in modern Arabic, *al-Ayyam* is not a novel. For all its irony and detachment, its vivid characterization, its humorous and pathetic situations, it is still no more than an inspired autobiography. It lacks one of the essential requirements of a novel, namely plot or unified structure, to say nothing of the discursive element in it which, while perfectly in keeping with autobiographical writing, would be found jarring in a novel. Anyway, the author did not intend it to be a novel and it would be fruitless to try to judge it as one. Taha Husayn, in fact, did write a number of straightforward novels, but the first one he published, *Duʿāʾ al-Karawān* (translated into English as *The Call of the Curlew*), did not appear until 1934.

Yet the years that separate the appearance of *Zaynab* and that of *Ibrahim al-Katib* were full of literary experiments in Arabic prose narrative. During these years, apart from the publication in 1926 of *Ibnat al-Mamlūk* (*The Mameluke's Daughter*) by Muhammad Farid Abu Hadid (1893–1967), the first fairly sophisticated Arabic historical novel set against the background of the conflict between Muhammad Ali and the Mamelukes in Egypt, the short story as a serious branch of Arabic literature also began to assert itself.

The short story had its beginnings in the short fictional pieces published by ʿAbdullah Nadīm (1854–96) in his weekly magazine *al-Tankīt wa'l-Tabkīt*: these dealt with contemporary social problems such as the blind imitation of Western manners, the dangers of drug addiction, the sufferings of the poor, the ill-treatment of women, and the exploitation of the nation's resources by European foreigners, and were written in a simple language, free from the cumbersome adornments that vitiated much conventional creative writing of the time and therefore more suitable for narrative. From these modest beginnings the short story developed gradually with a similar didactic end in view, either in a realistic, humorous, and satirical vein or in an emotional and sentimental mode, as shown in the work of the Egyptians Luṭfī Jumʿa, Manfalūṭī, Muṣṭafā Ṣādiq al-Rāfiʿī, and Muḥammad Taymūr as well as the Levantine Jibrān, Khalīl Baydas, and Nuʿayma. It can be said that this new form attained its maturity in 1929 with Maḥmūd Ṭāhir Lāshīn's *Ḥadīth al-Qarya* (*The Village Tale*), published in the collection *Yuḥkā Anna*. Many gifted writers like Maḥmūd Taymūr (who alone was to produce more than thirty collections of short stories), ʿIsā ʿUbayd, Lashin, and al-Mazini himself tried their hands at writing short stories, some of which were of considerable length, such as *Thurayyā* by ʿIsa ʿUbayd (published in 1922) and *Rajab Afandī* by Mahmud Taymur (published in 1928).

A group was formed, calling itself *al-Madrasa al-Ḥadītha* (The Modern School), setting up their own periodical *al-Fajr*, which appeared between 1925 and 1927, and in which they published their own work as well as translations from European writers. It included, together with Lashin, Ḥusayn Fawzī, Ḥasan Maḥmūd, and Ibrāhīm al-Miṣrī. Yahya Haqqi, who was old enough to have known some of them personally, left us a lively and sympathetic account of them in his important slim volume *Fajr al-Qiṣṣa al-Miṣriyya* (*The Dawn of Egyptian Fiction*), published in 1960, from which, as well as from other sources, some relevant facts emerge. In the first place they were passionately interested in Western and Russian literature. According to Haqqi they derived their 'intellectual nourishment' from Western, particularly French literature, but they subsequently found their 'spiritual sustenance' in Russian fiction. They were impressed and moved by Gogol, Pushkin, Tolstoy, Dostoevskey, Turgenev, Artzybashev, and Gorky. They found in Russian literature an impassioned treatment of life's tragedies, expiation and sacrifice, drinking and prostitution, crime and punishment, a comprehensive vision of life that combines a keen interest in social problems with a fascination with the mystery of the human soul and regards as fit to be a hero of a work a simple peasant (Turgenev) or an impecunious, hungry student (Dostoevsky). Thus, says Haqqi, Egyptian fiction 'passed from the stage of French literary influence, which it reached at the hands of Haykal to that of Russian influence at the hands of this Modern School'.

Secondly, these authors of short stories were possessed by an intense desire to write specifically Egyptian literature. This, of course, was among other things a manifestation of the growth of nationalism at the time. The feelings aroused and expressed by the 1919 revolts are, in fact, central in the literature and thought of the time. We have already noted the strength of nationalist feeling in *Zaynab*. In the work of the short-story writers immediately following Haykal, this trend is continued and together with Egyptian village types, characters from Egyptian urban life are introduced into their writing and they gradually dominate it. These range from the eccentric and abnormal types belonging to the lowest strata of society, which we find in the work of Mahmud Taymur (e.g. *al-Shaykh Jumʿa, ʿAmm Mitwallī*, 1925; *al-Shaykh Sayyid al-ʿAbīṭ*, 1926), to the lower middle-class characters created by Mahmud Tahir Lashin and ʿIsa ʿUbayd. There is indeed a tendency to produce a slice of life, to give what in effect is a photographic reproduction of social reality, especially in the early writings of Mahmud Taymur, and the result is often more sociology than art, for the social background stressed by these writers is not always organically related to the characters. However, by their emphasis on a specifically Egyptian social background, they helped the cause of the Egyptian novel and indeed in the writings of the more gifted among them such as Lashin in, for instance, his collection *Yuhka Anna*, which came out in 1929, and more so in his later work *Ḥawwāʾ bilā Ādam* (translated as *Eve Without Adam*), published in 1934, which is really a short novel, specifically Egyptian characters seem to arise naturally from, and react to, a specifically Egyptian social setting. This movement of short-story writing then provided a useful training in observing and recording interesting aspects of contemporary social reality, an indispensable training for a novelist.

Thirdly, these short-story writers were continually experimenting with the language of dialogue in an attempt to produce an effect of verisimilitude in their stories. Here again Haykal was a pioneer —we have seen how he boldly wrote the dialogue in *Zaynab* in spoken Arabic. They followed in his footsteps: for instance, in some of Lashin's stories the colloquial dialogue used is admirably expressive of the speaker or speakers. The Taymur brothers profitably experimented in both literary and spoken idioms. In the preface to his novel *Ibrahim the Writer* al-Mazini makes a point of defending his own solution to the problem of dialogue.

Ibrahim ʿAbd al-Qadir al-Mazini (1890–1949) had distinguished himself as a poet, critic, and essayist before he became known as a novelist and short-story writer. He published five novels: the first,

Ibrahim the Writer, appeared in 1931 while the other four—*Ibrāhīm al-Thānī* (*Ibrahim the Second*), *Thalāthat Rijāl wa Imraʾa* (*Three Men and a Woman*), *Mīdū wa Shurakāh* (translated as *Midu and his Accomplices*) and ʿAwd ʿalā Badʾ (translated as *Return to a Beginning*)—all came out in 1943, though they must have been written at different times before that date. Al-Mazini also published several volumes of essays, sketches, and short stories such as *Qabḍ al-Rīḥ* (*A Handful of Wind*) (in 1927), *Ṣundūq al-Dunyā* (*The Peep Show*) (in 1929), *Khuyūṭ al-ʿAnkabūt* (*The Spider's Web*) (in 1935), *Fī 'l-Ṭarīq* (*On the Way*) (in 1937), *ʿAl-Māshī* (*In Passing*) (in 1944), and *Min al-Nāfidha* (*From the Window*) (in 1949). He was an accomplished translator from English: he translated plays by Sheridan and Galsworthy, short stories and novels by Dickens, Wilkie Collins, R. L. Stevenson, Henry James, Hawthorne, Poe, Oscar Wilde, George Gissing, and H. G. Wells as well as works by Rousseau and the Russian writer Artzybashev.

In the preface to *Ibrahim the Writer*, apart from the question of dialogue, al-Mazini mentions a number of points: the peculiar order in which he wrote it, and his fictitious motive, revealing a playful and whimsical imagination, and a strange comparison he draws between himself and his protagonist in which he denies, while at the same time hinting strongly at, the autobiographical character of his novel. On the question of dialogue he explains that he allowed himself to use the colloquial word only whenever he felt that the literary equivalent would sound discordant and out of place, his reason being that the colloquial was unstable and incapable of expressing many things while the literary language was gaining in flexibility, scope, and polish all the time. Al-Mazini in fact managed to write his dialogue in a type of classical Arabic that has the simplicity and at times even the rhythm of the spoken language. This is one of his major achievements, in which he set an example for subsequent writers, notably Najib Mahfuz. In the Preface al-Mazini also tackles one of the major topics of discussion at the time, namely the position and future of the Arabic novel. Unlike some of his contemporaries he did not believe that the nature of Egyptian life, in which the sexes are socially separated, was not favourable to the development of the novel, particularly as it was not necessary for all novels to follow the pattern of the Western novel or for love to be the only emotion around which a novel revolved. He saw no reason why a specifically Egyptian type of novel should not arise, just as Russian novelistic art has developed, different from the English, French, German, or American. It was not imperative for all the events in a novel to occur in public places, where the Egyptian woman, who was to some extent still veiled, was unable to go, nor was the veil permanent or universal since it was found more in certain classes than in others and in towns rather than the country.

Yet, strangely enough, in *Ibrahim the Writer* love does occupy a central position: the novel, in fact, deals with the protagonist's relationships with three different women, relationships which help to define his character and pinpoint the crisis of the Egyptian intellectual. Ibrahim, a recent widower, goes into hospital for an operation, falls in love with his nurse Mary, a Syrian widow, with whom he has an affair which becomes a problem since he does not wish to marry her (we are not told exactly why), while she understandably cannot continue as his mistress. In an attempt to end this relationship he leaves Cairo for a while and goes to stay with his cousins in the country, where he develops a passion for his young relative Shūshū who reciprocates his feelings. He asks for her hand in marriage but his proposal is turned down because her older sister is still unmarried and custom and tradition make it unacceptable for a younger sister to marry before the older. Hoping to forget Shushu, Ibrahim, peeved and with his pride hurt, flees to Luxor where he meets at his hotel the emancipated and more mature Layla, with whom he has an affair. By chance Layla finds out about his earlier relationship with Shushu, for whom she soon feels great pity, and she decides to give him up for the sake of the younger woman, despite the fact that she is carrying his child about whom she tells him nothing. To make it impossible for him to pursue seriously his intention to marry her Layla lies about her past, gives him to understand that she has had several lovers, disappears from his life, has an abortion, and eventually marries her doctor. Ibrahim, shocked and disgusted, returns to Cairo, resumes his relationship with Mary and learns of Shushu's marriage to a family friend. However, his second affair with Mary does not last very long and the novel ends with a poetic passage in which Ibrahim, lost and baffled, takes refuge in the desert and meditates on the incomprehensible mixture of joy and sorrow in human life.

Like *Zaynab*, *Ibrahim the Writer* deals with love, but unlike the earlier novel it has no reformist intention. It is true that it contains too many general meditations and psychological observations, philosophical remarks, perhaps in keeping with the character of its protagonist who is a writer by profession. Nevertheless it does not primarily attempt to deal with any social or moral problem. In this respect al-Mazini takes the novel a step further than Haykal, he is not out to preach, but to produce primarily a work of the imagination. Furthermore, unlike *Zaynab, Ibrahim the Writer* is not a thoroughgoing romantic work: al-Mazini rejects Rousseau's romantic primitivism and Haykal's idealization of nature. 'The peace that is supposed to be found in the country', says Ibrahim, 'is only a myth for when nature is silent cows are aroused. Whoever seeks calm and tranquillity and deep sleep in the country must come to it armed with a supply of aspirins and pills.' He seems deliberately to provide a juxtaposition between the romantic and the anti-romantic; every romantic or pathetic scene in the novel is followed by a comic or humorous situation serving more as a deflationary device than simply as comic relief. The result is that the protagonist Ibrahim has the surprisingly modern appearance of an anti-hero, with al-Mazini often poking fun at him.

The novel is primarily one of character, and as such it displays a considerable degree of complexity, although this is largely confined to the autobiographical portrait of the protagonist, since the female characters are too westernized to be credible Egyptian women of the time. The plot suffers from major weaknesses, although it is possible to read into some of them a deeper significance and to regard them as revealing certain facets in the character of the protagonist. For instance, the absence of plausible conscious motives behind Ibrahim's rejection of Mary, or his running away from Shushu, and his indeterminate fate at the end of the novel (about which the author seems apologetic in the Preface) suggest that, like Hamid in *Zaynab*, although a much subtler creation, Ibrahim is a lost man who suffers from an inherent incapacity for happiness. They are both self-destructive characters whose ill-adjustment is a symptom of a malaise that characterizes a whole generation of Egyptian intellectuals during a period of cultural change from tradition to modernity, caught between two worlds in neither of which do they feel completely at home.

Al-Mazini's second novel, *Ibrahim the Second*, also concentrates on the character of the protagonist, again presenting him in relation to three women. But it lacks the humour and irony as well as the poetry and passion of the first novel and is full of rather tedious psychological analysis of his women, towards whom the extremely self-centred hero maintains an unbearably superior attitude. Instead of plot or organization we get disconnected episodes loosely linked together through Ibrahim's character, the events happening in a social vacuum. *Three Men and a Woman* has much more action and more interesting characters, providing a contrast with the previous works. Instead of depicting one man in relation to three women, this novel, as the title suggests, treats one woman, Maḥāsin, in relation to three men, but the action and characters in it belong to the less exacting world of romance. The plot is complicated and the different strands of the story are gathered together in the end in a manner more appropriate to artificial comedy than to the realistic novel. In *Midu and his Accomplices* al-Mazini abandons the position of an omniscient author, trying to give a slice of life or a semblance of reality and adopts the attitude of a raconteur, who keeps reminding his reader that he is telling him a story, thus breaking the illusion of reality. Written in a comic vein, the novel views with ironic detachment the characters, their follies, scrapes, whims, and idiosyncrasies. This attitude of a raconteur is firmly maintained in *Return to a Beginning*, which is a professed fantasy.

In *Return to a Beginning* after a long journey with his wife and prompted by a conversation at the dinner table with his family as well as a remark made to him by a friend they visited in Tanta, the author has a dream during his siesta, in which he has become a young boy again, smaller and weaker than his own sons, but retaining the outlook and experience of a man, despite the fact that at times he is driven by his physical condition to think, feel, and act like a child. The dream lasts until shortly before the end of the book. The humour arises from the juxtaposition of the grown-up man and the childish situation in which he finds himself. In his dream his wife appears as his mother, without however ceasing to look like his wife. Likewise, his two children appear as guests who come to his birthday party where they play all sorts of practical jokes upon him. His uncle appears as an unwelcome suitor to his mother/wife. Whereas a common theme in his other novels is that of a young woman falling in love with a man old enough to be her father, here the situation is reversed: the boy falls in love with his nurse and is sexually jealous of his uncle, resenting his designs on his mother. Here is a pure work of the imagination, free from any moralization or direct teaching. Yet more than any other of his works this novel, rich in Freudian significance, is deeply rooted in social reality: for all its humour the picture it affectionately draws of a middle-class Egyptian family is accurate in detail and pulsates with life. It admirably expresses the author's great humanity, his tolerance, his irony, and urbanity of spirit. Despite its shortness and the lack of development in its characters, *Return to a Beginning* provides a sensitive, though perhaps a limited comment on the human comedy: this tale ranks among the great works of humour in Arabic literature. It is really primarily as a humorist who is a master of Arabic prose alike in his description and his dialogue, that al-Mazini's contribution to the Arabic novel must be judged.

The autobiographical type of novel to which *Zaynab* and *Ibrahim the Writer* belong was continued in a major work which appeared in 1933, two years after al-Mazini's novel. This is *ʿAwdat al-Rūḥ* (translated as *The Return of the Spirit*) by Tawfiq al Hakim (1898–1987), the first of a series of works which were soon to secure for their author a distinguished place in modern Arabic letters. The dates of publication are misleading, since we are told that both novels were written a little earlier: *Ibrahim the Writer* between 1925 and 1926 and *ʿAwdat al-Ruh* in 1927. In his book *The Dawn of Egyptian Fiction* Yahya Haqqi opens his concluding chapter, which deals with al-Hakim, with these words: 'With the appearance of Tawfiq al-Hakim the dawn of the Egyptian fiction comes to an end', meaning that the Egyptian novel attains its maturity.

Al-Hakim was a prolific author who wrote plays, novels, short stories, essays, memoirs, letters, autobiography, and literary criticism as well as social and political commentary and philosophical speculations. Although it was primarily as a dramatist that he tended to view himself, his contribution to the novel was by no means negligible. He burst onto the literary scene in 1933 with the publication of his first play *Ahl al-Kahf* (*The People of the Cave*), which was hailed by the distinguished literary critic Taha Husayn as a landmark in the history of Arabic literature. Yet in the same year he published his major novel *The Return of the Spirit*, which was perhaps the most ambitious and most serious experiment in novelistic writing in Arabic at the time, and despite its shortcomings, still retains its popularity. Al-Hakim published a total of five novels between 1933 and 1944, after which date he devoted himself to writing plays. Of the novels the most interesting are the first three in order of their appearance: *The Return of the Spirit* (in 1933), *Yawmiyyāt Nā'ib fi'l-Aryāf* (translated as *The Maze of Justice*, published in 1937) and *ʿUṣfūr Min al-Sharq* (translated as *Bird of the East*, published in 1938).

The Return of the Spirit is the story of an ordinary middle-class Egyptian family, which, however, symbolizes for the author a whole nation. The main character, Muḥsin (clearly a portrait of the author), is an adolescent schoolboy, passing through the agonies of the first experience of love. Because his parents live in the country, he is staying for the convenience of his education with his relatively poor relations in Cairo. His two uncles occupy a flat in the traditional quarter of Sayyida Zaynab, which they share with a male cousin and their spinster sister, who keeps house for them, helped by a man servant who has been in the family service for a long time. The characters are an amusing array of different types: the head of the household, who is an unmarried, amiable school teacher of a rather weak personality; his brother, an earnest, highly strung engineering student; and a cousin, a vain and pompous police officer, who has been temporarily suspended from his post in Port Said, on account of his (unsuccessful) attempt to use his office and uniform to seduce an attractive Syrian woman. The sister is a woman in her forties, utterly lacking in beauty, who has been brought up in the country and whose mind is stuffed with superstitious belief in the power of magic and witchcraft, which she pathetically resorts to in a futile endeavour to obtain a husband, squandering most of the housekeeping money on the impossible and hilariously funny demands made by fortune-tellers and magicians.

Most of the action of the novel takes place in this setting: it consists of a series of exquisitely comic situations, through which the characters are revealed. They centre first on the men's dissatisfaction with the manner of their sister's housekeeping, then on the antics of the three men as one by one they fall in love, each in his own fashion, with the pretty daughter of their neighbour. The girl is flattered by the attention of these men, but she is shrewd enough to choose a better marriage prospect, a rich neighbour, whom the spinster sister, unaware of her own limitations, has been desperately trying to capture. When the girl's engagement is announced, Muhsin's heart breaks, the other men are united by their common disappointment, and the spinster is enraged, using all kinds of crudely comic devices to spoil the lovers' happiness. The novel ends with the preparations for their wedding and the unsuccessful suitors, now purged of their egoistic feelings, taking an active part in the 1919 revolution, which activities result in their arrest and temporary imprisonment.

Much of the novel, however, is taken up with matters not immediately related to the main plot. For instance, there is Muhsin's visit to his parents in the country during the mid-year school holiday, which occupies just under one third of the second part. Here the author gives a vivid, though highly idealized, description of life in the Egyptian countryside, demonstrating his sensitive and acute observation of the details of life in an Egyptian village. He offers a plea in favour of the Egyptian peasant, so ill-treated and despised by the Turkish ruling class, symbolized by Muhsin's mother. He also expresses his philosophy of life in which instinct and the heart are set above reason and intellect, as well as his own view of the unity of Egyptian history and the permanence of Egyptian identity, from the times of the Pharaohs to the present day. Egyptian nationalism is clearly reflected in al-Hakim's cataclysmic belief in the ability of the Egyptian people to shake off their lassitude from time to time and perform miracles, given the rise of a suitable leader with whom to identify themselves. He quotes from the Ancient Egyptian *Book of the Dead*, and the epigraph of Part II of the novel mentions the myth of Osiris, the god who was restored to life after his death and dismemberment. This intensity of nationalist feeling struck a chord in many Egyptians, including President Nasser, who in his youth was profoundly moved by *The Return of the Spirit*, to the extent that al-Hakim later believed his novel to have been an inspiration to the leader of the 1952 Egyptian revolution.

Although many of al-Hakim's ideas do not seem to grow naturally out of the action and despite much padding and irrelevance, *The Return of the Spirit* represents a giant step forward in the writing of the Arabic novel: the art of narration, the skill in characterization, and chiefly the management of dialogue, in which al-Hakim boldly opted for the language of speech rather than that of writing. Furthermore, the work is characterized by al-Hakim's intelligence and urbanity of spirit, as well as the ability to see and create comic situations in which humour is often combined with pathos.

The events of al-Hakim's next novel, *Yawmiyyat Na'ib* (*The*

Maze of Justice) cover a brief period of twelve days. It opens with an investigation of the mysterious murder of Qamar al-Dawla ʿUlwān and ends with the closing of the case, whose mystery not only remains unsolved, but is enhanced by the discovery of an earlier murder, that of his wife, and of the subsequent death (or murder) by drowning of his young and beautiful sister-in-law Rīm. *Yawmiyyat* shows al-Hakim's descriptive power at its best: in it the author succeeded in giving a remarkably vivid picture not only of his life as a district attorney, but of the entire machinery of justice as it operates in Egyptian villages. The life of the Egyptian peasant is no longer falsified by being romanticized, but is, on the contrary, clearly seen for what it is, with its attendant poverty, cruelty, and degradation.

The main theme of the book, from which much of its pathos derives, is the opposition between a highly elaborate legal system borrowed from a sophisticated modern European culture, and the simple and rather primitive villagers upon whom the system is imposed and who view its workings and its direct impact on their lives with helpless and inarticulate incomprehension. One person is fined for washing his clothes in the canal, while both the judge and the attorney know that there is nowhere else for him to wash them. Another, charged with stealing maize from a field, pleads guilty but says he was hungry and unemployed; when he hears the prison sentence passed on him, he amply demonstrates his gratitude because in prison he will at least be sure of a crust of bread. A decrepit, bent-backed old man, hobbling on a stick, is astounded to hear that he has been sentenced to one month's imprisonment with hard labour for having eaten his own wheat; the wheat has been reserved, pending the payment of tax. He cannot understand a law that brands him a thief for having eaten his own harvest, sown with his own hands, when he and his family were hungry.

Because the system has not arisen naturally from the needs of the community, those responsible for its application care more for the formalities than for actual justice. A fully documented report on a murder counts for more than the discovery of the murderer. Of the parliamentary institutions, only the outward forms and trappings of democracy, such as voting at polling stations, are preserved. Yet the voting is falsified and the result of the election is predetermined by the government of the day. Corrupt civil servants, police, and judiciary are vividly portrayed with many realistic touches and grim humour. Moreover, the narrator does not set himself apart: although not guilty of fraud and corruption, he does not exempt himself from responsibility in carrying out the duties of his office, in following the letter of the law, and observing the mere formalities. The effect is all the more horrifying, since we are made to feel that even the few individuals who have decent values can only further the inhumanity of a fundamentally bad system. Everyone appears caught up in a monstrous and dehumanizing machine.

As a living document of social criticism *Yawmiyyat* is unsurpassed in the history of modern Arabic literature. As a human document it does credit to the author's maturity of vision: evil is seen as such and is never symbolically transmuted into anything else. The novel is in many ways al-Hakim's most mature and satisfying work in this genre. Because it is cast in the form of a diary, the author's (narrator's) ideas and speculations do not strike the reader as being too obtrusive or arbitrarily imposed upon the narrative, but arise naturally from its course. Here there is no crude symbolism, no far-fetched philosophy. Instead the author gives his own direct response to contemporary social reality in an account marked by its deep compassion and humanity. The humour has risen above the level attained in *The Return of the Spirit* and has become permeated by a savage irony worthy of Jonathan Swift. Yet, unlike Swift's satirical writings, *Yawmiyyat* manages to combine with its savage indignation and revulsion from the loathsome aspects of physical human reality, a sensitivity to beauty and a sense of mystery.

Compared with *Yawmiyyat*, al-Hakim's *Bird of the East* is a rather disappointing novel. Its interest lies chiefly in its ideas, the theme being a comparison between the spirituality of the East and the materialism of the West, a common theme in early modern Arabic literature. Inspired by al-Hakim's sojourn in Paris, it depicts a brief love affair between the protagonist, named Muhsin as in *The Return of the Spirit*, an Egyptian student, passionately interested in Western culture, and a young French woman. Muhsin lives in a state of ecstasy for a few days, after which he is rudely awakened from his dream when she leaves him to return to the Frenchman she really loves and with whom she seems to have had a quarrel lasting those days she spent with Muhsin. The story, presumably designed to show the contrast between the infinite devotion of the man from the East and the calculated utilitarianism of the woman from the West, forms only a small part of the book, most of which is taken up with the meditations of the hero's friend, a self-exiled, dying Russian on the respective merits of East and West. *A Bird of the East* is decidedly inferior to *Yawmiyyat*.

The year after the publication of al-Hakim's *The Return of the Spirit* witnessed the appearance of two important novels: Mahmud Tahir Lashin's *Ḥawwāʾ bilā Ādam* (which appeared in English as *Eve Without Adam*) and Taha Husayn's *Duʿāʾ al-Karawān* (translated as *The Call of the Curlew*). Both represent a refreshing departure from the autobiographical novel. The protagonist of *Eve Without Adam* is Hawwa', a lower middle-class woman of 31, who has been denied a scholarship abroad, to which she was entitled, in favour of another woman from a rich and influential family. She now works as a schoolteacher and lives with her kind but superstitious grandmother, having lost her mother as a child, and an old relation al-Ḥājj Imām, together with the maid Najiyya. Ambitious, earnest, hardworking, and rigorously self-disciplined, Hawwa' joins a feminist society and spends all her free time helping to run a workshop for training orphan girls. She wins the admiration of the wife of a Pasha, who hears her deliver a powerful speech on education at a fête organized by the society and who subsequently employs her to give private tuition to her daughter. Hawwa' becomes a frequent visitor to the aristocratic family, and falls in love with Ramzī, the brother of her pupil who is ten years her junior. She imagines he reciprocates her feelings and, oblivious to the unbridgeable social gap between them, she even entertains secret hopes of marrying him. When she hears the news of his engagement to a woman of his own class she is overwhelmed by the shock, falls ill, and becomes unable to keep discipline in her class at school. Under the pressure of her grandmother and her old relation and partly to please them she is driven in vain to seek the help of magic charms and amulets and even to submit to an exorcism ceremony, about which she, the rational teacher of mathematics, subsequently feels shame and self-loathing. In the meantime she helps Ramzi's mother with the preparations for the wedding to which she has been invited. When, unable to contain her emotions, this self-repressed woman finds herself kissing the embarrassed Ramzi, she rushes home in a state of despair, puts on her wedding dress and commits suicide by taking an overdose of the sleeping drops prescribed to her by the doctor.

Eve Without Adam is a moving story, economically written in a simple but powerful and evocative language. While he does not ignore important social issues such as the corruption and social injustice of the system that is weighted against the less privileged, the unbridgeable gap between the social classes, and the question of women's emancipation, the author concentrates, like a true novelist, on individual human relationships. In the protagonist he paints a credible character of considerable complexity, showing particularly the conflict in her between reason and emotion, between her enlightened education and her attempt to educate others and her superstitious home background, where people still believe in witchcraft. Even the minor characters, such as the maid-servant Najiyya and the seller of charms and amulets Shaykh Muṣṭafā, are vividly sketched out. Their exotic humour is strictly functional and is not pursued for its own sake or introduced merely as comic relief. In fact the plot, though simple, is tightly organized, with nothing superfluous in it. Structurally, this short work is by far the most satisfactory Arabic novel to appear at the time. The characters, who are genuinely Egyptian, are placed in a genuinely Egyptian setting and the tragic ending is not forced upon the events, but seems to arise naturally from the interaction of the particular character of the heroine and the circumstances in which she finds herself. The dialogue, written in spoken Arabic, truly reflects the speakers' characters. It is indeed a pity that *Eve Without Adam* did not meet with the warm reception it deserved when it appeared: for it was nearly forty years later that scholars and critics rediscovered it. It must have been partly because of this neglect that Lashin did not try to write another novel: he only published one other collection of short stories (in 1940).

Like *Eve Without Adam*, the protagonist of Taha Husayn's novel *The Call of the Curlew* is a woman, though of a lower social class, a servant of bedouin stock. Amīna, her mother and sister are driven out of their village after the murder of their disreputable husband and father. They find employment as servants in another village: Amina with a kindly family who treat her more like a companion to their daughter Khadīja, a thing which gives her the chance to acquire some education with her, while her sister works for an unmarried agricultural engineer. When the sister is seduced by the engineer, the mother decides to take her daughters back to their village. On their way home they are joined by the girls' uncle, who has been summoned by their mother and who, to preserve the honour of the family, kills Amina's sister and buries her in the middle of the night, as the curlew happens to make its piercing call in the sky. Not long after their return to the village, Amina, having recovered from the shock of seeing her sister's murder, flees the village with the intention of wreaking revenge on her sister's seducer. She returns to Khadija's family and when she learns of Khadija's engagement to the engineer, prevents the marriage by revealing what he has done to her sister. Obsessed by her desire for revenge she then manages to work her way into his service without letting him know her relation to his victim and deliberately makes him fall in love with her, torturing him by remaining absolutely unattainable. In the course of this dramatic trial of wills between them, without her realizing it, her hatred of him gradually turns to love as he changes his character and becomes truly repentant, and she marries him in the end.

Although it deals with social issues such as the vulnerable position of women in a society that believes in honour and shame, the novel is written in a highly lyrical style of considerable beauty, with the call of the curlew being a recurrent motif that gives the work something of the quality of a musical composition: it is invoked by the heroine at several points in the work and is often an expression of her agitated soul. The novel is lacking in realism. For instance, it is exceedingly unlikely for three helpless women to be expelled by a tribe for the misdemeanour of their man. Only one character, that of Amina, is vividly portrayed, and she is not without her contradictions: she is far too articulate, too sophisticated for a girl of her circumstances. Yet the lyricism of the work has led some critics to overlook the absence of realism from this unusual novel.

Taha Husayn went on to write another four novels, one of which, *al-Ḥubb al-Ḍāʾiʿ* (*Lost Love*), is a love-story with French characters, set in France. These novels did not really constitute any significant contribution to the development of the Arabic novel, because of certain limitations in their novelistic technique. But they were not devoid of interest. For instance, in 1935, Husayn published *Adīb*, a work which is strongly autobiographical even though the hero is other than the author. The narrator is obviously Taha

Husayn himself, the author of *al-Ayyam*, an Azharite student disillusioned with the ancient religious institution, who attends lectures at the newly created secular university of Cairo where he meets and is befriended by Adib. Adib is a brilliant but unstable young Egyptian civil servant with enormous intellectual ambitions. He is bored with his job and determined to get himself sent on a government educational mission to France. Since scholarships are open only to unmarried men, he divorces his wife, of whom he is very fond. In France he does brilliantly in his studies at first, but soon signs of mental disorder appear: he is torn between feelings of guilt towards his ex-wife and his all-consuming passion for a French woman. When the First World War breaks out he refuses to obey his government order to return to Egypt but stays in Paris, with which he identifies himself completely. He neglects his studies, takes to drink, suffers from persecution mania, and finally ends in insanity. Structurally the novel seems lopsided as Adib does not arrive in France until three quarters of the way through the book. The style is heavily theatrical and instead of dialogue we are given inordinately long speeches and lengthy letters from the protagonist in lieu of narration. There is excessive psychological and moral analysis, or rather self-analysis of the hero's motives and states of mind, yet not enough analysis of the later and more serious stages of the moral and psychological disintegration that leads to his insanity. The novel, in a sense, is meant to point out the fatal attraction of European civilization for the young intellectual from the East who loses all his traditional values.

Unlike *Adib, Shajarat al-Bu's* (*The Tree of Misery*), published in 1944, is not autobiographical, although it has been claimed that some of its merchant characters are based on the author's own family. The events take place in an Egyptian village. Acting on the advice of the leader of their sufi order, two merchants, ʿAlī and ʿAbd al-Raḥmān decide to marry the former's son Khālid to the daughter of the latter, Nafisa, against the wishes of Khalid's mother who thinks Nafisa is too ugly and who therefore predicts that out of their marriage only a tree of misery will grow. The novel traces the growth of the various branches of this tree across three generations. In the course of the story the novelist points to certain changes in Egyptian society, such as the disappearance of the small merchant, incapable of competing against the inroads of large business, the growing importance of, and respect for, secular education, the waning influence of sufi Sheikhs, and the tradition of prearranged marriages. However, the novel is far too short and insufficiently detailed for such a large canvas. Yet structurally it seems to have had some influence on subsequent novelists, notably Najib Mahfuz, who attempted, much more successfully, to treat the fortunes of one family in three generations in his famous *al-Thulāthiyya* (Trilogy).

Such was the attraction of the novel in the 1930s that few among the major literary figures of the time resisted the temptation to try their hand at writing novels. This may explain why ʿAbbās Maḥmūd al-ʿAqqād, who clearly regarded the novel as by no means the greatest of literary forms, wrote his *Sāra* (*Sara*), published in 1938. In the introduction to the second edition he describes it as 'a novel of psychological analysis or an analysis in a narrative form'. Nothing much happens in it: we learn in retrospect that the protagonist Hammām had an affair with Sara, lasting a number of years, after which they grew bored and separated. When they meet again to resume their affair he suspects she has a lover, is wracked by jealousy, appoints a friend as a private eye to watch her and report on her movements, but Hammam's doubts are never dispelled and at the end he is left in a state of utter uncertainty. The novel is taken up with an exhaustive analysis of the protagonist's feelings and states of mind, written in a language that is generally dry and lacking in lyricism. *Sara* has been rightly described as 'a curiosity of literature', and ʿAqqad was never tempted to return to the novel form. One interesting feature of *Sara*, however, is the absence of social background; Hammam's love affair with Sara takes place in a social vacuum. In this respect it can be regarded as a product of romantic solipsism (also to be seen in some of the poetry written in the 1930s), for the hero who is completely absorbed by his own feelings will soon disappear from the world of Egyptian fiction, to be replaced by the protagonist who, when he falls in love, does so against a distinctly social and often political background.

There is, however, another novel which is clearly a product of romantic consciousness and which deserves to be mentioned here, namely Mahmud Taymur's *Nidāʾ al-Majhūl* (translated as *The Call of the Unknown*), which was published in 1939. It is an Arabic variety of the romantic Gothic novel: its action takes place against the mysterious and sublime background of Mount Lebanon. A

British woman, Miss Evans, who seems to have had some profoundly disturbing experience, sets out to explore a mysterious deserted castle on the mountain, accompanied by the narrator and others. She finds the castle inhabited by Prince Yūsuf al-Ṣāfī, a descendant of the family to whom the castle belonged, who has taken refuge in it after murdering the woman he loved, and whom he was not allowed to marry by her father, on the day she was due to marry another. Yusuf and his sweetheart had arranged that he should kill them both, but he was unable to kill himself. Yusuf is injured in his attempt to escape from the intruders and falls into a delirium, imagining Miss Evans to be the dead woman he loved. He is nursed by Miss Evans, who after his recovery returns with the party to their hotel, leaving him behind. Soon afterwards, however, Miss Evans quietly slips away to the castle and the Prince, who has held a strange fascination for her. The novel is written in a sensitive evocative style which succeeds in creating a powerful atmosphere of mystery and suspense, which does not preclude humour. Miss Evans's escape to the mountain castle is an expression of her rejection of corrupt civilized city life in favour of primitive nature, in her spiritual quest for meaning behind the artificialities of society.

The Call of the Unknown marks the end of a stage in the development of the Egyptian/Arabic novel. It is true that writers of the older generation continued to publish in the same vein; al-Mazini, for instance, as we have seen, published four of his novels in 1943, although clearly they were written earlier. Nevertheless from the 1940s onwards a new type of novelistic writing emerged and was soon to dominate the scene, a type in which social injustice is the common theme and the world of individual emotion and private sorrows recedes to the background. A new generation of writers appeared which concentrated on novel writing, unlike the older established writers, the pioneers in whose work the novel constituted only one of the several genres they attempted. Even the older generation began to devote more of their attention to social problems, whether in their short stories or the novel. Taha Husayn's collection *al-Muʿadhdhabūn fi'l Arḍ* (*The Wretched on Earth*, published in Beirut in 1949) was banned by the Egyptian Censor for its outspoken social criticism and call for higher taxation of the rich. Mahmud Taymur's *Salwā fī Mahabb al-Rīḥ* (*Salwa in the Eye of the Storm*, published in 1947) is more than the story of a woman who takes advantage of her physical attractions, it is a vivid comment on the harmful effects of class distinctions in Egyptian society and on certain difficult social circumstances which may drive a girl of Salwa's weakness of character to a life of immorality.

4

Najīb Maḥfūẓ (Naguib Mahfouz) and Other Egyptians

THE Second World War proved to be as important a landmark in the history of Arabic literature in general as it was a turning point in much of the social and political life of the Middle East. It signalled the waning of Romanticism in poetry and prose alike (see Chapter 2). For various reasons it was during the war that young Egyptian intellectuals became increasingly interested in Marxist philosophy and writers became more keenly aware of their social and political message. This was a reflection of their realization of the pressing need for political action, which came as a result of their disillusionment with political parties, their horror at the corruption at court and in public life, at the abysmal poverty of the masses due to the inflation created by the war, the profiteering which widened the gap between the rich and the poor, and the alarming growth of the lumpenproletariat as a result of the migration of the destitute from the countryside in desperate search of a livelihood in Cairo and Alexandria. Some turned to communism or socialism for a possible solution, while others found the answer in the teachings of the Muslim Brotherhood, both parties using the novel, amongst other genres, as a means of expressing their social and political commitment.

The 1940s also witnessed an important development in the history of the Egyptian novel, namely a dramatic rise in the number of novels written as well as published. This was due to a number of factors. First, the novel as a literary form was rapidly gaining in respectability: that it was becoming accepted by the literary establishment is attested by the fact that in 1941 the Ministry of Education initiated a novel-writing competition, with the judging committee being appointed on the recommendation of the august and conservative body, the Arabic Language Academy. Of the sixty-six entries submitted no fewer than fifteen were deemed worthy of consideration by the committee, who instead of awarding a first prize named the five best novels. Interestingly enough three of these were written by young university graduates, who later proved to be the most significant novelists of their generation: *Malik min Shuʿāʿ* (*A King of Sunbeams*) by ʿĀdil Kāmil (b. 1916), *Wā Islāmāh* (*Woe to Islam*) by ʿAlī Aḥmad Bākathīr (1910–69), and *Kifāḥ Ṭība* (*Thebes' Struggle*) by Najib Mahfuz (b. 1911). Secondly, the serious difficulty encountered by writers in getting their novels published, unlike authors of short stories, who found several outlets in the magazines and even newspapers of the day, was considerably reduced by the foundation in 1943 of a publishing establishment for university graduates by the young writer and novelist ʿAbd al-Ḥamīd Jūda al-Sāḥḥār (b. 1913), the Lajnat al-Nashr li'l Jāmiʿiyyīn, which published the work of young writers, mainly novelists, including Kamil, Bakathir, and Mahfuz. Likewise, the leading publishing house in Egypt, Dār al-Maʿārif, launched in 1943 a cheap monthly series *Iqra'*, which included many novels by established authors, such as Taha Husayn's *Aḥlām Shahrazād* (*The Dreams of Scheherezade*), al-Mazini's *ʿAwd ʿalā Bad'* (*Return to a Beginning*), and Yaḥyā Ḥaqqī's *Qindīl Umm Hāshim* (*The Saint's Lamp*). No doubt these ventures were embarked upon in response to the needs of a growing reading public, which was increasing at great speed with the spread of secondary and higher education, including the education of women, who were gradually becoming a significant percentage of the readers of fiction.

Before turning to the work of the younger writers of Mahfuz's generation it may be appropriate here to provide a brief discussion of *Qindil Umm Hashim* (translated as *The Saint's Lamp*), published in 1944 by the distinguished short-story writer Yahya Haqqi (b. 1905), who was a member of *al-Madrasa al-Haditha*. Besides conveying the feel of traditional life in Cairo at the turn of the century and indeed for many years to come, this novella belongs to the type of writing which in the field of the novel is known as the *Bildungsroman*, that is the type that deals with the education of the protagonist. The main character, Ismāʿīl, is a man who finds himself at the crossroads of civilization. He was brought up on traditional Muslim culture, which in its basic features remained largely medieval. But as a young man of impressionable years he was heavily subjected to the influence of modern Western culture, for he spent a number of years in England, studying medicine. The work treats in detail Ismaʿil's early background in an old quarter of traditional Cairo, where the sights, sounds, and smells of the Square of the Mosque of Sayyida Zaynab penetrate deep into his psyche, then in a brief manner his experiences in Europe where he falls under the influence of Mary, his fellow student, who for some time is infatuated with him. He loses his innocence as well as his religious faith, but acquires freedom from the shackles of tradition, a keen sense of individuality, a strong belief in science and rationality, and finally the ability to decide what to make of his life when seven years later he returns to his native country. The novella traces the spiritual development of this young man and the change that takes place in his social, moral, and mental attitudes. In so doing it indirectly places one set of cultural values in juxtaposition to another, illustrates the tension and dramatic clash between them and ends up with pointing to a possible resolution or synthesis. The work, therefore, is a deeply moving account of the devastating effect upon the soul of a sensitive and intelligent young man when he is caught in a clash between two different sets of cultural values.

Although he is a psychologically convincing character, Isma'il is more than an individual. *Qindil Umm Hashim*, as the title (which translated literally means 'lamp of Umm Hashim') suggests, is a symbolical work, in which the characters, no less than the Saint's lantern which gives the work its name, are partly designed as symbols or types of varying degrees of abstraction. Isma'il stands for Egypt at the turn of the century—the time during which the events take place. The tensions and stresses to which he is subjected are those to which Egypt was exposed; the agonizing choice between Eastern and Western values, which Isma'il finds he has to make, is the very choice which faced modern Egypt. Isma'il's salvation is therefore the kind of salvation which the author envisaged for the whole culture of his country.

The story, related by Isma'il's nephew, is written in a style of great lyrical beauty, utterly free from sentimentality. Rich in imagery, full of vivid impressionistic descriptive detail, it holds a unique place in modern Arabic prose fiction as a supreme example of the poetry of realism, sensitively in keeping with its spiritual and mystical theme. Its structure is marked by its elegance, relying as it does upon parallelism and recurrent motifs, as well as a subtle use of symbolism. Not surprisingly *Qindil Umm Hashim* soon occupied the position of a classic. Haqqi, who is primarily a short-story writer, went on to write another extended work of fiction, published in 1956 a novel: *Ṣaḥḥ al-Nawm* (translated as *Good Morning!*) is a fable embodying his mixed feelings about the effect of Nasser's 1952 revolution. It is an interesting, though by no means faultless novel, but it belongs to a later stage in the history of the Egyptian novel.

Despite their intense preoccupation with the social and political conditions of contemporary Egypt, the younger generation of writers began by producing historical novels. The three novels we have mentioned by Bakathir, Kamil, and Mahfuz, which were listed among the five best novels in the 1941 novel-writing competition, are historical: Mahfuz and Kamil (as well as al-Sahhar) first derived their plots from Pharaonic Egypt. This was partly due to the sudden resurgence in the 1940s of the vogue for historical fiction inspired either by Ancient Egyptian, Arab, or Islamic history, which was to be seen particularly in the work of the older generation, such as Muhammad Farid Abu Hadid (1893–1967), Muḥammad Saʿīd al-ʿIryān (1905–64), or ʿAlī al-Jārim (1881–1949)—no doubt an expression of Egyptian (Pharaonic) or Islamic nationalism and a desire to assert the glory of the past or to escape from the oppressive gloomy present. Mahfuz's first novel, *ʿAbath al-Aqdār* (*The Mockery of Fates*), was published as a special issue of *al-Majalla al-Jadida* whose editor Salama Musa was an exponent of the Pharaonic strand in Egyptian nationalism. It was also as if initially the younger generation did not wish to fall foul of the authorities and therefore chose to convey their criticism of society and their social protest indirectly, by using events of the past to illuminate the present. This is true especially of Bakathir, a prolific writer who is perhaps the least gifted of all these three novelists. In *Wa Islamah* (published in 1945) he used the defeat inflicted by the Mameluke Sultan Qutuz on the Tartars at the battle of ʿAyn Jalūt in 1260 to express his Islamic and Arab nationalist convictions. In *al-Thāʾir al-Aḥmar* (*The Red Revolutionary*, published in 1948) he chose an event from Islamic history, the Carmathian revolt, as a metaphor for the conflict between the Muslim Brothers and the extreme Left in contemporary Egypt.

ʿAdil Kamil's *Malik min Shuʿaʿ* (*A King Of Sunbeams*), published in 1941, employs Ancient Egyptian history, namely the reign of Ikhnaton, to give expression to a dark vision of Egyptian society in which scheming politicians and priests conspire to destroy upholders of noble ideals and spiritual values.

Kamil did not linger long at historical fiction, but soon turned to contemporary Egypt with the publication in 1944 of his second novel *Millīm al-Akbar*. Millīm, a destitute youth whose mother is dead and whose father is serving a prison sentence for drug-peddling, tries to earn an honest living as a carpenter's apprentice. When he goes to a Pasha's mansion to repair a window he is falsely accused of stealing a large sum of money (which in fact is taken by the Pasha's profligate son ʿUmar), and is sent to gaol despite the vain effort to exculpate him made by the Pasha's other son, Khālid, who has returned from his studies in England, full of socialist ideals. Khalid rebels against his father's materialist and selfish values and leaves his house. When Millim comes out of prison, eighteen months later, he is taken up by a group of young Marxist and anarchist intellectuals, and a medley of artists and writers who live in a commune in a historic building, forming what is apparently a secret communist cell. With the help of a young East European female painter who lives with the group, Millim tries to raise funds by all means, including cheating the gullible rich. He chances to meet Khalid who, despite his aristocratic background, decides to join the organization and who, to prove his total commitment, distributes subversive leaflets preaching revolutionary principles, at a popular café. He is arrested by the police, but is freed from prison through the intervention of his influential father. In return he agrees to abandon his socialist ideals. The organization is broken up as a result of the combined action of the Pasha and the police. In the mean time Millim marries the European member of the cell, becomes rich through trading with a British army camp during the Second World War, but uses his money to contribute generously to charity.

Millim aims at underlining the enormous gap between the rich and the poor, at showing the moral corruption and decadence of the aristocracy, and unmasking the collusion between the feudal system, capitalism, and the State police to crush the poor and suppress any revolutionary attempt to improve the lot of the masses. The novel, written in a clear, easy flowing style, paints a vivid picture of social injustice, as well as the debilitating confusion of the intellectuals in Egypt during the war years. It provides an interesting analysis of a fairly complex character, that of Khalid, whose dilemmas are presented in a convincing manner. The struggle between him and his father is shown as more than just a generation conflict but as having a symbolical value, although the author's socialist views tend to distort his vision somewhat, thus making him paint his characters in black and white: the aristocracy are shown to be either utterly wicked or hopelessly weak while the poor are honest and remain steadfast in their principles. It was probably because of these socialist views that the novel was not awarded the novel prize for 1944 by the Arabic Language Academy, who claimed that none of the novels submitted that year had reached a sufficiently high standard, a view which drove Kamil to write a lengthy (and interesting) introduction to his novel, attacking the judging committee's ignorance of the principles of literary criticism, amongst other things. This was a pity because Kamil's discouragement and his subsequent decision to write no more novels robbed Egypt of a most competent novelist whose work was in fact the closest to that of his friend, the great novelist Najib Mahfuz.

Kamil's portrayal of the dilemma of the alienated Marxist Egyptian intellectual during the war years was excelled only by Luwīs ʿAwaḍ's political novel *al-ʿAnqāʾ aw Tārikh Ḥasan Miftāḥ* (*The Phoenix*, written between 1946 and 1947, but not published until 1966), in which, using a supernatural and somewhat melodramatic framework, ʿAwad treats many of the political, psychological, and moral problems facing Egyptian revolutionaries, exemplified by his protagonist Hasan Miftah, a dedicated communist. These range from the difficulty of choosing between complete political commitment and action and personal relationships and private life to the question whether murder in the cause of the revolution can be morally justified. *Al-ʿAnqa*ʾ is a highly intellectual novel in which ʿAwad employs a subtle mixture of fantasy and realism, if not naturalism, and a sophisticated narrative technique: it was possibly the first Arabic novel to use the (Jamesian) technique of dramatized consciousness.

Like Kamil, Mahfuz too derived his material at first from Pharaonic history, but unlike him he continued to do so for another two novels: *ʿAbath al-Aqdār* (*The Mockery of Fate*, published in 1939), *Rādūbīs* (which came out in 1943), and *Kifāḥ Ṭība* (*Thebes' Struggle*, published in 1944). It has been said that it was under Kamil's influence that he gave up his original plan to deal with the whole history of Egypt in a series of novels modelled on Sir Walter Scott's work and turned for his themes to contemporary Egypt instead.

Few people will deny that Najib Mahfuz (Naguib Mahfouz) is the most significant figure to have arisen this century in the history of the Arabic novel. Yet paradoxically, of all writers he is perhaps the most peculiarly Egyptian in sensibility, outlook, and background—and that despite the underlying universality of the themes in many of his works. Other Arab novelists who produce works of literary merit appear from time to time, both in Egypt and elsewhere, and some have written truly outstanding novels, but no one has approached in output, variety, originality, and seriousness Mahfuz's achievement.

Born in 1911 in the old quarter of Cairo, al-Jamaliyya, the setting of several of his novels, Mahfuz began to publish as early as 1934, even before he graduated in philosophy from the secular university in Cairo, where he fell under the influence of Auguste Comte's positivism. He published mainly in *al-Majalla al-Jadida*, the journal edited by the Fabian secularist thinker Salama Musa. He began with popular articles on philosophy and the history of ideas, together with short stories, and subsequently turned to writing novels. It was not, however, until 1957, with the publication of his trilogy, that he received the acclaim he deserved. For two decades he continued to toil over his fiction in relative obscurity—his friends gave him the nickname *Ṣābir*, alluding to his infinite patience and his perseverance in devoting his spare time to writing (since for most of his life he worked to earn his living as a civil servant).

As has been mentioned, Mahfuz began his career as a novelist with historical fiction, publishing three novels in this genre between 1939 and 1944. In these works, the imaginative reconstruction of the Ancient Egyptian past is less important than Mahfuz's use of the distant Pharaonic setting as a vehicle for commentary on the political and social situation of contemporary Egypt. In this he succeeded to some extent: there is implied criticism of the tyranny of King Farouk in *Radubis*, and a pronounced feeling of nationalist resentment against the foreign (and hence British) occupation of Egypt in *Thebes' Struggle*. However, Mahfuz soon abandoned Pharaonic times for the contemporary Egyptian and especially the Cairene setting. This was a wise decision, not least because he was ill-suited to the historical novel. His venture in that genre, however competent it may be, is in no way superior to the work of others, even though there are perhaps signs of the future novelist in the breadth of his vision, which prevented him from painting his characters in black and white in *Radubis* and hence from witholding all sympathy for the dissolute monarch, and enabled him to rise above the limitations of narrow nationalism in depicting Egyptian defeat and victory in *Thebes' Struggle*. But it must be admitted that had he continued in this historical strain he might not have cut the figure he did in modern Arabic literature.

Mahfuz's next work, *Khān al-Khalīlī* (published in 1945) began a series of eight novels in which he emerged as the master *par excellence* of the Egyptian realistic novel, the chronicler of twentieth-century Egypt, and its most vocal social and political conscience. With titles taken from the names of streets of old Cairo, the novels offer a panoramic vista of the Egyptian lower and lower middle classes, with the minute details of their daily lives vividly and lovingly portrayed. Unlike Lawrence Durrell's Alexandria, Mahfuz's Cairo has more than mere romantic imaginative validity: it is a recognizable physical presence. Its powerful impact upon the lives of characters is as memorable as that of Dickens's London, Dostoevsky's St Petersburg, or Zola's Paris.

Mahfuz's realistic art reaches its pinnacle in his *al-Thulāthiyya* (*Trilogy*) (published in 1956–7, but clearly written before the 1952 revolution). With the exception of *al-Sarāb* (*The Mirage*, 1949), a somewhat superficial Freudian interpretation of the sexual difficulties of the upper middle-class narrator/protagonist, the earlier novels *Khan al-Khalili* (1945), *al-Qāhira al-Jadīda* (*New Cairo*, 1946), *Zuqāq al-Midaqq* (published in 1947 and translated into English as *Midaq Alley*), and *Bidāya wa Nihāya* (1951, translated as *The Beginning and the End*) deal in the main with the pressures and drama of life in Egypt shortly before and during the Second World War. *Khan al-Khalili* is a sensitive treatment of a middle-class family whose hopes of happiness slowly fade away, ending in death and sorrow, thus rendering utterly pointless the enormous sacrifices made by the pathetic middle-aged breadwinner Aḥmad ʿĀkif. *New Cairo* traces the fortunes of three philosophy graduates of Cairo university: ʿAli Ṭāhā, a secular liberal who believes in science and socialism, Maʾmūn Riḍwān, a devout Muslim, and Maḥjūb ʿAbd al-Dāyim, a self-centred nihilist. The novel concentrates on Mahjub, who is driven by poverty to accept employment in return for agreeing to marry the mistress of his boss, who continues his relationship with her. Although at first the future looks rosy and he obtains a promotion, they both soon come to a bad end when their arrangement is uncovered in a scandal. *New Cairo* paints a gloomy picture of a changing society suffering from moral and political corruption and desperately searching for values.

Midaq Alley, like *Khan al-Khalili*, one of his best novels in this vein, is set in Old Cairo which is described in loving detail: the alley with its inhabitants, men and women, their work and leisure, their intricate social relationships—all forming a close-knit community. Besides giving a vivid picture of the sights, sounds, and smell of the alley, Mahfuz paints here a gallery of colourful characters ranging from the hashish-smoking homosexual café-owner Muʿallim Kirsha, and his noisy quarrels with his wife Samiyya ʿAfifi, the rich middle-aged widow in search of a husband, who is cunningly manipulated by the matchmaker, the adoptive mother of Ḥamīda, the beauty of the alley to Zīṭa, who earns his living by counterfeiting defects on the bodies of the poor to enable them to become beggars, the demented ex-schoolteacher Sheikh Darwīsh, whose mystical utterances are interspersed with English words, and Sayyid Riḍwān al-Ḥusaynī who acts as mediator in the inhabitants' quarrels and represents the moral authority of the alley. The main plot shows the tragic impact the outside world has upon this community, as well as the destructive effect the presence of the British occupying army has upon Egypt during the war.

ʿAbbās al-Ḥulw, the young barber of the alley, is encouraged by his friend, Kirsha's son, to leave it and work in a British army camp to improve his financial situation so that he may be worthy of the alley beauty, the vivacious and ambitious Hamida, to whom he is engaged and who does not wish to lead a life of poverty and deprivation like the majority of the alley inhabitants. However, soon after his departure she is encouraged by her adoptive mother to break her promise and accept a proposal from a rich married man in his fifties who owns a grocery in the alley. Their marriage plans fall through due to a serious illness which renders him physically incapable. Not long afterwards she falls for a handsome, apparently rich young man with whom she elopes, but discovers, too late, that he is a pimp who runs a training school for high-class prostitutes to entertain the British soldiers. On a visit to the alley ʿAbbas learns of Hamida's disappearance and vows to punish her seducer. He runs into her and is horrified to see the manner of her dress and her heavy make-up. She arranges to meet him at a bar to show him her seducer, whom by now she has come to hate.

When ʿAbbas arrives at the bar a little early, accompanied by a friend, he finds her entertaining drunken British soldiers, becomes enraged and throws a bottle at her, and is immediately set upon by the soldiers who beat him to death. This is only one of the many sad changes in the lives of the inhabitants of the alley, which towards the end of the novel drive the saintly Sayyid Ridwan to go on a pilgrimage to Mecca to ask forgiveness for all their sins.

In *The Beginning and the End* a whole lower middle-class family gradually falls apart as a result of the sudden death of the bread-winner, a minor civil servant, who leaves behind him a widow, three sons, and a daughter. The widow makes heroic efforts to hold the family together and manage on a meagre pension, but not for long. The eldest son, who had hoped to become a singer, turns to a life of crime, smuggling drugs and living with a prostitute. The middle son has to give up any plans for a higher education or even marriage in order to help the family financially and enable his younger brother to become an army officer. The plain-looking daughter is jilted by the local grocer's son after he has seduced her and is driven by her strong sexual urges to resort to occasional prostitution. The young army officer is ruthlessly ambitious but his wild dreams of climbing up the social ladder and marrying the daughter of a rich family are dashed when his sister is discovered by the police in a brothel. He readily accepts her utterly unselfish offer to commit suicide to save his reputation, but after she has jumped to her death in the Nile he finds himself almost involuntarily following her example.

In all these novels individuals, men and women alike, desperately try to improve their lot, but are crushed by evil forces in society, as well as by a malignant fate, of which Mahfuz tends to make excessive use at this stage.

Mahfuz's last and most mature work in this realistic vein is his monumental trilogy *al-Thulathiyya*, published between 1956 and 1957, in separate volumes taking their titles from street names in Old Cairo where some of the characters lived: *Bayn al-Qaṣrayn, Qaṣr al-Shawq*, and *al-Sukkariyya*. It traces the fortunes of a middle-class Cairene family over three generations, beginning in 1917 with the growth of the nationalist movement that culminated in the 1919 revolution and ending in 1944, during the Second World War. *Bayn al-Qasrayn* begins with a detailed account of the family of a middle-aged merchant, Aḥmad ʿAbd al-Jawād, his wife Amīna, their two sons: Fahmī and Kamāl, aged 18 and 12 respectively, and two daughters Khadīja, aged 20, and ʿĀʾisha, 16, as well as his son by a previous marriage Yasīn (in his early twenties), whose mother was divorced before he was born. Ahmad ʿAbd al-Jawad rules his family with a rod of iron. At home he is a stern man, demanding absolute obedience from his children as well as his wife, whom he does not allow to go out of the house. On the one occasion when, during his absence on a business trip, at the instigation of her children she ventures to go out to visit the mosque of al-Husayn, she has an accident which necessitates a stay in bed to recover. She is severely punished after her recovery by being turned out of the house by him and it is only through the intercession of an old family friend that he agrees to have her back. Yet outside the house he reveals another facet of his character: his love of wine, women, and song in which he indulges in the evenings in the company of his merchant friends. Ahmad Abd al-Jawad, a bundle of contradictions, combining piety and discipline together with hedonism and amorous affairs, and to a lesser extent his silently loving, patient, and obedient wife Amina, are among Mahfuz's most impressive creations. In the course of the volume the daughters get married (to two brothers) and move out to their husbands' house in al-Sukkariyya. Yasin, who works as a junior-school clerk, is a skirt-chaser and to avoid any further scandals is forced by his father to marry the daughter of a friend, but the marriage does not put an end to his lechery and his wife runs away to her parents and subsequently obtains a divorce. He later inherits a house in Qasr al-Shawq, on the death of his mother. Fahmi, a law student, gets involved in nationalist politics against his father's wishes. The volume ends on a sad note when he is shot dead in a peaceful demonstration to celebrate the freeing of the leader of the nationalist movement by the occupying British forces in 1919.

The events of *Qasr al-Shawq* begin five years later. The shock of Fahmi's death has cast a shadow of gloom over ʿAbd al-Jawad's household from which it has never really completely recovered. Sorrow has put years on both him and his wife. He abjures wine, women, and song, though later, at the insistence of his former boon companions, he slowly resumes his hedonistic way of life. Yasin continues his life of debauchery and leaves the family house to live in his own house, marries and divorces again, and eventually marries an old flame who had been in the mean time his father's mistress, and has a son by his first wife. Khadija has two sons and ʿA'isha a daughter and two sons. Kamal, now a young man, falls in love with the sister of an aristocratic fellow student, but meets with disappointment. He is an intellectual, with an ambition to become a writer. His intellectual and spiritual development, including his loss of religious faith under the influence of logical positivism, become a major theme in the second and third parts of the trilogy, an expression of the religious doubts and uncertainties accompanying the transition to modernity. The volume ends on an equally sad note: ʿA'isha's sons, together with her husband, die suddenly in a typhoid epidemic and ʿA'isha moves with her daughter back to her parents' house.

The last volume in the trilogy, *al-Sukkariyya*, covers the period 1935–1944, concentrating upon the lives of the third generation. Ahmad ʿAbd al-Jawad is now an old man, a house-bound invalid who eventually dies of a heart attack during an air raid on Cairo. Amina, who has never got over the loss of her son, leads a gloomy existence in which she tries to comfort her bereaved daughter ʿA'isha. Kamal, now a schoolteacher, leads an emotionally sterile life, not having recovered from his disappointment in love. He watches with keen interest the development of his nephews, all of whom have had a university education: Yasin's son becomes a shrewd and compromising politician, while Khadija's two boys embrace two diametrically opposite ideologies, the one becoming a Muslim Brother, while the other joins the Left (with which Kamal finds himself more in sympathy), and meets and marries a fellow journalist, Sawsan, a communist. The hapless ʿA'isha loses her daughter, who dies in labour, and her death almost unhinges her mind. The novel ends with both the communist and Muslim Brother in goal for their political activities, the dying Amina in a coma, and Khadija's grandson about to be born.

The trilogy stands as a unique monument in the history of the modern Arabic novel. Nothing quite like it or on a similar scale had been attempted before. The work, covering such a huge canvas, with a gallery of unforgettable characters, offering a panorama of Egyptian society, keenly sensitive to the passage of time, and recording the minutest changes in social and political life testifies to Mahfuz's admirable architectonic sense and reveals his ability to design almost in epic dimensions. As the work develops the emphasis on environmental description grows noticeably less and more space is accorded to the inner lives of the characters and their intellectual and political preoccupations. Amongst the changes recorded are those in the position of women: there is a world of difference between the docile and submissive Amina and the emancipated communist journalist Sawsan.

The destinies of the individual characters in the trilogy are the microcosm, but the macrocosm is the destiny of modern Egypt. The tragedies, the sufferings, the conflicts of the men and women who people these novels reflect the larger social, political, and intellectual changes in one significant part of the modern Arab world. The struggle of the younger generation to attain their domestic freedom, to shape their own lives, mirrors the nation's struggle to achieve political independence and to free itself from the shackles of outworn and debilitating, almost medieval conventions in a gigantic endeavour to become part of the modern world. The slow unfolding of events, the meticulous enumeration of detail, the heavy sociological documentation, the anxious concern to produce a tightly knit plot, the scrupulous care to maintain an objective stance, give these novels, despite their unmistakable Egyptian character, the air of nineteenth-century European fiction. To the criticism that they took no account of modernist techniques Mahfuz replied that although he was not unaware of modernism, he felt that technique was determined by the writer's material and vision of life. Herein lies Mahfuz's strength: unlike lesser writers he has never been dazzled by the latest literary fashion.

Between the completion of the trilogy and the appearance of *Awlād Ḥāratinā* (translated as *The Children of Gebelawi*) in 1959 Mahfuz wrote nothing for more than five years, a silence all the more baffling in view of the prolific output of earlier and later years. His own recorded explanation is that with the coming of Nasser's revolution he felt he had nothing further to say, since it was pointless to continue to criticize the *ancien régime*. But clearly the novelist must have experienced something of a spiritual crisis, partly responsible for the change in emphasis, form, and theme which occurred in his work when it was later resumed—the kind of crisis related in his short story *Zaʿbalāwī* (1961), which deals with man's compulsive search for God after all other remedies have failed. *The Children of Gebelawi* is one of the few allegorical novels in Arabic. The events, true enough, still take place in Cairo, but unlike the earlier novels, which are set in a particular place and at a particular juncture in modern Egyptian history, *The Children of Gebelawi* evokes the general atmosphere of Old Cairo, in an almost timeless period, although it is clearly before the late nineteenth century. The timelessness is perhaps appropriate since the theme is, in fact, the whole of human history and man's quest for religion from Adam and Eve, Cain and Abel, Moses, Jesus, Muhammad, right down to the last of the prophets, the modern man of science, the man indirectly responsible for the death of their ancestor, Gebelawi, the Mountain Man, who clearly stands for God. These figures are given thinly disguised Arabic names, which, together with a brief outline of the main events in their lives, immediately reveal their true identity. They are portrayed as the heroes of an imaginary alley who from time to time rise up in rebellion against the violent tyranny of the *status quo*. Structurally it is an interesting work: instead of the slow tempo of the earlier novels, we have in effect a number of very fast-moving short novellas, held together by means of certain parallelisms and continuities, and, of course, one unifying concept. Significantly, the novel is divided into 114 chapters, the same number as that of the chapters or *Suras* of the Koran. This cannot be dismissed as mere coincidence: Mahfuz here is giving modern man's view of the stories of prophecy narrated by the Koran.

Yet, although *The Children of Gebelawi* deals primarily with metaphysical questions, such as the nature of evil and the meaning of life, the moments of spiritual illumination or religious ecstasy are few and far between. The driving force behind all the prophets is not so much the sense of man's essential need for God's comfort in a frighteningly insecure universe, as a keen awareness of social injustice and the evil perpetrated by man against man. In this respect *The Children of Gebelawi* forms a link with the rest of Mahfuz's work. The conflict between science and religion, and the influence of Auguste Comte's logical positivism are clearly marked in his early writings, particularly, as we have seen, in the character of Kamal in the trilogy. And it is this interpenetration of the philosophical/religious and the social, political, and psychological that gives Mahfuz's novels, particularly his later works, their peculiar resonance and richness of texture, their many layers of meaning. As a novel *The Children of Gebelawi* suffers from serious defects: it is too repetitive, too full of fighting, too fast-moving, too thickly populated to allow for convincing characterization and, for a work on man's religious quest, it is too explicitly prosaic and lacking in the poetic spirit. Yet, despite its imperfections, it constitutes an impressive landmark in the development of Mahfuz's novelistic art. Its spiritual preoccupations, its existentialist terror of death, point forward to future works.

The next novel Mahfuz published, *al-Liṣṣ wa'l-Kilāb* (in 1961, translated as *The Thief and the Dogs)* marked the beginning of a new phase of shorter novels, generally concentrating on one protagonist, more dramatic in nature, more lyrical in style, more symbolical in mode, employing interior monologue and some of the stream-of-consciousness techniques, dreams and flashback, as well as other modernistic devices in keeping with the nature of their subject. In them we have the poetry of realism, an indissoluble mixture of the political, the psychological, the metaphysical, and the mystical. These novels include *al-Summān wa'l-Kharīf* (published in 1962 and translated into English as *Autumn Quail*), *al-Ṭarīq* (published in 1964 and translated as *The Search*), *al-Shaḥḥādh* (published in 1965 and which came out in English as *The Beggar), Tharthara fawq al-Nīl (Chattering on the Nile*, in 1966), and *Mīramār* (in 1967, translated as *Miramar)*, even though the last mentioned, instead of presenting one protagonist, describes its events through the eyes of four characters.

In some of these shorter novels the obsessive spiritual quest leads to disturbing states of consciousness in which the borderline between illusion and reality is blurred and the distinction between past and present obliterated. Yet despite their metaphysical dimension, they provide an eloquent and sensitive index to the mood and temper of Egypt since Nasser's revolution, a revolution which was welcomed with considerable enthusiasm by the Egyptian intellectuals who had hoped that it would put an end to the social injustice and the corruption of the *ancien régime*. Later they were disenchanted, frustrated, and alienated by the turn the revolution took, first in imposing military rule and banning political parties, then in establishing the one-party state, suppressing individual freedoms, and ruthlessly crushing all opposition, which resulted in the rise of a new, cynical class of self-seeking opportunists who paid only lip service to the revolution's socialist slogans.

The Thief and the Dogs, to take but one example, is a study in depth of the mind of its protagonist, Saʿīd Mahrān. On one level it can be viewed as a psychological study, a portrait of a revolutionary nihilist, or a disenchanted revolutionary idealist; nearly all the events are presented to us as seen through his eyes. The boy Saʿid grows up in extreme poverty (there is a harrowing description of his feelings as he witnesses his mother dying of a haemorrhage because she could not afford the doctor's fees). His parents are the caretakers of a Cairo students' hostel, in which he falls under the influence of the dynamic character of Ra'ūf ʿIlwān, a student with revolutionary ideals, who instils in his mind the spirit and principles of revolutionary action, trains him, together with others, militarily, encourages him to read revolutionary literature and, when he learns that the youth has robbed the rich, provides him with the necessary intellectual and moral justification. Saʿid falls in love with and marries a servant girl from the neighbourhood and has a child by her, called Sanā'. Soon afterwards he is caught by the police and gaoled for four years, in the course of which Nasser's revolution is successfully staged. On the anniversary of the revolution, as a result of an amnesty, he is freed from gaol. The book opens with his emerging from the prison gates, an angry man possessed by a desire for revenge, for while he is in gaol his wife divorces him and marries his assistant ʿIlīsh, whom he suspects of having seduced her and informed on him to the police.

Saʿid's first thoughts turn to his daughter whose vague image in his mind grew ever lovelier and more adorable during his absence in prison. So he goes to the house where she has been living with her mother and stepfather. After a painful scene in which his daughter naturally enough turns away in fear from her real father, whom she hardly knows, Saʿid threatens to apply to the Law Court for the custody of the child. The following day he goes to see his old mentor Ra'uf ʿIlwan, but to his horror he discovers that, instead of the revolutionary journalist who wrote fiery and idealistic articles attacking the political system in a progressive newspaper of slender means, his friend has now become a rich and successful corpulent man, who occupies the plush office of sub-editor in a leading newspaper, and works as a columnist specializing in writing on trivial matters such as women's fashions. He now lives in great luxury in an imposing house in the very street Saʿid used to frequent as a burglar before his prison sentence. During an uncomfortable meeting, Ra'uf makes it clear that he now has no time for Saʿid, and he concludes the meeting by giving him a little money to tide him over until he finds himself an honest job. Enraged at what he regards as the ultimate in treachery in his old mentor, who has betrayed all the values he taught and become a bourgeois opportunist under the new revolutionary regime, Saʿid resolves to avenge himself on him, posing as the champion of the exploited masses. He goes to burgle his house at night, but is caught by Raʾuf, who has been expecting his raid, and who thoroughly humiliates him and orders him to pay back the money he has given him. Still resolved to punish his ex-assistant and his unfaithful wife, Saʿid manages to procure a gun, goes to ʿIlish's house, and fires a shot at a person he is convinced is ʿIlish, but it turns out that, anticipating trouble, ʿIlish had already moved out with his family the previous day and that the person killed is a new tenant, a totally innocent man. Now the police are after Saʿid the murderer, against whom Raʾuf's newspaper vigorously whips up public opinion. Saʿid subsequently tries to shoot Raʾuf, but again he bungles the affair and kills his door-keeper instead. Saʿid is given a temporary home and some comfort by an ex-flame, a prostitute, who soon disappears mysteriously and Saʿid is left a hungry captive in her flat overlooking the cemetery. He is finally caught and shot by the police who, with their dogs, chase him in the cemetery where he has been hiding.

This very brief account of the story of the novel inevitably does not do justice to a work of great density of texture and remarkable powers of suggestion, written in a style that is highly evocative and poetic with its multiple symbolism and subtle imagery, its contrast between light and darkness, its balanced structure, its feverish and nightmarish atmosphere. I have here deliberately given the bare outline of the plot to show that it is fundamentally the story of a disappointed criminal with revolutionary aspirations, who fails in his attempts to avenge himself on those who have betrayed either him or his ideals. Seen in the light of this, the book may appear as a purely secular tale, a study in criminal/revolutionary psychology. Yet how far from the truth such an account of the novel would be.

In the first place, apart from his poverty, the only important fact about Saʿid Mahran's childhood that the author gives us is that when his father was alive the boy used to accompany him often to the mystical sessions (*dhikr*) in which his father, a disciple of the mystic (sufi) Sheikh ʿAlī al-Junaydī, participated. Sheikh al-Junaydi's primitive home in an outlying part of Cairo provides

Saʿid with a roof over his head on his first night of freedom, simply—on the realistic level—because there is nowhere else for him to go, and it is in the Sheikh's home that he seeks refuge after committing his first murder. From the sufi Sheikh's cryptic and enigmatic utterances it is clear that he is mysteriously aware of the murderous thoughts that go on in Saʿid's mind. When Saʿid asks him for comfort after telling of the painful manner in which he has been betrayed by his wife and his best friend and spurned by his only child, the Sheikh advises him to perform his ritual ablutions and recite from the Holy Book, the Koran. Thus a contrast is established between this advice of the mystic and that of his worldly teacher, the revolutionary student leader who constantly counsels him that what he (and the country) need most are two things: a book (to enlighten the mind with—obviously a different sort of book from the Holy Book) and a gun to fight with. Saʿid cannot bring himself to do as the Sheikh tells him and he is incapable of comprehending his language, which contains double meanings and allusions indicating a spiritual level of reality, higher than, and beyond, this mundane world. The Sheikh views Saʿid as a man beyond redemption, and in this respect the novel can be regarded as a study of damnation: Saʿid is a lost soul who has been abandoned by God. He is trapped; the world he inhabits is feverish and nightmarish. All this is emphasized by the style and imagery of the work. At the beginning of the novel, when he threatens to wreak vengeance on his wife and her lover, he says at the conclusion of a passage that receives peculiar emphasis by the author's use of the same rhyme in a number of sentences, 'I shall attack at the right moment just like Fate'. But in a series of mishaps all his attacks misfire and he is doomed to failure. In other words, the man who has the audacity to compare himself to Fate is reduced to mere helplessness *vis-à-vis* Fate. What, therefore, could have been a mere secular novel, has been endowed with a spirital dimension by Mahfuz. Saʿid Mahran is not merely a victim of economics, nor merely of politics, but he is also a hapless victim of Fate, and this, among other factors, makes us feel that in some ways he is more sinned against than sinning.

Autumn Quail explores the mind of ʿĪsā, a prominent member of the Wafd party, a somewhat unscrupulous, high-flying bureaucrat under the *ancien régime*, whose career as well as personal life are dashed by the outbreak of Nasser's revolution and the subsequent dissolution of the Wafd party. It is a study in alienation, even though the protagonist, an utterly selfish man who cruelly abandons his pregnant mistress, shows at the end signs of beginning to come to terms with the revolution. In *The Search* Ṣābir, a playboy whose mother, a former prostitute, reveals to him on her deathbed that he is the son of a wealthy aristocrat whom he should seek for financial support, sets out on a search for his father, whose mysterious whereabouts no one knows for certain. He never finds his father, but in the course of his search he gets involved with two women and ends up by committing double murder for which he receives a death sentence, but which he hopes be commuted to life imprisonment. The story, full of spiritual significances, paradoxes, and tragic irony, treats amongst other themes the problem of religious belief. In *The Beggar* ʿUmar, a successful and happily married middle-aged lawyer with two loving daughters, finds himself bored with work and suddenly unable to enjoy life, having lost his religious faith which gave a meaning to his life. He tries in vain to find consolation in sex, then in mysticism, gives up his work, runs away from his family, and lives like a drop-out and a recluse, lost in his wild visions. The novel describes an existentialist experience relating to loss of the meaning of life.

The same spiritual emptiness and desolation pervade the closed world of *Chattering on the Nile*. Set in 1964, it depicts a group of intellectuals who meet in the evening for drugs and occasional sex on a Nile houseboat, rented by Anīs Zakī, a middle-aged minor Civil Servant, who, not having recovered from the loss of his wife and baby, is almost permanently drugged and escapes from harsh reality, a boring job, and the pressures of modern life by thinking about periods of past history, hashish-inspired reflections on the mysteries of an absurd world. They are joined by a young woman journalist in search of material for a play. Unlike the others who are either cynical, morally corrupt, or escapist, she is an idealist. Yet when they are faced with a moral dilemma regarding the need to report an accident in which their car has been involved, resulting in the death of a pedestrian, they all fail the test, except Anis Zaki. The novel, full of moral ambiguities emphasizing the absurdity of life, is at the same time a criticism of Egyptian society, particularly its cynicism and moral disintegration, lack of commitment, and fatal apathy, the result of lack of political power and suppression of freedoms. These qualities are even more visible in *Miramar*.

Through the delineation of characters representing current political trends (those of the 1960s) who happen to be staying in a pension of that name in Alexandria, and using the multiple viewpoint of narration, *Miramar* paints a gloomy picture of a society utterly lacking in values; it is a bitter attack on the shortcomings of the revolution and on the hollowness of its socialist slogans, and undoubtedly prophesies Egypt's military defeat of 1967.

The shock of the 1967 defeat had a stunning effect upon the Egyptian literary scene, from which Mahfuz was no more immune than other Egyptian writers. Although he wrote many short stories marked by their dark, irrational, and surrealistic vision of reality Mahfuz did not write any more novels until 1972, when he published *al-Marāyā* (translated as *Mirrors*), which signalled yet another phase in his development as a novelist, a phase which is characterized by bold experimentation in form and mode of writing, ranging from fantasy to unadorned realism or documentary. He has been writing prolifically, producing more than twenty novels, since then. Many of these are of considerable interest, both culturally and politically. To take but a few examples, *al-Karnak* (published in 1974) describes the harsh and repressive methods used by the police state and the ruthless onslaught on the dignity of the individual; *Ḥaḍrat al-Muḥtaram* (published in 1975, and translated into English as *Respected Sir*) portrays the attempt of an ambitious civil servant to climb up the ladder in a corrupt social system, perceived in religious mystical terms, material promotion being the necessary accompaniment of spiritual aridity. In *Malḥamat al-Ḥarāfīsh (The Epic of the Riff-Raff)* which came out in 1977, Mahfuz uses the fantasy and realism of the folk-tale to express what is in essence transcendental spiritual experience, the human dream of salvation and immortality. However, it must be admitted that Mahfuz's later novels often betray clear signs of decline in creativity, originality, and fervour. Several are indeed close to direct commentary on political events: for instance, *Yawm Maqtal al-Zaʿīm (The Day the Leader was Assassinated)*, published in 1985, which treats the Egypt of President Sadat. A younger generation of novelists who had benefited greatly from Mahfuz's achievement were beginning to emerge in the 1960s and early 1970s and to outstrip him in their imaginative experiments.

Since the late 1950s Mahfuz's reputation as a novelist has grown steadily in Egypt and the whole Arab world, but it is important to remember that Mahfuz was only one of many novelists writing in Egypt at the time, some of whom indeed enjoyed for a while even greater popularity than he did and were not much less prolific in their output, though they did not attain his range and degree of artistic skill. Mention has already been made of ʿAbd al-Hamid Jawdah al-Sahhar (b. 1913) who in each of his two novels *Fī Qāfilat al-Zamān (In the Caravan of Time)* and *al-Shāriʿ al-Jadīd (The New Street)*, published in 1947 and 1952 respectively, attempted to give a realistic account of a large Egyptian middle-class family through three generations, chronicling briefly the social and political history of the country, pointing out the major changes in Egyptian society, and stressing the effect of time on people's lives. He covers some aspects of the world depicted with greater skill by Mahfuz in his realistic period, and in *The New Street* he brings the story up to the revolution of 1952.

Mention may also be made of Muḥammad ʿAbd al-Ḥalīm ʿAbdallah (1913–70), Yūsuf al-Sibāʿī (1917–78), and Iḥsān ʿAbd al-Quddūs (1919–90), authors of popular romances in which love figures prominently and is treated in a manner not always free from sentimentality. ʿAbdallah chose his characters from the poorer and lower middle class, and despite his Maziniyan humour portrayed his generally idealized women as the hapless victims of a cruel society, often exploited by the very men to whom they are devoted. In his later and more mature novels, such as *al-Bayt al-Ṣāmit (The Silent House*, published in 1962) he extended his horizon to include themes of more universal significance such as the nature of evil and the relation between the sexes. Al-Sibaʿi and ʿAbd al-Quddus, on the other hand, tended to derive their characters from the higher strata of society and to concentrate on the struggle of women against the stifling constrictions of social conventions. ʿAbd al-Quddus, in particular, liked to pose as the champion of women who called for their emotional and sexual liberation. This he did at the expense of realism, as we see for instance in his novel *Anā Ḥurra* (*I am Free*, published in 1954) which depicts Egyptian woman not as she was but as he wished to see her.

Much more realistic in their portrayal of Egyptian society were a group of novelists who became prominent after the 1952 revolution, many of whom were leftist in their politics. They include the Marxist ʿAbd al-Raḥmān al-Sharqāwī (1920–87), Yūsuf Idrīs (1927–91), and Fatḥī Ghānim (b. 1924), as well as the woman writer Laṭīfa al-Zayyāt (b. 1925) in her single novel *al-Bāb al-Maftūḥ (The Open Door,* which was published in 1960, and deals with women's emancipation set against the background of the 1956 Suez crisis). Because of the avowed populist aims of the revolution, writers felt freer to write about the poor and the oppressed classes. Indeed it became fashionable to write in the socialist realist mode during the 1950s and the early 1960s.

Al-Sharqawi's best known and most satisfactory novel is *al-Arḍ* translated as *Egyptian Earth*), which came out in 1953 and was his first venture in the genre. The events, narrated partly by a schoolboy during his holidays in his village, partly by the omniscient author, take place during the autocratic government of Sidqi Pasha in the early 1930s. The villagers are enraged by the government's decision to limit their irrigation period for the benefit of the nearby big landowner and to cut a road leading to his estate through their fields. The novel describes the heroic but fruitless efforts made by the villagers to stop the execution of the government's orders, in the course of which the author gives a panoramic view of village life and the different types of village inhabitants: the landless peasant and the small-holder, the headman and the police chief, the clergyman, the school-teacher and the grocer, the ex-Azharite, the prostitute, and the village beauty. It is an epic relating their intricate interrelationships, their plots, their rivalries and quarrels as well as their solidarity and cooperative efforts, their daily preoccupations, their loves and their sorrows, their fight over irrigation water and their current struggles against the brutal authorities, all in vivid detail with a lively dialogue in which the colloquial language is employed to good effect. The novel suffers from structural defects and the characterization seems to follow a simplistic Marxist formula, according to which the rich landowner and his men are hopelessly wicked and the clergyman (*Imam*) only serves the interests of the ruling class. Nevertheless *al-Ard* was instantly hailed as a success and that not merely because of the date of its publication, i.e. so soon after the army revolution and its land reform laws. *Al-Ard* is not just a novel in which events take place against a village background: it is a novel in which the protagonist is the Egyptian village itself; for the first time we find a wholly convincing and sympathetic portrait of a village. Unlike *Zaynab*, with which it is deliberately contrasted, *al-Ard* does not falsify village life by excessive romanticization and that despite the lyrical descriptions that al-Sharqawi sometimes provides and the Egyptian peasant's love of the soil he shows, which borders on the mystical.

Al-Sharqawi's three other novels lack the energy that pervades *al-Ard; Qulūb Khāliya* (*Fancy-Free*, 1957), *al-Shawāriʿ al-Khalfiyya* (*The Back Streets*, 1958) and *al-Fallāḥ* (*The Peasant*, 1967), particularly the last mentioned, adhere mechanically to the rules of socialist realism; they are politically committed to the extent that they come perilously close to mere propaganda. *Fancy Free* and *The Peasant* are set in the countryside. The former deals with the village moral code and the dangers to which it is exposed when it comes into contact with the city, together with the corrupting influence of foreigners, while the latter treats the mismanagement of the Revolution agrarian reform by the rural middle class who work against the welfare of the peasants. Although the setting of *Back Streets* is the city, the themes are similar to those of the other novels, namely the moral corruption of the former ruling classes and the virtues of the political struggle, to which is added the need for a democratic system of government.

Yusuf Idris, a physician who gave up medicine to devote himself to writing and journalism, whose distinguished contribution lies mainly in the field of short story and drama, wrote a number of extremely interesting novels which view politics in relation to the drama of individual human relationships: *al-Bayḍā*ʾ (*The White Woman*, written in 1955 but not published in book form until 1970), *Qiṣṣat Ḥubb* (*A Love-Story*, published in 1956), *al-Ḥarām* (translated as *The Sinners*, published in 1959), and *al-ʿAyb* (*Shame*, 1962).

The first two have much in common: they both deal with politics and love. In *A Love-Story* the protagonist Ḥamzah is a young man engaged in the guerrilla fight against the British forces of occupation in the Suez Canal Zone in 1950–2, he falls in love with Fawziyya, a female schoolteacher, who professes an interest in the nationalist struggle and brings him some money she has collected for the cause at her school. When he later declares his feelings for her, she severely rebukes him for not being seriously interested in the cause and leaves him in fury. At first he feels ashamed, but subsequently, when she admits that she reciprocates his feelings he realizes that commitment to wider causes does not necessarily mean complete self-denial. *The White Woman*, which seems to be in parts autobiographical, is a subtler and more complex work. Yaḥyā, a doctor, who belongs to a group of Marxists active in producing a radical newspaper for which he contributes articles, is charged with the task of teaching Arabic to Xanthe, a Greek girl, belonging to the group. He soon develops a passion for her, but she tells him she is married and does not love him. However, the more unattainable he finds her, the more obsessed he is with her, and his obsession does not cease until she eventually leaves the country. The novel is taken up with a detailed and sensitive analysis of his feelings about the girl, the gradual destructive effect his obsession has upon his person and his work, as well as with his relationship with his Marxist colleagues, particularly his struggle not to follow blindly the orders he receives from above, but to assert his freedom and his right to independent judgement.

In the other two novels Idris turns away from the problem of the relation between politics and love and concentrates on moral issues. *Shame* relates the story of the slow and deliberate corruption of an innocent and morally upright young woman. Sanā' is one of a small group of girls appointed in a Government department where no woman has been employed before. Being the only girl in her office, she is made to feel uncomfortable by the men who regard her with a mixture of amusement and resentment, particularly as they fear that her presence might hinder them in pursuing their shady business of selling illegal licences. She is paid unwelcome attentions by al-Jundī, a married man with two wives, who has designs on her. When her colleagues ask her to join them in the shady business of accepting bribes, she is horrified and feels insulted. She complains to the chief clerk, who only responds by saying that no one, including himself, could support his family on his salary alone. She decides to get on with her work and have nothing to do with her colleagues' illegal activities. However, overhearing her telling a girl colleague that she desperately needs money to pay her brother's school fees to enable him to sit for the examination, al-Jundi decides to set her a trap: he sends her their experienced customer, making sure that there is no one else in the room, who slips a bundle of banknotes into the drawer of her desk. She accepts the money, though not without some hesitation. When her colleagues return to the room she realizes that they know, and instead of anger, she finds relief in the thought that she now belongs. Her moral disintegration is complete when she agrees to go out with al-Jundi. Once more Idris provides a subtle analysis of the heroine's feeling that mysterious things were happening behind the scenes in the office, of the air of moral corruption that she was breathing in, of her gradual awareness that the forces of evil were closing in on her—all done in a natural way, devoid of melodrama or surprises. There is even a hint of irony in that, at the time Sana' accepted the bribe, al-Jundi was half hoping that she would be able to resist the temptation.

Irony is much more pronounced in *The Sinners*, the only novel by Idris set in the countryside, and it does not revolve round one chief character. It is ostensibly about the poorest section of the Egyptian population, the seasonal migrant workers (*tarāḥīl*), imported by contractors whenever work on the soil is needed and paid miserable daily wages: they are even worse off than the exploited local landless peasants. But this theme of the appalling conditions of the migrant labourers, described by the author in moving and memorable terms, forms only part of a complex web of themes which renders *The Sinners* one of the most skilfully organized Arabic novels with an impressively dense texture. The *tarahil* world of outsider labourers is set against that of the local village with its richly diverse elements, and through the interaction between these two worlds as well as the interpersonal relationships within each, Idris probes deeply into the secret springs of human actions, thus casting an ironic light on human nature and on group psychology.

The novel, set some time before the 1952 revolution, opens with the general excitement following the discovery at dawn of the body of an illegitimate new-born baby near the village irrigation canal by the night-watchman. While the angry villagers immediately assume that the mother must belong to the migrant labourers, who as a group are despised, reviled, and regarded as sub-human, some are troubled by the possibility of her being one of their own womenfolk, in particular Linda, daughter of the estate chief clerk Masīḥa, who has taken to her bed complaining of colic. The villagers are relieved and confirmed in their prejudices when the mother is discovered to be ʿAzīza, one of the migrant labourers. Her fellow workers have been screening her: they have taken pity on her as she is lying there, suffering from puerperal fever. She badly needs her wages, having to support her sick husband and children at home. Even the villagers are moved by the suffering of the woman, who has accidentally strangled her baby and in her feverish, conscience-stricken state eventually commits suicide, and they begin to change their hostile attitude to the migrant labourers. Pleased to be reassured about his daughter's innocence, Masiha allows her to pay a visit to Umm Ibrāhīm, the wife of the local teacher, of whom he generally disapproves. (Unbeknown to him Umm Ibrāhīm is arranging a clandestine meeting between Linda and the Don Juan of the village, and Linda in fact will elope with him later on.) The hypocrisy of the village, where, we are told, immorality is rife, but behind the scenes, is underlined by the author who shows the gap between public morality and private conduct, as well as the complexity of human motives. Even the rape of ʿAziza by her local landlord's son while she is digging for potatoes left over from the harvest to satisfy a craving of her sick husband, which resulted in her pregnancy, is not presented as a simple matter of sexual assault: although an unwilling victim, she was powerless to run away, partly, the author suggests, because of her long period of sexual deprivation on account of her husband's prolonged illness. She herself is aware of it and cannot forgive herself for her moment of weakness. It is such complexity that bestows credibility on Idris's characters, just as his irony serves not only as a binding structural device for *The Sinners*, but as an expression of a vision of mankind that is rich in understanding and sympathy, and which sees human beings as full of imperfection, but at the same time truly deserving of pity.

Pity is not the dominant feeling one detects in the novels of Fatḥī Ghānim, a writer who was acutely aware of the moral imperfections of his characters: usually professional middle-class men, often with sophisticated tastes, who have achieved considerable success as journalists, senior Civil Servants, or executives. They pursue their career goals in society with single-minded determination, caring more for material comforts, good food, drink, and pretty women than for matters of the spirit or intellect. The world they inhabit is presented in several of his novels, for example *Min Ayn (Wherefrom, 1959), al-Sākhin wa 'l-Bārid (The Hot and the Cold,* 1960), *al-Rajul alladhī Faqad Ẓillah* (1962, translated as *The Man who Lost his Shadow), al-Ghabiyy (The Dunce,* 1966) and *Tilka 'l-Ayyām (Those Days,* 1966), although it is fair to point out that a more charitable view of mankind is expressed in his later novels such as *Bint min Shubrā (A Girl from Shubra,* published in 1986).

Ghanim's first novel, *al-Jabal* (*The Mountain*, 1958), which is based on a true story, is a subtle and fascinating treatment of the theme of tradition and modernity, or the relation between town and country, pointing out the problematic nature of modernization and the need to relate reform to local, indigenous conditions, instead of imposing it from above. The narrator is a Civil Servant, sent to al-Gurna, an Upper Egyptian village near Luxor, to investigate a complaint by a certain villager against the Government, accusing it of destroying the villagers' homes. What has happened is that in an attempt to improve the living conditions of the villagers the Government has built for them a model village with modern, salubrious houses, designed by a brilliant architect, to replace their cave dwellings in the mountain. However, the villagers refuse to move into the model village or give up their primitive hovels and their centuries-old way of life, particularly as they secretly derive their livelihood largely from the theft of antiquities, made possible by their close proximity to the ancient Egyptian remains, and which they sell to tourists, together with fakes of their own making. The narrator listens to the points of view of the Government, the architect, and the local chief, but after spending a day in the mountain with the villagers he undergoes a sort of spiritual experience from which he emerges a wiser man and resigns his post as investigator. He feels that the needs of the villagers were not sufficiently considered either by an insensitive Government or an ambitious architect in pursuit of success and self-aggrandisment.

Wherefrom is a fantasy with some melodramatic and detective-story elements about a visit paid to the earth by a pretty young woman from the moon. It is related by the protagonist, Muṣṭafā Ḥamdī, a journalist who pursues success at any price and as he himself admits, is prepared to break promises, betray his trust, and even sell his soul for a journalistic coup, and to 'get rich quick'. Right at the end, somewhat unconvincingly, some criticism of the ways of the earth's inhabitants, particularly their absurd veneration of money, is made by the girl from the moon. *The Hot and the Cold*, also narrated by the protagonist, is the story of a passionate affair between an Egyptian, Yūsuf Manṣūr, an executive in an import firm on a business trip to Sweden, and a Swedish married woman, Julia. Yusuf falls in love for the first time in his life, and feels truly loved also for the first time in his life, since his mother died young and his father married again soon after; he was therefore brought up by his grandparents. The young businessman is driven by his love to run the risk of sacrificing his career. But at the last minute his lover decides to go back to her husband, an older man who needs her. Once more, and despite several weaknesses and improbabilities, the novel shows that the author is a good story-teller. There are some very good descriptions of Scandinavian land-scapes and skyscapes. The title signifies the difference between the hot-blooded man from the East and the lonely and cold rational behaviour of Western man, i.e. the husband. The novel is at times reminiscent of al-Hakim's *Bird of the East*.

The Dunce consists of papers written by an unknown person, meant to be a study of an idiot and of idiocy. They are presented by an editor with very few comments, tracing the development of an idiot even before his conception and birth, until he becomes a prominent Civil Servant: clearly a biting satire on Egyptian Civil Service. The treatment is occasionally humorous, but the humour is generally of the sardonic variety: poking fun at serious, academic, and methodical studies. It becomes a bit tiresome sometimes, though clearly the author is experimenting with modes of nar-ration, posing as editor of the papers. *These Days*, on the other hand, is an extremely readable novel, employing experimental techniques in modes of narration, dramatic consciousness, and non-chronological sequence of events. The protagonist is a distin-guished professor of history, concerned with problems of histori-ography, namely the relation between history and truth, the danger of relating the whole truth, and the need for the historian to know himself before investigating the history of his own country. Related to this is the professor's consuming jealousy and his obsession with finding out about the various love-affairs of his much younger wife, who he knows is unfaithful to him. The two themes become inter-twined when in the course of his investigation into the use of terror-ism in modern Egyptian history he interviews an ex-terrorist and it occurs to him, as a means of avenging himself on his wife, to engineer an affair between them in the hope that when jilted by her, he may kill her. The novel suffers from a lack of a unified clear vision as a result of excessive multiplicity of themes and side issues.

Ghanim's best known work is *The Man who Lost his Shadow*, a novel in four parts, each viewing from a different angle the main character Yūsuf, a journalist who, employing most unscrupulous means, rises to the position of Editor-in-Chief of a leading Cairo newspaper. In Part One he is seen through the eyes of his peasant stepmother Madīḥa, in Part Two he is viewed by Sāmiya, the starlet whom he loves but whose love he regards as standing in the way of his career, in Part Three by Nājī, the sensual, worldly-wise editor he ousted, while in the final part Yusuf himself gives a first-person account of his own character and actions. The title is meant to indicate how Yusuf lost his conscience or moral integrity. While giving us a glimpse into the minds of several characters, but chiefly Yusuf himself, the novel affords us a panoramic view of Egyptian society, from shortly before the Second World War until a few years after the Egyptian army revolution of 1952. The multiple viewpoint narrative technique, which allows each of the four narrators to speak frankly to us, enables us to see how all the characters are in varying degrees guilty of mendacity. Ghanim here excels in portraying the moral and spiritual aridity of Egyptian society. Although he returns to the theme of the pursuit of self-interest under the guise of slogans of social reform in later novels (as in *Zaynab wa'l-'Arsh, Zaynab and the Throne*, 1976) it is in *The Man who Lost his Shadow* that Ghanim gives his most convincing and fullest character study of the self-interested type. In it too he uses most successfully several modernistic novelistic techniques such as the multiple viewpoint, the flashback, and other cinematic techniques, thus making *The Man who Lost his Shadow* one of the best examples of the Arabic experimental novel. Apart from his experimentation in the novel form which, it must be admitted, sometimes remains on the level of external features without touching the substance of a work, Ghanim is a born story-teller, who has the ability to arouse the reader's curiosity and sustain his suspense.

The tendency to experiment began to spread in the late 1960s with the rise of a new generation of novelists who also happened to be directly or indirectly influenced by developments in European literature, for example Kafka and Faulkner, and experiments in the new French novel, and who found in the modernist techniques a suitable medium to express their experiences arising from the new political and social condition of their society. Other influences were the vogue of the Theatre of the Absurd and the growing popularity of Existentialist literature, which was being translated into Arabic and published on a fairly wide scale in Beirut. The result was a reaction against social or socialist realism, examples of which we have already encountered in the later work of Mahfuz, starting from *The Thief and the Dogs*.

A spate of novels appeared, expressing alienation at all levels and a sense of political impotence as a result of living under a steadily authoritarian regime, a mood of disillusionment made worse by the traumatic defeat in the Six Day War. Unlike the heroes of the 1940s and 1950s who, in their commitment to a socialist or nationalist ideal, stood for certain positive values, amply expressed in their desire to change society and their confidence in their ability to do so, the protagonists of the later novels tended to be anti-heroes, diffident and emasculated, who had lost their sense of direction, were also wracked by self-doubt, and were utterly incapable of mastering their own fate or determining the destiny of their country. The emphasis therefore was placed on their inner world, on an analysis of their feelings and attitudes, the external world having lost its solidity, sharp contours, and definite direction. To express this inner world novelists abandoned the traditional devices of a well-constructed plot, moving along a chronological line of progression, related by an omniscient author, in favour of an indeterminate shape with no clear beginning, middle and end, the blurring of the line separating dream from reality, breaking up the chronological sequence of events and resorting to flashbacks, employing a poetic language which relies more upon imagery and suggestion than plain statement, together with making full use of the creative potentialities of indigenous myth, folklore, and the Arab literary heritage. Thus in their best works, some of these writers display a remarkable fusion of the modernist techniques derived directly or indirectly from the West and the creative use of the classical Arabic tradition.

Naturally novelists vary in the degree of experimentation they use. They range from the relatively traditional such as ʿAbd al-Ḥakīm Qāsim to the most modernistic or post-modernistic, such as Idwār al-Kharrāṭ. Al-Kharrat gathered around him a group of young writers who rebelled against the establishment and published specimens of their work in a new literary magazine, *Gallery 68*, which ran into eight issues appearing between April 1968 and February 1971. Many of them were soon to number among the leading short-story writers and novelists of their generation. In the editorial to the last issue of the magazine, al-Kharrat writes that he regards the experimental and the avant garde not as a mere fashion, but as an artistically dire necessity, as the product of the need to face squarely and honestly the reality and beauty of the sufferings of the self, the other and, on a larger scale, the whole of the wounded nation.

The first work by the younger generation of novelists, which expresses what is generally referred to by Egyptian critics (for example al-Kharrat and Ṣabrī Ḥāfiẓ) as the New Sensibility, is the novella *Tilka 'l-Rā'iḥa* (translated as *The Smell of It* and published in 1966) by Ṣunʿallah Ibrāhīm (b. 1937), author of several novels, short stories, and science fiction for children. It was apparently written in 1964 immediately after the author's release from five years' imprisonment for his political activities. It was banned after its publication in Egypt had caused a heated controversy, and only a damagingly expurgated edition from which passages containing either direct political criticism or explicit sexual description (of heterosexual, homosexual, or masturbatory activity) was allowed to appear in 1968. It is a remarkable work, expressing a state of utter alienation on a political, social, as well as a metaphysical level. The narrator, a young journalist, about to be released on parole from prison (where he has been kept presumably for political reasons) is met by his sister who has rented a room for him in town. He then leads a completely aimless existence, going to the cinema or sitting in cafés, visiting friends and relations, occasionally calling at a magazine office, constantly on the move because of his restlessness. Without enthusiasm or interest in anything, by chance he learns of his mother's death, at which like the hero of Camus's *l'Étranger*, he shows no emotion. There is no plot worth mentioning, but the protagonist provides a record of the trivial details of his daily life in a singularly bare language, interspersed with past memories and flashbacks. He is easily sexually aroused and yet he is subject to impotence. His prison experience under the dictatorship has sapped his energy and robbed his life of all meaning.

Sunʿallah Ibrahim's next novel *Najmat Aghusṭus (August Star*, published in 1974), represents a further stage in formal experimentation. It too has no real plot: the narrator, again a young journalist, recently discharged from long political detention, who is trying to earn his living as a free-lance, describes a visit he makes to the Aswan High Dam and its environs during the last stages of its construction. The novel consists of three parts: the first and the third parts are written in a matter-of-fact style, almost like a travelogue, or reportage, in which the author offers an extremely slow-moving and highly detailed technical account of the construction operations, observations on and conversation with other journalists, interviews with Russian experts, Egyptian technicians, and manual labourers, and impressions of European tourists, particularly women. The first and longest part deals with the building of the High Dam, while the third concentrates on the attempts to save the Abu Simbel temple of Rameses II. The second and shortest part, on the other hand, is one long sentence, slightly reminiscent of the final monologue by Molly Bloom in James Joyce's *Ulysses*, written in a more emotive language, in which the description of external reality merges with dreams and reverie, all transcending time and place. The successful consummation of the dam's construction and its meeting with the gushing flood-waters blending with the narrator's managing to make love to a Russian girl, the protagonist's painful memories of his experiences in prison, particularly his physical torture, are mixed with his reflections on Michelangelo (he has been reading a book on him during his trip), on David, the biblical figure, as well as the sculptor's statue, on the opposition between the fluidity of life and permanence of art; Egypt's Nasser and Rameses II are juxtaposed with Shelley's 'Ozymandias'.

Although it can be read as a straightforward account of a journalist's trip to the High Dam and Abu Simbel *The August Star* is in fact a satirical novel in which irony is used as a subtle device that rises to the stature of a structural principle. The dead-pan, matter-of-fact description of the construction operations in which, as he acknowledges in his Appendix to the novel, the author makes use of official handouts, leaflets, and Government sources, is clearly meant to represent the official view which paints a highly romanticized picture of the noble and dedicated efforts by patriotic and idealistic Egyptians, This is sharply contrasted with the way the workers on the site see their dull, harsh, and miserable life. The Russian experts are motivated by the desire to make money and so are the Egyptians, whether technicians or unskilled labourers, unless they happen to be conscripted and have no choice. Young men are sexually starved and spend unconscionable time and effort in pursuit of sex which more often than not prove fruitless. The narrator's affair with the Russian girl, brief as it is, is utterly without love. Young men clearly brag of imaginary sexual adventures with allegedly easy European women. Whatever the advantages of the dam, its construction meant the destruction of Nubian communities and the loss of their traditional ways of life. The giant proportions of Nasser's dam bring to mind Rameses II's huge temples and gigantic figures, and by implication the quotation from an article on the worship of Rameses II suggests the personality cult in modern Egypt and the worship of Nasser. Self-glorification of absolute rulers is juxtaposed with the oppression of the masses and the abuse of their individual freedom, whether under Rameses or Nasser. Likewise, the official propaganda image of Rameses is contrasted with the real historical Rameses who is described as 'the Pharaoh of lies'. Last but not least the cutting of stone from the quarries in the mountain on an enormous scale with huge mechanical devices is contrasted with the sensitive carving of stone with a delicate chisel by Michelangelo in his statues of David and the Pietà.

Sunʿallah Ibrahim pursues his attack on the abuse of individual freedom under dictatorship in his most powerful novel *al-Lajna (The Committee,* 1981). Outwardly it is written in a conventional mode of narrative, with a clear plot, the story progressing in a straight line, uninterrupted by flashbacks or stream-of-consciousness devices. In reality, however, the entire novel is one continuous ironic statement. The narrator/protagonist has to face the Committee of Investigators, before whom every citizen knows that he has to appear sometime, to prove that he has the 'correct' answers to questions put to him. He therefore chooses the time of his test for which he has been preparing himself for a whole year, learning the special language used by the Committee at their interviews and studying philosophy, art, chemistry, and economics as well as television quizzes and general-knowledge programmes. He is intimidated first by being made to wait a long time after his appointment, then by the humiliating behaviour of the members of the Committee who consist of solemn-looking military personnel and civilians of both sexes and who keep consulting papers before them, containing full information about him.

They first order him to dance, then after hearing that he has spent a certain year in prison, they ask him to explain why he was incapable of having sex with a certain woman and order him to strip naked and submit to an examination of his sexual organs and his anus, which leads them to believe that he is a homosexual. They proceed to ask him questions to which he tries to give the detailed lengthy answers he has prepared beforehand, while standing naked before them. The questions vary from 'What is the most important thing by which the twentieth century will be remembered?' to 'What do you know about the Great Pyramid?' To the first question the answer he gives, after eliminating on detailed logical grounds Marilyn Monroe, Arab oil, space travel, several revolutions, and Vietnam, is the double-barrelled word Coca-Cola, giving a lengthy disquisition on the history and world-wide spread of Coca-Cola, and its reappearance, after a long ban, on the Egyptian market. When the Committee has heard another disquisition on the Great Pyramid and the theory that Jewish architects must have designed it as the Egyptians are not thought intelligent enough for such a difficult task, they bring the ordeal to an end, telling him that they will let him know their verdict in due course.

After a long period of silence he receives an order from the Committee to write a study of the most brilliant contemporary Arab personality. After considerable thought the protagonist chooses a public figure whose career he proceeds to research, finding all sorts of unsavoury and dishonest details, but just before he begins to write down his results he is surprised by the Committee visiting him in his flat, searching his possessions and private papers, confiscating some of his notes, advising him to choose some other personality, and leaving one member with him until he makes up his mind. The member left is the most hostile and ugliest, with apparently homosexual leanings. He follows him around, even when he goes to the bathroom, and insists upon sharing his bed. After a lapse of days, the protagonist cannot stand it any longer and finding his companion armed with a revolver, he kills him with a sharp kitchen knife. He is then summoned before the Committee, threatened with torture, and finally condemned to the worst punishment, namely to eat himself. After further humiliating experiences the protagonist returns to his flat, listens to the music of certain European classical composers, and proceeds to consume his own body, beginning with his arm.

The intensity and savagery of this political satire, the dead-pan style of writing is worthy of the pen of Jonathan Swift. Specious rigorous logic is used to argue extensively that Coca-Cola is the most signficant single mark of the twentieth century and that the brilliant Arab personality he has chosen to study has achieved the goal of Arab Unity by managing to make the entire Arab world consume American goods. The Committee keeps reminding the protagonist that he is a free agent: free to choose the time of his investigation, free to answer any of the questions put to him, free to select for his study any Arab personality, and yet he knows full well that he is not in a position to disobey any of its orders and behaves all along like a captive man, robbed of any freedom of action. Even the punishment meted out to him, he has to carry out himself: he literally eats himself. In its utter absurdity, its complete inner consistency, its claustrophobic self-enclosed world, the whole thing is like a Kafkaesque nightmare, in which the protagonist is trapped, but with sufficient allusions to contemporary Egyptian and Arab society to make it immediately relevant to the real world.

Less experimental in form is the work of ʿAbd al-Ḥakīm Qāsim (1935–90), whose output is small, but of a consistently high quality. He is the author of one of the best long short stories produced by his generation: *Al-Mahdī (The Convert)*, published in 1977, is a courageous, sensitive and deeply moving account of a poor Copt's religious conversion to Islam as a result of subtle organized coercion practised by over-zealous Muslims. Qasim's first and best novel *Ayyām al-Insān al-Sabʿa (The Seven Days of Man,* 1969) relates through the eyes of a village boy, ʿAbd al-ʿAzīz, the annual pilgrimage made by his folk to the shrine of al-Sayyid al-Badawī in the town of Tanta during the fair held on the occasion of the Saint's birthday *(mawlid)*. The seven days are those of the planning for the journey by the men, the preparations of the necessary food by the women, the actual journey, the stay at the hostelry, the attendance at the fair festivals, the visit to the Mosque shrine, and the return to the village. Each of these days, however, is chosen by the author to fall in a different year, representing a different stage in the boy's development. Whilst giving a detailed account of village life embracing both men and women, the novel therefore traces the development of ʿAbd al-ʿAziz from a state of total acceptance of the values of his father, a prominent member of a sufi order, and his associates to his gradual rejection of these values, the superstition, and sub-human conditions of life in his village, as he grows up to be a secondary-school boy in Tanta and subsequently, a university student in Alexandria.

This interesting use of the seven-day device also enables the author to show the effect the passage of time has on the adult villagers: the ageing and impoverishment of the spendthrift father and the gradual break up of the community, the slow erosion of the traditional way of life. In this novel Qasim, who himself grew up in a village, provides perhaps the most sensitive and convincing insider description of Egyptian village life in Arabic fiction, written in a language of considerable emotive and poetic power. He also offers a sympathetic portrayal of the crisis experienced by the intellectual of peasant origin who, as a result of his exposure to urban living and modern secular education, becomes alienated from the belief system of the community to which, however, he is deeply attached, and who is therefore torn between two worlds. It is an eloquent statement of the universal theme of the generation gap as well as the conflict between tradition and modernity and the impact of town on country, which is common to much modern Egyptian and Arabic literature.

In *Muḥāwala li'l-Khurūj (An Attempt to Get Away)*, which appeared in 1980, the narrator has a brief affair with a European girl-tourist whom he shows round Cairo and takes to visit his village. The novelist paints a vivid picture of the grim reality of life in Cairo and the countryside against the harsh political background of the 1970s, particularly its authoritarian Government. Once more the protagonist is torn between his loyalty to his own people and rejection of the inhuman living conditions imposed upon them. In *Qadar al-Ghuraf al-Muqbiḍa (The Fate of Depressing Rooms,* 1982), clearly an autobiographical work, Qasim's point of departure is the village world of his first novel, the protagonist even bearing the same name: ʿAbd al-ʿAzīz; the young boy is overpowered by the heat and afraid of the prevailing silence of the village, depressed by the ugliness of the neglected homes and dusty smelling hovels around him. The feelings of the boy towards the men, women, and animals are delicately described, especially his adolescent dream of a cheerful room and house of his own—which for him seems the focus of human happiness. The boy longs for the beautiful home from which his father was expelled, together with his family, by his angry grandfather. As an adult ʿAbd al-ʿAziz spends the whole of his life in a vain attempt to recover this lost happiness. The novel, which is picaresque in form, is taken up with a graphic description of the various appalling rooms and flats he has had to occupy in the countryside, as well as in Cairo and Alexandria, and finally in Berlin where he, by now a fairly well-known writer, has been invited to lecture by the university. He decides to stay on to do doctoral research, but after a while falls ill and is diagnosed as diabetic. A long chapter of this gloomy novel is devoted to a vivid and detailed account of the horrifying conditions of the prison cells which he was made to occupy for more than three years as a political prisoner in different prisons all over Egypt: this is one of the most memorable parts of the book and it contains some lyrical passages of considerable beauty, albeit not always free from marks of hasty writing. On a deeper level the novel can be taken to be a modern parable of man's expulsion from Eden and his constant and fruitless search for beauty and happiness.

Like Qasim, Yūsuf al-Qaʿīd (b. 1944) gives an insider's account of village life. His first novel *al-Ḥidād (Mourning*, 1969), a story of revenge, begins soon after the mysterious strangling at a water-wheel, on his estate, of al-Ḥājj Manṣūr Abū'l-Layl, a wealthy and powerful farmer, an object of fear and envy to all around him. The novel consists of a series of four monologues: by his daughter ʿĀ'isha, his illegitimate son Ḥasan, ʿA'isha's unsuccessful suitor Zahrān, and lastly his legitimate son Ḥāmid, which employ the stream-of-consciousness method and make generous use of the colloquial language. The speakers record their (mostly ambivalent) feelings towards the murdered man, their reflections on their situation, and their relation to one another, as well as bits of dialogue, in the course of which the characters are revealed and life in the village is evoked. Clearly the dead man was a tyrant: he did not allow his daughter to complete her education and his son only managed to continue his in Tanta against considerable opposition. He treated his unacknowledged illegitimate son like an unpaid servant and rudely refused the proposal of marriage to his daughter made by Zahran. It is widely believed that he was murdered by the spirit of a small-holder, whose land he had grabbed and in whose murder he was instrumental, as water-wheels are commonly held to be haunted places. ʿA'isha, his devoted daughter, is Electra-like bent on revenge for her father's murder: she drives both Hasan and Zahran to their death in their unsuccessful pursuit of revenge. The novel ends with Hamid, a dreamer who suffers from Hamlet-like irresolution, on his sister's insistence, making his way with his loaded gun to the water-wheel site, where the victims had been strangled, to meet the murderous spirit. This structurally interesting novel, which makes extensive and at times highly emotive use of the colloquial language, succeeds in creating suspense and in building up a mysterious atmosphere, which allows for a symbolical interpretation of certain events, such as the tyranny of authority as represented by the father, or the attempt of the scholar Hamid to kill the murderer who belongs to the world of superstition.

Qaʿid's second novel is connected, albeit tenuously, with the first. In *Akhbār ʿIzbat al-Manīsī (What Happened on the Manisi Estate,* published in 1971) we hear about the murder of al-Hajj Mansur and about his irresolute son Hamid. It is much less melodramatic and although just as steeped in folklore and teeming with popular sayings, is more realistic and less reliant upon the supernatural. The main theme is also revenge, this time revenge for the honour of a peasant's family. Ṣabrīnī, the pretty and beloved daughter of the night-watchman ʿAbd al-Sattār, is seduced and made pregnant by Ṣafwat, the son of al-Hajj Manisi, the owner of the vast estate, although she is engaged to Abū'l-Ghayṭ, the farm labourer who has been away for a long time to make enough money for the wedding. In spite of the fact that Safwat's father arranges for an abortion and pays ʿAbd al-Sattar some money, Sabrini's brother al-Zanātī murders her to save the honour of the family by administering rat poison under the guise of medicine. The novel is remarkable not only for its pervasive pathos arising from the degree of sympathy with which all the main characters, including the seducer, who has failed alike in love and in his university education, are portrayed, but also for the extended warm description of the Egyptian countryside, which serves more purposes than merely as a background to the action. Formally the novel makes an interesting use of time: it starts at the time of the investigation of the murder, then it goes back to the time of seduction, then further back to the time of Sabrini's engagement, then jumps forward five years to the murder, before returning to the present.

In the short novel *Ayyām al-Jafāf (Arid Days)*, which came out in 1974, the narrator is a young and impecunious schoolteacher starting his first job in a village school in which he is the sole teacher. Incapable of relating to anyone around him, he spends his monotonous days in solitude and emotional and sexual starvation. After four years he gradually sinks into a world of make-believe, hallucination, and madness. In his desperate attempt to create excitement he is even driven to write letters to himself. Unlike its predecessor *Ayyam al-Jafaf* offers no experiment with time, but straightforward chronological narration. The same is true also of *al-Bayāt al-Shitawī (Hibernation)*, also published in 1974, which does not represent a considerable advance in Qaʿid's art. It depicts the clash between town and country, the unsettling effect upon a village of a visit by an enthusiastic young engineer, prospecting for oil, and thereby arousing the villagers' fantastic expectations and wild dreams of a life of plenty, only to be disappointed by the authorities' shelving the engineer's plans; a considerable part of the novel is narrated from the engineer's point of view.

In *Yaḥduth fī Miṣr al-Ān (It is Happening in Egypt Now,* written 1974–5, but not allowed by the Egyptian Censor to be published until 1977) Qaʿid deliberately avoids any attempt to create the illusion of reality: he invites the reader to participate in the act of creating a novel, based upon a set of documents, a device which the author resorts to all too often. Inspired by President Nixon's trip to Egypt in 1974, which arouses the author's wrath, al-Qaʿid is keen to unmask the Egyptian Government's conspiracy and its deliberate attempt to mislead the people into believing that their erstwhile American foe, the closest friend and ally of Israel, is now their friend, whose intention is to bring instant prosperity. Against this background of colossal deception, al-Qaʿid feels it is his primary duty as a committed intellectual to break the silence and speak directly to his readers, instead of using the indirect method of a novelist. The result is a flawed novel, which lacks subtlety and is closer to a political tract, attacking the greed and rapacity of the new class that has benefited from the revolution and has thereby widened the gap between the rich bureaucrats and the poor peasants. The misery and helplessness of the latter are portrayed in the melodramatic form of a hungry peasant, beaten to death by the police, whose crime is successfully hushed up by the authorities: they simply concoct documents to prove that the peasant never existed.

Al-Ḥarb fī Barr Miṣr (translated as *War in the Land of Egypt*, written in 1975, but not published until 1978), is a much more successful, more subtle, and better-constructed novel. In it the story is told by several nameless characters, each contributing a bit while being partly aware of his role in creating the whole. One character alone is given a name, the significant name Maṣrī (indicating Egyptian); he is the son of the night-watchman, who is made to pose as the village headman's son in order to serve in the army in his place, in return for a piece of land. The deal is concluded through a broker by the fathers of the two young men, but subsequently complications arise: the deception is discovered when Masri is killed in action and his body returned to the village. However, as in the previous novel, the investigation is arbitrarily stopped by orders from above.

Qaʿid's most ambitious work is *Shakāwā al-Miṣrī al-Faṣīḥ (Complaints of the Eloquent Egyptian,* 1983), a huge novel in three parts, which, unlike his earlier novels, has an urban setting. A destitute Cairene family with numerous members, having been evicted from their rented flat because of the need to build a new road, take shelter in the City of the Dead. They have now been ordered to clear out of it, as they have been caught digging for treasure hidden in the tombs. They decide to march to the main city square and offer themselves up for public auction, are promptly arrested by the police, whose agents suspect them of organizing a riot and plotting against the state. The action takes place against disturbing political events, such as the food riots in 1977, Sadat's dramatic visit to Jerusalem in a bid to end the Arab–Israeli war, and the negative consequence of his policy of political liberalization, *infitāḥ*, which encouraged greed and self-seeking beyond measure. The novel is characterized by its bitter and courageously frank satire, which is exceedingly comical in places, on the political and social conditions of modern Egypt, its passionate concern about the plight of the urban poor, their lack of food and shelter and basic amenities, their sexual starvation, as well as the predicament of the honest creative writer who lacks the resources for publication and the right reader for his novels.

In *Shakawa* al-Qaʿid carries his experimentation to extraordinary lengths. Intent on destroying any possibility of an illusion of reality he addresses the reader directly about the novel he is writing, offers him alternative beginnings and endings, includes among his characters an imaginary author of his novel, thereby making his work a novel about the writing of a novel, and has a literary critic commenting in full upon the defects of the work. Events are not narrated chronologically, but through flashbacks, characters are revealed by means of extensive use of stream of consciousness and the author includes the private papers of one of the characters, together with a large number of newspaper items and advertisements, designed to document and enforce his themes. This self-indulgent experimentation, however interesting in itself, has certainly resulted in a sprawling work that lacks the necessary economy of great art and has turned *Shakawa*, despite its impassioned writing, into a literary curiosity.

One of the most original experimental novelists of the 1960s generation is Jamāl al-Ghīṭānī (b. 1945), a prolific writer who has evolved his own unmistakable distinct style of writing, even though at times he risks the danger of becoming too manneristic. In a series of works he used the framework and linguistic apparatus of medieval Arabic historical writings, or sufi literature, or other non-fictional genres such as official documents or newspaper reporting to make a trenchant and profoundly ironic comment on contemporary Egyptian society and politics. The narrative is non-linear and modernist in tone, and the style is abrupt as a result of the omission of traditional connective particles which bestows a dramatic quality and a sense of urgency, even though it makes for relatively difficult reading. The emphasis throughout is on states of consciousness and the shifting of levels and types of discourse, from the archaic and parodic to the contemporary idiomatic, from the detachment of irony to the direct statement of passionate commitment which, apart from the effect of rich and colourful mosaic it creates, contributes to the multiple viewpoint. It also blurs the line separating fact from fiction, history from legend, thus enhancing the complexity of reality, while placing the modern and relevant work of fiction securely within the classical Arabic literary tradition.

The first of al-Ghitani's novels is *al-Zaynī Barakāt* (translated as *Zayni Barakat*, published in 1974). Though not a historical novel, designed primarily to recreate a period of the past, it is set in Cairo at the end of the Mameluke reign just before and immediately after the Mamelukes' defeat at the hands of the Ottomans in 1517, thus establishing an obvious parallel with Nasser's Egypt, al-Ghitani's real subject, before his humiliating defeat by the Israelis in 1967. Deriving some details from, and even on one occasion quoting the words of, the chronicler Ibn Iyās (who gave an eye-witness account of the Ottoman conquest of Egypt in *Badāiʿ al-Zuhūr fī Waqāiʿ al-Duhūr*), al-Ghitani portrays a police state with an intricate spy system which crushes the intellectual and yet makes possible the survival of a cunning tyrant such as the muḥtasib (the inspector of markets and trade and supervisor of public morality) Zayni Barakat, who even manages to retain his high office under the conquerors, the Ottomans.

The novel begins and ends with an account of Cairo given by a fictitious Venetian traveller both before and after the Ottoman invasion. Through his eyes and those of local characters we are given a description of Zayni Barakat, whose thoughts the novelist does not allow the reader to enter into and yet who dominates the novel while remaining an enigma. Barakat, who in many respects has been taken to represent President Nasser, is a complex creation: driven by what seems to be an excessive zeal for virtue and reform he pries into the private lives of the citizens and ends up by striking terror into their hearts. Not only the idealistic young Azhar student, who initially enthusiastically welcomed his assumption of office, gradually becomes disillusioned in him and ends up by being destroyed by him, but also the sufi Sheikh who was instrumental in Barakat's appointment, at some point in disgust has him beaten up. Barakat's arch enemy, the Chief Spy eventually joins forces with him when he realizes that they need each other. The multiple viewpoint, the variety of styles ranging from the poetic and emotionally charged description, to the bare and unadorned government proclamation, the interplay of past and present enhance the moral ambiguity, contributing to the complexity and universality of evil in this remarkable novel which contains some of the most vivid and haunting descriptions of physical torture of political prisoners in modern Arabic fiction.

Equally enigmatic is the central character of *Waqā'iʿ Ḥārat al-Zaʿfarānī* (translated as *Incidents in Zafrani Alley*, published in 1976), the sinister Sheikh ʿAṭiyya, whom the reader never sees, and to whom all the men of the alley go, initially separately for advice on the affliction of sexual impotence, and who manipulates and gradually takes control of their lives. The novel, narrated mostly in the form of official reports and files, is set in the old medieval quarter of Cairo, but in modern times. It uses a brilliant mixture of realism and fantasy, of sardonic humour and pathos to satirize Egyptian society, in particular the abuse of freedom and the coercion of the individual, as well as the spread of obscurantist religious fundamentalism. Needless to say al-Ghitani shows considerable courage in choosing for his theme a taboo subject such as men's impotence, whether viewed sexually or in its obvious political symbolism. Sheikh ʿAtiyya, who is credited with supernatural powers, summons all the men who have sought his help to a meeting at which he convinces them that he has willed their impotence as part of his grand plan to create a brave new world. Through his messenger he issues instructions for them, giving the times when they are allowed to rise, to sleep, to go out, to eat their uniform communal meals, in short to regulate every minute detail of their lives. This eventually drives some of them to a rebellion, but the rebellion is only half-hearted, so thoroughly emasculated have they become. Because it is believed that any man who enters the alley or has sexual relations with its women will be similarly afflicted, the alley becomes ostracized, life in it slowly grinds to a virtual halt, and misery prevails among the women no less than the men. The authorities who learn of these events typically issue official proclamations denying their occurrence, as they are afraid of their possible negative impact, especially on tourism. However, news leaks abroad and by the end of the novel the plague of impotence seems to have spread to other parts of the world, under the influence of Sheikh ʿAtiyya and his disciples.

As the incidents take place in an alley, a fairly close-knit community consisting of members of the lower and middle classes, the author has the chance of presenting a vivid picture of people engaged in the business of their daily lives, acting and reacting upon one another. Apart from Sheikh ʿAtiyya, who almost belongs to the world of legend, the characters, both male and female, are most sympathetically drawn, with their needs and desires, their foibles, their rivalries, their pathetic and comic quarrels. It is the warmth of al-Ghitani's sympathy in treating his creations that makes the novel such pleasurable reading. Among the gallery of fascinating and colourful characters is a Government employee by the name of Ḥasan Anwar (which suggests to some President Anwar Sadat), who suffers from illusions of grandeur, dreams of great military exploits with great military commanders from history such as Napoleon, working under him, and who ends pathetically in a mental asylum, much to the distress of his devoted wife and loving son.

Like *al-Zayni Barakat, Khiṭaṭ al-Ghīṭānī* (1981) employs the technique of the medieval Arab chronicler and annalist, *khiṭaṭ* being a type of topographical-cum-historical writing. Al-Ghitani uses it as a parody designed to paint a picture of contemporary Egypt, tracing its history from the beginning of Nasser's revolution to Sadat's conclusion of peace with Israel. Here again the main character, referred to as 'al-Ustādh' (i.e. The Master), is a mysterious figure whose name is not known to anyone: he is the Editor-in-Chief/Director of a powerful newspaper *al-Anbā'* (i.e. *News*), established after the fall of the monarchy. *Al-Anbā'* stands for the Government (as through its censorship and direct control of the press the revolutionary Government ruled the Egyptian people) just as *Khitat* represents Egypt. Al-Ustadh is an absolute tyrant who inspires awe and admiration in his subordinates, all of whom, men and women alike, are in varying degrees corrupt. As is to be expected, he is aided by a highly efficient and inhumane police system. Al-Ustadh, who clearly stands for Nasser, disappears half way through the novel and is succeeded by al-Ṭanūkhī, his second in command, an inferior and much more vicious man. Both directors of *al-Anba'* persecute their political opponents: the *ʿAjam* (a medieval term for Persians/foreigners) standing here for Marxists in particular and intellectuals in general, who are described as purveyors of foreign enemy ideas, as well as the *Murabiṭūn* (a term with sufi associations, indicating here Muslim dissidents). Under al-Tanukhi the country is plunged into yet another war against the Enemy (i.e. Israel), which surprisingly ends in welcoming the Enemy into the country as friends. However, all is not lost: a group of dissidents (*ʿAjam* and *Murabitun*) who have fled into the desert, organize themselves into a fighting force and manage to storm the Establishment and destroy the *Anba'* building, but they fail to take over the Government. Nevertheless their leaders remain alive and will one day rescue the country from disaster. The novel is the nearest of al-Ghitani's works to a political allegory, a savage attack on the authoritarian regime of Nasser and Sadat, but it is not as bare and contrived an allegory as it may sound. Rich in mystical and folkloric allusions it is a poetic lament on the passing of a fairer and more peaceful Egypt before its destruction at the hands of tyrannical rulers. It is a phantasmagoria of characters and caricatures presented in the author's usual mixture of sardonic humour and deep pathos. Al-Ghitani has continued to express his passionate concern about his country in works of fiction of varying degrees of experimentation, the latest of which bears the archaic rhyming title *Risālat al-Baṣā'ir fī 'l-Maṣā'ir* (1989) and deals with the predicament of Egyptian migrant labour abroad and the ever-growing tide of cynicism and the prevalence of materialistic values in Egyptian society.

It is clearly impossible to discuss here, however briefly, the work of the very large number of Egyptian novelists who have attained fame in the last two or three decades, such as Muḥammad Abū 'l Maʿāṭī Abū 'l-Najā, Sulaymān Fayyāḍ, Saʿd Makkāwī, Nawāl al-Saʿdāwī, Sharīf Ḥitāta, Sabrī Mūsā, Yaḥyā al-Ṭāhir ʿAbdallah, Muḥammad Mustajāb, Jamīl ʿAṭiyya Ibrāhīm, Bahāʾ Ṭāhir, Ibrāhīm Aṣlān, Ibrāhīm ʿAbd al-Majīd, ʿAbduh Jubayr, and Khayrī Shalabī, to mention but a few names. However, it is necessary to end this discussion of the contemporary Egyptian novel with the extremely experimental and original work of Idwār al-Kharrāṭ (b. 1926), because of his own distinctive narrative voice, and his unique contribution to the Arabic novel. A brilliant short-story writer and an early pioneer of modernism, al-Kharrat turned to novelistic writing late in his career. He has published three novels so far, *Rāma wa'l-Tinnīn (Rama and the Dragon)* in 1979, *al-Zaman al-Ākhar (The Other Time)* in 1985, and *Turābuhā Zaʿfarān* (translated as *City of Saffron*) in 1986. The protagonist of all of them is an Egyptian Copt named Mīkhā'īl. While the first two works contain certain autobiographical elements, the last is predominantly autobiographical, although the author warns us that the flights of fancy and the artifice it contains take it far beyond the bounds of an autobiography.

Al-Kharrat's work constitutes an interesting and welcome change from the claustrophobic political atmosphere of that of many of his contemporaries; he concentrates on individual personal relations, on the inner life of his characters, on man's awareness of time and place, on emotional, sexual, spiritual, and metaphysical issues, though not to the total exclusion of political considerations. He combines extreme modernistic formal devices with a daring and original use of language, the result of his passionate interest in words. His novels are marked by a total absence of unilinear narration, a constant movement backward and forward in time, a structure that closely resembles that of a musical composition. External events, reduced to a bare minimum, are presented in a series of flashbacks and filtered through the main character's consciousness, memories triggered off by discrete sensations: sounds, smells, taste, touch, and vision. It is a purely subjective world, delineated, in long convoluted sentences in a highly sophisticated language of extraordinary richness, colour, and fervour which combines immediacy and a precision of describing the details of external objects, even the shape and feel of a Chianti or Alsace wine bottle or the unique appearance of smoked salmon, with Pharaonic, Greek, and Arab mythical allusions. The resultant atmosphere, in which past and present, reality and dream, fact and fiction are inextricably intertwined is reinforced by a highly poetic use of language which drives the author to introduce into his work what in effect are passages of prose poetry. He even writes whole paragraphs in which one letter of the alphabet is used in every word, thus creating a harmonious world of interrelated sounds, aspiring to the unity of the mystical experience he is at pains to show in his novel. Kharrat's verbal dexterity, albeit at times a little too self-conscious, is in fact a modernist development of the medieval verbal games of al-Ḥarīrī's *maqamas*.

Rama and the Dragon treats the love-affair between two middle-aged people, a Copt, Mikha'il and a Muslim woman, Rama, an unusual and indeed a daring theme, since Islam does not allow a Muslim woman to marry a non-Muslim. They are both archaeologists by profession and Marxists in political affiliation, although he has ceased his political activities, while she has remained a revolutionary. The love-affair is described in vivid physical detail without any moral judgement, interspersed by discussions of contemporary Egyptian and Arab politics and Egypt's ancient Pharaonic past, particularly the place of the Copts in Egyptian culture. Rama, a divorcée, is an emancipated woman of remarkable vitality and zest for life, who has affairs with men, but refuses to commit herself to any one man. Symbolically she is meant to be an embodiment not only of the Female Principle, but also of Eternal Egypt, as well as of elusive Truth. Mikha'il's love-affair, described in strongly sexual terms, also has its mystical dimension as is indicated in the title as well as the epigraph from al-Ḥallāj, the celebrated mystic of medieval Islam. Because he cannot have her all to himself Mikha'il, despite his overwhelming love for her, decides at the end to break off the affair and spends the rest of his days in a state of inconsolable grief and utter loss.

In *The Other Time* al-Kharrat reworks the theme of the first novel. Mikha'il and Rama resume their relationship eight years later after a chance meeting at a conference. The author develops and delves deeper into their relationship. Although the technique remains the same, we are given more facts about their lives and early revolutionary activities. The characters become more intellectual: they read T. S. Eliot and listen to a Beethoven Quartet after making love. We hear more about politics, about Nasser, Sadat, and the Palestine writer Ghassān Kanafānī, and issues like whether or not political assassination is ever justified are discussed. Their love-affair is now more self-consuming and their sexual experience even more overtly mystical in its implications. Although his quest for the ideal, for total spiritual and physical union is not diminished, Mikha'il has left behind him the unbearable feeling of utter loss which marked the earlier novel. He is now permanently in a state of love, with his passion and his senses all aglow. The language is even more poetic with a more frequent use of the potentialities of alliterative prose passages, a language aspiring to the function of music in keeping with the musical structure of the entire novel.

It is, however, in his semi-autobiographical *City of Saffron* that al-Kharrat manages to produce his best work, a work of greater spontaneity which, although it employs his usual technique, remains more accessible to a wider readership. Once more the protagonist is called Mikha'il and the novel, set in Alexandria, tells the story of the little Coptic boy's development from boyhood until his undergraduate days, from his incipient awareness of sexuality as a child, until his revolutionary activities in the nationalist struggle against the British forces of occupation. It traces his change from innocence to experience, from the magic world of childhood which bestows a sense of higher reality upon details of everyday living and sees as shrouded in mystery the actions of grown ups, to the more mundane world of adulthood with its countless suffering and sorrow. It is all delicately described in the form of memories of the past which reveal an almost Proustian sense of the passing of time.

5

Other Arab Writers and Further Developments in the Short Story

OUTSIDE Egypt the novel of literary merit was slow to appear. In the Lebanon, which witnessed the very first experiments in the novelistic genre, it is not until 1939 with the publication of *al-Raghīf* (*The Loaf*) by Tawfīq Yūsuf ʿAwwād (1911–89) that we find a novel of more than historical significance. However interesting in other ways works such as Jibrān Khalīl Jibrān's romantic *Al-Ajniḥa il-Mutakassira* (*The Broken Wings*, 1912) or even Mārūn ʿAbbūd's patriotic and revolutionary *al-Amīr al-Aḥmār* (*The Red Prince*, 1948–53) which has plenty of external action, but little or no characterization, they cannot be seriously considered as novels.

The Loaf, set mainly in a Lebanese village during the First World War, revolves round two main themes: Arab nationalism and social justice. These themes are interrelated in that the few feudal and rich local landlords side with the foreign Turkish military authorities against the starving masses who are desperately struggling to obtain a loaf of bread. The hero, Sāmī ʿĀṣim, a poet and a member of a secret revolutionary organization, is hunted by the Turkish authorities; disguised as a monk, he hides in a cave where he is discovered and taken prisoner, but he manages to escape and although reported dead he in fact survives and plays a leading role in the struggle by Arab forces against the Turkish troops, but falls in battle during the last stage of the war.

The novel is well constructed; the events move in a clear progression with plenty of suspense, the setting is vividly and subtly described, and there is considerable pathos in the delineation of the character of the grandfather, Abū Saʿīd. The author is at pains to maintain an attitude of detachment: he does not hesitate to show that amongst the Lebanese there were collaborators and spies, although his hero and heroine are a shade too idealized. The description of scenes of deprivation, misery, and starvation, particularly of the heroine Zayna's little brother Ṭām, is at times a little overdone, bordering on the sentimental, and the novel is packed with melodramatic happenings, ranging from Zayna's shooting of the deceived Turkish commander, just when, in response to her encouragement, he is about to make love to her, to the screechings and ravings of a mad woman, Abu Saʿid's daughter-in-law, who was driven to insanity by her ill-treatment in prison. However, the author cannot be accused of overall sentimentality, since he judiciously avoids the temptation of contriving a happy reunion between the hero and heroine at the end.

More than thirty years separate ʿAwwad's *The Loaf* from his other novel *Ṭawāḥīn Bayrūt* (translated as *Death in Beirut*, published in 1972) which relates the story of a tragic love-affair between two university students, a Shiʿi Muslim girl and a Maronite Christian boy, whose decision to get married in spite of their religious differences is frustrated, against the background of the aftermath of the Arab–Israeli war of 1967. Set in 1968 when Lebanon was under constant attacks by Israeli forces, with the politicians rendered powerless by their internecine squabbles, the pursuit of self-interest and illicit pleasure, student demonstrations and calls for revolution, and the growing activity of the Palestine Liberation movement, the novel paints a powerful picture of the moral and political corruption and the intellectual confusion and sectarian strife that bedevilled Lebanon and presaged the imminent civil war. Tamīma, an ambitious Muslim girl from an impoverished family in a Southern Lebanese village, intent on continuing her education in Beirut and making a life for herself, is injured in a student demonstration, rescued by Ḥānī, a Maronite engineering student with whom she eventually falls in love when they meet again, but after she has been seduced by a popular journalist Ramzī Raʿd, who excercises a profound influence on the young through his nihilistic ideas. She has met the journalist when visiting the house where her good-for-nothing student brother lives which is owned by Mme Rose Khūrī, a retired whore. Her house is virtually a brothel, to which many of the characters, pimps, thugs, prostitutes as well as journalists, lawyers, and aspiring politicians are directly or indirectly connected. When told of his sister's relationship with the Maronite, the incensed brother goes to murder her, but kills instead her girlfriend, Mary. Grieving for Mary's death and horrified at the shocked condemnation of Hani when she tells him of her seduction by Ramzi, Tamima decides to join the Palestine Liberation resistance, resolved 'to fight against all legal codes and traditions made by the society' which 'has denied her the right to life'.

The novel, written in a language of great sensitivity, is carefully structured with the two themes, the personal and political, inextricably intertwined. The characters are vividly portrayed, the contrast between the nihilist Ramzi and the cultural right-wing Hani is convincing because they are not drawn in black and white: the liberal Hani is not liberal enough to accept the loss of virginity of his beloved, and the nihilist Ramzi is not always portrayed unsympathetically. The writing is powerful as is exemplified in the scene of the heroine's seduction, the moving account of her tragic predicament, or the effect of Israeli raids with their resultant destruction and death of the innocent, or in the biting satirical description of the demonstrating students' speeches. We are shown how the grinding millstones of Beirut roar noisily, but they produce nothing, as the Arabic title suggests. Modernist technique is used sparingly as in the stream of consciousness in the feverish ravings of Tamima after her abortive suicide attempt, or Ramzi's random thoughts by Mme Rose's death bed. On the whole, however, the novel is fairly conventional in form: events are related chronologically with little experimentation in time.

Much more experimental is the fiction of Ḥalīm Barakāt (b. 1933), written in a staccato style, with the normal Arabic connective particles constantly omitted to enforce the dramatic effect, a feature which has become increasingly common in fiction since the 1960s. Other modernist devices are used, chiefly poetic prose, repetition of phrases, stream of consciousness, and symbolism. His first novel, with the prophetic title *Sittat Ayyām* (translated as *Six Days*, published 1961) is set in Dayr al-Baḥr, a coastal town which is given an ultimatum by the Israelis in 1948 to surrender within six days or face annihilation. The novel, divided into six sections, each devoted to one day, traces the various reactions and preparations of the inhabitants and the development of the events which end in the storming and burning of the town and the killing of most of the characters. *Six Days* shares some features with ʿAwwad's later novel: both stress the contradictions within Arab society, visibly expressed in the differences in dress between modern Westernized women and veiled traditionally dressed ones, the backwardness of its men, armed with antiquated weapons and their minds stuffed with superstitions. They both depict a daring love-affair between a Muslim girl and a Christian young man, an affair which shocks the people around them. As in ʿAwwad's novel, the two themes are interrelated, the message being that you cannot fight the enemy without until the enemy within has been vanquished. Barakat uses as a symbol of the stagnation of society a clock in the village that had stopped for a very long time, to which he makes frequent references. The hero of the novel, Suhayl, is a Westernized Christian intellectual, who becomes an atheist and an admirer of Nietzsche. He suffers, however from an existentialist type of ennui and therefore welcomes the excitement of the heroic challenge of facing death, so that life may flow into his being again. He falls in love with the Muslim Nāhida, but their love is opposed by those around him, most of all by the girl's mother, the widow of a famous nationalist martyr. They defy society and initiate a passionate love-affair described in physical detail. Suhayl is assigned by his resistance comrades a mission which, as a result of betrayal, ends in his capture by the enemy, his interrogation and torture. He refuses to inform on his people just as the village decides not to surrender and is finally destroyed by the enemy. The novel gives a powerfully vivid and moving description of the panic, fleeing, cupidity, and treachery no less than the heroism and self-sacrifice of the villagers, together with the butcheries and brutality of the enemy. At the end all Suhail's friends are killed, but he alone remains alive, held captive by the enemy. However, when he is shown by his interrogator the smoke arising from his burning town in the distance, his reply is that out of the ashes will come life, thereby asserting the author's basic optimism.

Barakat's next novel deals with the 1967 Arab–Israeli war. *ʿAwdat al-Ṭāʾir ilaʾl-Baḥr* ('The Return of *The Flying Dutchman* to the Sea', translated as *Days of Dust*, 1969) is more sophisticated in its structure and use of time. It is divided into three parts: the first and third parts, which are more in the nature of Prologue and Epilogue respectively, take place in the immediate aftermath of the war, and are dated 11–20 June 1967, while the second part, which is the main body of the novel, is dated 5–10 June 1967, that is the period of the actual fighting, and is divided into six chapters, each dealing with one day. Moreover, the first two parts contain a parody of the Book of Genesis designed to emphasize the horrifying chaos and the utter gloom that pervaded the whole Arab world in the wake of their crushing defeat. In the first part the protagonist tells us that 'Earth was a desolate wasteland and there was darkness on the face of the deep; but the spirit of God did not move upon the waters.' In the third and last part we are told 'The Arab saw all that he had done and behold, it was very bad. Then it was that on the seventh day he did not rest.' Sandwiched between these two parts are fast-moving brief accounts of events, snapshots of the war, the atrocities committed by the invading soldiers with their napalm bombs, the fleeing of the panic-stricken Palestinian civilians, men, women, and children strafed by warplanes in their scramble for safety, the pathetic futility of ill-equipped, badly organized resistance, the lies about the progress of the war put about by Arab governments in their official communiqués, the reaction, euphoric or violent to the events, especially Nasser's resignation speech, of the masses in Beirut or Amman. The novel also shows some of the factors that led to the Arab defeat, as seen through the agonized eyes of the main protagonist, Ramzī Ṣafadī, a Palestinian professor at the American University of Beirut, a thoroughly Westernized man who received his higher education in America. Like most Arab intellectuals, he feels frustrated and wasted in his society because of the authorities' inefficiency, lack of organization, fatal self-deception, and addiction to words and slogans. As a somewhat pathetic gesture to help, he collects medical supplies in Beirut and leads a team of social scientists from his university to travel to Amman to investigate the causes of the refugees fleeing from their homes, to prevent the possible repetition of the Israelis' spreading any false accounts in the future.

In the midst of this turmoil Ramzi is shown as having an affair with Pamela, an American painter touring the Middle East, separated from her sick husband. The author introduces this love interest not only to provide for Ramzi a means of escape from grim reality, and pinpoint the irony of his love-making in Beirut while people are slaughtered in Jerusalem, but also to use Pamela as a convenient interlocutor to whom Ramzi can express his views on, and attitude to, the Arab predicament. One of these, in fact, serves as a structural symbol for the novel, namely the story of *The Flying Dutchman* which lends its name to the work. Ramzi believes that like Wagner's *The Flying Dutchman*, who is doomed to perpetual exile and to sail the seas until he finds a woman prepared to love him unto death, Palestine has to suffer exile until she finds those whose devotion to her is absolute and who in his opinion are represented by the guerrillas, individuals prepared to sacrifice absolutely everything for her. The novel ends with the two themes, the Biblical and the Wagnerian, coming together: 'The Arab could not rest on the seventh day' and 'the crew of *The Flying Dutchman* could not remain exiled and rootless for ever'. Even Pamela decides to put an end to her wandering and go back to her roots in America. Barakat's *Days of Dust* is at once an intellectual's *cri de cœur* against the tragic shortcomings of the military, administrative, social, and intellectual structure of the Arab world, and a moving and powerful record of the sufferings of the Palestinians during the 1967 war, even though as a novel it suffers from a serious lack of characterization, with the possible exception of the protagonist's character.

In his third novel *al-Raḥīl bayn al-Sahm wa'l-Waṭar* (*Travelling between Arrow and Bowstring*, 1979), Barakat pursues his analysis of the problems of Arab society, though he concentrates mainly on the problems of the Arab woman and the relation between the sexes. Attending an Arab conference held in Palestine Hotel in Alexandria in the mid-1970s to discuss the future of the Arab world, two Egyptian married women have an affair, one with an Iraqi Marxist revolutionary journalist (married, with children) and the other with a Moroccan intellectual divorced from a French woman. The Egyptian women, although liberated enough to take advantage of their absence from their husbands to go to a nightclub and drink alcohol with men, are in search of freedom from the chains of a man-made world, particularly sexual freedom. They regard their marriages (arranged for them) to men they do not love as 'a perpetual rape' and spend hours arguing with their left-wing companions about whether the problems of Arab women are part of the more general problems of oppressed and underprivileged classes of society and their liberation therefore requires a more comprehensive social, economic, and political revolution, or their own personal problems, particularly sexual ones, the result of their living in a coercive society, with outworn institutions. Although some of the women in the novel are shown as not particularly suffering from sexual taboos, the author concentrates on the difficulties one couple have in coming to terms with their sexual needs. Zaynab, who admits she has never experienced sexual pleasure, is relentlessly pursued by her admirer the Iraqi Nā'il, to whom she has been physically attracted for some time, but she does not give in, preferring to remain faithful to her husband whom she does not love. After his final unsuccessful attempt to seduce her at the end of the novel and their parting from one another, she makes up her mind to opt for freedom and life and give herself to him the next day, but it is too late for he has left the country, having decided to learn to accept her purely as a friend and rise above his sexual feelings for her. *Travelling* is an interesting novel which makes use of the narrative technique of the *Thousand and One Nights*, to which it makes several allusions. It also provides several comments on Sadat's Egypt, its politics and culture, including the Egyptian literature of protest and the gap between the opulent world of the smart hotels and the poverty, sordidness, and filth of the old quarters of Cairo. But it is inordinately long and self-indulgent, quoting whole popular poems and songs of protest. It is also too cerebral with whole pages devoted to what amounts to bare discussions of the problems of the Arab woman, with little action or drama.

Also connected with the difficulties confronting the Arab woman is the work of Suhayl Idrīs (b. 1924), the editor of the influential literary periodical *al-Ādāb*, although in it he also deals with other issues, political, social, and cultural. His three novels have some autobiographical elements: *al-Ḥayy al-Lātīnī* (*The Latin Quarter*, 1953) describes his experience as a student in Paris after the Second World War; *al-Khandaq al-Ghamīq* (*The Deep Trench* (the name of a Beirut district), published 1958) deals with his childhood and adolescence, his education in a theological boarding school in Lebanon, and his rebellion against his father and the narrow confines of a religious education in favour of secular schooling; *Aṣābiʿunā allatī Taḥtariq* (*Our Burning Fingers*, published 1963) treats his experiences after his return from Paris to Beirut, his editing of one of the leading literary journals in the Arab world, his thoughts on literature, politics, sex, and marriage. It is mainly the story of his love and marriage to Ilhām, the woman who becomes his secretary and subsequently co-editor of his journal, told against the background of literary and political events in the Lebanon and the Arab world until just after the Anglo–French–Israeli aggression against Egypt and the Suez War of 1956. It is a *roman à clef*, with recognizable literary figures, both men and women, given thinly disguised names. In fact parts of it read more like memoirs than a novel, with extensive discussion of general issues such as the relation between literature and society, literature and politics, freedom of speech and of criticism in an open society, Arab Marxists, and the Soviet Union.

The most accomplished of these novels is *The Latin Quarter*, in which he uses the relationship between a number of male Arab students and French women in Paris, not only to comment on the sexual starvation of the young Arabs (as a result of the hypocrisy of Arab society and the damaging repression of its women's sexuality) but also as a means to trace their development, marking a stage along the road to emotional and psychological maturity and hence their assumption of responsibility to promote the Arab nationalist ideal. The main character has to learn to shake off the restricting influence of his tradition, in the form of his conventional powerful Lebanese mother, and to act independently to atone for the harm he was driven to cause the French woman Jeanine Montreux, who loved him deeply and conceived his child. His mother makes him reply to Jeanine's loving letter in which she informs him of her pregnancy and asks him for advice during his holiday in Beirut, by denying all responsibility for the pregnancy in a language that is both cowardly and offensive. The shocked Jeanine has an abortion, but when after a long search he manages to trace her, and offers her marriage she declines his offer and disappears from his life altogether, not wishing to stand in his way, as he struggles for his great cause (of Arab nationalism). Despite some romantic excesses (for example making Jeanine end as a prostitute) and obtrusive existentialist echoes, this is, on the whole a well-written, well-constructed novel in which the psychological, cultural, and political anxieties of the young Arab intellectuals of the post-Second World War years, as well as the contrast between the emancipated Western woman and the repressed woman of the East, are vividly and convincingly portrayed.

But it is in the writing of women novelists in the Lebanon (as in Syria and Egypt) that the problems of the suppressed Arab woman figure most prominently. The first to attain wide celebrity and even notoriety in the Arab world was Laylā Baʿalbakī (b. 1936) with her *Anā Aḥyā* (*I Am Alive*), which appeared in 1958. The story is told by Līnā, a rebellious, abrasive, highly strung, and extremely egoistic young woman, who suffers from near existentialist ennui and fear of death. Her hypersensitive mind registers strange sensations emitted by ordinary objects in a language which is at times vivid and vibrant. She despises her affluent family, particularly her father, whose wealth has been made out of profiteering from international crises and whom she thinks to be a liar and a voyeur, lacking principles and integrity, and her mother whom she regards as a submissive wife whose main purpose in life is to provide sexual gratification for her husband. All the people around her, especially the men who give her lascivious looks, inspire nothing but nausea and she does not miss any opportunity to shock her parents by her outrageous behaviour. Although her consciousness is suffused with eroticism, she rejects angrily the traditional view of woman, which constricts her role to her biological function of meekly providing sexual pleasure for her husband and bearing his children. A part-time university student, she finds herself a job (in an anti-communist organization) in order to be financially independent of her rich father. She meets and falls in love with an Iraqi fellow student, Bahā', a Marxist revolutionary, and that relieves some of her boredom, but in pursuit of the freedom to live, as she puts it, she first gives up her university studies and then her job. When she realizes that Baha' is wholly absorbed by his revolutionary plans, she tries to kill herself in despair, but having failed to do so she is forced to go back to the home and family she loathes.

Al-Āliha al-Mamsūkha (*Deformed Deities*, 1960), Baʿalbaki's second novel, describes in unusually frank language a love-affair between a young girl and a middle-aged man and the girl's rebellion against the authority and conventional values of a tyrannical father. These two novels proclaim loudly the Arab woman's need to liberate herself from the tyranny of the male and the taboos and constraints of society, but they are written in a rather melodramatic style, their structure is seriously flawed, and because of the author's blinding self-absorption, the characterization is weak.

Unlike Layla Baʿalbaki, Laylā ʿUsayrān moved beyond the stage of portraying the existentialist young woman in rebellion against man-made society and in pursuit of total freedom shown in works such as *al-Ḥiwār al-Akhras* (*Dumb Dialogue*, 1963) and *al-Madīna al-Fārigha* (*The Empty City*, 1966). In *ʿAṣāfīr al-Fajr* (*Birds of Dawn*, 1968), she includes other major themes such as the Palestinian resistance. Maryam, a young Palestinian, is converted from a life of idle pleasures full of parties and dancing to a commitment to the Palestinian cause, breaking off her relationship with ʿIṣām, who has been driven by despair to an utterly defeatist position. Suhayr, the young woman teacher, loses her faith in a just God for allowing the Palestinian tragedy to happen, becoming a rebel, acquiring a powerful *raison d'être* through taking an active part in the Palestinian resistance in occupied Jerusalem, alongside men, instead of confining her work to women's organizations, and thereby asserting her sexual equality with men. The novel, written after the 1967 Arab defeat, contains graphic descriptions of the horrors of the war, the suffering of the Palestinian war victims, as well as vivid accounts of the various forms of torture used by the Israelis in interrogating Palestinian Arabs. It puts forward the thesis that the only hope for the Palestinians is for themselves to fight as guerrillas which will also restore Arab honour after their shameful defeat. These views are expressed by the author directly in the concluding pages of the novel to the extent that one is made to feel that she used the novelistic form only for the sake of convenience. The novel suffers not only from weak characterization, but also from the excessive idealization of the young men in the resistance, 'the birds of dawn', who are the symbol of hope, and who are all like the heroes of popular medieval romances, not sufficiently distinct from one another. The language is predominantly lyrical, indeed at times it becomes damagingly poetical and sentimental.

In *Khaṭṭ al-Afʿā* (*The Snake's Line*, 1972) this lyricism is pushed to the extreme; the writing becomes far too figurative, ornate, verbose, and self-indulgent. The novel is a celebration of armed resistance, pinpointing the spiritual value of dying for the cause. The author's point is to prove that a woman can become a real fighter in the Palestinian resistance, just like a man, and need not be satisfied with the traditional female passive role of a nurse. The narrator/protagonist, Maryam, who as a child had seen her mother butchered by the enemy, was brought up by her grandmother, and educated at a boarding-school, relates how she becomes a guerrilla fighter. The novel delineates the process of her military training and describes in detail everyday life in a resistance camp. A subsidiary theme is a chaste love-affair between Maryam and the mysterious leader of the group, Abū 'l-Layl, an affair that is given a strongly symbolical significance. This is not a novel in the usual sense: there is no plot or characterization. Even the narrator/protagonist Maryam is less of a character than a bundle of sentiments, aspirations, and emotional attitudes, expressed in an impassioned language. In these two works Layla ʿUsayran offers an exceedingly romantic and idealized apologia for a guerrilla's death.

One of the best novels written by a woman novelist is *Ṭuyūr Aylūl* (*September Birds*, 1962) by Emily Naṣrallah (b. 1938). The narrator, Munā, a village girl who moves to the city, recalls nostalgically, many years later, her childhood and adolescence in her native village. In so doing she paints a vivid picture of a closely knit village community, their quiet monotonous life, their daily preoccupations, their festivals, their superstitions, and their gossip —mostly seen from the female point of view. Hence the criticism of the stifling social conventions and attitudes which discriminate against women, denying girls the chance of a city education allowed to boys, impose prearranged marriages on women against their wishes, and make it impossible for love between young people of a different class or religious denomination to end in anything but frustration or tragedy. Nevertheless, the village is favourably, but not simplistically, contrasted with the ugly, impersonal, and materialistic city, even though the idyllic life in the village is tinged with sadness. This is largely caused by the emigration of many young men to America to better themselves, which brings about much heartache to their village relatives, particularly their elderly parents who make a daily pilgrimage to the local post office in the hope of finding letters from them to allay their anxieties. The novel is written in a style marked by great sensitivity; the events and characters of the Lebanese village are exquisitely and lovingly described and set against the background of nature. The relation between the migratory birds moving southward in September in search of a warmer climate and the young villagers feeling the urge to emigrate to America is expressed in poignant, poetic language. As the whole novel is cast in the form of memories a keen sense of time is revealed, nostalgia is mixed with irreversible change, felt by the protagonist, who on a visit to the village, realizes that she is hardly recognized by the villagers she knew.

Nasrallah went on to write three more novels, two of which were produced after the outbreak of the Lebanese civil war. Although the theme is largely that of migration from the village either to the city or overseas, the contrast between town and country loses much of its significance, and the need to demonstrate allegiance to the Lebanon and earn the right of belonging by resisting the temptation to migrate and bravely opting to remain, despite danger, is passionately enunciated. A similar sentiment is expressed in *Kawābīs Bayrūt* (*Beirut Nightmares*, 1976) by Ghāda al-Sammān (b. 1942), a Syrian woman writer of short stories resident in Beirut. The narrator is a liberated woman journalist of obviously Marxist views, engaged in writing a novel called *Beirut Nightmares*, describing her experiences during the Lebanese civil war. Her lover, a schoolteacher who belonged to a different religion from her own, has just been shot dead by the street militia who humiliate her for going out with the wrong side. Living opposite The Holiday Inn, she is virtually a prisoner in her flat, not daring to go out for fear of being caught in the cross-fire or shot by a nearby sniper. Her brother, who has ventured to go out to fetch some food, never returns. Her flat is hit by a rocket which sets it aflame and she loses her most precious possessions, her books. The novel is an account of the protagonist's thoughts, feelings, fantasies, and nightmares during the ten days or so of her forced confinement to her flat until her rescue by the army. It is a powerful account of the atrocities of the civil war, written in the poetic style of magic realism, making use of symbolical devices such as the nearby pet shop, with its caged animals being likened to Beirut's citizens like herself, although the comparison may be a bit overdone. As a novel *Beirut Nightmares* suffers a little from excessive length, repetitiveness, and some structural weakness which at times renders it not much more than a series of surrealistic, albeit very disturbing, sketches, loosely strung together.

Perhaps the most accomplished novel by any Arab woman to date is *Ḥikāyat Zahra* (translated as *The Story of Zahra*, published 1980) by the Lebanese Ḥanān al-Shaykh (b. 1954). Zahra grows up in a lower-middle-class Shiʿi family, terrified of a tyrannical father with a Hitler-like moustache, who brutally beats up her mother. For her own protection, her mother takes her with her to her meetings with her own lover, where Zahra is virtually forced to watch the two of them making love; meanwhile at home she is discriminated against in favour of her spoilt and good-for-nothing brother. After her schooling, lacking self-confidence, her face full of pimples, she is sent to a friend of her brother's to help her find a job, but the friend seduces her, gets her pregnant twice, and each time she has to have an abortion. Although she finds no pleasure in sex, she is completely dominated by the friend. Because of her fear of being murdered by her father for her loss of virginity, she has a nervous breakdown when she receives a proposal of marriage and has to undergo electro-convulsive therapy. As a way out of her dilemma she accepts an invitation from her uncle, who has settled in Africa after fleeing his country in the wake of a failed *coup d'état* in which he was involved in the name of his Syrian Nationalist Party. In Africa, alarmed at what she feels to be her uncle's sexual molestation, she agrees to marry a lonely Lebanese emigrant, but the marriage proves a disaster and she suffers a recurrence of her nervous complaint. Back in Beirut after her divorce, she is horrified by the events of the civil war and in the mistaken hope of stopping the killing by a sniper on the roof of the building opposite where she lives, she develops a relationship with the sniper, which brings her sexual satisfaction for the first time in her life and by a curious chance, in keeping with the irrational logic of the situation, seems to bring her back to normality. She becomes pregnant, but, realizing it is too late for her to abort she decides to kill herself. When she breaks the news of her pregnancy to the sniper, his reaction causes her to have a nervous fit. However, feeling secure as he has promised to marry her, she asks him if he is a sniper, a thing which unleashes his anger and alarm and he naturally replies in the negative. As she walks home, happy at the thought that her engagement will be formally announced the next day, she is cut down by several bullets, clearly from the sniper's gun.

In this novel Hanan al-Shaykh makes a masterly use of modernist technique in narrative discourse, such as the multiple viewpoint, the stream of consciousness, bold handling of time and chronology, use of montage and flashback, together with subtle irony and imaginative freedom from taboos, sexual and otherwise. Against the background of the horrors and absurdities of the Lebanese civil war and the alarming political, social, and economic conditions that led to it, the author lets the personal tragedy of her heroine Zahra unfold. Because the emphasis remains on the individual character or characters, their interrelationships and their pathetic struggle to make some sense of their absurd life or to snatch a drop of happiness from a hostile world and against great odds, *The Story of Zahra* is a good novel and not another political tract disguised as a work of fiction. Yet Zahra's mental illness is in a sense a metaphor for the tragically diseased Lebanese society. Moreover, because of its relatively more direct treatment and greater intelligibility, its account of the Lebanese civil war and the nightmare of life in Beirut is much more telling than the near-surrealistic presentation in *al-Jabal al-Saghīr* (translated as *Little Mountain*, published in 1977) or the even more experimental Samuel Beckett-like *Abwāb al-Madīna* (*The City Gates*, 1981) by the Lebanese avant-garde novelist Ilyās Khūrī (b. around 1940).

The mature Palestinian novel was not to appear until a couple of decades later than the Lebanese: it began to make its impact only with the work of Ghassān Kanafānī (1936–72). Kanafani published four short novels in his lifetime: *Rijāl fi'l-Shams* (translated as *Men in the Sun*) in 1963, *Mā Tabaqqā Lakum* (*What Remains for You*) in 1966, *Umm Saʿd* in 1969, and *ʿĀ'id ilā Ḥayfā* (*Going Back to Haifa*) also in 1969, all of which revolve round the plight of the Palestinians, which is hardly surprising considering Kanafani's deep involvement with the activities of the Popular Front for the Liberation of Palestine, for which he was assassinated by Israeli agents. Of these the first, *Men in the Sun*, is the best known and arguably the most accomplished novel inspired by the Palestinian tragedy. Three Palestinian men of different generations and circumstances have left their refugee camps and are desperately trying to enter Kuwait illegally to make their fortune, crossing the desert from Iraq. A water-tank driver, Abū Khayzurān, also a Palestinian, has agreed to smuggle them inside his tank, for a fee: he too is intent on making as much money as he can. The plan was for the men to hide inside the closed tank in the blazing heat of the sun, but only for a few minutes, while Abu Khayzuran gets the necessary papers signed by the Kuwaiti officials at the frontier post. Unfortunately he is delayed by the bored officials who take no notice of his appeal for urgency, but fool about, making jokes about his alleged sexual adventures in Iraq—all the more ironic as we know that he is impotent as the result of a surgical operation to save his life after he was wounded by the Israelis in the 1948 war. When he finally gets away and opens the tank he finds to his horror that all the men have died of suffocation. Abu Khayzuran then dumps the bodies on a rubbish heap after stripping them of their valuables. The novel ends with his bewildered cry: 'Why didn't they beat on the side of the tank?' Utterly free of sentimentality the novel is written in a poetic style, pregnant with symbolism and employing several aspects of modernist narrative technique. In a series of flashbacks the characters are presented, fully drawn and differentiated, with their weaknesses and sufferings, their dreams and aspirations. With his deep attachment to the homeland, the novelist shows the futility of the quest for individual salvation pursued by fleeing Palestinians, and condemns the tragic passivity of their suffering, as well as their betrayal by unsympathetic Arab authorities.

In *What Remains for You* Kanafani chooses a Palestinian refugee camp in the Gaza strip as a setting for his characters. Using a more daring experimental narrative technique in which, as he warns the reader in an explanatory prefatory note, there is no clear dividing line between points in time and place, he is driven to the device of differing typefaces to distinguish between different speakers and narrator as there is constant shifting of pronouns, and the dramatization of the consciousness of characters, their thoughts, feelings, and memories is rendered as one continuum in which characters are portrayed largely through flashbacks. The protagonists of his novels, he tells us, are Ḥāmid, Maryam, Zakariyyā, Time, and the Desert, and these do not move in parallel lines but intersect. The result is a highly condensed work of a dense texture and symbolical imagery: the events move swiftly in less than twenty-four hours, taking place mainly in the dark and ending somewhat surprisingly and melodramatically.

Hamid and his older sister Maryam have been living in a refugee camp with their grandmother, who dies at the beginning of the novel: they were separated in the confusion of the 1948 war from their mother, who lives now in Jordan. Maryam, who is thirty-five, is seduced by Zakariyya, a married man with children, and she becomes pregnant. To avoid scandal he agrees to take her on as his second wife, but because her brother Hamid has no respect for him, as he is known to be a coward and a traitor to the cause, he (the brother) decides to leave for Jordan, to join his mother, embarking on an extremely hazardous journey across the desert at night. He meets and overpowers an Israeli guard and knows that he will have to kill him at some point if he is to pursue his journey. In the mean time Maryam, who is spending the night with Zakariyya, learns to her disgust that he wants her to have an abortion and that unless she agrees to that he threatens to divorce her. When he proceeds to beat her, she grabs the kitchen knife and kills him. Echoes to and parallelism between the actions of Maryam in the camp and her brother in the desert are linked as all along there is indeed what seems like telepathy between them. Although it does not gloss over the misery and wretchedness of the Palestinians, the novel projects a more positive image of them. Unlike the men in *Men in the Sun*, neither Hamid nor Maryam is prepared to endure passively their suffering.

Kanafani's two later novels were written in 1969, after the shocking and humiliating Arab defeat of 1967. They clearly express Kanafani's need to raise Palestinian morale and advocate the value of the armed struggle. In *Umm Saʿd* the mother, who lends the novel her name, is idealized almost beyond belief: she positively enjoys the prospect of her sons' deaths as guerrilla fighters. *Going back to Haifa* describes a visit by a Palestinian couple to their home in Haifa, made possible by the Israeli victory in 1967, in the vain hope of finding out what has become of their son, whom they were forced to leave behind as a child in 1948, only to discover that he has been adopted by a childless European Jewish couple, brought up as an Israeli, and is now a soldier in the Israeli army. That, they learn, is the heavy price they have had to pay for fleeing the land: they should never have left their home and their city Haifa. Weeping bitter tears, they make their way back to Ramallah, the father expressing his dear wish that his other son will have already joined the guerrilla movement, although, not wanting to lose him, he has hitherto done everything within his power to stop him doing so. *Going back to Haifa* is an interesting novel, unusual in that it presents credible Israeli characters, but the political message is too palpable: compared with the first two novels, it is lacking in subtlety. How Kanafani might have developed as a novelist if he had not been cut down so tragically young is obviously impossible to say. But at least in his first two works, his contribution to the Arabic novel has been original and impressive.

Other Palestinian novelists include Emile Ḥabībī (b. 1921) and the younger Saḥar Khalīfa (b. 1941), both of whom dealt with the life of Arabs under Israeli rule. In *Sudāsiyyat al-Ayyām al-Sitta* (*Sextet on the Six Days*, published in 1969), more a series of short stories than a novel proper, Habibi presents a pathetic account of the reunion of Arabs in Israel and their relatives who were settled in neighbouring Arab countries, using a style pregnant with symbolism and folklore. Habibi's later work, *Al-Waqāʾiʿ al-Gharība fī Ikhtifāʾ Saʿīd Abū al-Naḥs al-Mutashāʾil* (translated as *The Secret Life of Saeed, the Ill-Fated Pessoptimist*, published in 1972), is a novel of considerable originality, employing a variety of devices borrowed from the picaresque as well as the traditional *maqama*, from science fiction and farcical situations, modern idiom, and pastiche of mediaeval Arabic, to paint a bitterly ironic and even tragic picture of the life of Palestinian Arabs in Israel. In *al-Ṣabbār* (translated as *Wild Thorns*, published in 1976) and its sequel *ʿAbbād al-Shams* (*Sunflower*, 1980), Sahar Khalifa describes the change of mood in the Arabs under Israeli occupation from one of cooperation and concern with the business of everyday living, with the will to struggle undermined, to one of resurgence of resistance. The first novel ends with the blowing up of the family house of the freedom fighter while the second concludes with a violent demonstration by Palestinian men, women, and children throwing stones at armed Israeli soldiers. Among the themes dealt with by this feminist writer is the need for the Arab woman to be emancipated in order that she may contribute to the liberation of Palestine. The hardships encountered by the occupied Arabs are vividly portrayed: Saʿdiyya, who managed, by the sweat of her brow, to buy a piece of land to build her dream house for herself and her orphaned children, is ruthlessly forced by Israeli soldiers to give up her land to make room for a settlement.

But the other major figure in the Palestinian novel, to be compared with Kanafani, is without doubt Jabrā Ibrāhīm Jabrā (b. 1919), who has lived in Baghdad since leaving Palestine in 1948, and is one of the most sophisticated and cultured modern Arab writers. Distinguished alike as a poet, critic, translator (particularly of Shakespeare), and painter, he even wrote a novel in English, *Hunters in a Narrow Street* (1960). His first Arabic venture in fiction is the short novel *Ṣurākh fī Layl Ṭawīl* (*A Cry in the Long Night*), written in Jerusalem in 1946, but published in Baghdad in 1955. The actual events of the novel occupy one day in the life of the protagonist, the rest are recalled as memories. The narrator, Amīn Sammāʿ, is a young journalist and novelist of humble origin who marries Sumayya, the daughter of a rich businessman, against her parents' wishes. After two years she runs away, obviously with another man. Sammāʿ is thoroughly shaken by her desertion, which sours his view of women, even though he is still in love with his unfaithful wife. He slowly goes back to his journalistic work after a period of absence, and is employed by a rich aristocratic old lady to write the history of her family by which she is obsessed. When the lady dies, her younger sister, the only survivor who inherits the large family fortune and mansion, reacts violently against this unhealthy obsession with the past, burns the family papers and sets fire to the mansion. Intent on living her present to the full she proposes marriage to the stunned young author. He is tempted by the incredible offer for a short while, but his wife's sudden return and his full realization of her adultery not only drives him to turn her out of the house, but also enables him to decline the rich heiress's offer. The burning of the mansion, which represents freedom from the dead hand of the past, is parallelled by Amin's recovery from his own past, his emotional enslavement to his unfaithful wife. The chief interest of the novel lies in its adumbration of several features of Jabra's later and more mature work. The protagonist is typically an intellectual, who talks to other intellectuals (a painter and an academic) about Rabelais and Rubens. The dialogue tends to be a discussion of general issues such as the differences between men and women, as regards the attitude to the body and sex. The city is a powerful, rather ominous presence, full of corruption and contrasted with an idealized countryside and there is a strong element of melodrama, and a powerful atmosphere of mystery.

It is, however, with the publication in 1969 of *al-Safīna* (translated as *The Ship*) that Jabra began his serious contribution to the Arabic novel. The five main characters ʿIṣām, Lumā, Fāliḥ Wadīʿ, and Emilia meet seemingly by chance on a Mediterranean cruise ship sailing from Beirut, but in reality all but ʿIsam have secretly planned the trip for their amorous encounters. ʿIsam is a brilliant young Iraqi architect deeply in love with the beautiful and intelligent Oxford-educated Luma, whom he met while they were students in England. When they later learn that ʿIsam's father had long ago killed Luma's uncle in a dispute over land, their marriage is rendered unthinkable due to tribal social pressures. Luma instead marries Falih, a successful Iraqi surgeon of a gloomy temperament and self-destructive tendencies. While attending a medical conference in Beirut Falih is introduced by his Lebanese medical friend Mahā to the Italian Emilia, who has been deserted by her Lebanese husband, and he and Emilia fall in love. Maha is the fiancée of Wadiʿ, an exiled Palestinian businessman who has made his fortune in Kuwait and who dreams of returning with Maha to Jerusalem, where he lost his closest friend and fellow fighter during the 1948 war, and of setting up a farm in his native land. ʿIsam has decided to take the ship on his way to England in a desperate attempt to run away from Baghdad and cure himself of his passion for Luma. The others, however, have joined the week-long cruise in order to be united with the persons they love.

During the cruise a number of events take place, including an unsuccessful suicide attempt by a Dutch passenger, which prompts a discussion on suicide, one of a great many discussions in which these highly Westernized Arab characters engage and which reveal the moral, philosophical, cultural, and political preoccupations and dilemmas of the modern Arab intellectuals. The novel ends somewhat melodramatically, like much of Jabra's fiction, with the suicide of Falih, partly as a result of his discovery of Luma's love for ʿIsam. The story is told by two narrators in turn, ʿIsam and Wadiʿ, with one chapter related by Emilia in which she explains her affair with Falih. The background of the action and the past experiences of the characters which determine the course of the events, are given largely in a series of flashbacks. The novel is written in a sensitive, highly evocative prose, rich in symbolism and irony as well as in graphic description, as in Wadiʿ's account of his experience of the 1948 war in Jerusalem. The tone is profoundly melancholic. Despite moments of ecstasy, the characters experience no real fulfilment. Falih's suicide causes ʿIsam to return with Luma to Baghdad instead of pursuing his journey to England, but it in no way removes the obstacle to their marriage; and it constitutes a tragic loss to Emilia. Wadiʿ is joined by his fiancée Maha, but their plan for a return to Palestine remains a seemingly impossible dream. There is an element of artificiality about *The Ship*, which is due in part to its highly contrived plot and its web of complexity and deception, reminiscent of the work of Iris Murdoch. Although we are given sufficient information about the main characters to render them distinct from one another, they all seem to speak in the same voice, which is the intellectual voice of their most sophisticated westernized author. They discuss Thomas Aquinas and Bergson, Dostoevsky and Camus. Jabra cannot resist the temptation of revealing his detailed knowledge of various aspects of Western civilization: from architecture and sculpture to painting, music, and literature. So intent is he on educating his Arab reader, almost in the didactic manner of an early novelist like Yaʿqūb Ṣarrūf, that he feels the need to explain certain allusions in the course of ʿIsam's conversation with Luma by making ʿIsam unconvincingly explain the point to Luma, who herself talks about

Dostoevsky and T. S. Eliot no less than Ibn ʿArabī, and who therefore, one would have thought, did not need such explanations.

Jabra's next novel *al-Baḥth ʿan Walīd Masʿūd* (*In Search of Walid Masʿud*, 1978) is happily less cluttered with such allusions than *The Ship*, even though the characters still belong to the class of westernized Arab intellectuals. Here again Palestine forms an important, if not the most important theme. Although he by no means ignores completely the social and economic problems of the poor and underpriviliged in society, as is clear from his first novel *A Cry in the Long Night* Jabra concentrates on the predicament of the Arab intellectuals and their frustrated attempts to change reality and attain freedom and self-fulfilment, with Palestine becoming increasingly the point of reference in his world.

In Search of Walid Masʿud opens with the mysterious disappearance of the successful Palestinian banker, thinker, and author Walid Masʿud, who has settled in Iraq, and the discovery in his abandoned car of a tape on which he has recorded in a disconnected stream-of-consciousness manner fragments of his memories, mainly of his childhood, his jumbled thoughts and feelings about his insane wife, his love-affairs, his friends, male and female, several of whom are mentioned by name, his grief over the killing of Marwān, his freedom-fighter son, at the hands of the Israelis. The tape is played to his assembled friends at a party given in an attempt to decipher it for the benefit of Dr ʿAwaḍ Ḥusnī, who is writing a study of the vanished man. Walid has had an enormous impact upon the lives of his friends, men and women alike, all of whom, in common with Jabra's other novels, belong to the upper stratum of society and are mainly intellectuals: creative writers, journalists, artists, academics, and senior members of the professions. Using his favourite multiple-narrator technique Jabra allots separate chapters to different characters, in which they give an account of their reaction to one another and particularly to their vanished friend; he also assigns three autobiographical chapters to Walid himself. The result is a brilliant gallery of sophisticated Arab men and women, sufficiently liberated to form and have extra-marital affairs. The sex, however, is not pursued for its own sake, but either as a means of consolation for people afflicted with existentialist sorrows, or even as the passport to spiritual experience.

Towering above them is the character of Walid, who, although the novel begins with his disappearance from the scene, in fact dominates the entire work. Larger than life he is a Dionysian character of immense energy and prodigious talent. Of humble origin, as a child his talent is spotted and he is given the chance of an education in a Palestinian monastery, then sent on an educational mission to Italy to study theology. Despite his early spiritual cravings he gives up theology in Italy and works in a bank instead, gaining experience which prepares him for his later spectacular success as an international banker. He inspires deep feelings of loyalty in men and he is irresistibly attractive to women. His fate is not known for certain; some assume he has been killed, but his latest and youngest lover Wiṣāl is convinced that, disguised and under an assumed name, he has joined the freedom fighters in the occupied land and she even flies to Beirut to join him in the struggle. Walid is portrayed as the ideal uprooted Palestinian, free from the shackles of narrow ideologies, committed to freedom and liberal values, who puts his gifts, fortune, and indeed his life at the service of his homeland. (In fact such is the strength of the author's Palestinian nationalism that he makes one of his characters attribute all notable modern Arab achievement in art, thought, culture, and administration to distiguished Palestinians of the diaspora.) However, because of the centrality of the Palestinian cause in the Arab experience, Walid also stands for the Arab intellectual, who despite physical torture at the hands of authoritarian governments remains steadfast in his commitment to his ideal. Brilliantly and neatly constructed, the novel is written in a language of great poetic power, which describes admirably not only the beauty of natural landscape, but also the fine shades of feelings of the various characters, who in their search for Walid Masʿud are introspectively engaged in an arduous and painful adventure of self-discovery.

Even more impressive is Jabra's *ʿĀlam bilā Kharāʾiṭ* (*Mapless World*, published 1982) which he wrote jointly with another distinguished writer who until recently had settled in Baghdad, ʿAbd al-Raḥmān Munīf, a Saudi oil economist trained in Egypt and France. While in *In Search of Walid Masʿud* the character of Walid seems to attain mythic dimensions, in *Mapless World* the fusion of the mythic and realistic is more striking, and there is even an epic quality about the later work, which is probably the contribution of Munif. Just as *In Search of Walid Masʿud* begins with the mysterious disappearance of Walid, *Mapless World* opens with the equally mysterious murder of Najwā. At the end of the earlier novel the fate of Walid remains unknown, likewise the later novel is concluded with a report by the investigating police in which it is stated that there are more than one likely suspects with sufficient motive, even though the protagonist, Najwā's lover ʿAlāʾ al-Dīn Najīb, seems to believe at the beginning that he himself has shot her at her own behest. Amongst the many themes these two rich novels contain is obviously the metaphysical *angst* arising from the uncertainty of truth.

The events take place in the imaginary city ʿAmmūriyya, a name with strong ironic literary associations, but, we are told, it stands for any Arab city 'spoilt by easy money'. The narrator ʿAlaʾ al-Din Najib, a novelist and lecturer in history of art, a graduate of Manchester University, in his early forties, is madly in love with Najwā al-ʿĀmirī, the wife of his friend Khaldūn. In the past he has been politically active, but now he is more concerned with fundamental questions to which, according to his uncle, there is no answer, although, like most Arab intellectuals, he has been profoundly disturbed by recent tragic events, such as the 1967 Arab defeat, which he describes as an 'earthquake', and which seems to have impaired his sense of reality, making him unable to distinguish clearly between fact and fantasy. His family has been dogged by misfortune for several generations, some were possessed by a sort of madness. From his great-grandfather he inherited this madness, as well as an enormous appetite for life, particularly for women. Ignoring the advice of his closest friend, ʿAlaʾ carries on his illicit affair with Najwa in spite of the scandal caused. Although he continues to find her irresistibly attractive, he begins to be repelled by her hitherto unnoticed overwhelming desire to make money: he refuses to join her and her family in their financial schemes. In an attempt to liberate himself from his enslavement by her he develops a relationship with one of his attractive female students and he takes her to face Najwa in her cottage by the sea, where earlier in the day Najwa has insisted upon making love with him. But when they arrive at the cottage they find Najwa dead from a gunshot wound in the neck.

This is the bare outline of a novel rich in themes and conceived on an enormous scale with action moving boldly backward and forward in time, but without sacrificing either clarity or concentration. The passionate love-affair is vividly and sensuously described in erotic detail against a background of wider issues, ranging from the inevitable impact of the Palestinian tragedy and the Lebanese civil war to the place of the Arab intellectual in an authoritarian revolutionary society. The narrator's younger brother Adham, a dedicated freedom fighter in Beirut, makes the prophetic statement that the civil war will not be confined to Lebanon but will engulf the whole Arab world, and unlike the Arab–Israeli conflicts of 1948, 1967 or 1973, wars will be fought not by the Israelis, but by their agents, the Arabs themselves. The title of the novel *Mapless World* refers to the absence of any clear vision of the future for the Arab world: there is only a vague desire to change reality. ʿAla' himself and his intellectual friends lament the fact that once a revolution, the product of the intellectuals' ideas, has taken place the intellectuals themselves become marginalized by the new regime. In the course of the events, which are full of surprises and melodrama, the reader's suspense is constantly aroused and characters larger than life emerge, such as the narrator's uncle or the mysterious semi-demented figure of his aunt, whose mind is filled with superstitious thoughts about the devil and the wicked ancestor whom, in her view, ʿAla' resembles. She seems to possess preternatural knowledge and Cassandra-like warns ʿAla' against impending doom as a result of his relationship with Najwa. The novel is full of tragic irony, almost like a Greek tragedy.

Mapless World has clearly benefited from the co-operation of Jabra and Munif, an unusual phenomenon for two novelists to co-author a work of fiction (although we find a precedent in the history of modern Arabic fiction in *al-Qaṣr al-Mashḥūr*, written jointly by the Egyptian writers Taha Husayn and Tawfiq al-Hakim in 1937). The novel seems to contain the best aspects of the art of both novelists. Jabra's subsequent novel *al-Ghuraf al-Ukhrā* (*The Other Rooms*, published in 1986) is a much slighter, more cerebral work, an experiment in surrealist writing, in which André Breton is quoted to justify the author's dwelling on the subconscious of his character, the absence of logic being in the order of episodes and not in verbal structure. Described as a black comedy, the novel deals with the painful experience of the narrator, a young doctor who seems to be suffering from amnesia and hovering on the brink of insanity. In it the dividing line between the real world and that of hallucination and dreams is deliberately blurred and the concept of a person's single identity is seriously challenged.

ʿAbd al-Rahman Munif (b. 1933) is a prolific writer whose large output displays a high degree of originality and a remarkable variety of themes and structures, although nearly all his novels have several features in common, in particular the author's passionate concern for the freedom of the individual *vis-à-vis* an oppressive totalitarian regime (in fact, the only novel in which this does not appear as a prominent theme is *Qiṣṣat Ḥubb Majūsiyya* (*A Magian Love Story*), which is set in Europe and deals overtly with the theme of love at first sight, the narrator's romantic obsession with a highly idealized and unattainable Western woman).

Munif's first novel *al-Ashjār wa Ightiyāl Marzūq* (*Trees and Marzuq's Assassination*, published 1973) consists of two parts and a conclusion. In Part One Manṣūr ʿAbd al-Salām, a history lecturer in his thirties, dismissed from his university post for refusing to teach his students the official distorted version of recent Arab (and by implication Iraqi) history, is after three years of unemployment finally allowed to leave his country to take up the post of a translator for a French archaeological expedition in a neighbouring country. On the train taking him to this country, he meets Ilyās, a strange gipsy-like man with an almost mystic reverence for trees. Profoundly disturbed when he finds that the trees in his old yard have been cut down by the new proprietor, Ilyas spends his life restlessly doing a variety of jobs, the last of which is smuggling second-hand clothes across the border. Most of this part of the novel, which covers the time taken by the train journey, is devoted to Ilyas, slightly inebriated, narrating the story of his life to Mansur, who plays the passive role of listener to the strange tale of this Zorba-like exuberant man. In Part Two Mansur tells the reader his own very different story: a broken-down intellectual, a victim of political oppression, he tries to drown his sorrows and flee from his terror of the secret police in alcohol, daydreams, and sexual fantasies. The narrative takes the form of flashbacks and nightmarish memories from the time of his orphaned childhood to his unhappy love-affairs, both at home and abroad, and his imprisonment for his revolutionary political ideas. During his exile Mansur's behaviour while working for the archaeological team, shows signs of growing abnormality, until finally his mind is unhinged when he reads in a local newspaper the devastating news of the assassination of his friend Marzuq, a geography teacher who clearly stands for all revolutionary intellectuals at home. In The Conclusion a journalist relates what he has heard at his hotel about Mansur's being hauled off by the police to a mental asylum after being found shooting at his own reflection in the mirror in his hotel room. Here, in his very first novel, Munif gives a powerful portrait, the first of many, of an Arab intellectual, psychologically maimed or destroyed by a ruthless despotic regime for refusing to compromise his intellectual integrity. At the same time the ironic contrast between its two parts, the parallelism between the cutting-down of the trees and the assassination of Marzuq, the faint underlying symbolism of the events lend this novel considerable structural and technical interest.

In *Ḥīna Taraknā al-Jisr* (*When we Abandoned the Bridge*, 1976) Munif gives his oblique comment on the Arab defeat by the Israelis. It is a strange novel, set in a vague country that might be Iraq, in which nothing much happens: the protagonist, Zakī Nadawī, a solitary young man who suffers from an acute sense of personal and national failure, escapes from the boredom of his life by hunting birds, accompanied by his dog, his closest associate, to whom he confides his random thoughts and anxieties. He cannot forgive his Government for ordering him and other soldiers to abandon ignominiously a bridge which they had built with loving care, instead of destroying it before their disorderly retreat. His mind bordering on insanity, Zaki spends his time talking to birds, trees, and stones besides his dog. However, when the dog dies in an accident at the end of the book, he is suddenly flung out of his solitude and made to realize that people around him whom he has hitherto been shunning, share his feelings about the bridge and are only biding their time to do something, though we are not told exactly what. The intimate relation between man and animals, and the minute aspects, the joys and disappointments of hunting game, so admirably described here, are themes that will be further developed in Munif's later works.

Munif's *cri de cœur* denouncing political persecution is undoubtedly *Sharq al-Mutawassiṭ* (*East of the Mediterranean*, published in 1977), in which by way of preface he quotes several clauses from the United Nations Charter of Human Rights and uses as an epigraph lines from the Chilean Pablo Neruda's poetry. The novel consists of six chapters, narrated alternately by the thirty-year-old protagonist, the ex-political prisoner Rajab Ismāʿīl, and his older married sister Anīsa. It opens with a lyrical description of Rajab on board a Greek ship taking him to France for medical treatment for the serious illness he has contracted as a result of the torture to which he was subjected in prison over a period of five years and which eventually drove him to give in to his torturers and sign the required confession that branded him, especially in his own eyes, as a traitor to the revolutionary cause. While abroad he decides to resume the struggle and he informs the Red Cross in Geneva about this torture of prisoners in his country. The novel ends with his death after he has been further tortured and blinded on his return to his country: he has had to come back to save from gaol his brother-in-law Ḥāmid, who has been made to guarantee his return from France. In the end, however, Hamid is taken away from his wife and children for daring to reveal the cause of Rajab's death. *East of the Mediterranean*, which consists mainly of reminiscences of the past, interlaced with present happenings, is a most powerful indictment of the methods of torture employed by a police state, a remarkably vivid account of the destructive effect of political tyranny on the lives of innocent human beings while at the same time being an eloquent expression of man's unconquerable spirit. It stands comparison with the best-known works of a similar vein in Soviet literature. For obvious reasons of censorship the state east of the Mediterranean is not mentioned by name; it is meant to stand for any Arab state, but clearly refers in the first instance to Iraq.

One of the most original of Munif's novels is *al-Nīhāyāt* (translated as *Endings*, published 1977). Al-Ṭība, a fictitious village on the edge of the desert, in which there is an idyllic cohesiveness among its inhabitants and to which even its children, who emigrate to the city, remain loyal, is struck by severe drought, which drives its inhabitants to hunt for game in the desert. A group of visitors from the city descend upon the village for pleasure hunting and despite the growing scarcity of wild life, are welcomed by the local people according to the traditional code of hospitality. The visitors are given as a guide the strange solitary ʿAssāf, known for his unequalled skill in hunting and intimate knowledge of the desert. ʿAssaf reluctantly agrees to accompany the party, but only after he has warned the villagers against the folly of overhunting and thereby endangering their very survival. Driven by reckless greed, the party decides to stay longer in the desert, against ʿAssaf's advice; as a result of a sudden sandstorm they are lost and are found the following day by a rescue team, the guests nearly dead in their cars, while ʿAssaf, who has been hunting on foot, is discovered dead and buried in the sand, with his dog, also dead, shielding him from the vultures. The villagers feel they are responsible for ʿAssaf's death. His body is carried to the village chief's house where he is laid out with the grieving chief and other villagers keeping vigil overnight. They spend the time telling anecdotes from personal experience and folk tradition, including two stories from *The Book of Animals* by the great classical Arabic author al-Jāḥiẓ relating to birds and animals, wild and domesticated, pointing out the need to maintain the balance and harmony between man and the animals in his environment and showing an exquisite sensitivity and affection in describing animal and bird behaviour. The narrative, suspended during the telling of anecdotes, is resumed with an account of ʿAssaf's funeral procession, during which he is transfigured from an almost social outcast to a mythical hero whose death inspires the villagers with the resolve to get the city authorities to build the dam that has been promised to save them from future droughts. Alike on the realistic and symbolical levels *Endings* is rich in themes; besides underlining once more the uneasy relation between town and country/desert, it dramatizes the primordial balance and near mystical affinity between man and nature. It is yet another manifestation of Munif's originality of conception and execution: the different modes of narration, the 'pastiche' use of the classical literary tradition (comparable to the technique adopted by the Egyptian novelist Jamal al-Ghitani), the transmutation of the realistic to the magical, of the individual to the collective. The hunter and his dog of the earlier novel *When we Abandoned the Bridge*, where the interest lies in the inner world of the individual, has now become a metaphor for the collective world of a whole community.

Sibāq al-Masāfāt al-Ṭawīla (*The Marathon*, 1979) is set in Iran during the turbulent rule of Mosaddeq (1951–3), although neither Iran nor Mosaddeq is mentioned by name. The background is the events leading to the fall of Mosaddeq and the return of the autocratic rule of the Shah with the help of the Americans (and the British). It describes the machinations and the various subtle methods used by the British and the Americans to engineer the end of the Nationalist Government and the return of the *ancien régime*, but the novel is ultimately about human beings. The narrator is a British agent, Peter McDonald, a supporter and faithful servant of the British Empire, who displays the traditional Western prejudices against the mysterious East: the men, he feels, are wily, but stupid and sheep-like, to be despised and never to be trusted; the women voluptuous and sexually insatiable. It is an unusual novel, in that its main character is a European, and although by implication it condemns the unscrupulous methods used by the West to promote its own interests at the expense of the local people, because the events are viewed through the eyes of McDonald, a certain measure of sympathy is aroused for him as a human being. In spite of himself, his passion for the 'Oriental' woman Shirīn gets the better of him and his sense of personal failure, as a result of his ultimate rejection by the authorities in London, as well as his painful awareness of the decline of the British Empire (to which his devotion is absolute), and its supplanting by the crude and vulgar but rich and powerful Americans, are sensitively described by the author.

Munif's most impressive work to date is *Mudun al-Milḥ* (*Cities of Salt*, 1984–9), a work of gigantic proportions, consisting of five large volumes running to more than 2,400 closely printed pages (Volume I has been translated, as *Cities of Salt*). This marathon work has no parallel in modern Arabic fiction: not even Mahfuz's trilogy is comparable in length and epic breadth. Its main theme is the psychological dislocation and distortion which mark the impact of the discovery of oil and development of oil interests on the individual, social, cultural, and environmental life of the author's native country Saudi Arabia, although typically names of actual places or rulers are not given, but are to be inferred from internal evidence. No dates are cited either, but the period covered is roughly from 1933 to 1975. In many ways *Cities of Salt* is the summation of Munif's work, containing several themes and features of his earlier novels. *Al-Tīh* (*The Wilderness*), the first volume, covers the period from the beginning of prospecting for oil by the Americans to the celebration of the completion of the Trans-Arabian Pipeline. It begins with a highly idealized description of Wādī'l-ʿUyūn, a bedouin village, that lies on a caravan route, where people's uncomplicated lives are lived in harmony with the rhythms of nature and traditional caring values have reigned from time immemorial. It is a simple idyllic existence in which natural joys and sorrows are evenly balanced, to some extent reminiscent of the world we encounter in the beginning of *Endings*. It is a community of proud, dignified, largely unmaterialistic individuals with their own folk heroes, in particular the al-Hadhdhāl family, who in the past terrorized the Turkish forces of occupation. This peaceful existence is upset by the arrival of Americans prospecting for oil, but under the pretext of searching for water—something which arouses the suspicion and hostile reaction of Mutʿib al-Hadhdhal, one of the leaders of the community, who, endowed with uncanny prescience, feels that the Americans constitute a serious threat to their way of life. The local people view these foreign infidels, some of whom can speak a little Arabic and even quote the Koran, with total incomprehension. Amusingly enough their morning exercises are mistaken for daily prayers and their scientific notes concerning the rocks and soil assumed to be black-magic formulas. In the course of time al-Hadhdhal's fears are justified: trees are cut down, villagers are forcibly uprooted to make room for various oil installations, simple trade and subsistence agriculture are replaced by capitalist enterprise and industrial strife.

The Wilderness is a truly remarkable novel, with its own peculiar, almost magical atmosphere, so different from anything else in Arabic fiction. The narrator assumes the character of a contemporary chronicler with the consciousness of a local man, which enables him to present the changes in the environment brought about by modern technology with the freshness, wonderment, and lack of comprehension which mark the naïve vision of people cut off from the main stream of modern civilization for many generations. The Emir and his people view the miracles of new technology such as the telescope, the radio, the telephone, and the motor car, not to mention the oil drills and the electricity generator, with utter fascination, mixed with fear. But despite their technological innocence, they are fully human, with all the psychological complexities, emotions, and intelligence of men. And in the course of time innocence gives place to experience and with sophistication moral corruption creeps in. *The Wilderness*, which begins with a harmonious community, ends with the brutal suppression by the Emir's soldiers, trained by their American mentors, of a demonstration staged by the oil construction workers (who live in unpleasant housing conditions, separated from their families and fed on empty promises) against the redundancy of some of their men and lack of proper investigation into the murder of their medicine man. The novel is a moving lament on the destruction of traditional society and its replacement by the 'cities of salt', i.e.

ephemeral artificial creations lacking any roots and bound to dissolve into nothingness once the oil is exhausted.

Munif's prodigious inventiveness is seen, not least, in the endless procession of characters that move before our eyes, characters vividly drawn such as Mutʿib al-Hadhdhāl, Umm al-Ḥūsh, Ibn al-Rashīd, or Dr Subḥī al-Maḥmaljī, to mention but a few. Al-Hadhdhal, a man incapable of compromise, watches from a distance with tears in his eyes the first trees of the village being brutally mown down by the American bulldozers and angrily disappears into the desert on his white camel, armed with a gun, nobody knows where, and is gradually transported to the world of legend. He later, no less mysteriously, makes fleeting visits to the site of the vanished village without speaking to anyone, only to be glimpsed from afar. His haunting appearance strikes fear into the hearts of those engaged in working for the oil company and acts of sabotage are attributed to him. His figure, real or imaginary, runs like a leitmotif in a musical composition through the story and continues to be a source of inspiration in the people's struggle against the forces of corruption until the end of the novel. Umm al-Hush, pathetically driven to distraction because of the lack of news of her long absent son, is constantly calling upon the local hostelry and pestering every passing caravan with questions about him. Her sudden and moving death occurs significantly on the very day the community is forced to leave the village. Ibn al-Rashid, the proprietor of the hostelry, sees in the arrival of the Americans an opportunity to line his pockets, is subcontracted to provide labour for the oil company: he entices bedouin with false promises to come to Ḥarrān (i.e. Dhahran) to work for the Americans, buys off their camels (thus making it very difficult for them to return home), which he sells at considerable profit to the Americans, but he himself is ultimately destroyed by a bigger entrepreneur, al-Dabbās, and killed, largely by fear.

But it is Dr Subhi al-Mahmalji, later to be known as al-Ḥakīm (the Physician), who in the course of subsequent volumes emerges as Munif's finest character creation. Here he is introduced as a cynical Syrian physician, who resorts to lying and scheming, worming his way into the favour of the ruler, amassing a fortune for himself by setting up a modern private hospital, buying cheap extensive land, the value of which he knows to be rising to astronomical heights, and having a mansion built for himself and his family.

Al-Mahmalji's character is further developed in the second volume *al-Ukhdūd* (*The Trench*), where he is shown employing a mixture of diplomacy and subtle tricks, including a skilful use of his wife and children, to attain a position of great power as the trusted and indispensable counsellor to the Sultan Khazʿal (i.e. King Saʿud). Unlike *The Wilderness*, which consists of a large number of fast-moving vignettes, showing various aspects of tribal society, the pace of narrative in *The Trench* is slow, largely because it describes in considerable detail life under Sultan Khazʿal, including the beginning of the physical changes in town planning and the general modernization of the capital Mūrān (i.e. Riyadh), the building of wide streets, and the replacement of horses and camels by motorcars as status symbols to which were subsequently added large palaces. *The Trench* concentrates on the role of Dr al-Mahmalji during this period, giving a full account of his machinations, his ability through nepotism and corruption to appoint his friends and relatives to responsible positions at the Court and to set up his dishonest and opportunistic relations in lucrative businesses, to form large international commercial companies for import and construction so as to get rich quick, exploiting the locals' naïveté and fast-growing wealth, and the lack of serious competition, in short to turn the country into a jungle of capitalist enterprise.

Al-Mahmalji feels all along that he has been entrusted by the Sultan with the task of creating a whole modern state. He therefore sets up a system of secret police for security reasons as well as local journalism for propaganda purposes. The only thing that the state lacks in his view is an ideology, which he sets about trying to formulate on the basis of his own philosophy, which he calls the Theory of the Square, or of the Four Pillars, four being the sacred number to be seen in nature in the four seasons and the four elements (humours): the pillars are reason, heart, stomach, and sex. In the new society money and sex are the dominant values, particularly among the princes. *The Trench* lacks the tragic sense of *The Wilderness*, but it possesses satiric intensity in the masterly portrait of Dr al-Mahmalji, complete with his bogus philosophy of the Four Pillars. Ironically enough, despite his insight into human nature, which enables him to manipulate people, he is totally unaware that he is being cuckolded by his own highly sexed wife.

The Trench ends with the fall of Dr al-Mahmalji and his expulsion from the country after the deposition of his patron, the extravagant and much-married Sultan Khazʿal, during the latter's absence abroad on his honeymoon with his latest wife (Dr al-Mahmalji's 15-year-old daughter Salmā), and the Sultan's replacement by his brother Finar (i.e. Faisal). The third volume entitled *Taqāsīm al-Layl wa'l-Nahār* (*Division of Day and Night*) goes back in time and treats Finar's childhood and upbringing under the watchful eye of his father Sultan Khuraybit (i.e. King Ibn Saʿud), the founder of the Kingdom with the help of the British. The novel describes the role of the British (in the person of Mr Hamilton) in the early history of the Kingdom and generally reads more like a chronicle than a novel proper.

Much more accomplished as a novel is the fourth volume *al-Munbatt* (*The Uprooted*), which deals with the life of the deposed Sultan Khazʿal in exile in Baden-Baden and the estrangement of Dr al-Mahmalji. The latter loses his power and influence as a result of the persistent advice of the Sultan's family to dissociate himself from the Physician, who is regarded as the source of the Sultan's unpopularity and the disaffection of his people. Under pressure from his close relatives and his favourite and influential wife, the deposed Sultan divorces his latest wife, ordering her to return to her father, whereupon the anguished Dr Mahmalji decides to leave Baden-Baden immediately, accompanied by his wronged and humiliated daughter. They take up residence in a house in Switzerland where he sadly broods over what he feels to be his wasted life and his unhappy daughter commits suicide. He is abandoned by his son Ghazwān, who takes the side of the new Sultan Finar, and his wife, who joins Ghazwan first in America, then in Muran. Ironically enough in betraying him his son and wife are only applying the philosophy of life which makes money the be-all and end-all of existence and which he himself has diligently taught them. The slow and subtle development of Dr al-Mahmalji from a satiric portrait to an almost tragic figure betrayed not only by his patron but also by his own wife and son, makes him one of the major creations in modern Arabic fiction, to be compared only to characters like al-Sayyid Ahmad ʿAbd al-Jawād, the paterfamilias of Mahfuz's trilogy. The 'uprooted' of the title refers as much to him as to the deposed monarch, forced to live with his retinue in exile where he pathetically dies at the end of the volume.

The last volume, *Bādiyat al-Ẓulumāt* (*The Desert of Darkness*), like the third volume, goes back in time, dealing with the formation of Prince Finar, particularly the influence upon him of his English mentor Mr Hamilton, with his amoral modern version of Machiavelli's *Prince*. It is narrated at first in the form of memories ('Memories of the Distant Past' and 'Memories of the Recent Past'), then it traces Finar's reign until his assassination by his crazed young relative. Here the author resumes his very leisurely chronicle narration, interspersed with apt verse and prose quotations from classical Arabic sources as well as extracts from allegedly foreign journalists' diaries and correspondents' accounts of the general situation and catastrophic changes in the Kingdom of Muran. It gives further information about the recent history of Muran, such as the attempt on the life of Sultan Khuraybit, showing how Khazʿal's risking his own life to defend his father has led the Sultan in gratitude to declare him heir to the throne instead of the expected Finar, much to the disappointment of Finar and Mr Hamilton. It also shows the details of Finar's successful plot to oust Khazʿal. The picture painted is that of a jungle which is replete with greed, corruption, deception, and tyranny, in which men prey upon one another and summary executions are normal events.

Of the five volumes of this impressive work the most outstanding as novels are the first and the fourth, the first as a lament on the passing of the old order and the fourth for its tragic human interest. *Cities of Salt* has undeniably epic breadth, but it does not reveal the same poignant sense of time as Mahfuz's trilogy. However, it is pervaded by a distinctly elegiac tone, arising partly from the author's attitude to the manner in which the oil wealth has been used, or misused, by the desert Arabs, to the wanton and irreversible destruction of permanent, albeit meagre, natural resources of wealth in keeping with the recurrent rhythm of living nature and their attendant humane values and social harmony, and their replacement by impermanent structures, senseless consumerism, and capitalist greed and strife. Apart from his contribution to the Arabic novel of political repression Munif, with his sensitive handling of the Arabic language, his deep insight into individual human behaviour, and broad vision of history, has made his own the novel of the Arabian desert, which in turn has its own unmistakable atmosphere and distinct flavour.

*

We have discussed the work of some Syrian novelists in our account of the Lebanese novel. In fact it is not always easy to separate the two regions where fiction is concerned, since several Syrian writers moved to Lebanon where they settled, using Lebanese characters and setting in their fiction. However, it may perhaps be necessary for our survey to say a brief word about the Syrian novel as such. It was slow to appear. There is general agreement that Shakīb al-Jābirī's *al-Naham* (*Greed*), published in 1937, is the first proper Syrian novel and it is often compared to Haykal's *Zaynab*. However, *al-Naham*, a love-story, is set in Germany and its characters are all German. Likewise, its sequel *Qadar Yalhū* (*Fate Plays*, 1939), although its protagonist ʿAlāʾ is a Syrian medical student in Berlin who has an affair with Elsa, resulting in her carrying his child, is set mostly in Europe and is permeated by the spirit of European Romanticism. It contains descriptions of wild natural scenery, improbable events, and rather implausible characters. The hero, though an Arab, is a hypersensitive sentimental who is described by the author as suffering from *Weltschmerz*. Furthermore, the language of narration is far too 'literary'; obscure words requiring explanation in footnotes are employed. For a proper Syrian novel, with Syrian characters and setting we have to wait until Ḥannā Mīna (b. 1924) appears on the scene, a truly remarkable man, who as a child knew real poverty and deprivation and who had held a series of tough manual jobs before he turned to writing novels.

Mina's *al-Maṣābīḥ al-Zurq* (*Blue Painted Lamps* (i.e. blackout)) was published in 1954. Like Mahfuz's *Midaq Alley*, by which he seems to have been influenced, it is a fictional account of the effects of the Second World War on the lives of the (largely Christian) inhabitants of a poor district in Lattakiya, with an admixture of nationalist feeling against the French forces of occupation. Although it lacks the depth of Mahfuz's psychological analysis, it shows Mina's admirable power of observation, of recording details of the daily life and work of humble Syrians. The novel does not have a tightly knit plot, but reads like a series of descriptive sketches written in the manner of social or socialist realism, which shows the influence of the current translations of Russian literature, in particular Maxim Gorky, for whom Mina had great admiration. Despite the realistic description of details of daily life, the novel displays a romantic element in the presentation of its young hero and heroine: Fāris and Randa. As in *Zaynab*, she dies of tuberculosis while her beloved is killed in action in Libya, where he has volunteered to raise sufficient money to enable him to marry her. However, compared with al-Jabiri's language of narration, Mina's shows a remarkable maturity: instead of drawing excessive attention to itself, his simple language flows smoothly as a fit tool of narrative discourse.

Hanna Mina was to return to novel writing after a gap of twelve years, with *al-Shirāʿ wa'l-ʿĀṣifa* (*The Sail and the Storm*, 1966) and went on to produce a large number of works, which render him arguably the leading novelist of his generation in Syria, but of that more will be said later. In the mean time his first novel can be regarded as having started a trend of social and socialist realism which, inspired by the Egyptian example and translations from Russian, dominated the Syrian scene for two decades. Amongst the best known representatives of this trend were Adīb Naḥawī (b. 1924), whose *Matā Yaʿūd al-Maṭar* (*When Will Rain Return*, 1958), a novel full of direct political teaching, is in truth no more than a parable about the need for the peasants to rebel against local feudalism in the name of the ideal of socialism and Arab unity, and a celebration of the union of Egypt and Syria under the leadership of Nasser and the consequent arrival of land reform. Nahawi went on to write more developed, but no less political novels in which he lamented the dissolution of the union between Egypt and Syria and attacked the corrupt reactionary forces responsible for the 1967 defeat. In his description of the plight of the Palestinians as in *ʿUrs Filisṭīnī* (*A Palestinian Wedding*, published 1969) he resorted to the use of folklore and the supernatural. In *al-ʿUṣāh* (*The Rebels*, 1964) Ṣidqī Ismāʿīl (1924–72) treats the development of Syrian society and politics over the first half of the twentieth century, an ambitious undertaking, motivated mainly by the author's desire to point out the backwardness and political and moral corruption that led to the 1948 Arab tragedy of defeat by the Israelis.

Walīd Midfaʿī's (b. 1932) *Ghurabā' fī Awṭāninā* (*Strangers in our Homeland*, published in 1965) is a satirical attack on the tyranny of the male head of the traditional family. It describes, albeit rather superficially, the attempts made by the younger generation of a Damascene family, both male and female, to stand up to their father and lead their own lives. The family, however, is only the microcosm and the loss of freedom and individuality within the family is an expression of its absence from the State and society at large. The novel ends with the European-educated doctor-son driven to emigrate and another son, the narrator, a young revolutionary undergraduate journalist, being arrested in his home by the State security police.

In 1960 Muṭāʿ Ṣafadī (b. around 1930) published his influential novel *Jīl al-Qadar* (*The Generation of Destiny*), a highly rhetorical voluminous work pervaded by a mixture of existentialist thinking and Arab nationalism. The period covered runs from the last year of Shishaykli's despotic rule to the arrival of Nasser in Damascus after the union of Egypt and Syria. The hero, Nabīl, a student of philosophy at Damascus University, is portrayed as a highly idealized character: an intellectual *par excellence*, an accomplished violinist, and an active revolutionary, plotting with young fellow intellectuals to assassinate the military dictator Shishaykli. In every respect he dwarfs the men around him and is adored by the women with whom he has affairs in his search for an impossible mixture of absolute personal freedom as well as freedom for his people. This inordinately long novel employs every possible novelistic technique available from straightforward narration to diaries, the stream of consciousness, and interior monologue. The same themes are pursued in Safadi's second novel *Thāʾir Muḥtarif* (*A Professional Revolutionary*, published 1961), in which we meet the mixture of revolutionary Arab nationalism, sex, and endless philosophical discussion, inspired by French existentialist revolutionary thinking.

Despite their shortcomings these two novels had a powerful impact upon many young writers, both formally and thematically. The self-indulgent revolutionary intellectual, obsessed with sex and the search for meaning in life, became a common feature of many novels. Likewise, novelistic experimentation became the vogue, no doubt aided by French ventures into the new novel: it reached its extreme form quite early in the work of Walīd Ikhlāṣī (b. 1935), regarded by the scholar Ḥusām al-Khaṭīb as the undisputed pioneer of the *nouveau roman* in Syria. *Shitāʾ al-Baḥr al-Yābis* (*Winter of the Dry Sea*, published in 1965) is a series of disconnected episodes taking place in Alexandria, the only link between them being a dominant tone of sadness, rising to a tragic feeling of loss and futility, enhanced by poetic imagery. Events have the immediacy and absence of logic of dreams. The introduction to the novel, written by the distinguished short-story writer Dr ʿAbd al-Salām al-ʿUjaylī, explains how in the new form narration is subservient to atmosphere, chronological narrative or logical sequence are replaced by the association of ideas, the stream of consciousness, originality of expression, and poetic imagery. In his second short novel *Aḥḍān al-Sayyida al-Jamīla* (*The Fair Lady's Bosom*, 1968) Ikhlasi displays in his protagonist a mixture of revolutionary commitment, philosophical and existential anxiety about the meaning of life, together with a preoccupation with sex. Ismāʿīl, a middle-aged teacher in a girls' school, suffers from guilt feelings for failure to rise to the standard of his fellow revolutionaries who sacrificed themselves for his sake, and is driven by despair, in spite of his unexpected marriage to a rich attractive widow, to imagine himself being stoned for his treachery. The story is narrated unrealistically in a poetic style of considerable lyricism, with echoes from *Fi'l-Manfā* (*In Exile*, 1963) by Jūrj Sālim (b. 1933), an obscure Kafkaesque symbolical novella about a teacher with whom a woman falls in love, but who ends up by being stoned to death for a crime he has not committed. In both novels the themes include guilt and innocence and philosophical questioning concerning life and death.

In *Sharkh fī Tārīkh Ṭawīl* (*A Crack in a Long History*, published in 1969) Hānī al-Rāhib (b. 1939), who had begun his novelistic career with the publication in 1961 of *al-Mahzūmūn* (*The Defeated*), dealing with the changing and troubled attitudes of university students towards society, politics, and sex, the narrator Asyān, a student at Damascus University, is shown in relation to his friends and fellow students, male and female, particularly the latter, who include Palestinians and a Jordanian engaged mainly in discussion of issues, both national and universal, psychological and philosophical. Asyan believes that the nationalist cause is primarily the struggle to change the age-old mentality. The men use the existentialist/revolutionary vocabulary of the times, while the female students insist upon the males keeping their distance. Yet the men suffer from obsession with sex, even sex with prostitutes, which is described in idealized Lawrencian terms. There are quotations from and allusions to Keats, *Moby-Dick*, Van Gogh, and Freud and Marx dominate the intellectual scene. The tempo is slow, nothing much happens, with insignificant details from everyday life patiently recorded in the manner prescribed by Alain Robbe-Grillet. The author deliberately avoids action or event, stating that in modern writing there is room for neither action nor event, but only sensations. However, the last third of the novel becomes more lively as things begin to happen. Asyan, a ratiocinative, tough, self-centred, and at times ruthless young man, has an affair with a married woman, Lubnā, his Palestinian friend's sister, during her husband's absence on a Government mission in Moscow. He regards the affair not as adultery, but as an expression of freedom, of breaking a taboo. The affair turns into a love-affair and they decide to marry after Lubna has obtained a divorce. However, when the husband returns, she does not have the courage to ask him for a divorce and Asyan feels badly let down, his dreams of a new and liberated life shattered. The group of friends sadly break up: one is put in gaol for his attempt to overthrow the Government, another meets his death in the heart of Africa, a third emigrates to West Germany. The novel ends with the narrator's being rudely woken up by a neighbour, who breaks to him the shocking news of the Syrian military coup to end the union with Egypt. In his later work published in the 1980s such as *al-Wabā'* (*The Plague*) al-Rahib develops far beyond the confined and somewhat etiolated world of students, to embrace the wider aspects of society and the drama of individual human relationships, which he treats in a style combining the virtues of rich realism, the poetry of legend and the haunting call of the past.

Close to the early work of al-Rahib is *al-Zaman al-Mūḥish* (*Desolate Time*, 1973) by Ḥaydar Ḥaydar (b. 1936), which has no plot in the proper sense; the narrator as well as the other characters are Syrian intellectuals, committed Arab writers with existentialist sorrows which they drown in alcohol and sex, mixed with mysticism. They incessantly talk about literature and revolution and the need to rebel against the Third-World backwardness of the Arab world, with frequent allusions to Freudian psychoanalysis, Western and Russian writers, poets and composers. One character, Rānī, is a novelist writing what is described as 'a novel of Arab nationalism redolent of sex'. *Desolate Time* is written in a poetic style with the line between reveries and reality blurred and characters, particularly women characters, merging into one another in the narrator's consciousness. Towards the end the tempo quickens, murders are committed and the style acquires surrealistic density, the narrator's dreams multiply, turning into nightmares which reveal his disturbed personality as well as the malaise of the Arab nation, whose stagnation renders it powerless before the Israeli aggression. The novel has as appendices a quotation from Jeremiah, and a lengthy prose poem, a lament on the Arab people. As in al-Rahib's *Sharkh*, Haydar's message is that the salvation of the Arab world can only come by means of a fundamental revolution in all its institutions and attitudes and that the test of a genuine revolution is a change in sexual mores and attitudes to women. Hence the prominence of the themes of sex, adultery, and breaking of taboos.

Related to this group of Syrian novelists is the work of the Jordanian Ghālib Halasā (1939–89). He prefixes his novel *al-Ḍaḥik* (*Laughter*, 2nd edn. 1981) with two extracts from classical Arabic sources: *The Book of Songs* and al-Jāḥiẓ on the subject of castration. The main theme of the novel, the action of which takes place in Cairo, is the castration of the narrator, a Jordanian intellectual, whose passionate love-affair with Nādiya, a liberated Marxist Egyptian woman, gradually loses its ardour and finally disintegrates against the background of political persecution by the Egyptian State. Although the couple's intention to marry is not realized, the author gives explicit descriptions of their sex acts as well as the narrator's sexual adventures with other women. The form is rather self-consciously experimental, the laughter of the title is sardonic and pathological rather than a spontaneous expression of genuine mirth and happiness. It is the narrator's only response to what in the final chapter is described as the terror of the world. In that Halasa's fiction resembles the wave of contemporary Egyptian novels of disillusionment and despair.

It is time now to return to Hanna Mina. His second novel *The Sail and the Storm* shows a striking development in his artistry. The same power of observation is amply demonstrated, this time of the sea and seamen's life, which will become one of his favourite subjects. But the novel is better structured, despite its length and excessive discussion of Syrian politics by secondary characters with whom the reader is not emotionally involved. Unlike the first novel it is conceived more like an epic: the protagonist, al-Ṭurūsī, is a larger-than-life character, but vividly drawn, with his love of the sea, his tenacity, his attachment to his mistress and friends, his mixture of kindness and ruthlessness. Through three fights against great odds he establishes his authority, revealing his heroic stature, his sheer physical prowess and extraordinary courage. Having lost his ship in a storm, Turusi, a born seaman, cannot bear to be away from the sea, so he sets up a café in Lattakia harbour where he is exposed to the dangerous effects of the ruthless rivalry between corrupt capitalist factions who have torn the community apart, and who use thugs to protect their interests. At the beginning of the novel one such thug is employed to ensure Turusi's subordination to the capitalist employer and prevent any concerted action by the workers. In the fight Turusi scores a spectacular victory which soon wins him the admiration and loyalty of most, particularly the poor dockers. Turusi later pits himself against the power of the sea by rescuing his friend Raḥmūnī from his sinking ship in the midst of a raging storm. In a flashback Turusi is shown scoring another victory abroad on behalf of fellow Arab seamen against an Italian sailor. Thus Turusi's almost legendary heroism is established not only through his victory over the sea, but also his championship of the Arabs and of the poorer classes. Before he returns to the sea as captain of his partly owned ship at the end, thus realizing his ten-year-old ambition, he contributes to the nationalist struggle against the French forces of occupation by smuggling arms to the guerrilla fighters.

The protagonist of the next novel also goes through a series of painful trials before he fulfils himself. In *Al-Thalj Ya'tī min al Nāfidha* (*Snow Comes From the Window*, published 1969) Fayyāḍ a writer, wanted by the Syrian authorities for his revolutionary socialist views, flees to Lebanon where he continues to be hunted by the police, and is sheltered by several Lebanese friends of similar political views. To escape the attention of the authorities he does a number of arduous manual jobs until finally he is caught by the police, with his underground press and subversive writings, and put in goal for a while. The novel, formally more like picaresque fiction, ends with his decision to go back to Damascus, having realized that self-exile is not only a cause of his personal unhappiness, but an escape from his real duty, which consists in staying at home to conduct the political struggle, whatever the suffering this might entail.

The extent of the price that has to be paid by the true revolutionary is the theme of *al-Shams fī Yawm Ghā'im* (*Sun on a Cloudy Day*, 1973). Using an experimental method relying upon a mixture of realistic presentation and stream-of-consciousness technique, symbolism and folklore, Mina describes the rebellion of a young man against his rich semi-feudal home background on the political, social, and psychological levels. His rebellion takes the form of his turning his back on the bourgeois values of his wealthy landowner father who oppressed the poor peasants and collaborated with the French forces of occupation of Syria, his association with the poor and destitute, including prostitutes in the poorest quarter of the town, his dancing the folk 'dagger dance' which he has learned from his revolutionary tailor friend. The novel ends with the murder of the tailor on the orders of the young man's scandalized father, and the final rupture between father and son. Despite a certain amount of repetition it describes vividly the turmoil in the soul of the idealistic young man as he grows away from the intellectual stagnation, the moral corruption and materialism of the world into which he was born.

Mina returns to the sea for the setting of *al-Yāṭir* (*The Anchor*, published 1974) which bears some resemblance to *The Sail and the Storm*. The narrator is a huge and impressive Syrian fisherman of phenomenal courage, Zakariyya al-Mirsanlī. He kills a whale that has been threatening the harbour, but is tricked by the Greek owner of a tavern into giving him the contents of the whale's stomach in return for a barrel of wine. Angered by the realization that the contents of the stomach must include gold and egged on by his mates, Zakariyya, in a fit of drunkenness, rushes to disembowel the Greek. He then flees to the woods believing that the police must be after him for his crime. In the woods he leads a primitive, solitary life, living on the fish he catches, but eventually meets and falls in love with a Turkish shepherdess whose husband is away in Turkey. Due to a misunderstanding, she avoids him after their first meeting when they made love. However in the end they are reunited but only after he has barely survived unimaginable physical hardships, his first experience of love as different from mere lust having fully humanized him, presumably providing his turbulent life with the anchor of the title. The novel ends, however, with Zakariyya returning to the harbour to save the community from another whale, which he has heard is threatening the people. Basically a romantic story with a message, *The Anchor* is related by the protagonist in a manner which, despite the external physical adventures, concentrates on the narrator's inner world of feelings and thoughts, with considerable use of flashbacks. It is a unique work in modern Arabic fiction, which testifies to Mina's range and richness of imagination.

Baqāyā Ṣuwar (*Remains of Images*, 1975), described on the title page as a novel, like its sequel *al-Mustanqaʿ (The Swamp*, 1977) reads more like an autobiography, written from a child's point of view, than a clearly structured work of fiction. As autobiographical writing both books make fascinating reading on account of the wealth of sociological details they afford of Syrian life, manners and customs, and politics, particularly the suffering and near starvation of the poor prior to and during the Great Depression, an account obviously based on the author's first-hand experience. The second volume ends with the departure of the narrator's family, while he is still a youth, from Alexandretta after it has been annexed by Turkey. The books contain several memorable and vividly painted portraits such as that of the weak, alcoholic father and his mistresses; the prostitute with a heart of gold; the saintly, self-effacing mother who, though illiterate like her spouse, insists on sending her son to school, incurring thereby appalling hardships; the sensitive young schoolboy, facing countless embarrassing and humiliating situations on account of his poverty, avoiding coming out top of his class, despite his academic brilliance, to save himself from appearing in the limelight in his tattered clothes. The author also provides profoundly moving descriptions of cruelty and persecution by the authorities, unimaginable suffering, poverty, disease, and death as well as scenes of great moral and physical courage and heroism. Mina deals with more recent history in his *al-Marṣad* (*The Observation Tower*, 1980), which is really a celebration of the heroic struggle put up by Syrian forces in the Golan Heights during the 1973 Arab–Israeli war and a condemnation of what is regarded as Sadat's treachery in ordering a cease-fire on the southern front of Sinai. *The Observation Tower* is somewhat vitiated by its overt political propaganda.

A much purer work of the imagination is Mina's trilogy *Ḥikāyat Baḥḥār* (*A Seaman's Tale*) written between 1980 and 1983. Volume I, *Hikayat Bahhar*, opens with Saʿīd, a seaman in his fifties, leading a group of seaside holiday-makers. In a series of flashbacks he goes over his past feats as a swimmer, but most of the novel is about Saʿid's father, also a seaman, larger than life, performing heroic deeds against the background of Arab nationalist struggle, first against the Turks, then against the French. There is a strong erotic component not only in the accounts of the seamen's love-making, but also in the strikingly sexual imagery in which the sea itself is described. As in much of Mina's work, the two main themes of the sea and women are closely intertwined, both as potent life symbols. Structurally the novel consists of several interesting episodes, memories of the past loosely strung together. In Volume II (*al-Daqal* (*The Mast*)), the narrator in the beginning is not the omniscient author, but Saʿid himself. The story begins where the first volume ends, namely with Saʿid's brave attempt to retrieve the body of what was thought to be his dead father from the sunken ship which was used for smuggling arms for nationalist guerrillas fighting the French. Saʿid discovers that the corpse is that of some other seaman and he is punished by the French authorities and sentenced to three years' imprisonment. The omniscient author returns and thenceforth the narrative alternates between the author and the protagonist. Memories of the prison experience are mixed with those of Saʿid's first sexual encounters, with Katherine, the ex-mistress of his father, who is now married to his captain. The volume ends with a vivid description of a sea storm leading to abandonment of the ship, on which Saʿid serves as seaman and whose owner and captain is his sexual rival. Only the captain remains on board after he has treacherously cut off the rope to the lifeboat for Saʿid, both men facing what seems to be certain death.

In the last volume, *al-Marfa' al-Baʿīd* (*The Distant Port*) (the title refers to a Latin-American port, where the seaman witnessed an anti-Government demonstration led by a young woman, ending in violence) the narrator is Saʿid throughout. The main theme is Saʿid's fruitless search for his missing father in his compulsive sea wandering as well as his equally unsuccessful attempts to free himself from his enslavement by the sexually insatiable and much-married ex-mistress of his father, who in the end discards him and marries a Greek captain with whom she emigrates to Athens. Saʿid's sense of failure in living up to the example set by his father after several years of sailing round the world, his feeling of guilt for having betrayed his father with his mistress, his morbid obsession with her, his long unemployment because of his political views, all eventually lead to his nervous breakdown. The novel ends with Saʿid, as a result of a hallucinatory vision, sailing yet again in search of his father. It is a story of a mind teetering on the brink of insanity, rich in Freudian implications.

Mina's last novel to be considered here *al-Rabīʿ wa'l-Kharīf* (*Spring and Autumn*, written in 1984) belongs to some extent to the tradition of the 'romantic' encounter between East and West: it attempts to describe the suffering of exile. The protagonist, Karam, aged forty, is a Marxist Syrian novelist, self-exiled, first in China and now in Hungary, earning his living as a university lecturer in Arabic and desperately trying to write a novel about the suffering of exile undergone by an author. He has affairs with two European women (one a twenty-year-old student, hence the title), but feels dried up and incapable of true passionate love. When the disastrous Arab defeat of 1967 occurs he goes to pieces and then decides to return home to Syria to take part in the struggle against the authoritarian Government. Ironically he is stopped by the immigration officers at Damascus airport, handcuffed and sent to detention as a politically subversive person. The novel is set in a highly idealized communist Hungary, in which Arab and Third-World students and refugees abuse the country's hospitality and allow the life of ease to blunt their political commitment. However, the main point is to show that exile has a paralysing effect upon an author's creativity and that an author's place is in his country where he should stay to pursue the fight for freedom and democracy—a message in some ways similar to that of *Snow Comes From the Window*.

In none of his works does Mina lose sight of his political message. However, it is to his credit that he does not always let the propagandist dictate to the novelist. The novels may suffer from excessive length and structural defects, but they are impressive by their wide range and the rich variety of their settings and indeed by their occasional epic quality. What is more they perform the basic function of a novel: namely to tell a story and create suspense. In many of them Mina concentrates on the drama and mystery of human relationships, creating in the process a gallery of memorable characters, unusual, damaged, and fascinating. Indeed, some are larger than life: they acquire their legendary dimension not only by their heroic deeds, but also through the author's increasing use of an adventurous novelistic technique and a sensitive, at times even poetic language, which help to create a powerful atmosphere, particularly in the descriptions of the sea. Mina is clearly the Arab novelist of the sea just as Munif is the novelist of the desert.

Iraq has still to produce a novelist of the calibre of its great poets or short-story writers. Indeed quite a few Iraqi novels have appeared since Dhu'l-Nūn Ayyūb (b. 1908) published the first serious Iraqi novel, *Dr Ibrāhīm* (1939) in which he painted a portrait of a thoroughly unprincipled opportunist who takes advantage of his higher educational qualifications and the weaknesses and corruption of Iraqi society under British occupation to reach the top and amass a fortune. Ayyub himself published later other novels, in which he either attacked the greed of semi-feudal landlords, who exploited the wretched peasants, or denounced the backwardness and lack of democratic institutions in the Arab world. Subsequent writers followed his example of using the novel to comment on the social and political ills of their society, writers such as Ghānim al-Dabbāgh (b. 1923) and Ghā'ib Ṭiʿma Firmān (1927–90), who in their turn were succeeded by a younger generation of novelists, more adventurous in form and technique, more deeply influenced by the modernist political-cum-existentialist novel in vogue in the rest of the Arab world discussed above. They include ʿAbd al-Raḥmān Majīd al-Rubayʿī (b. 1939) and Ismāʿīl Fahd Ismāʿīl (b. 1940), among others.

The protagonist of Rubayʿi's *al-Washm* (*The Tattoo*, 1972), for instance, is Karīm al-Nāṣirī, a young man recently discharged from a camp for political detainees after he has agreed to sign a declaration to renounce his revolutionary political activity. Psychologically damaged and incapable of forming real relationships, he finally decides to emigrate to Kuwait to start a new life. Karim is a familiar type in more recent Arabic fiction, a young revolutionary intellectual, frustrated, alienated, and obsessed with sex and the search for meaning in life. Al-Rubayʿi's treatment is somewhat pedestrian: it lacks the profundity and the poetry achieved by some other Arab novelists. As for Ismaʿil's work, despite its more skilful use of the modernist technique of flashback, interior monologue, and stream of consciousness, in it the political interest and the desire to render a faithful picture of a period of Iraqi history are often satisfied at the expense of the exigencies of novel-writing, such as deep characterization and clarity of vision. This is amply illustrated in his quartet of novels (1970–3), which give a vivid, grim description of life in Iraq in the 1960s during the brutal regime of the dictator ʿAbd al-Karīm Qāsim. After his sympathetic analysis of this quartet in his study *The Arabic Novel: An Historical and Critical Introduction* (see Bibliography), Roger Allen justly remarks: 'The author seems to allow his political agenda to insert itself too obtrusively into the narrative.'

It is arguable that the most significant Iraqi novelist to date is Gha'ib Tiʿma Firman, particularly in his *Khamsat Aṣwāt* (*Five*

Voices, 1967), which, however, is not without its shortcomings. *Five Voices*, which is set in pre-revolution Baghdad under Nuri al-Saʿid, has no single protagonist, but five main characters reasonably distinguished from one another, the five 'voices', which are treated in separate chapters, although they are brought together in the final chapter. They are a group of friends, young educated men: two journalists, working for a leftist newspaper, a poet, a well-read Government employee and a bank clerk. Suffering from boredom and sexual frustration, they indulge in alcoholic drink and sexual fantasies and meet in cafés and bars to discuss their literary ambitions as well as the social and political problems of the day, particularly the position of women and the need for the younger generation to assert their independence from their parents. The poet is a Bohemian rebel, who claims to be against not only the old traditional metrical forms in poetry, but all the values of a whole generation. A dreamer, he talks about Baudelaire to his favourite prostitute who is illiterate. The only narrative thread in the novel relates to the bank clerk, who, we learn later, was forced into an early marriage by his father. He hides from his friends the fact that he has a wife and children, whom he treats scandalously, letting them practically starve while he irresponsibly spends his income on drink and entertainment. His wife, however, secretly writes about her plight to his friend, the journalist who happens to run the readers' problems feature in the newspaper. Partly in response to his shocked friend's confrontation, the bank clerk eventually divorces his wife. The novel ends with the closure of the opposition paper on the orders of Nuri al-Saʿid, the journalists and the Government employee losing their jobs. The group of friends is disbanded: one journalist emigrates to Syria in search of employment, the bank clerk is rejected by the female colleague on whom he has had designs, becomes an alcoholic, and is dismissed by his bank, while the impecunious poet continues to lead his aimless Bohemian existence after he has been thrown out of the prostitute's room.

Although the author is a Marxist, the novel, which deals with poverty, sickness, and death, reads more like a work of Zolaesque naturalism than of socialist realism. It is a competent work that paints a vivid picture of a sick society crying out for reform. However, it is full of obtrusive literary allusions to Gogol and Gorky, Flaubert and Marcel Proust, Mark Twain and Faulkner. It is also written in a somewhat bare style without any particular felicities. On the whole, Iraqi fiction writers showed a distinct preference (and aptitude) for the short story rather than the novel, although it is also arguable that the most impressive Iraqi novel to date is *al-Rajʿ al-Baʿīd* (*The Distant Echo*, 1980), which was written by Iraq's leading short-story writer Fuʾād al-Takarlī (b. 1927); to my knowledge it is his only venture in writing novels.

The events of *The Distant Echo* take place in Iraq during the last days of the regime of the tyrant ʿAbd al-Karīm Qāsim, whose assassination occurs just before the end of the novel. Despite its sporadic references to Qasim's rule, *The Distant Echo* is not a political novel: it is primarily an account of the life of an extended Iraqi middle-class family in Baghdad, whose members, children, parents and grandparents, as well as cousins, all live together in the same house. The details of their daily life, their ritual-like actions, the communal meals in which they partake, the interests and preoccupations, especially of the elderly women, are all described in a leisurely and almost naturalistic fashion. The dialogue, of which there is a considerable amount, is written in Iraqi colloquial, which is a bold naturalistic device, but risks some unintelligibility outside Iraq. The characters are a closely linked group of people, forming a self-enclosed, claustrophobic world. The father, the head of the family, is virtually an invalid, looked after by his wife, who runs the household. The main characters are their two sons, a daughter, and a young cousin.

The older son, Midḥat, is a Civil Servant, a rather unfulfilled law graduate and unmarried, the younger ʿAbd al-Karīm, a university student still suffering from the shock of seeing his closest friend killed in a car accident next to him, which has robbed his life of all meaning and ambition. The daughter, Madīḥa, has moved in with her two daughters after her husband, Ḥusayn, an alcoholic journalist, has deserted them. The cousin, Munīra, a schoolteacher who has fled with her mother to Baghdad, to which she is in the process of being transferred, after having been raped by her wild, loutish nephew. She has kept her rape secret from everyone, including her mother, convinced that because of the loss of her virginity she has now lost all hope of getting a husband and leading a happy, normal life. Both young men fall in love with her, but she makes it clear to them that she cannot marry because of her illness, although she does not specify the nature of the disease. They are all in some way or other broken-down people, or as Munira tells ʿAbd al-Karim: 'all the people in their world are sick and deformed'.

After a hard struggle Munira, in a state of panic because of her secret, yields to the pressure put upon her by the whole family to accept Midhat's offer of marriage. However, on their wedding night, as soon as he discovers she is not a virgin, his world collapses around him: he flees in horror without saying a word to anybody. He lives rough, sharing the sordid lodgings of his brother-in-law, loses all desire to live, and is haunted by nightmares in which he sees himself killing his wife to wipe away the dishonour. Gradually, however, after considerable soul-searching and profound thinking about the harmful effect of the value society sets on virginity and the injustice done to innocent women, he learns to reconcile himself to the thought of going back to his wife. Ironically enough on his way to his house, he is shot dead by a sniper during the chaotic street fighting following the murder of ʿAbd al-Karim Qasim.

The Distant Echo is a powerful novel which demonstrates the author's remarkable powers of description and of creating atmosphere and tension already amply revealed in his short stories. It expresses a bleak vision of society, unrelieved by humour, a society populated by highly conscious individuals dominated by fear of death and a sense of failure. It is full of memorable descriptive passages, such as that of a dog run over by a car (paralleling the earlier killing of ʿAbd al-Karim's friend in a car accident), which leaves a deep impression on the mind of Midhat, or the visit to the sick and apparently dying Husayn in his sordid room by his deserted wife and daughters and brother-in-law. It is a craftily constructed novel: the events are related by different characters, each from his or her point of view; yet the novel builds up to a tragic climax. Suspense is masterfully created and successfully maintained. The reader suspects early in the novel that Munira harbours a sad secret, but it is not until half way through that the author reveals her secret, when the full horror of her rape is described. The main characters are portrayed in all their complexity, largely through their interior monologues. They are convincing individuals and therefore their behaviour and development are never completely predictable. The hopeless alcoholic Husayn suddenly musters enough determination to seek hospital treatment when he is gripped by the fear of dying. After a prolonged and painful process the conventional Midhat learns to accept his wife's loss of virginity and to see through society's harmful and inhuman fossilized attitudes, though he does not live to demonstrate to her his change of heart. Munira, who has borne her sorrow and humiliation in silence eventually becomes enraged at the thought of her husband running away without having the courage to say a word to her, and when, after his death, his brother professes his love for her, she turns away from him in disgust, accusing him and all around her of weakness and cowardice. She, far from planning to commit suicide as he fears she might do, is determined to go on and make something of her life. Although rape and loss of virginity are central to the events and politics have an impact upon the characters, at least in being instrumental in the death of Midhat, *The Distant Echo* is primarily not about social or political issues, but about the drama of human beings and herein lies its great merit as a novel.

In the rest of the Arab world, even in those parts which have made a late appearance on the literary scene, authors have been turning their attention increasingly to writing novels. In North African countries several names have impressed themselves on the attention of the literary world: the Libyan Aḥmad al-Faqīh, the Tunisians Maḥmūd al-Masʿadī and al-Bashīr Khurayyif, the Algerians ʿAbd al-Ḥamīd bin Haddūqa and al-Ṭāhir Waṭṭār, the Moroccans ʿAbd al-Karīm Ghallāb, ʿAbdallah al-ʿArwī (Laroui), Muḥammad Barrāda, Aḥmad al-Madīnī, Mubārak Rabīʿ, and Muḥammad Zifzāf, and the list is by no means comprehensive. Their work displays a wide variety of mode and style, ranging from straightforward traditional realism to the bold experimentation of modernism. In their different ways they explore aspects of modern Arab consciousness, the psychological stresses, the spiritual agonies, the political dreams and nightmares experienced by the Arabs, men and women, in their dramatic confrontation with the issues posed by the modern world. Clearly in this brief survey it would be impossible to deal with all these writers. There are, however, two novelists who have made such a distinct contribution to the modern Arabic novel that they merit a separate, albeit short treatment: the Sudanese al-Ṭayyib Ṣāliḥ (b. 1929) and the Algerian al-Tahir Wattar (b. 1936), both of whom are careful craftsmen who have not published a great deal.

Al-Tayyib Salih's work, his novels and short stories alike, shows an almost unparalleled unity of setting and continuity of character: the action nearly always takes place in the little northern Sudanese village of Wād Ḥāmid. The theme is often the conflict between town and country, tradition and modernity, East and West, and at a deeper level between good and evil, heart and mind. The events are enveloped in an atmosphere of mild mysticism and popular Islam and the action is not unusually intertwined with myth and legend, mystery and the supernatural. Al-Tayyib Salih's world is entirely his own, it is at once Sudanese, Arab, and African, described in a limpid style, rich in texture, poetic in its symbolism and suggestiveness and yet is of classical precision and economy. His vision remains unclouded; even when the events narrated are violent or melodramatic his tone is generally serene.

Al-Tayyib Salih is not a prolific writer: he produced only three novels, *ʿUrs al-Zayn*, translated as *The Wedding of Zein*, 1966) *Mawsim al-Hijra ilāʾl-Shamāl* (translated as *Season of Migration to the North*, 1969), and *Bandershāh* in two short volumes: *Ḍawʾ il-Bayt* (1971) and *Maryūd* (1977). *The Wedding of Zein,* which is really a novella, provides a picture of the close community of Wad Hamid, drawn with humour and irony but always sympathetically; despite their normal squabbles and petty jealousies the villagers form an integrated and harmonious society. Behind the apparent realism, however, lies a deeper spiritual reality and characters seem to have an allegorical dimension, sometimes indicated by their names. The main event around which the narrative revolves is the amazing wedding of Zayn, (Zein) an ugly buffoon, to Niʿma, the village beauty who has turned down all her rich and handsome suitors, a thing which the entire village found incredible, but which was predicted by the mysterious holy man Ḥanīn before his death. But both Zayn and Niʿma have other aspects to their characters: Niʿma, whose name means 'blessing', used to dream that one day she would make some great sacrifice, and she is drawn to Zayn who, she feels, as an orphan is in need of being cared for. Similarly, Zayn is more than the village buffoon: he is possessed of almost superhuman strength and clearly stands for the life force, *joie de vivre* and especially laughter, but, more importantly, he has been blessed by Hanin, who has performed extraordinary deeds for the whole community, which they regard as miraculous. The novella ends with Zayn disappearing during the wedding festivities, only to be found in the cemetery crying by Hanin's grave, so sorry was he that the blessed man of God could not attend his wedding.

The harmony that marks Wad Hamid is brutally shattered by the intrusion of an outsider in *Season of Migration to the North*, al-Tayyib Salih's best-known and most accomplished novel. It is a novel rich in themes, complex in structure, relying upon devices such as parallelism, juxtaposition, and contrast, sophisticated in narrative technique, with a brilliant use of stream of consciousness, a skilful handling of time, cunningly mingling past and present and developing character most vividly through flashbacks. It begins with the Narrator returning to his native village Wad Hamid after a seven-year absence successfully studying in England. He is happily reunited with his own people: 'By the standard of the European industrial world', he says, 'we are poor peasants, but when I embrace my grandfather I experience a sense of richness as though I am a note in the heart-beats of the very universe'. He notices, however, a stranger in the community, Muṣṭafā Saʿīd who, he is told, is a respectable man from Khartoum, married to a local woman, Ḥusnā, farming his own land and performing a valuable service to the community. Mustafa Saʿid arouses his curiosity, not only by his different manners, but also because one day, under the influence of drink, he proceeds to recite in excellent English several lines of English verse. Eventually Mustafa tells him his story, after extracting a promise from him to keep it a secret from the villagers.

As a young boy Mustafa, whose father died before he was born in 1898, was brought up by his mother who strangely enough showed him no real motherly feelings and to whom he was not attached. In fact, many years later, when the news of her death reached him in England, like the hero of Camus' *L'Étranger*, he remained completely indifferent. At a time when school was not popular, he chose himself to go to school and he did so well that his English headmaster arranged for him to continue his education in Cairo and the young boy travelled to Cairo all by himself, with a bundle of his belongings prepared by his mother, who showed no feelings at his departure. In Cairo he was treated kindly by an English couple, the Robinsons, and from Mrs Robinson, about whom he developed some adolescent sexual feelings, he received something of a mother's affection. After Cairo he was sent by his benefactors to pursue his study in England, where his brilliant academic achievement and his 'knife'-sharp intellect earned him a London University lectureship in economics. In England he was resolved in a calculated cold-blooded manner to make use of his exotic appeal as an African, avenging the wrong done to his colonized people by his conquest of the women of England, to whom he told fanciful stories and fabricated lies. To his African friends he used to say that he was going to liberate Africa with his penis. Three of the women he had affairs with committed suicide on his account and the fourth, Jean Morris, an elusive woman with a violent streak, with whom he was besotted, became his wife. The marriage proved to be a tempestuous affair, in which she was unfaithful to him, and he ended up by killing her. It was almost a ritual murder, mixing sex and violence: at her invitation he plunged his knife between her breasts, while she lay naked in bed, ready for him. Although he wanted to die to atone for the lie that was his life, at his trial at the Old Bailey, he was valiantly defended by his lawyers and ex-teachers, and was sentenced to seven years' imprisonment. After his release he wandered all over the world and finally settled in Wad Hamid, having decided to turn a new leaf and live like an ordinary Sudanese farmer.

After having been told this story the Narrator goes to Khartoum to take up his duties as a schoolteacher, visiting his village only during his holidays. Two years later he learns that Mustafa Saʿid has drowned in the Nile (though his body has not been found), having left him a sealed envelope in which he entrusts him with the task of looking after his wife, his two sons, and all his worldly goods. He has also left him the key to the one locked room in his house which none of his family is allowed to enter. The Narrator continues to keep an eye on his charges, but after a lapse of time he is approached by the village womanizer Wad Rayyis: he wishes the narrator to persuade Mustafa Saʿid's widow, Husna, to agree to marry him (even though Wad Rayyis is nearly forty years her senior). Reluctantly the Narrator broaches the subject with Husna, who immediately warns him that if she is made to marry Wad Rayyis, she will kill him and herself. This is exactly what happens when her father, who approves of the idea and is ashamed of his daughter's disobedience, forces her into this marriage. The grisly double murder occurs when, not being allowed to touch his new wife for several days and unable to contain himself, Wad Rayyis tries to rape her. The whole village is shocked at the murder and the two bodies are hastily buried without a proper funeral. At the news of Husna's death the Narrator returns to Wad Hamid, but nobody is willing to give him the details and circumstances of the deaths, except Umm Majdhūb, an unshockable elderly woman, who keeps men's company and shares their dirty talk, after he has plied her with drink. He is also told that he bears part of the blame, because he should himself have married Husna, as indeed Husna herself had informed his shocked parents that that was what she wanted him to do. The Narrator, though married, with a child, now apparently convinced that he was in love with Husna, goes to the locked room which he unlocks to find to his amazement that it is furnished exactly like the study of an English gentleman don, stacked with books in various disciplines, not a single Arabic work to be seen; it is a piece of England kept secretly in his house, a perfect illustration of Mustafa Saʿid's alienation and his indissoluble tie to the past. The Narrator also finds his papers and diaries, from which he pieces together the rest of the story he was told. Deeply disturbed by the experience the Narrator does not stop to finish reading all the papers, but rushes late at night to the Nile, takes off his clothes, and plunges into the river, apparently about to commit suicide. However, in the midst of the river he changes his mind, decides to continue to live at least out of a sense of duty, unconcerned whether or not life has meaning, so he screams for help at the eleventh hour.

From this brief summary it is clear how the lives of the two men, the Narrator and Mustafa Saʿid, are closely intertwined. At certain points in the story it is difficult to tell, even for the Narrator himself, whether Mustafa Saʿid really existed at all outside the Narrator's mind, or represented the Narrator's subconscious, his *alter ego*. For instance, when he enters the secret room he sees in the dim light the frowning face of the man whom he now calls his 'adversary', Mustafa Saʿid, but it turns out to be his own reflection in a mirror. While the themes of cultural conflict and misapprehension (on the part of both Saʿid and his European victims) are never entirely absent from much of the novel, it would be unfair to reduce it merely to a novel on the perennial theme of opposition between East and West. Besides the clash of cultures *Season* treats alienation, the imbalance of heart and mind, the question of identity, the relation between the conscious and unconscious self, and the nature of evil. Mustafa Saʿid is not just an African intellectual in Europe; he is an individual with a specific history, his character comes alive through a skilful use of his own words, his thoughts and memories, shreds of words said at the trial, of his conversations with his various women victims, all of which cumulatively contribute to build a vivid portrait of a tragically torn man, an emotional cripple with an overdeveloped, cold intellect, whose attitude to women has been determined in part by the absence of a father and the total lack of a mother's affection. His evil outlives him, resulting in part in the brutal murder of Husna and Wad Rayyis. In *Season* al-Tayyib Salih has written a novel which combines suspense and melodrama with depth of thought and profound psychological analysis to a remarkable degree. While betraying the influence of Conrad and D. H. Lawrence as well as Freud, *Season* is a genuinely Sudanese novel, the originality of which is beyond dispute. Because of its many layers of meaning, it has been subjected to varied interpretations.

A different kind of stranger to Wad Hamid appears in *Bandershah*, which we will, for lack of space, only very briefly discuss here. He is a more positive and mysterious figure, Daw al-Bayt (literally 'The Light of the House'), a wounded white soldier, suffering from amnesia, who has been swept by the Nile waves onto the banks of Wad Hamid. He is nursed, cured, circumcised, and converted to Islam and is then married to the girl who has nursed him. He becomes a successful farmer and contributes significantly in many ways to the development of the village, bringing in new goods and introducing new crops from his wide travels. One day however, he disappears in the Nile, just as mysteriously as he appeared, and his disappearance is described in mystical language. But he leaves behind his blessed progeny: his son Bandershah, who fathers Maryud, who is said by all to bear an uncanny resemblance to his legendary grandfather. In many ways we are back in the world of *The Wedding of Zein*, only two decades later, with the younger generation taking over from the old, bringing in modernization and its attendant problems. There is the same mixture of realism and legend, the same narrative technique relying upon flashback, which we have encountered in al-Tayyib's earlier works. *Bandershah* represents a later stage in the development of al-Tayyib Salih's vision of the microcosm of the world, Wad Hamid, a stage more strongly marked by mysticism. It contains some of the most lyrical and poetic prose al-Tayyib Salih has published. However, as a novel it does not possess the human density, the ambiguity and wealth of meanings of *Season*.

Al-Tahir Wattar made his mark as a novelist through his very first novel *Al-Lāz* (*The Ace*, the name of the protagonist), which was published in 1974 although we must remember that it took him, as he says in the Introduction, seven years to write (1965–72). In the same Introduction he claims that he is no historian, but a novelist, contemplating a stage in the history of his country's revolution, stretching from the formation of the provisional Government of the Algerian Republic in 1958 until the appearance of dissension and conflict within the ranks of the Front for National Liberation. *The Ace* is not a historical novel chronicling the events of the Algerian war of independence, yet more than any history book it gives the feel and spirit of that war, the tensions it created, and the sacrifices it entailed for individuals, families, and social groups alike, as well as the barbarities committed in the name of ideology, be it imperialism, nationalism, or anti-communist religious fundamentalism. Considering the fact that Wattar, a self-professed socialist writer, took an active part in the nationalist struggle, it is remarkable that he managed to maintain a novelist's objective stance towards his characters and the events. Nothing is presented in black and white here: there are no perfect heroes or unredeemed villains, even though the author's patriotism is never in doubt.

The novel begins and ends with an elderly man standing in a queue to draw his Government quarterly pension, recalling with others the heroic deeds of the revolutionary martyrs, including his son, the main events of the novel being sandwiched between the brief beginning and conclusion. The form is experimental, the narrative is multilinear, the action shifts from the present to the past and vice versa, from the Algerian guerrillas to the camp of the French occupiers and their Algerian collaborators. Things are not what they seem: collaborators turn out to be nationalists in disguise; events take an ironic twist, having a logic of their own. Acts of horror committed by a self-seeking collaborator, Baʿṭūsh, under his commanding officer's orders (such as murdering one guerrilla's mother or raping another's, who also happens to be his own aunt), prove too much for the human mind to bear and drive him to a state of insane desperation, leading to his murdering his officer and blowing up the entire camp, thereby becoming a national hero. Al-Laz, an illegitimate thug, hardly out of gaol, hated by most, and enjoying privileges as a result of his homosexual relations with a French officer, turns into an important revolutionary, performing in secret a valuable service for the guerrillas. When his secret is discovered he becomes an almost legendary national hero, although the sight of his leader Zaydān, who, he learns in the course of the action, is his real father (he has been separated from him by cruel circumstances) being butchered before his eyes robs him of his reason. After Independence al-Laz roams the streets like an idiot, shouting all the time one slogan he learnt from his father. Zaydan, the second most important character, who managed to get an education in France, is the only intellectual among the guerrillas, many of whom are illiterate. He is a valiant and noble freedom fighter, but because of his refusal to obey the order from the Supreme Command to renounce his communism and despite his heroic achievement and his commitment to the nationalist cause he is slaughtered, together with fellow communists, Europeans who have volunteered to fight on the side of the revolution. The novel ends tragically with this execution, after the author has created a powerful and menacing atmosphere of mystery and suspense, marked by an ironic contrast between the niceties displayed by the communist intellectuals in preparing their statement and defence, and the brutality of the summary execution meted out to them by their executioners, who are not even prepared to listen to what they have to say. Alike in conception and in execution, *The Ace* is a work of considerable originality written in a simple language which at times rises to poetic heights.

Wattar's second novel, *al-Zilzāl* (*The Earthquake*, 1974), the only other work by him to be discussed here, deals with Algeria after Independence, with the achievements of the revolutionary Government and the changes brought about in social and political attitudes and values. Here too Wattar's originality is amply revealed. Instead of offering us a picture of the new society painted by an omniscient author, Wattar chooses to introduce us to the changes as seen through the disapproving eyes of one single character, Sheikh Bu'l-Arwāḥ. A wealthy landowner and teacher, imbued with the values of the *ancien régime*, Bu'l-Arwah, having heard of the impending land reform, returns after a long absence to his home town, Constantine, to give away to members of his family as much of his land as he can before the Government seizes it. As he travels round in search of his relatives whom he has not seen for many years, he is shocked at the changes that have occurred in Constantine since the departure of the French and at the extent to which his several relatives have one by one in their different ways embraced the values of the new regime. Horrified at the betrayal of all he has held dear, he wishes the city could be destroyed by an earthquake, similar to the one that struck it in 1947, and he repeatedly recalls the Koranic description of the horrors of earthquakes (in *Sura* XXII), which is reiterated like a *leitmotif* throughout the novel. The action of the novel lasts only the few hours of his visit to the city, during which his state of mind grows steadily and rapidly worse so that he finds he is lost in hallucination and is brought to the brink of madness. The novel ends with his desperate attempt to kill himself by throwing himself from a bridge, but he is saved by the police who take him to a mental hospital.

The Earthquake is a fine description of the mind of one man during a few hours on a crucial day, through a subtle use of the stream-of-consciousness technique, interior monologue, present sensations, and past memories, all rendered in a concise language and pregnant style, that has some of the depth, concreteness, and indeed the physical directness of poetry. It opens ominously with the protagonist's awareness of being overpowered by the smell of the place, an indication of his sharpened senses and his greater receptivity, foreshadowing his growing excitement, his consuming emotions, particularly of anger, building up in a crescendo of nightmarish hallucination, leading to his attempted suicide. Although the author's enthusiasm for the new society is unmistakable, because of his sensitive description of Bu'l-Arwah's state of mind, he manages to enlist our sympathy for him, despite our condemnation of his antagonistic attitude to the reforms brought about by the new regime. *The Earthquake* is a tribute to the broad humanity of Wattar the novelist, and an eloquent testimony to the high standard the modern Arabic novel has reached.

Practically all the novelists discussed here have written short stories which naturally embody the same ideas, proccupations, and attitudes as their novels, although they vary widely in the degree of their mastery of the different narrative technique required by the exigencies of the shorter genre. Some indeed excelled more in the short stories than in the novels; obvious examples are the Egyptians Yahya Haqqi and Yusuf Idris, about whom more will be said later. This also applies to the Lebanese Tawfiq Yusuf ʿAwwad, whose stories reveal deep psychological insight and a sensitive handling of the emotion of love and of family relations in the context of the opposition between town and country, together with patriotic love of an idealized beautiful Lebanon set against the desire for emigration. They also contain much social criticism, especially of the hypocrisy of self-professed men of religion. Likewise, this is true of the stories of the Syrian Dr ʿAbd al-Salām alʿUjaylī (b. 1919), with his keen powers of observation, developed no doubt by his medical training, his sensitivity, melancholy, and occasional irony, no less than of the work of the Palestinian Samīra ʿAzzām (1927–67), with her eloquent and moving descriptions of the suffering of the Palestinians, particularly of her vulnerable female characters whose idealism is crushed by the outworn values of a male-dominated aggressive world. Very few writers confined themselves to the short story: notable examples are the Egyptians Maḥmūd al-Badawī (1908–86), Yūsuf al-Shārūnī (b. 1924), Shukrī ʿAyyād (b. 1921), and the Syrian Zakariyyā Tāmir (b. 1931).

The writer who is commonly regarded as chiefly responsible for the development and popularization of the genre of the short story in Arabic is the Egyptian Maḥmūd Taymūr (1894–1973), who was a member of *al-Madrasa al-Haditha* (the New School) in the 1920s and who during his long and productive career published nearly thirty collections of short stories (in addition to his numerous plays and novels discussed elsewhere in this book). Something has already been said in Chapter 3 about his early stories, which he used to sign in magazines with the pen-name 'The Egyptian Maupassant.' These dealt with social problems, such as the greed, ignorance, and hypocrisy of the men of religion, the ill-treatment of women by their irresponsible husbands, the conflict between town and country, innocence and experience, the Arab variety of the Noble Savage. Both the setting and the characters are emphatically Egyptian. The characters tended to come from the weak and eccentric, the poor and the downtrodden strata of society and were viewed from outside, in a realistic vein with a touch of sentimentality, although occasionally the author succeeded in portraying a character's thoughts and feelings, bringing out the pathos underlying a human situation. Taymur's later stories (of the 1930s and 1940s) underwent a change. The emphasis shifted from social criticism and didacticism to preoccupation with chaste and idealized love against the background of beautiful natural scenery, as well as with the world of art and artists. Characters from the lower classes were replaced by the aristocracy, artists, and intellectuals and the opposition between the idealized country and the ugly town is greatly enhanced.

While the romantic and sentimental element in Taymur's work was continued in the enormously popular, but superficial innumerable stories of the lawyer Maḥmūd Kāmil (b. 1906), whose name became synonymous with the Arabic short story particularly during the 1940s, more importantly the realism of some of Taymur's stories was further developed in the work of many writers, of whom Mahmud al-Badawi is a good example. Al-Badawi began by translating Chekhov, but went on to publish no fewer than nineteen collections of his own stories. He expanded the scope of the Arabic short story considerably, not only by setting his action both in town and country and especially seaside towns and Upper Egyptian villages, but also by choosing his characters from minority groups such as gypsies and foreigners, together with the poor, destitute, and tramps. Among the themes he explored with great sensitivity are the relation between man and nature, be it the sea or the rugged Upper Egyptian countryside, man and inscrutable fate, human suffering whether it is caused by class divisions, poverty, and failure or by sex, which is treated both as a life force and a force of destruction. In dealing with the taboo subject of sex al-Badawi showed considerable courage.

But it is in the stories of Yahya Haqqi (b. 1905) and Yusuf Idris (1927–91) that we find the greatest achievements of the Arabic short story in Egypt. Haqqi is not a prolific writer: he published no more than half a dozen collections throughout his career, which began in the 1920s. He is such a meticulous craftsman that even his earliest stories show a remarkable maturity in structure, characterization, mood, and especially language. His later work is marked by a constant desire for experimentation: it is this openness to the new, both thematically and formally, that explains the great influence he has exercised on the younger generation of writers, whom he constantly encourages and who hold him in great esteem and affection. The setting of Haqqi's stories is presented in such rich detail that the spirit of Egypt breathes in them; this is done through the use of evocative language and imagery, often derived from the animal kingdom, which he observes with a keen and sympathetic eye. As a result his stories constitute a perfect example of the poetry of realism, with a hint of mysticism. With great ease and unlimited sympathy he enters into the minds of his characters, who belong to all the classes of society, in both town and country, and include children, women, men of all types and mental states, ranging from the mystic to the criminal, from the normal to the morbid. They are all painted not in black and white, but in their full complexity, their contradictions and foibles, their frailties and their strengths, their joys and their sorrows, their simple actions as well as their enigmatic behaviour.

Unlike Yahya Haqqi, Yusuf Idris was a prolific writer: he produced more than a dozen collections of short stories, besides a large number of novels and plays, dealt with elsewhere in this book. His very first collection *Arkhaṣ Layālī* (translated as *The Cheapest Nights*, published in 1954) established at once his reputation as a short-story writer, a reputation sustained and strengthened by his later stories with their rich variety of themes and mastery of structure; he was soon recognized as the greatest short-story writer in the Arab world. Full of social criticism in which his keen power of observation, aided by his medical training and boundless sympathy for the poor and underprivileged, not surprising in a Marxist, Idris's first volume represents much of his early output. This is characterized by a mixture of humour and pathos and a daring choice of the most expressive word, often a colloquialism, to bestow liveliness, credibility, and realism. Despite his political commitment, however, he refrained from pointing a moral, letting the situations and characters speak for themselves. Idris's earlier stories dealt with many problems of contemporary Egyptian society, such as over-population, child labour, extreme poverty in primitive villages or city slums, torture of political prisoners—all sensitively treated with an eye on the telling, moving detail and in a manner which shows deep humanity, psychological insight, as well as irony. As in the case of Haqqi, human reality is viewed here in all its complexity and not reduced to a simplistic formula. Poverty and deprivation lead a police sergeant to fantasy and debilitating daydreams and drive a servant woman to theft, immorality, and prositution, but they can also awaken a sense of family responsibility in a schoolboy. Sex figures prominently in Idris's vision of the world: it is a means of defining human relationships and generally unmasking hypocrisy, either enhancing the human comedy or shifting the balance in the direction of tragedy.

In his later stories Idris's preoccupation with sex continued unabated, but his vision grew darker, more sombre, and even absurdist and surrealistic, the emphasis being placed on the conflict between an individual, often a secretly damaged or vulnerable individual, and a hostile and menacing crowd or a cruelly indifferent institution. The style of writing became more economical, the narrative mode more experimental in its use of time, its reliance on the stream-of-consciousness technique, on suggestive imagery and symbol, with the line of demarcation between reality and dream (or nightmare) often blurred. In this respect Idris's later stories bear some resemblance to the work of more self-conscious modernists such as al-Sharuni and al-Kharrat. While dealing with basic human situations and psychological truths, Idris's stories, however, tended to have a further political significance.

Sex is also one of the dominant themes in the stories by the Iraqi Fu'ād al-Takarlī (b. 1927), which are among the most artistically accomplished in the genre. Full of suspense and tightly organized with a carefully painted setting and a powerfully evocative atmosphere, his stories often explore by means of a highly developed narrative technique the darker side of sexuality, particularly illicit sex, incest, and rape, themes which amply illustrate the author's courage in dealing explicitly with such a taboo in his society. Al-Takarli's treatment of the subject, however, is such that besides its inherent psychological interest, it is meant to reveal the pathological state of contemporary Iraqi society, with its social injustice, political repression, and brutality, issues which provide themes for many of his stories.

Like al-Takarli, Zakariyya Tamir (b. 1931), a self-educated Syrian worker of a poor background, has established himself as one of the major short-story writers in the Arab world. Tamir has been described by the historian of the modern Arabic short story, Sabry Hafez, as 'the poet of the Arabic short story *par excellence*' and that is not only because of his use of lyrical language, dense imagery, metaphor, allegory, and irony, but also because poetry 'penetrates every aspect of the narrative, inspires its structure, liberates the action from the shackles of realistic plausibility, and suggests a new logic and a different order' (see his chapter 'The Modern Arabic Short Story' in the *Cambridge History of Arabic Literature: Modern Arabic Literature* listed in section 2 of the Bibliography). Tamir's use of fantasy is therefore not an escape from reality, but a means of reaching a deeper level of reality and of probing the appalling inhumanity of man in the modern world. His work reveals a marked development in the exploration of the darker side of experience, a progression in the use of violence. The poor, unable to realize their dreams, resort to absurd acts of violence as the only means left to them to assert their rebellion, acts perpetrated in a folkloric and ritualistic setting. Shocking murders are committed to satisfy not only material hunger, but also a need resulting from a spiritual malaise. Particularly after 1967 the political dimension of Tamir's stories became more pronounced: they loudly proclaimed the author's unreserved condemnation of an inglorious and corrupt Arab world. In their nightmarish and violent vision they bear a close affinity not only to much of the poetry written at the time, but also to many of the novels of alienation and political dissidence, which were written in the wake of the shocking Arab defeat in the Six Day War and which we have discussed in the preceding pages. In an uncanny way, together they all form a harbinger of the tragic and bloody events that have swept the Arab world since then.

Part Three

Drama

6

Early Developments

THE birth of modern Arabic drama is well documented both in the Lebanon and in Egypt. Unlike other literary forms in modern Arabic literature, drama did not develop gradually under the impact of the West, but was consciously and deliberately imported from it wholesale by Mārūn al-Naqqāsh in Beirut in 1847 and Yaʿqūb Ṣannūʿ in Cairo in 1870. This is not surprising since in spite of a growing number of highly speculative attempts to prove the opposite, classical Arabic literature did not know drama in the sense of an established art form which provides an imitation of an action on a stage through dialogue in verse or prose by human actors. This, of course, does not mean that the medieval Arabic literary tradition was devoid of all dramatic elements both on the level of highbrow culture and of popular entertainment, elements which, as we shall see in the course of this chapter, went some way in determining how the imported form was initially conceived and in affecting its subsequent development, whether in structure, theme, or language.

The specifically Arabic form of *maqāma* often related the picaresque adventures of an eloquent rogue who lived by deception and impersonating other characters. Out of the *maqama* and probably under Far Eastern influence, the nearest approximation to drama in the sense defined above which seemed to develop was the shadow play, *Khayāl al-ẓill*, in which characters are represented by shadows cast on a screen by flat, coloured leather puppets held in front of a torch by a hidden puppet-master, who introduced the characters and, with the help of assistants, spoke the dialogue in a mixture of rhyming prose and verse, some of which was sung to well-known tunes. Although the shadow theatre was known in Fatimid Egypt, the earliest surviving shadow plays are the three works of the Mosul-born Cairo oculist Ibn Dāniyāl (1248–1311), which show a considerable measure of sophistication. In spirit and technique they are not too far from medieval Western drama such as miracle plays, moralities, and the *sotties* (the French satirical farces) and they definitely belong to the category of Fool literature. Although they have several features in common, such as singing and dancing and their interest in lower orders of society, structurally all three are different, ranging from a reasonably well-constructed plot to a loosely connected procession of interesting human types, and they can at times attain a remarkably high level of characterization.

The next instances of shadow plays which we encounter show that by the seventeenth century the standard of their writing had sharply declined and that the shadow theatre had definitely joined the ranks of popular folk entertainment, the work not of a single sophisticated author, but of several hands. There was no longer any attempt at subtle characterization or a well-organized plot, the dialogue was written in *Zajal* (colloquial verse) and was meant to be sung throughout. Other popular entertainments with a dramatic ingredient included the dramatic recital of medieval romances, such as *ʿAntara* and *Abū Zayd al-Hilālī*, by rhapsodes to the accompaniment of primitive string instruments, the relatively more modern Punch-and-Judy-like puppets of *Qaraqoz*, as well as what was known as *faṣl muḍḥik* (a comic act): a brief farcical scene relying upon mimicry with the bare minimum of dialogue, often with satirical intent. Mention perhaps ought to be made here of the annual ceremony of *Taʿziya*, celebrated by the Shiʿites (the followers of the Fourth Caliph ʿAlī), a kind of passion play in which, by a mixture of crude symbolism and naturalistic self-torture, the murder of al-Husayn, ʿAli's son, by the Ummayyad Caliph is re-enacted. This, however, never developed into drama, but remained an extension of religious ritual, and was more relevant to Persian than to Arabic literature, even though al-Husayn was to become the subject of many an Arabic play later on.

Both al-Naqqash and Sannuʿ were fully aware that they were introducing their Arab audience to a completely new and alien form of art. Marun al-Naqqash (1817–55), a well-to-do Lebanese businessman who knew foreign languages, had the chance in the course of his travels to see the European theatre, particularly the Italian opera with which he fell in love. In 1847 he performed with the help of members of his family, males in disguise playing female parts, and on a makeshift stage he had erected in his own house in Beirut, before an invited audience, *al-Bakhīl* (*The Miser*), a play he had written under the influence of Molière's *L'Avare*. He introduced his performance with a speech explaining to his fellow countrymen what drama was, in which he emphasized the civilizing influence of the theatre. After enumerating the various types of theatre arts in Europe, he went on to explain that he had opted for musical drama, because he believed that the Arabs, including himself, had a distinct preference for singing. *Al-Bakhil* was written mostly in verse in simplified classical Arabic and it contained many songs based mainly, but not exclusively, on well-known Arabic tunes. It tells the story of a father who, against the advice of his own son, is intent on marrying his daughter to an ugly, old miser because of his wealth and the plot consists of the complicated tricks the younger generation employs to stop this marriage. The play ends with the old suitor being stripped of all his wealth and the daughter marrying the young man she loves.

The favourable response with which *al-Bakhil*, with its plentiful action and lively and often farcical humour, met, encouraged al-Naqqash to write and produce two more plays and even have a proper theatre constructed, close to his house, after obtaining the necessary licence from the Ottoman authorities. *Abu'l Ḥasan al-Mughaffal* (*Abu'l Hasan the Fool*, 1849–50) easily the best of the three, written in a mixture of classical Arabic verse and rhyming prose, is based upon a tale from the *Arabian Nights*. Overhearing a merchant who wishes he could be made Caliph for one day to reform the world and punish all those dishonest people who were responsible for his financial ruin, Harun al-Rashid has him drugged and brought to the palace where he is made to believe he is the actual Caliph. To this al-Naqqash adds an elaborate love interest, and the action of the play consists in the amusing and intricate complications and misadventures in which the foolish and gullible merchant is embroiled, and which end in the virtual unhinging of his mind when, after he is brought back to his humble dwelling, he is no longer able to distinguish dream from reality. Together with the interesting portrait of this merchant, the play offers in his man-servant a character of enormous vitality and humour who has been compared to Scapin and the valet in classical French comedy as in Molière's *Fourberies de Scapin*. In the last play *al-Salīṭ al-Ḥasūd* (*The Sharp-Tongued Envious Man*, 1853), also written in a mixture of verse and rhyming prose, not all of which is meant to be sung, the protagonist is modelled on Alceste of Molière's *Le Misanthrope*.

The play has an exceedingly complicated plot, which contains several intrigues and disguises, duels, elopement, an attempted poisoning, stealing, and hair's-breadth escape. Yet besides its protagonist, it too offers a lively portrait in the resourceful character of the male servant. In fact, despite their loose structure and excessive padding, these first attempts at writing Arabic drama are quite remarkable, not least because of their author's powers of characterization and his lively humour.

To al-Naqqash goes the credit of not only being the father of modern Arabic drama, but also of determining the course it was to take for a long time to come, and that in two respects: firstly in introducing the element of singing and secondly in drawing upon the *Arabian Nights* as a source for drama. Although after his early death his theatre was turned into a church, as he had instructed in his will, al-Naqqash's family maintained this interest in drama. His brother published his plays in 1869 and his nephew Salīm performed them as well as his own plays, in a newly built theatre in Beirut where he had formed a troupe which, incidentally, included actresses. This troupe he eventually took to Egypt in 1876, attracted by what he had heard of its ruler Khedive Ismail's generous encouragement of the theatre, thus setting an example which many Lebanese and Syrian troupes were to follow.

Egypt had known theatres long before Salim al-Naqqash's arrival. During the brief French occupation (1798–1801), French troops were entertained by theatrical performances given (in French) in a makeshift theatre: the historian al-Jabarti left us in his chronicle a bemused account of one such performance. With the increase in the European population, as a result of the modernizing policy of Muhammad Ali and his successors, European plays and operas were often performed by visiting or local amateur companies before a Western or Westernized audience, in theatres built for the purpose. The most impressive of these was the Cairo Opera House, which Ismail had built in 1869 as part of the celebrations of the opening of the Suez canal. (The plan had been for the first performance of Verdi's *Aida* to be given in it, but because this opera was not ready in time *Rigoletto* was performed instead.) Among those who witnessed and even took part in such performances of European works was Yaʿqub Sannuʿ (1839–1912), a young polyglot Egyptian Jew, who had received part of his education in Italy where he had developed a passionate interest in the theatre, and who on his return worked as a schoolteacher in Cairo. Like Marun al-Naqqash, Sannuʿ believed in the civilizing influence of the theatre, and was resolved to create an Arabic theatre, apparently unaware of the efforts of his Lebanese forerunner. Interestingly enough the inspiration for both men was Italian opera and their work was strongly influenced by the comedies of Molière.

Sannuʿ formed a troupe out of his old pupils in 1870 and managed to arouse the interest of Khedive Ismail before whom he performed a show, now lost, which clearly involved complicated intrigues and disguises and much singing. The performance was attended by the Court, foreign diplomats, and local dignitaries whose enthusiastic response encouraged Sannuʿ to reconstitute his troupe and even include (non-Muslim) actresses. According to his probably exaggerated estimate he produced no fewer than thirty-two plays, with the result that the honorific title of the Egyptian Molière was conferred upon him by Ismail. It was not long, however, before Ismail withdrew his patronage, allegedly because of the playwright's implied criticism of the Khedive, in his play attacking polygamy. Whatever the reason, Sannuʿ was ordered to close his theatre and cease his dramatic activities in 1872. Subsequently he turned to satirical journalism and politics, becoming involved in the Egyptian nationalist movement.

Much of Sannuʿ's theatrical output is unfortunately lost, but what has survived shows clearly Sannuʿ's considerable talent as dramatist. Unlike Marun al-Naqqash, Sannuʿ did not use the *Arabian Nights* as a source for the plot of any of his works, but sought his material in contemporary Egypt, using colloquial Egyptian as the language of his dialogue. In the work of both dramatists love and marriage, money, and greed are recurrent themes. Where the plot requires the mixing of the sexes, for obvious reasons Christian characters are introduced. As a rule the main characters in Sannuʿ's plays are Levantine Christians while the minor ones such as servants and doorkeepers are Egyptian Muslims, whether they are Alexandrian, Cairene, or Nubians. His plays also contain much less singing than those of al-Naqqash. He informs us that before writing his first play in Arabic he had made a study of Molière, Goldoni, and Sheridan and indeed it is not difficult to see the influence of the comedy of manners and intrigue upon his entire work. Apart from two short pieces, one of which is a farce attacking polygamy, the surviving plays consist of six works, mostly half the size of full-length plays (as apparently it was his practice to put on two plays each evening). *Burṣat Miṣr* (*The Cairo Stock Exchange*), which satirizes money speculation, prearranged marriages and the foolish imitation of Western manners, revolves round the rivalry between two young suitors for the hand of a rich banker's daughter, which ends in the success of the good suitor (who is not after the girl's fortune) as a result of the machinations of his servant. *Al-ʿAlīl* (*The Invalid*) attacks quack medicine and the practice of parents forcing their daughters to marry against their wishes. *Al-Ṣadāqa* (*Fidelity*), a lightweight variation on the Griselda theme, depicts the strange way in which a young man tests his fiancée's constancy.

By far the two most impressive plays of Sannuʿ's are *Abū Rīda wa Kaʿb al-Khayr* and *al-Amīra al-Iskandaraniyya* (*The Alexandrian Princess*). These are not at all what one might expect from a nascent theatre, but are competent plays, which have more than historical value: the former is a delightful comment on the human comedy while the latter represents the first major frontal attack on the blind imitation of Western manners, which will prove to be one of the recurrent themes in Egyptian Arabic drama. *Abu Rida* deals with the desperate passion the Nubian servant Abu Rida has for the recalcitrant Nubian maid Kaʿb al-Khayr and the attempt made by their mistress, Banba, a rich young widow, to bring about a union between them, as well as with the successful manner in which the wily and cunning matchmaker-cum-saleswoman Mabrūka gets Banba to accept the offer of marriage made by her admirer, the eligible merchant Nakhla. *Abu Rida* is a well-constructed play with enough action to sustain our interest; all the necessary information is given indirectly through the lively dialogue, which is written in a most colourful type of spoken Egyptian Arabic that faithfully expresses the speaker's temperament, sex, origin, and station in life. The humour arises not only from the traditional linguistic sources, such as dialect, mispronunciation, and malapropism, but also from situation and character. In this play Sannuʿ managed to create two most memorable characters, namely Abu Rida, and more particularly Mabruka the matchmaker, who is strongly reminiscent of Umm Rashịd, the matchmaker in Ibn Daniyal's shadow play *Ṭayf al-Khayāl*.

In *The Alexandrian Princess* a prosperous Alexandrian merchant of humble origin is henpecked by his wife Maryam, a social climber and a snob, and is forced by her to adopt the outward form of the French way of life at home down to the minutest and most ridiculous detail. Maryam is determined to marry her daughter to a young French aristocrat and will not allow her to marry the young man of her choice, because he is a mere Egyptian and a commoner. The plot consists of the successful attempt, involving intrigues and impersonation, made by the young couple to deceive the mother and secure their marriage. Here the author exploits to the full the twofold source of humour, namely the sex war (eventually won by the husband) and the ridiculous aping of Western manners. *The Alexandrian Princess* is a skilful work which makes its point concisely without ceasing to be entertaining.

Sannuʿ's last play *Molière Miṣr Wa Mā Yuqāsīh* (*The Egyptian Molière and What He Suffers*), inspired by Molière's *L'Impromptu de Versailles*, the only play he published in his lifetime (1912), was obviously revised some forty years later, and despite the interesting light it sheds on his theatrical activities, represents a decline in his dramatic art. By employing rhyming prose in the dialogue he denied himself the full use of one of his greatest gifts, namely his ear for the colloquial, which helped him to write realistic dialogue and hence create convincing characters.

As far as dramatic technique is concerned the art of the pioneers Marun al-Naqqash and Yaʿqub Sannuʿ was not improved upon by their immediate successors. With the closure of his theatre Sannuʿ's plays were soon forgotten (they were only retrieved from oblivion by Dr Muḥammad Yūsuf Najm when he published them in 1963). As for Marun al-Naqqash, he had his followers in Lebanon (as we have seen) and in Syria, in the figure of the popular Syrian actor/dramatist Aḥmad Abū Khalīl al-Qabbānī (1833–1902). Like Salim al-Naqqash, al-Qabbani moved to Egypt in search of greater appreciation, where he produced Marun al-Naqqash's plays as well as others of his own. The work of these two immediate successors was marked by a combination of the dominance of love themes, a romance-like quality of events, a passion for singing and the desire to point out overtly the moral significance of the action. They adapted or translated freely European works: for instance Salim used the libretto of Verdi's opera *Aida*, and Corneille's *Horace* and *Le Menteur*. Al-Qabbani, although he knew no European language, wrote works based on Corneille, Racine, Victor Hugo, and Alexandre Dumas, as well as a large number of plays derived from traditional Arab sources, particularly the *Arabian Nights*. Both dramatists contributed towards the reinforcing of two strands in the growing Arabic dramatic tradition: singing and music as well as emotionalism and the predominance of the theme of love. Al-Qabbani's further contribution lies in his establishing the traditional Arab heritage as a rich source for the plots of plays.

These Lebanese and Syrian dramatists/actors/managers and their successors and Egyptian imitators with their various splinter troupes played a major role in the development of the Arabic theatre in Egypt, making possible the subsequent appearance of great acting talents such as Salāma Ḥijāzī, Jūrj Abyaḍ, and Najīb al-Rīḥānī, who contributed greatly to the popularity of the Arabic theatre. To meet the demands of the public countless musical plays were produced, mostly free translations or adaptations from Western works. It is interesting to note that the more serious dramatists such as Faraḥ Anṭūn, Ibrāhīm Ramzī, Muḥammad Taymūr, Anṭūn Yazbak, and even Tawfīq al-Ḥakīm began writing for this unsophisticated public. As the theatre became a more permanent feature of Egyptian urban life it came to be used for political ends, mainly in Egypt's nationalist struggle against British occupation. This intense theatrical activity may to some extent account for the fact that it was in Egypt that Arabic drama eventually reached its maturity in the second and third decades of the twentieth century. No doubt the fairly continuous history of dramatic or semi-dramatic popular entertainments in that country, from the early medieval shadow theatre to modern primitive farces, helped in creating a more receptive audience. At the same time the birth of modern drama in Egypt coincided with the rise and growth of Egyptian nationalism with the consequent drive to create a specifically Egyptian literature and drama in particular to give expression to the Egyptian ethos and character. With the movement of religious, intellectual, and social reform, a new concept of literature was emerging towards the end of the nineteenth century, which departed from the still dominant medieval view that regarded literature as polite entertainment displaying verbal skill and inculcating a moral lesson. Instead of a ruler or a notable the patrons of modern literature were the newly created secularly educated middle classes, who were increasingly expecting literature to reflect their contemporary social reality and indeed to attempt to change or reform that reality.

The search for Egyptian identity became the guiding principle of the serious dramatists, both in their theoretical writings and in their practice. For instance, Farah Antun (1874–1922) wrote that the need for drama to reflect contemporary social reality should be given top priority at the expense of historical drama or translations of European plays. As an example of *al-riwāyāt al-ijtimāʿiyya* (plays dealing with social issues), which he was advocating, he wrote his own *Miṣr al-Jadīda wa Miṣr al-Qadīma (Egypt, New and Old,* 1913) a play in which he tackled a wide variety of problems in Egyptian society, but which, however, despite several lively scenes depicting details of Egyptian life, was too didactic to qualify for good drama. Because he believed in the immediate relevance of drama to contemporary Egypt he faced courageously the problem of diglossia of Arabic in writing dialogue. His analysis of the problem shows critical acuteness, but the remedy he prescribed, namely the use of three levels of language, classical, colloquial, and heightened classical in the same play proved far too cumbersome. Ibrahim Ramzi (1884–1949) wrote six history plays, four social comedies, and two serious dramas, all of which deal with Egypt, past or present. For his historical drama he wrote his dialogue in classical Arabic, while he did not hesitate to use the spoken Egyptian for his social comedies and satires, convinced as he was that that is the proper medium for such works. The most articulate advocate of the movement of the Egyptianization (*tamṣīr*) of the theatre at the time was certainly Muhammad Taymur (1891–1921). He too was converted to the view that to write convincing plays, comic or tragic, about contemporary Egypt it was essential to use the spoken Egyptian in the dialogue.

It was in the work of this generation of Egyptian playwrights that modern Arabic drama reached its maturity. They completed the process of Egyptianization which began with the superb adaptation of Molière's *Tartuffe* in *al-Shaykh Matlūf* (1873) by ʿUthmān Jalāl (1829–1894). Ibrahim Ramzi was a prolific writer who translated, amongst other works, plays by Shakespeare, Sheridan, Shaw, and Ibsen. In his plays we find a surprisingly high level of sophistication in dramatic writing, which is reflected in the playwright's keen awareness of the exigencies of drama, including full stage directions coverning the minutest details. In *Dukhūl al-Ḥammām mish zayy Khurūguh (Admission to the Baths is a Lot Less Difficult than Coming Out of Them,* 1915) it can safely be said that

Ramzi produced the first fully-fledged truly Egyptian comedy. *Admission to the Baths* deals with the perennial theme of the opposition between town and country; it shows how the economic difficulties caused by the First World War drive certain poor sections of Cairenes to resort to cheating foolish country folk to eke out a living, as well as satirizing the malpractices of the courts of law. Set in a public bath in a poor quarter of Cairo, the play describes how the manager of the bath is driven by lack of custom to give up his job, and sell some of the bath equipment to buy clothes to smarten up his appearance so that he may take up the more lucrative job of 'an official false witness in the court of law'. His wife, Zaynab, prevails upon him to let her try her luck in running the bath herself with the help of the assistant. Chance brings them a village chief (*ʿUmdah*) who has just sold his cotton crop and has come to Cairo, laden with money, accompanied by his bailiff to pay homage to a high official. Despite his caution and his almost pathological fear of being conned by the proverbial tricksters of Cairo, he falls an easy prey to Zaynab who, spotting his weakness for women, uses her seductive charms and, with the help of her husband and the Assistant, manages to fleece him of all his possessions. At the end the horrified village chief is only too pleased to escape alive and the tricksters sing that 'in such hard times the poor have to live off fools'.

Admission to the Baths is so well written, so close knit, that not a word is out of place. Events are so well organized that we are never taken completely by surprise either at the turn of events, or the behaviour of characters. Action moves so fast that despite the fact that the play is not divided into acts or scenes our attention is never allowed to flag. Yet the characters are drawn in depth, particularly that of the wife Zaynab who, with her endless resourcefulness and remarkable vitality and charm, is surely one of the most memorable portraits of the Egyptian female of the traditional lower orders of society. The humour arises from a variety of sources ranging from word-play to situation and character, from popular devices and horseplay to subtle overall irony. Yet despite its hilariously comic effect the author never loses sight of his serious satirical intent.

Ramzi can also be credited with having written the first fully mature historical drama, *Abṭal al-Manṣūra (The Heroes of Mansura,* 1915). Inspired by the ill-fated Sixth Crusade of 1248 by Louis IX of France, it is an eloquent and subtle expression of Egyptian nationalist feeling and democratic aspiration. It is no accident that its production was banned by the British Censor for several years. The two main themes of the play are the heroic struggle of the Egyptians/Muslims to drive out the Western invaders and the successful attempt to curb the autocratic rule of the Sultan. Both themes were of immediate relevance to Egypt at the time. Yet the author's nationalism does not drive him to paint characters in black and white, but on the contrary his characters, who are sufficiently distinguished from one another, are complex human beings who act from mixed motives. The play is packed with action—fighting, spying, plotting, intrigue, and romance-like elements—yet it is well constructed and it moves in a clear line of progression with few melodramatic surprises. The style of writing is classical Arabic at its most dramatic: free from the bombast and hollow artificial rhetorical devices which often marred the verse and rhyming prose of the author's predecessors, yet at times rising to poetic heights. The poetic atmosphere of the play is enforced by certain ceremonial and almost ritualistic actions as well as by the use of symbolism, as in the game of chess with which the play opens, with significant phrases running like *leitmotifs* being reiterated at certain crucial moments in the play.

Muhammad Taymur, whose premature death robbed Egyptian drama of a figure that held much promise, wrote three full-length plays. *Al-ʿUṣfūr fi'l Qafaṣ (The Bird in the Cage,* 1918) is a domestic drama treating life in an upper-class Egyptian family; its main theme is the conflict between generations, particularly the tyranny of the head of the family, with the relation between town and country and the state of flux of the social values at the time as minor themes. Much lighter in tone and richer in humour is *ʿAbd al-Sattār Afandī* (1918), in which the situation is reversed—the tyranny is practised by the spoilt good-for-nothing son against his father—and where the setting is a middle-class family. It underlines the threat to traditional values posed by a veneer of Westernization which allows the erosion of parental authority, while exposing the evil traditional practice of forcing young women to marry against their wishes. The play is marked by its crisp dialogue and depth of characterization, although traces of *Tartuffe* can be detected in a couple of situations. These two plays met with little success on the stage, as they could not compete with the commercial theatre: they lacked the titillation of the cheap revue, what was known as 'Franco-Arabe' farce and the sensationalism of the popular melodrama. Dejected by his failure, Taymur concentrated on editing his periodical *al-Sufūr*, publishing a series of humorous but thoughtful critical articles on contemporary Egyptian dramatists, which constitute the best account of Egyptian drama at the time.

In 1921, however, he went back to writing plays, producing his best work, *al-Hāwiya (The Precipice). The Precipice*, a bourgeois tragedy, has for its immediate theme the tragic problem of drug addiction in Egyptian high society, but it is at the same time a plea for responsible relations between marriage partners in modern Egyptian society. Amīn, a wealthy dissolute young man, who as a child had lost his father and was therefore spoilt by his widowed mother, lives in the family home with Ratība, his superficially Westernized wife and his weak conservative mother. To his list of vices of drinking, gambling, and whoring he has added cocaine addiction, neglecting his wife and paying no heed to the advice offered him by his mother and uncle. He introduces his wife to his male friends as a proof of being a 'modern' man. His closest friend, who has been virtually stealing his land, begins to have designs on his wife as well, and he manages to invite her to his house where she nearly commits adultery but saves her honour in time, when they are disturbed. Believing that she has been unfaithful to him, Amịn tries to force a confession from her in a scene of confrontation, where she stands up to him and accuses him of being partly responsible for her behaviour. The shock of his discovery that she has been with his friend in his house, coupled with the deleterious effect of cocaine, prove fatal to him. *The Precipice* is a well-constructed play with all the characters vividly portrayed, particularly those of Amin and Ratiba. They both develop convincingly, but in different directions: Amin deteriorates rapidly, is driven to self-destruction by his self-indulgence, and his rebellion against traditional family values, while Ratiba grows under the impact of events from a spoilt, superficial middle-class girl interested only in frivolities such as women's fashions, to a more healthily liberated Egyptian woman with a sober realization of the duties of marriage who stands up against her neglectful husband, without any feeling of inferiority. Here Taymur certainly struck a blow for women's emancipation in Egypt.

The use of the spoken Egyptian language reaches truly poetic and tragic heights in an even more impressive play, *al-Dhabā'iḥ*

(The Sacrifices), written by the lawyer Anṭūn Yazbak and produced on stage in 1925. It is the most tragic work written in the colloquial in the first half of this century. The problems of marriage and the question of the emancipation of the Egyptian woman, are also among the themes of *The Sacrifices*, although the relation between husband and wife is seen here in the context of a mixed marriage (an Egyptian husband and a European wife). After a brief marriage to the Egyptian Amīna, Hammām, an Egyptian general, now retired, fell in love with and married the European Noreska with whom he has been living for twenty years. The second marriage proves a disaster but partly for the sake of their son (as well as a niece, who has been living with them after the death of her parents) he soldiers on. He regards his unhappiness as a divine punishment for having wronged his first wife. Now in poor health and in need of nursing he employs a nurse who turns out to be none other than Amina in disguise: she has been driven to take up nursing to earn her living. On discovering this the contrite Hammam decides to make amends, takes her on as a second wife, which as a Muslim, he is allowed to do. In an angry scene the enraged Noreska is declared divorced, the unhappy son is removed from her custody. When Hammam realizes that his son and his niece are in love he decides to send the girl away to be safe from temptation, a thing which drives the hypersensitive youth to suicide, and the shock of the suicide unhinges the niece's mind. At first, unable to face the consequences of his actions, Hammam himself contemplates putting an end to his own life, but the sight of his pathetic helpless niece makes him decide to stay alive to look after her. Just at the moment when the proud and authoritarian Hammam, now humbled by suffering, has decided to face up to his responsibilities, the irate Noreska, on receiving the news of her son's suicide, suddenly arrives and shoots him dead.

Despite the melodramatic sound of these events, *The Sacrifices* is a carefully constructed and sensitively written play. The events are so highly organized that more than any other Egyptian drama hitherto, it is permeated by tragic irony. The colloquial reaches such poetic heights that a powerful atmosphere is created, enhanced by the use of certain objects as potent symbols for the characters' moods and feelings. The characters are drawn in depth, they are complex and credible and are capable of enlisting our sympathy, not least Hammam who is a truly tragic character, painted in heroic dimensions. While raising larger issues about the need for the emancipation of Egyptian women, Noreska remains an individual whose feelings and suffering arouse our profound sympathy. Although *The Sacrifices* is set in a specific social context and deals with certain problems of Egyptian society, such as the position of women or the tyranny of fathers, it is primarily about human relations. It describes the destructive impact of the clash between the self-absorbed older generation upon the lives of the impressionable and sensitive young, who are often thoughtlessly sacrificed by their elders. No one who has read *The Sacrifices* can possibly doubt that Arabic drama in Egypt has definitely come of age. Compared with it the few Arabic plays written outside Egypt that have survived, such as the Lebanese Mīkhā'īl Nu'ayma's *Al-Ābā' wa'l-Banūn (Parents and Children,* 1917) or Sa'īd Taqiyy al-Dīn's *Lawla'l-Muḥāmī (But for the Lawyer,* 1924) are singularly immature works.

7

The Period of Maturity

THE Arabic theatre did not assert itself in Egypt without a struggle. Even when good plays were being written drama was generally regarded as mere entertainment and not as serious literature, and the theatre for a long time continued to be looked upon as a place of immorality with which no self-respecting man (or woman, for sure) should be associated. As late as the early twenties Tawfīq al-Ḥakīm had to hide the fact that he was the author of plays, and when his secret was revealed his scandalized father decided to send him off to Europe to pursue his higher legal studies in France (in 1925), in the hope that his absence might help him to break his link with the disreputable theatre world at home. It was not until the early 1930s that drama and acting acquired a modicum of respectability. This was due to the increasing number of well-educated and highly born young men who became involved in the theatres, either as authors, or actor/managers, together with the rapid growth of theatre criticism in newspapers as well as in several magazines, devoted to the theatre, which began to appear in increasing numbers in the 1920s. Of particular relevance was the interest taken in drama, ancient and modern, by the influential literary critic Ṭāhā Ḥusayn and his enthusiastic reception of Tawfiq al-Hakim's play *Ahl al-Kahf* (*The People of the Cave*, 1933), which he regarded as a landmark in the history of Arabic literature, since in his view it signalled the appearance of a fully fledged Arabic drama.

No less relevant was the fact that the great neo-classical poet Aḥmad Shawqī, who was regarded as the supreme poet throughout the Arab world, turned to writing verse drama during the last four years of his life. Shawqi wrote seven plays in all, six tragedies and historical dramas on Egyptian and Arab historical subjects, as well as a comedy inspired by contemporary life in Egypt. In them he used traditional classical Arab verse, with its rigid adherence to specific metres and often to monorhyme in each speech, a medium more suited to rhetorical flourishes and public declamation than the exigencies of drama, such as the subtle nuances of character or the half-uttered intimate thoughts and fleeting emotion which mark complex dramatic experience. The result is that in general his verse drama sounds more lyrical than dramatic and indeed some of the speeches, particularly from *Maṣraʿ Kilyūbaṭra* (*The Fall of Cleopatra*, 1929) and *Majnūn Laylā* (*The Mad Lover of Layla*, 1931) were set to music and have become among the most popular songs in the whole of the Arab world. Despite their defects, however, the mere fact that Shawqi wrote dramas, perhaps more than anything else, helped to render drama an acceptable form of literature in the opinion of many people. The Government began to send scholars on educational missions to Europe to study drama and acting. In 1935 the National Theatre Troupe was formed under the direction of the poet Khalīl Muṭrān, with the help of many distinguished men of letters. The first play they performed was al-Hakim's *Ahl al-Kahf*.

When al-Hakim appeared on the scene the main problem which had faced dramatists, and indeed modernist writers in general, namely how to produce specifically Egyptian Arabic literature, was gradually being resolved. As we have seen, Egyptian Arabic drama came of age with Ibraham Ramzi's comedy *Admission to the Baths*, and his historical drama *The Heroes of Mansura*, Muhammad Taymur's tragedy *The Precipice*, and Antun Yazbak's tragedy *The Sacrifices*. Making good use of the dramatic potentialities of either classical or colloquial Arabic, these plays, in their different ways, deal with genuinely Egyptian problems, be they political, cultural or psychological.

Al-Hakim's remarkably long career as dramatist, during which he wrote more than eighty works, spans over half a century, from the 1920s to the 1970s. This is the period which witnessed the full flowering of modern Arabic drama. While still a student, al-Hakim wrote for the popular stage musical dramas and amusing satires on current political or social issues, such as the British occupation of Egypt, or women's emancipation. During his stay in Paris, however, he learnt, amongst other things, to regard drama not as cheap, ephemeral entertainment, but as a serious form of literature; when he returned to Egypt, he was bitterly disappointed to find that the Egyptian theatre, which had been bursting with activity when he left for France only three years earlier, was for various reasons, economic, political, and cultural, virtually dead. It is true that, as stated above, when he started publishing his work in the early 1930s, drama was slowly becoming a respectable form of literature. Nevertheless, partly because of the world economic crisis, the Egyptian theatre world was shrinking rapidly, and only the popular commercial stage with its cheap diet of sensational melodrama and sexually titillating farce had managed to survive. The rift between drama as literature and drama as a stage performance was becoming ever wider. To his credit, however, al-Hakim resumed writing plays, both in the classical and the Egyptian colloquial, knowing full well that they were not likely to be performed on the stage in the immediate or near future.

The plays he wrote at the time already show a remarkably wide variety of themes and types, ranging from the comedy of manners, with an emphasis on the war of the sexes, such as *Sirr al-Muntaḥira* (*The Secret of the Suicide*, written in 1928) or the much underrated *Raṣāṣa fi'l-Qalb* (*A Bullet in the Heart*, 1931), which attacks materialistic attitudes to marriage and upholds traditional moral values such as loyalty and friendship, or dark comedies of social criticism such as *Ḥayāt Taḥaṭṭamat* (*A Wrecked Life*, 1930) or the fascinating one-act play *al-Zammār* (*The Piper*, 1930), in both of which the playwright is also clearly interested in probing into the psychology of his protagonists, the former being a study of failure and moral disintegration, while the latter is a charming and sympathetic delineation of the artistic temperament. To this period also belong al-Hakim's dramas of ideas, two of his best-known works. *Ahl al-Kahf* (*The People of the Cave*, written in 1928, but published in 1933) and *Shahrazād* (written in 1927, but published in 1934), in which al-Hakim puts forward his thoughts on time and place, art and life, illusion and reality.

The last two plays in particular demonstrate quite clearly al-Hakim's major contribution to Egyptian Arabic drama, namely the philosophical dimension he has added to it and for which he was partly indebted to the avant-garde European dramatists whose work he came to know in Paris, notably Luigi Pirandello. *The People of the Cave*, an elegant and well-constructed work of considerable originality, which displays exquisite sensitivity and humour, is based on the Koranic version of the Christian legend of the Seven Sleepers of Ephesus. It shows how only love and the heart can triumph over time, while reason and the intellect fail.

Apart from dealing with one of al-Hakim's favourite themes, namely the opposition between the intellect and the heart, the play is meant to illustrate his conception of the specifically Egyptian tragedy; this, unlike the Greek, which he believes represents man's struggle against fate, depicts man's conflict with time. In *Shahrazad,* which is more of a dramatic poem (with its own unique atmosphere) than drama proper, the action takes place after the passing of the thousand and one nights of the *Arabian Nights*, and it depicts the tragic results of man's attempt to live on the level of intellect alone to the total disregard of the emotions and the demands of the material world. To this category belongs a later work, *Pygmalion* (1942), a dramatization of the Greek legend, showing one of al-Hakim's main preoccupations: the relative importance of art and life, and the need to choose between them. Because of his constant indecision, Hakim's Pygmalion ends up both smashing his statue and destroying his own life.

In 1950 under the title *Masraḥ al-Mujtamaʿ* (*Plays on Social Themes*) al-Hakim published a collection of twenty-one plays of varying quality, mostly one-act plays which originally appeared in the newspaper *Akhbār al-Yawm* between 1945 and 1950. Apart from their lively dialogue, these plays have in common a keen observation of the social problems that confronted Egypt immediately after the Second World War. In them al-Hakim satirizes corruption in politics and the machinery of Government, favouritism, nepotism, abuse of power, war profiteering, the ugly face of unbridled capitalism, and the prevalence of materialistic attitudes, particularly in marriage. Perhaps the most impressive of these is *Ughniyyat al-Mawt* (*Song of Death*), arguably the best-constructed and the most skilfully written one-act tragic play in Arabic—a moving dramatic statement of the clash between the values of traditional peasant society where revenge, honour, and shame reign supreme and those of the educated urban class intent on modernization.

In some ways al-Hakim's plays, published after the 1952 army revolution, represent a new stage in his development. Although the difference in their political message from the earlier work has been somewhat exaggerated, it is a fact that from now on he came to be regarded as having effected a true marriage between the so-called theatre of the mind and the popular theatre, and indeed many of these plays were performed on the stage. Clearly al-Hakim evinced an enthusiastic espousal of the cause of the Revolution in the beginning. In *al-Aydī al-Nāʿima* (*Soft Hands*, 1954), he made a plea for reconciliation between the classes of society, in *Ṣāhibat al-Jalāla* (*Her Majesty*, 1955), he somewhat crudely attacked the corruption of the *ancien régime*. *Shams al-Nahār* (1964) is a Brechtian didactic play, preaching the values of work, egalitarianism, and the need for the military to respect the law. Perhaps the most successful were *al-Ṣafqa* (*The Deal*, 1956) and *al-Sulṭān al-Ḥāʾir* (*The Sultan's Dilemma*, 1960), both of which employ traditional folkloric elements and appeal to the intellectual and the common man alike. It is noteworthy that in *The Deal* al-Hakim made a bold experiment with the language of dialogue, resorting to what is called the third language, which, while retaining the basic rules of classical grammar, can with the slightest modification be made to sound like the colloquial on stage. He also tries to dispense with stage scenery by setting the action of all three acts in a village public square.

Al-Hakim's experimentation continued unabated. As a result of his later sojourn in France as Egypt's permanent representative at Unesco, he fell under the spell of the Theatre of the Absurd, and in 1962 he wrote his *Yā Ṭāliʿ al-Shajara* (*The Tree Climber*) which reveals some of its influence. Al-Hakim's fascination with the Absurdist technique coincided with his disillusionment with the cause of the revolution, clearly revealed in a series of works, full-length plays such as *Maṣīr Ṣarṣār* (*The Fate of a Cockroach*, 1966) and *Bank al-Qalaq* (*Anxiety Bank*, 1967), as well as gloomy one-act parables or allegories such as *Riḥlat Qiṭār* (*A Train Journey*, 1964), *Kull Shayʾ fī Maḥallih* (*Not a Thing Out of Place*, 1967). Their mood is best expressed in the message of *The Fate of a Cockroach*, which is a strange work, consisting of two deliberately juxtaposed plays: the grotesque and fantastical political world of the first play—a fable marked by the savagery of its political satire—provides the context for the absurd human relations of the second play. A society ruled by a cockroach king will end up making its individuals feel like cockroaches. However, al-Hakim seemed to have recovered a little from this mood of unmitigated gloom. His final comment was couched in the wry humour of the title of his last full-length play, *al-Dunyā Riwāya Hazliyya* (*The World is a Farce*, 1971), a lightweight pastoral fantasy. For a detailed analysis of the achievement of al-Hakim, who is without doubt the greatest figure in the history of Arabic drama, see my study *Modern Arabic Drama in Egypt* listed in section 5A of the Bibliography.

Al-Hakim's prolific output and constant experimentation tended to overshadow the more traditional work of two important writers who also wrote plays: Maḥmūd Taymūr (1894–1973) the brother of Muhammad, the author of *The Precipice*, and ʿAlī Aḥmad Bākathīr (1910–69). Although Taymur turned to writing drama late in his career and is mostly thought of as a novelist and short-story writer rather than as a dramatist, he wrote a very large number of plays, and some of the most interesting in Arabic drama. He often published his works in two versions: colloquial and classical, the latter clearly for the benefit of the non-Egyptian Arab reader. He first published (in 1941) a collection of one-act plays, predominantly satirical comedies in which the weaknesses and pretensions of the Egyptian upper classes are unmasked, their false respectability and their hypocrisy. This he followed with a longer play *al-Makhbaʾ Raqam 13* (*Shelter No. 13*), dealing with the question of social class and the extent to which it is artificially maintained, in a manner reminiscent of J. M. Barrie's *The Admirable Crichton*. In 1942 he published three vaguely historical plays (*Suhād, ʿAwālī*, and *al-Munqidha*), whose theme is romantic love, but their chief interest lies in the way he portrays his young women, which reveals a changing attitude to women: they are regarded not as mere chattels, but as persons in their own right, responsible for their own actions and to be treated with respect. It is an attitude more relevant to the modern movement of the emancipation of the Egyptian woman.

In 1943 Taymur published two of his best works in which he returns to the subject of modern Egypt, *Ḥaflat Shāy* (*A Tea Party*) and *Qanābil* (*Bombs*). *A Tea Party* is perhaps the best Arabic farce of a superior kind, a hilarious, though scathing satire on the follies of certain sections of upper-class Egyptian society, their trivial pursuits and silly quarrels, false values and snobberies, and particularly their blind imitation of Western manners. *Bombs*, which is more thoughtful than *A Tea Party*, is without doubt Taymur's greatest comedy: its scope is larger, since the action in it takes place in Cairo as well as in the countryside, and it has a wider range of characters, representing a variety of types from different social classes, both in town and country. The events take place during the Second World War, when there was fear that Cairo would be bombed by the Axis in the wake of the severe air raids on Alexandria. The play describes the antics of a prosperous Cairene family and their hangers-on when they flee Cairo to their country house only to encounter a typhus epidemic in the neighbouring village, and the threat of being placed in quarantine. Taymur skilfully manages to create a whole world with its convincing characters and an atmosphere, subtly evoked, which is reminiscent of Chekhov's plays. The dramatist's stance is ironic, characters are incapable of understanding either themselves or other groups, and the gap between the town and the country could not be wider. Yet the treatment is sympathetic and humane throughout.

Taymur wrote other plays on contemporary Egypt: *Kidh fī Kidb* (*A Pack of Lies,* 1951), dealing with the upper echelons of Egyptian society, but in a more cynical spirit, and *al-Muzayyafūn* (*The False Ones,* 1955), his only overtly political play, the theme of which is the corrupting influence of power in a corrupt society. He also wrote a large number of historical plays, the most interesting of which is *Ṣaqr Quraysh* (*The Hawk of Quraysh,* 1955), which describes the rise to power of the Umayyad prince who escapes the massacre of his family to seize power in Muslim Spain. It is better constructed than most and in its hero Taymur managed to create one of the most fascinating and memorable characters in modern Arabic drama, with his single-minded determination, his obsession with power, his relentless pursuit of his goal, together with his superstition, insecurity, vanity, and sensitivity about his physical defects, his complex and unconscious reaction to the incalculable suffering he had to endure as a fugitive, hunted by his enemies, his ambivalent feelings about women, and his fits of sentimentality.

As for Bakathir, he wrote his dialogue only in classical Arabic, and his enormous output encompasses a wide variety of subjects, ranging from Pharaonic history, ancient legend, and the *Arabian Nights,* to modern Egypt and Iraq. Much of it consists of historical plays, a very large number of which retell Islamic history in dialogue form, rather than drama proper. Unlike Taymur's plays, his tend to be structurally weak. But he created two most interesting characters: Al-Hakim bi Amrillah, the third Fatimid ruler of Egypt, the hero of *Sirr al-Ḥākim bi Amrillāh* (*The Secret of al-Hakim,* 1947), a fascinating psychological study of a tyrannical religious maniac, endowed with extraordinary sensitivity, who yet commits atrocious murders in obedience to his principles. The other character is the old eccentric, rich Turkish widow, Lady Julfadān in *Julfadān Hānim* (*Lady Julfadan,* 1962).

Unlike Bakathir, Fatḥī Raḍwān (d. 1988) wrote only a small number of plays, but they are of considerable interest. Although he wrote his early plays in classical Arabic, he tended to use the colloquial more and more in his later plays. His early work betrays the profound influence of al-Hakim, dealing primarily with moral and philosophical ideas, but his later work revolves around social and political issues. His mature plays are marked by breadth of outlook, basic sanity, and warm sympathy with, and sensitivity to, human failings, qualities which enabled him to rise above narrow political sectarianism and crude preaching and create complex and convincing characters.

Taymur, Bakathir, and Fathi Radwan continued to write after the 1952 revolution. But it was a new generation of dramatists who, together with al-Hakim, tended to dominate the scene. The Egyptian revolution, was in fact, a landmark in the history of modern Egyptian and Arabic drama. A remarkable revival of the Egyptian theatre occurred during the late 1950s and 1960s, following the mood of euphoria and optimism that swept over the country in the years immediately after the revolution.

The new dramatists were young men more eager to experiment with the form and language of drama than their older contemporaries, with the obvious exception of al-Hakim. They were less inhibited about the use of the Egyptian colloquial in their 'serious' plays, particularly as the new regime adopted socialist and populist slogans. The mood of optimism was expressed in several plays in which playwrights contrasted the hopeful present and future with the corrupt *ancien régime*. Writers seemed to turn spontaneously to drama instead of other genres, as the most suitable form in which to express their preoccupations and impart their message. Because of the banning of political parties and the consequent absence of free exchange of opinion, the theatre became, as it were, an ersatz parliament in which authors expressed their political views, often obliquely, particularly later on with the increasingly active censorship, the growing disillusion with the revolution, and anger at the crushing of the individual by a totalitarian regime.

Despite their intense nationalism these dramatists were open to foreign influences. Either directly or through translations they were introduced to the work of playwrights such as Ionesco, Samuel Beckett, and John Osborne, and they followed with avid interest the news of contemporary experimental productions on the Western stage, such as *Oh, What a Lovely War*. The two European dramatists whose works were most often discussed in the recently established influential monthly periodical devoted to the theatre, *al-Masraḥ* (*The Stage*), were Pirandello and Brecht, the latter as much for ideological as for artistic reasons. The interest they took in Western theories about 'total' theatre, theatre in the round, 'alienation', and the like, coupled with the deepening mood of Egyptian and Arab nationalism, led these new Egyptian dramatists to raise fundamental questions about the nature of drama and the role of the theatre in society, and to search for a specifically Egyptian and Arab form of theatre. They tried to establish their plays on the basis of popular traditional village entertainment such as *al-Sāmir* (a village evening gathering for singing, dancing, and story telling), or relate their work to medieval Arabic forms such as the *maqama*, or shadow theatre.

From the start the new regime was aware of the importance of cultural propaganda, and therefore pursued a policy which soon led to the flourishing of the theatre. The newly created Ministry of Culture and National Guidance set up palaces of culture and the General Foundation for Theatre and Music (1960), which established theatres, including an experimental theatre, encouraged actors, invited distinguished Western directors, and financed the stage production of plays, indigenous and foreign, classical and modern alike. It also founded in 1964 the *al-Masrah* monthly review devoted to the serious discussion of issues related to the theatre, together with two series of texts of plays, one consisting of original Arabic plays, while the other specialized in translations of masterpieces of world drama. One particularly significant development was the publication, on a regular basis, of the texts of plays recently produced on the stage: these included many works written in the Egyptian colloquial, a fact which helped considerably towards the acceptance of the colloquial as a medium for serious drama.

Critics are agreed that the appearance of *Il-Nās illi Taḥt* (*The People Downstairs*) by Nuʿmān ʿĀshūr (1918–87) in 1956 marks the beginning of the new wave. The play is characterized by a new note of harsh realism, of urgency and commitment, together with a bold use of the colloquial. Set in an apartment building in a popular quarter of Cairo, it contrasts the materialism of the self-seeking older generation with the idealism of the young who reject a secure but soulless life in favour of a more meaningful altruistic socialist future. The tragic failure of the Chekhovian character of Ragāʾī, the only aristocrat in the play, signals the eclipse of the old aristocratic order. The same combination of social and political criticism and popular comedy can be seen in ʿAshur's other works, which for a while he produced almost at the rate of one a year. The most distinguished of these is perhaps *ʿĀʾilat al-Dughrī* (*The Dughri Family*, 1962), in which, using a middle-class Egyptian family as a symbol for Egyptian society as a whole, he gives a vivid picture of the disintegration of society through lack of idealism and social responsibility and the pursuit of pure self-interest, thus revealing his disillusionment with post-revolutionary Egypt.

Social realism is also the hallmark of Luṭfī al-Khūlī (b. 1928), who provides a vivid portrayal of Egyptian life, together with naturalistic colloquial dialogue, but in his plays, such as *Qahwat al-Mulūk* (*Café Royal*, 1958), politics seem to be somewhat arbitrarily superimposed. Unlike al-Khuli, Saʿd al-Dīn Wahba (b. 1925), another playwright who used colloquial Arabic and who began by writing within the social realist school, concentrated on the Egyptian village, at least in his early work, but his sombre comedies gradually acquired an admixture of symbolism which at times attained considerable subtlety. Among his best known plays are *al-Maḥrūsa* (the name of an estate owned by the King, 1961) and *al-Sibinsa* (*The Guard's Van*, 1962), in both of which he portrays the flagrant miscarriage of justice under the corrupt administration of the *ancien régime*. The humour in them does not hide the author's indignation. In *Kubrī al-Nāmūs* (*The Mosquito Bridge*, 1963) the mixture of symbolism and realism takes a more subtle form. Nothing much happens in the play: near the bridge a young girl with the significant name Khaḍra (green, i.e. Egypt) keeps a little coffee-stall and dreams of an ideal husband/lover. On the bridge all sorts of people assemble and chat in the way they do in an Egyptian village, and are all waiting for something or someone. In spite of its interesting gallery of defeated characters the message of the play is not pessimistic: the author manages to create a powerful atmosphere of expectation: someone, possibly a redeemer, is sure to come.

ʿAshur's *The People Downstairs* was one of the two plays which had a seminal effect upon Egyptian drama, the other being *al-Farāfīr* (*The Flipflaps*, 1964) by Yūsuf Idrīs (1927–91), who began as a realistic dramatist as early as 1954. In *The Flipflaps* he claims to have attempted to write specifically Egyptian drama, based upon the indigenous folkloric theatrical tradition, such as the licensed Fool, Juḥā, and the shadow theatre, and more particularly the village *al-Sāmir*. But the play in fact owes as much, if not more, to the modern western dramatic experiments of Pirandello and Brecht. In an attempt to make drama a genuinely collective, shared experience, Idris deliberately breaks down the barrier between actors and audience, thereby destroying the dramatic illusion of reality. The play begins with the Author, dressed in ridiculous costume, explaining to the audience what they are about to see. He is rudely interrupted by the sudden noisy appearance of the clown, Farfūr, a servant in search of a master, and a master is promptly found for him by the Author. The play proceeds to give an account of the tempestuous relation between servant and master. In the mean time the Author's part grows gradually smaller, until he disappears altogether, leaving the two to work out their own destiny. The servant's problem is not solved by his exchanging of roles with the Master, or even by their deaths at the end, which only turn Farfur into an electron spinning round the proton of his Master. Despite its prolixity and digressions *al-Farafir* is a deeply disturbing play on the social, political, and metaphysical levels. The themes it tackles are not only authority and freedom, the hierarchical structure of society, and the tendency of power to corrupt, but by the gradual shrinking into nothing of the Author of the play, Idris hints at a world which is deserted by God and in which men are left to their own devices. The final image of Farfur spinning dizzily round his master like an electron round the proton suggests the all too gloomy conclusion that the division of beings into master and slave is a cosmic law. Yet, despite this very depressing conclusion *al-Farafir* is full of humour: through his licensed Fool the author ridicules social injustice and political tyranny and all forms of hypocrisy and cant, current intellectual and artistic fashions.

Idris's rejection of the form of realistic drama, which began with *The Flipflaps*, continued to mark his later plays in which the author's vision grew noticeably darker, culminating in his *al-Mukhaṭṭaṭīn* (*The Striped Ones*, 1969); besides 'striped' the title also means 'planned' or 'programmed', a deliberate *double entendre*. It is an 'absurdist' political allegory, lashing out savagely at the totalitarian one-party State and it reminds one of George Orwell's *1984*. It is one of the most outspoken political satires written during the Nasser era, and it is amazing that its publication was not banned by the Censor. In it Idris is primarily interested in *homo politicus*, man is reduced merely to his political role, thereby becoming a caricature.

Similar satire on corruption and tyranny in contemporary Egyptian society can be found in the work of Fārūq Khūrshīd (b. 1924), and Mikhā'īl Rūmān (1927–73). Khurshid created in *Habazlam Bazāza* (1967) a character who is a perfect personification of amoral Machiavellian opportunism. Ruman concentrated on the theme of the freedom of the individual, depicting in more than one eloquent and moving drama, notably his Kafkaesque *al-Wāfid* (*The Newcomer*, 1965) and *al-Khiṭāb* (*The Letter*, 1965), the way this freedom is crushed under moral, psychological, and political pressure. Ruman began as a realist in his full-length play *al-Dukhkhān* (*Smoke*, 1962), a study of a somewhat existentialist rebel struggling to break free from drug addiction. As his art developed, Ruman relied increasingly on Symbolist and Absurdist techniques. A curious feature of his work is that he gave the same name, Ḥamdī, to the protagonists of many of his plays, who are all highly strung, hypersensitive men, usually of creative artistic talent, driven to the edge of insanity by extreme, often nightmarish experiences. They are all rebels against various forms of oppression.

Alfred Faraj (b. 1929), on the other hand, avoided the excesses of the Theatre of the Absurd, and sought his inspiration in Arab popular and folk literature such as the *Arabian Nights* and the medieval romances, which he treated in a manner, slightly influenced by Brecht, to comment on contemporary social and political reality. He satirized the abuses of the socialist State and attacked dictatorship. Like ʿAshur he acknowledged his debt to Tawfiq al-Hakim. He produced one of the best and most thoughtful comedies of the period, *ʿAlī Janāḥ al-Tabrīzī,* (1964), as well as an interesting study of a tragic character in *Sulaymān al-Ḥalabī* (1964). ʿAli Janah, a young and carefree prince, a dreamer who had lost all his fortune on extravagant living and unlimited hospitality, sets out on a journey to a legendary place to try his luck, accompanied by his follower, an itinerant shoemaker, who has taken a liking to him. They pretend to be a rich merchant and his servant arriving ahead of their caravan. ʿAli Janah gives away the life-savings of his follower to all and sundry, thereby acquiring a reputation for fabulous wealth. All the rich merchants of the city and even the king are deceived by them: they all rush to lend ʿAli Janah money, which he continues to give away to the poor to start businesses with, and the King even allows him to marry his daughter. As time passes and the caravan does not arrive, ʿAli Janah's trick is finally revealed by his disappointed servant and he is sentenced to death. However, while he is awaiting his execution his servant takes pity on him and falsely announces to the city that the caravan has at long last been sighted, approaching its destination. Immediately the delighted merchants offer ʿAli Janah their abject apologies and they set him free. In the ensuing confusion he makes his escape, accompanied by his servant and the Princess who finds in him many loveable qualities, more valuable than material wealth. Despite being an entertaining work, making full use of the popular dramatic and literary Arabic tradition, *ʿAli Janah* has a deeper social, political, and psychological significance. Both the protagonist and his fictitious caravan lend themselves easily to symbolical interpretation. The author raises several interesting questions such as the relation between illusion and reality, the thin line of demarcation separating the prophet or social reformer from the impostor, deception from self-deception.

In marked contrast to the predominantly political drama is the work of Rashād Rushdī (1912–83), who in a number of plays concentrated on the predicament of the modern Egyptian woman, but later turned to more political issues. In his subsequent plays Rushdi employed rather precious, and at times irritating experimental techniques, making his plays look too contrived, straining after effect.

Of the next generation of dramatists the two most interesting are Maḥmūd Diyāb (1932–83), arguably the most outstanding dramatist of his generation, and ʿAlī Sālim (b. 1936). Diyab's contribution to the theatrical revival was both varied and original. His first play is *al-Bayt al-Qadīm* (*The Old House*, 1962) written in distinguished classical Arabic, which won him the Arabic Language Academy Award (1963). Ostensibly it deals with social questions such as class and social climbing, but in reality it treats psychological issues: acute social embarrassment, parental anxieties, fraternal jealousy and resentment, and the strange pull of the past, in a manner revealing dramatic insight and free from sentimentality and melodrama. But it is his second play *al-Zawbaʿa* (*The Storm*, written in 1964 but published in 1967) which made Diyab famous. Unlike *The Old House* which is set in Cairo, *The Storm* uses as the background of its action an outlying Egyptian village which was to be the setting of many of his subsequent plays. It is also written in the sinewy and authentic language spoken by villagers.

A villager, Abū Shāma, is falsely accused of robbery with violence, sentenced to twenty years' imprisonment with hard labour and before he is taken away, swears that he will avenge himself on the wicked village that has wrongfully testified against him, by murdering one man for every year he spends in gaol. The action starts many years later when it is rumoured that he has been released and panic sets in among the villagers, so scared are the real original culprits and those who have ill-treated the prisoner's family and stolen his property in his absence. Murders are committed to prevent the discovery of the truth, which are ascribed to the freed prisoner, who never appears on the scene, and yet his presence dominates the play. At the end it is revealed that the rumour about the freeing of Abu Shama is utterly groundless, for, in fact he has died in prison four years earlier, having got over his desire for revenge, wanting above all to be reunited with his family. Most of the villagers feel ashamed that they have wronged Abu Shama again in his death as they had done in his life. *The Storm* is certainly one of the best plays to be produced by the new wave of dramatists. The dialogue, realistic to the point of faithfully reproducing the local dialect, rises to poetry in moments of deep emotion. In it Diyab, unlike most of his contemporaries, does not preach a facile political or moral lesson. Yet by concentrating on the drama of human relationships and probing deeply into human motives, he manages to raise, in the close and confined world of a tiny far-off Egyptian village, large questions relating to justice and conscience, individual and collective responsibility. Despite its earnestness, however, the play is not solemn or devoid of humour.

After *The Storm* Diyab changed his dramatic technique, moving away from the traditional form of realistic drama to experiment with the indigenous, local mode of entertainment, *al-Samir*, as advocated by Yusuf Idris. In *Layālī al-Ḥiṣād* (*Harvest Nights*, 1967), Diyab employs a complex structure using three planes of reality. The characters, all villagers, are introduced by a one-man Chorus/Presenter, who calls upon other characters to do a bit of improvised acting, himself taking part, impersonating one another, as well as well-known village personalities, re-enacting situations from their real life. Things go badly wrong when the line of demarcation between acting/illusion and reality is blurred. In their play-acting the villagers condemn to death a beautiful young woman who has been a source of trouble and annoyance to the village, but suddenly the young man who is obsessed by her, steals away with the intention of actually murdering her; in the dark of night, however, he kills by mistake another, innocent woman. The same deliberate confusion of illusion and reality is to be found in *al-Halāfīt* (*The Worthless People*, written in 1969, but published much later in 1986), a variety of the Carnival genre, in which play-acting turns into serious action. Because it was felt to be a politically subversive work, inciting the destitute to rise against the oppressive rich, the play was banned after its first performance.

In his later work, with one exception, Diyab returns to the use of literary Arabic. *Rajul Ṭayyib fī Thalāth Ḥikāyāt* (*A Good Man in Three Tales*, 1970), a trilogy of one-act plays, set in modern Cairo, makes use of the technique of the Theatre of the Absurd, and clearly expresses the mood of dejection and near despair in the wake of the defeat of 1967. They are separate works, each with a different plot, but they have in common a character called Man, described as *ṭayyib* (good and easily put upon), who stands for the little man, the underdog, the victim of oppression and authoritarian government. They are characterized by economy of dramatic writing, and deadpan treatment of nightmarish, grotesque, and outrageous events, an unnerving air of uncertainty and mystery, and what may be described as Harold Pinter-like poetry of terror.

Diyab's most outspoken contribution to the agonizing process of political self-examination after the 1967 defeat is his Brechtian epic play *Bāb al-Futūḥ* (*Gateway to Success*, 1971, which for obvious reasons was banned by the Censor). The play, which features a huge number of actors, opens with a group of young men and women who bitterly and openly complain about their despotic rulers, who have deprived them of all freedom of self-expression and action. They cheer themselves up by play-acting, imaginatively reconstructing a period of their glorious past, the age of Saladin. The action takes place on two levels: present-day Egypt as well as the Middle Ages. By contrasting the present and the past, the author provides not only an ironic comment upon the present, but indirectly delivers his revolutionary message. Formally the play is interesting in that it provides a cathartic experience for author and audience alike. Instead of offering the audience a well-made, finished work, the dramatist shows a play in the making, mixes past and present, actors and authors, and destroys the distance between stage and reality. In so doing he helps the audience identify more easily with the young men and women who are making the play, and therefore pass with them from despair and despondency to hope and self-confidence. As a theatre experience it is no mean achievement as it restores to drama its original collective therapeutic function.

Just as *Gateway to Success* caught the mood of the nation after the Arab defeat of 1967, *Rasūl min Qaryat Tamīra* (*A Messenger from the Village of Tamira*, published 1975) was inspired by the Arab–Israeli war of 1973. In it Diyab returns to the world of the little Egyptian village and hence to the colloquial Arabic. It expresses the nation's jubilation over the crossing of the Suez canal and destruction of the Bar-lev line, with the resultant recovery of national self-respect and dignity as well as bafflement at the sudden cessation of fighting. Despite the tragic death of one of the main characters, the play does not end on a note of despair. Diyab pursues his comments on Egyptian/Arab politics in his last published play, written in 1974, but published in 1975, *Ahl al-Kahf 1974* (*People of the Cave 1974*), the title of which bears an obvious ironic relation to Tawfiq al-Hakim's well-known play, *Ahl al-Kahf*. Here, in the form of an amusing dramatic fantasy taking place in a Cairo mansion, Diyab provides a warning on the dangers of Sadat's policy of *infitāḥ*, the open-door policy of economic liberalization after 1973, which he felt could lead to the return to power of the pre-revolution class of the unprincipled and exploiting rich and the loss of all socialist gains.

The last-published play by Diyab is *Arḍ lā Tunbit al-Zuhūr* (*Flowers Won't Grow in This Soil*), first published in the periodical *al-Masraḥ* in 1977, and in book form in 1986; it is in some ways difficult to place in the corpus of Diyab's work, as the date of its writing is uncertain. It is the only historical play he wrote, based on the Arabic version of the story of Queen Zenobia, who ruled Palmyra in the third century, and it uses a fairly conventional form of drama. It is not an intensely political play. What it has in common with much of Diyab's work, however, is that it celebrates the value of ordinary unheroic man, safe from the damaging or destructive demands of power or public life. It is a plea for love which can only survive when the heart is cleansed of all desire for revenge. Diyab's significance as a dramatist lies in the fact that while deeply interested in social and political issues, at his best he is not a mere preacher delivering directly a sermon, but he employs his interesting dramatic technique in treating important psychological, moral, and even metaphysical questions.

ʿAli Salim, who had first-hand experience of the theatre where he began as actor, is a most distinguished satirist, who has aimed his merciless attacks at three main targets: bureaucracy, corruption, and despotism. He is at his best in his one-act plays, for instance *Bīr al-Qamh* (*The Wheat Well*), *Ughniyya ʿalā 'l-Mamarr* (*Song on the Mountain Pass*), and *il-Bufayh* (*The Buffet*), all written between 1967 and 1968. The first is a bitter satire not only on the dead hand of bureaucracy, but also on the utter selfishness of most of mankind, the total lack of integrity even in scientific research. *Song on the Mountain Pass* describes the last moments of resistance before dying by five Egyptian soldiers besieged by the enemy in Sinai during the 1967 June war and cut off from their command. It succeeds in creating the claustrophobic, tense and dramatic atmosphere of the trenches. The characters are entirely free from false idealization: they fight and are prepared to die, yet they bicker among themselves, and are scared of dying. Despite his obvious patriotism the author gives a plausible and unsentimental account of the war and the pity of it. *The Buffet*, a Kafkaesque work reminiscent of Ruman's *The Newcomer*, shows how a playwright is brutally coerced by a tyrannical authority to alter his work thereby sacrificing his integrity as a writer and as a human being. It is a powerful play, with its crisp dialogue, fast moving action building up to a climax, its poignant images, and rich texture and has the frightening inner logic of a nightmare. Salim has also written full-length plays in which he attacks the same targets, such as *Kūmidiyā Ūdīb* (*The Comedy of Oedipus,* 1970) and *Bakalūriyūs fī Ḥukm al-Shuʿūb* (*B.A. in Ruling Peoples*, 1979). Despite their competence and humour, these owe their popularity less to their great artistic value than to their political message, which is generally a denunciation of military dictatorship, as exemplified in the Nasser regime.

To the same generation as Diyab and Salim belongs Shawqī ʿAbd-al-Ḥakīm, who began to write plays in 1960 and who derived his inspiration almost exclusively from the Egyptian folk-tale and popular ballad. Although not written in verse, his plays, mostly one act, are closer to dramatic poems than to dramas proper. Each is based on a popular tale, dealing with an extreme situation, often involving murder and violence, through which the dramatist expresses his thoughts on political and, more importantly, larger moral and metaphysical issues concerning man's powerlessness *vis-à-vis* fate and his ineradicable anxieties concerning death. They are a blend of rural realism and poetic sensitivity. Full of haunting and near surrealistic images, they are presented by an experimental method: events do not unfold before the audience in a chronological sequence, but are either related by a narrator or a chorus or re-enacted in a series of flashbacks, or simply assumed to be known to the audience with the characters themselves providing comments on them in the form of monologues. In his work Shawqi ʿAbd-al-Hakim represents one of the distinguishing features of the new wave of drama, namely its creative use of folklore.

Another distinguishing feature is the flourishing of poetic drama which answers all the requirements of good drama, including above all actability, probably for the first time. As we have noted in Chapter 2, recent experiments in metrical forms had liberated Arabic verse from the traditional constrictions of monorhyme and monometre which tended to make earlier attempts at writing verse drama sound more lyrical and declamatory than truly dramatic. Thus it was possible to use the new, immeasurably more flexible, forms which were much more satisfactory for purposes of drama, with the result that there was an interesting large-scale revival of verse drama. A spate of plays soon appeared, beginning with the work of the Egyptians ʿAbd al-Raḥmān al-Sharqāwī and Ṣalāḥ ʿAbd al-Ṣabūr; other Arab poets from Egypt and elsewhere, such as Najīb Surūr, Muʿīn Basīsū, and Samīḥ al-Qāsim joined in and the vogue spread even to several poets who seemed to know little about the exigencies of drama.

Although al-Sharqawi, already an established novelist, wrote his *Maʾsāt Jamīla* (*The Tragedy of Jamila*) in 1959 it was not produced on the Cairo stage until 1962, when it made a strong and immediate impact on the audience. This was partly because of its subject, the story of the Algerian female resistance fighter, Jamila Buhrid, and partly on account of the freer verse form in which it was written, which, through the author's sensitive and skilful handling, revealed the rich possibilities the new form had for drama. *The Tragedy of*

Jamila is a chronicle play which contains many moving scenes, much dramatic suspense, and fairly complex characterization: the author does not allow his Arab nationalist and socialist sentiments to distort his vision by making him paint all the French as inhuman bullies. However, because it lacks dramatic structure or plot, it reads more like a documentary than a play, and even as a documentary it is excessively long. Al-Sharqawi went on to produce several other verse dramas which suffer from the same prolixity: they are the work of a novelist used to employing a large canvas, and despite their dramatic content they are, as it were, verse novels in dialogue form. Al-Sharqawi indeed succeeded in making Arabic verse relevant to the events of everyday life and therefore not sound too artificial on the stage. However, all too often the poetry does not seem to arise organically from the nature of the action, but is superimposed upon it with the result that it does not seem to add an extra dimension to the plays.

Unlike al-Sharqawi's poetic dramas, which are generally far too long, often prosaic and didactic, those of ʿAbd al-Sabur, who was an immeasurably better poet, tend to be short, more concentrated, and in his later works, more experimental and obscure. His first play *Maʾsāt al-Ḥallāj* (*The Tragedy of al-Hallaj*, 1965) is based on the story of the celebrated mystic and martyr al-Ḥusayn ibn Manṣūr al-Ḥallāj (858–922), who was executed for his heretical views. It describes the last phase of al-Hallaj's life, beginning at the end with the crucified body of al-Hallaj hanging from a tree, then showing in flashback the events that led to his imprisonment and death. ʿAbd al-Sabur's interpretation is that al-Hallaj was not really executed for his theological or religious heresies but for his political commitment, his decision to cease shutting himself off from the external world and to identify with the cause of the poor and the hungry, whom he has been encouraging to rebel against the ruler. It is an interpretation in keeping with the general theme expressed symbolically, often through stylized gesture and ritualistic action and with varying degrees of clarity, in the poet's other plays, namely the relative position of thought and action, the pen and the sword, in saving Egypt. At times he intimates the need to combine both in the person of the militant intellectual. *Laylā waʾl-Majnūn* (*Layla and the Madman*, 1970) ends with the poet Saʿīd spending his time in gaol dreaming of the future redeemer of the country, who will bring about social justice, prosperity, and happiness for the poor and the deprived and who, he hopes, will not forget to carry his sword with him. In *al-Amīra Tantaẓir* (*The Princess Waits*, 1971), the Princess, a symbol for Egypt, is actually saved by the Poet with a dagger. ʿAbd al-Sabur's plays, all five of them, mark the most serious development of Arabic poetic drama to date. Because of its density of texture, its conciseness and suggestiveness, its richness of imagery and euphonious music and, above all, the sense of mystery it evokes, the poetry in them is a much more sensitive and suitable medium for symbolic drama than any prose.

The Egyptian theatrical revival had its impact upon many parts of the Arab world where there soon developed a keen interest in the theatre. In Syria the National Theatre was established by the Government in 1959. In Lebanon the influential Contemporary Theatre Troupe was founded by Munīr Abū Dibs in the following year. In Iraq the General Foundation for Cinema and Theatre was created in 1960, and in Tunisia a Drama School was set up in 1959, which was further developed into an important National Institute in 1966, and festivals for North African Drama have been held since 1961. In Morocco drama institutes were established by the Government in 1956, two troupes in 1957, and a centre for dramatic art in 1959. The first permanent Sudanese theatre was opened in Khartoum in 1961, and in Jordan the Ministry of Information formed the National Theatre Troupe in 1965.

Partly under the influence of the Egyptian theatre there developed a corresponding search for specifically Arab dramatic forms, based upon either traditional folk modes of entertainment or the medieval Arabic *maqama*. The emphasis, however, no doubt inspired by the Western example, tended to be more on staging, acting, and improvisation, on the theatre as 'a happening' and a living communal experience, than on drama as a written text or a form of literature. Several playwrights and directors of theatre companies distinguished themselves, for example al-Ṭayyib al-Ṣiddīqī in Morocco, ʿIzz al-Dīn al-Madanī in Tunisia, Yūsuf al-ʿĀnī in Iraq, and Munir Abu Dibs and others in Lebanon. However, in Syria the theatre retained its close links with the literary text, and interestingly enough classical Arabic tended to dominate the stage. This may be due in part to the continued efforts to write verse drama in the tradition of Ahmad Shawqi by poets who are as different as ʿUmar Abū Rīsha in the 1930s and ʿAdnān Mardam later on, but whose plays show little understanding of the exigencies of writing for the stage.

The most outstanding of the Syrian dramatists is Saʿdallah Wannūs (b. 1940), who received his theatre training in Cairo and Paris. Wannus attained instant fame with his experimental play *Ḥaflat Samar min Ajl Khamsa Huzayrān* (*An Evening Party for June the 5th*) first published in 1968, a bitter and courageous satire on the politics which led to the Arab defeat in the Arab–Israeli war of June 1967. Prior to *An Evening Party* Wannus had written a number of interesting one-act plays in the tradition of Tawfiq al-Hakim's drama of ideas, but employing the technique of the puppet-theatre. The most notable of these are the sinister *Juththa ʿalā'l-Raṣīf* (*Corpse on the Pavement*, 1977), a somewhat surrealistic portrayal of the callous manner in which the authorities side with the rich against the poor and destitute, and *al-Fīl yā Malik al-Zamān* (*The Elephant, O King of the World!*, 1971), a didactic parable, demonstrating how people can be totally emasculated and terrorized by a tyrannical and despotic ruler.

Under the influence of Piscator, the theatre producer who evolved the 'epic' play and of Brecht, Wannus had been calling for the need to politicize drama, *tasyīs al-masraḥ*, i.e. to use drama as a means of politically educating the theatre audience. In several experimental plays he tried, with varying degrees of success, to put into practice his principles, employing various techniques from traditional as well as modern Western sources to ensure the participation and education of his audience. For instance, *Mughāmarat Ra's al-Mamlūk Jābir* (*The Adventure of Mameluke Jabir's Head*, 1969), *Sahra maʿa Abī Khalīl al-Qabbānī* (*An Evening's Entertainment with Abu Khalil al-Qabbani*, 1972), and *al-Malik Huwa'l-Malik* (*The King's the King*, 1977) are all set in the world of the *Arabian Nights* and carry overt revolutionary political messages. In *Ḥaflat Samar*, by strategically placing the actors amidst the audience, Wannus extends the stage to the entire auditorium. At an official performance of a play intended to deal with the June war, actors representing eyewitnesses of the war, rise from the audience to object to the misrepresentation of the events by the author and director and proceed to give a more factual and less flattering account. The lively and open discussion about who was to blame which ensues leads the authorities to stop the show and to place the entire audience under arrest. Despite its shortcomings as a play *Haflat Samar* had a strong impact, because of its topicality: it was a powerful expression of the mood of disillusion and anger, of self criticism and soul searching which enveloped the entire Arab world in the wake of their shocking defeat.

The Adventure of Mameluke Jabir's Head is described in the Preface by the author as another experiment in *Masraḥ al-Tasyīs*, not 'political theatre', but politicized theatre, theatre which engages with actors and audience in a lively dialogue. In it Wannus uses multiple planes of reality. At a café customers order various drinks, listen to popular songs on the radio, while waiting for the *ḥakawātī* (the Story-teller) to come and entertain them for the evening. The Story-teller arrives, but instead of their favourite medieval romance, which relates the heroic victory of Baybars over the Crusaders, he insists upon telling them the earlier story of the cunning and resourceful Mameluke Jābir, who during a serious quarrel between a late Abbasid Caliph and his Vizier, manages to get out of Baghdad, bearing a secret message from the Vizier for the Persian King, written on the skin of his head after his hair has been first shaved and then allowed to grow again to cover it. When he arrives in the Persian Court, instead of being recompensed for this ingenious device, as he has been promised, with wealth and marriage to the woman he loves, Jabir is instantly put to death by the Persian King in accordance with the Vizier's instruction, which, unbeknown to Jabir, is part of the message, the other part being an invitation from the Vizier to the Persian King to invade Baghdad and help him depose the Caliph. These events in the Story-teller's narration are acted out by actors with the Story-teller performing the function of chorus and the café customers commenting on the action. The audience of the play share with the audience of café customers the same interest in popular songs, but are obviously differentiated from them, and the latter in their turn are distinguished from the characters who enact the Story-teller's tale. The dramatist provides many links between all three planes of reality, using various devices, including many topical allusions to the contemporary Arab world. On the whole this rather complicated structure, in which the same actors are made to play several parts, works reasonably well, despite the author's inability to resist the temptation to bring in a series of very brief scenes depicting the abject misery of the common people, totally neglected by their rulers who are selfishly engaged in their struggle for power. One also questions the wisdom of making the fate of the Mameluke Jabir the central theme in a play dealing with events of such magnitude and import as the struggle for power between the Caliph and Vizier, and the treachery of the rulers and their readiness to conspire with foreign governments against the national interest.

Wannus makes another attempt to use history to comment on the present in *An Evening's Entertainment With Abu Khalil al-Qabbani*. Here his immediate object is threefold. First, to recreate the theatre of Abu Khalil al-Qabbani the Father of Syrian drama (in which Wannus believes there was a kind of direct communion between actors and audience, which he wishes to recreate in his own work) through a presentation of a slightly modified version of his play derived from the *Arabian Nights, Harun al-Rashid maʿ al-Amīr Ghānim ibn Ayyūb wa Qūt al-Qulūb*. Secondly, to dramatize the (idealized) career of al-Qabbani as dramatist in Syria, including a semi-documentary episode showing his struggle to establish a theatre, the encouragement he received from the Ottoman Governor, the opposition he met with from the conservative men of religion, who eventually managed to close down his theatre. Thirdly, interspersed with this is Wannus's political commentary on the corruption and chaos of the Ottoman rule of Syria. The result is a sprawling work which lacks the necessary dramatic concentration and which even the author himself suggests in the Preface could be abridged on the stage.

By far the most satisfactory of Wannus' experiments is *The King's the King*, which uses as its framework the very tale which Marun al-Naqqash, the father of Arabic drama, had used for *Abu'l Hasan the Fool*, but with a difference. Here Harun al-Rashid's attempt to amuse himself, by having the impoverished and disgruntled merchant Abū ʿIzza drugged and placed on the throne for a day, turns sour: once on the throne Abu ʿIzza assumes absolute authority, becomes even more tyrannical than the real king to the extent that the latter's men are forced to acknowledge him as their real monarch, and the tale ends with Abu ʿIzza actually replacing Harun al-Rashid. Using a variety of techniques, including farce and puppetry, the play opens and closes with the actors forming a chorus informing the audience what they are about to perform for them, in the true Brechtian manner deliberately destroying the dramatic illusion. They comment on the action and at the end point out that the people can, and should, get rid of the very system that makes kings possible, because all kings are the same.

No less political in content are the plays of Muṣṭafā al-Ḥallāj.

For instance, *al-Ghaḍab* (*Anger*, 1959) deals with the Algerian struggle for independence and depicts the methods of torture employed by the French colonists. Torture is also the theme of *al-Darāwīsh Yabḥathūn ʿan al-Haqīqa* (*The Dervishes Seek the Truth*, 1970): a totally innocent man is subjected to unspeakable torture and finally condemned to death, because he happens to bear the same name as a political activist sought by the secret police, the primary concern of the secret police being not to establish a man's guilt or innocence but to prepare a file which they can submit to their superiors on anyone they can force to admit guilt. It is a powerful play, though overwritten in parts, with not enough action, but its protagonist undergoes a character development, becoming a symbol of the heroic struggle of the innocent individual against an all-powerful unjust system.

Other Syrian playwrights include Mamdūḥ ʿUdwān (b. 1941) who in *Muḥākamat al-Rajul alladhī lam Yuḥārib*) (*The Trial of the Man Who Did not Fight*) employs, in a Brechtian manner, events from early Islamic history, namely the Mongol sacking of Baghdad (an obvious metaphor for the easy Israeli victory in the June 1967 war), to make comments on modern Arab political reality, attributing the defeat of the demoralized Arabs to the permanent state of fear in which they live as a result of their persecution by their oppressive governments. ʿUdwan is also capable of producing a neatly constructed play with a strikingly cynical twist at the end: *Ḥāl al-Dunyā* (*That's Life*), written throughout in the interesting form of monologue, punctuated by the ringing of the doorbell or the telephone. ʿAlī ʿUqla ʿArsān (b. 1940) wrote several plays with political themes such as *al-Ghurabāʾ* (*The Strangers*, 1974), a rather naïve allegorical treatment of the Zionist immigration to Palestine, and the more subtle *al-Sajīn Raqam 95* (*Prisoner No. 95*, 1974), which ruthlessly attacks political persecution in the Arab world by showing the complete arbitrariness with which sentences, be they death or imprisonment for a limited period of time or for life, are passed on the innocent and even indiscriminately changed around by the authorities. *ʿArrāḍat al-Khuṣūm* (*The Enemy Demonstration*, 1976), is more of a political parable or illustrated sermon than drama, a defence of political idealism and genuine self-sacrifice for the nationalist cause against cynicism and hypocrisy and use of slogans to promote self-interest. Characters are mere types and undergo conversion instantly, against all probability. It can be argued that the impact of the documentary and Brechtian theatre on Arabic drama, as is clearly shown here, has generally resulted in dramatists abandoning any serious attempt at portraying characters in depth. On the whole the effect has been rather damaging.

Much less politically charged and, on the whole, less sombre and more comical in spirit are the plays of Walīd Ikhlāṣī (b. 1935), although they are by no means free from satire or social criticism. *Kayfa Taṣʿad Dūna an Taqaʿ* (*How to Climb without Falling*, 1973) is a study of the making of an opportunist who, through sheer cunning and resourcefulness, dishonesty and unscrupulousness, manages to rise to the position of Cabinet Minister. *Hādha 'l-Nahr al-Majnūn* (*This Mad River*, 1976), described by the author as 'an original tragedy', portrays an elderly woman of a domineering personality belonging to the expropriated class of the *ancien régime*, unable to come to terms with the new situation created by the recent land reform laws, which limited her property and reduced her status; despite personal tragedies she is determined to struggle on in a world that bears no relation to reality. In *al-Ṣirāṭ* (*The Path*, 1976) the protagonist is a humble theatre-cleaner and general factotum who, due to the illness of an actor, is asked to stand in for him and he proves such a success as a stage clown, that he is encouraged to go on playing the role. But he discovers to his disillusionment that he can only maintain his popularity as a comedian on the stage, and hence his huge financial success, by means of hypocrisy and affirmation of the false values of the Establishment. In the end he opts out and is punished by the authorities by not being allowed either to leave or remain in his country, thereby being forced to inhabit an impossible no man's land. It is through his portrayal of such interesting human types that Ikhlasi presents his criticism of society and reveals its corruption.

The work of Ikhlasi as well as that of other dramatists often contains poetic elements, but it is in the surrealistic play *al-ʿUṣfūr al-Aḥdab* (*The Hunchback Sparrow*, 1967) by the poet Muḥammad al-Māghūṭ (b. 1932) that we find one of the most powerful and haunting dramatic statements of political oppression and tyranny in the modern Arab world. It is a surrealistic play in four acts with an enormous cast which includes, besides human beings of all ages ranging from grandparents to children, birds, a Birdwoman, as well as Voice of the Wind. Characters change from one act to another. In the beginning they all appear as political prisoners in a huge cage, but the Old Man of Act I is rejuvenated as the tyrannical Prince of Act III, and likewise the sex-obsessed Bachelor is transformed later into the Holy Man. The violence of al-Maghut's imagery and syntax is paralleled in the action of the play which includes the flogging of prisoners and the shooting of children by a firing squad. However, the absence of a clearly defined plot, a single action with logical progression, would certainly make the staging of *The Hunchback Sparrow* an exceedingly difficult task; it is clearly a work more suited for the study than for the theatre.

Al-Maghut went on to write a savage satire on Arab regimes in *al-Muharrij* (*The Jester*, 1973), a much more easily actable drama, which makes its point in a less surrealistic language. A fantasy in three acts, *The Jester* is a black farce which mercilessly ridicules by means of buffoonery and zany methods modern Arab society, exposing all the sham and hollowness in its cherished values as well as the horror of its oppressive authoritarian governments. It is a powerful, well-constructed play, with plenty of action and humour to sustain the interest of the audience, and yet has the rare advantage, for an Arabic play, of concentrated style and manageable length. It opens noisily with the beating of drums and clinking of a dancer's castanets announcing the arrival of a troupe of penniless itinerant players (clowns who have turned to acting after having failed in every other trade), who appear on a cart which constitutes the mobile stage, in the open space next to a café in an old slum quarter of an unnamed Arab city. The troupe is run by a semi-literate Drummer who acts as Presenter and Commentator, and includes a woman dancer. The inhabitants are attracted by the noise and fascinated by the garish costumes and the gyrations of the female dancer. The Drummer introduces the troupe to the people as young committed actors, with a highly developed social conscience, determined to bring the theatre to the people's doorsteps, and they proceed to entertain them. Their acting is punctuated by angry protests from the owner of the café, patrons' orders called aloud by the waiter, shouts of annoyance by a solemn elderly schoolmaster because of the actors' constant breaking of the rules of classical Arabic grammar, and critical comments from the audience. They first act a thoroughly distorted scene from *Othello*, leading to the murder of Desdemona. The part of Othello is played by the actor referred to as *Muharrij* (the Jester), who will play subsequent leading parts. He is a comic version of Othello in the exaggerated melodramatic tradition of the famous Egyptian actor Yūsuf Wahbī, while the female dancer plays Desdemona, appearing in modern costume, swinging her handbag and chewing gum. In a comment on the action the Drummer attacks Shakespeare for bringing about the downfall of the Arab national hero Othello, which he sees as a British imperialist plot, in collusion with America, with her nuclear bases. This gives rise to several anti-American and anti-NATO shouts from the audience. The Drummer urges his audience never to give in to such imperialist plots, but to derive inspiration and comfort from the innumerable national heroes of their past.

At the audience's suggestion the troupe then play Harun al-Rashid, the paragon of Arab justice and chivalry. The Jester then appears as Harun al-Rashid comically devouring his food at a feast, dispensing mock justice in an absurdly arbitrary manner to the noisy approval of the audience. This is followed by the Jester's impersonation of the Arab founder of Muslim Spain, the Umayyad ʿAbd al-Raḥmān, known as the 'Hawk of Quraysh', who is presented, contrary to historical facts, as a spoilt prince given solely to the pursuit of sensual pleasure. This prompts a comment from someone in the audience that this interpretation would make the Hawk turn in his grave. Immediately the telephone rings and Act I ends when the proprietor of the café announces that the Hawk is on the phone, wishing to speak to the Jester. Accompanied by thunder and lightning, the Hawk's voice is heard to the amazement of the stunned audience. From now on the mood of the play becomes more sombre and macabre.

In Act II the Jester has been transported in a coffin to the court of the Hawk who is intent on punishing him. The Jester humbly begs for mercy and by a clever trick manages to distract the Hawk and his courtiers by arousing their interest in the wonders of modern civilization, showing them some of the modern gadgets which, like a travelling salesman, he has brought with him in his coffin. Impressed by the Jester's knowledge and expertise, the Hawk wishes to make use of him by appointing him Governor in one of the Arab provinces. He offers him first Spain, then Alexandretta, then Palestine, but he is told that these provinces no longer belong to the Arabs. The Hawk asks for the reason of the modern Arabs' failure and the Jester explains how, using the excuse of the Palestinian cause, their despotic rulers have emasculated them, turning them into mere mice and cockroaches, by abusing their freedoms, and subjecting them to torture, robbing them of their dignity, and destroying their self-respect. He even gives him a practical demonstration of how this is done by inflicting gruesome torture on one of the Hawk's incredulous men, who volunteers for the purpose. The Act ends with the disgusted Hawk deciding against the Jester's advice to come back from the dead to restore Arab dignity and manhood and liberate Palestine.

In Act III the Hawk is stopped by immigration officers at the frontiers of an Arab state, on the grounds that he has no passport. He is first taken to be mad when he declares his identity, then his story is believed, and he is surrounded by media men who, uninterested in his mission, ask him all manner of silly questions in the way of media men. But soon he is put under arrest by the Arab authorities and a deal is struck with the emissary of the Spanish Government; in return for the significant sum of thirty thousand tons of onions, the authorities will hand the Hawk over to the Spanish who are keen to try him for the war crimes he committed when he originally invaded their country in the eighth century. Suspecting the worst the Jester makes a desperate attempt to persuade the Hawk to escape, but of course he refuses to listen to him.

As we can see the play presents a topsy-turvy world in which values are completely reversed. Othello is viewed as an Arab hero destroyed by Shakespeare as part of a British imperialist plot backed up by the Americans with their nuclear bases and Phantom jet fighters. Harun al-Rashid's Arab chivalry and sense of justice are displayed in his order that a plaintiff brought before him for trial be paid a thousand dinars and then have his head struck off for being too talkative. A great Arab national hero from the medieval past is humiliated for not owning a passport and is betrayed by his people and sold to the enemy. Past and present are mixed. The Jester is taken back to the early Middle Ages, and the medieval figure of the Hawk is brought into the twentieth century. Metaphors are literally translated into the physical reality of their verbal components. The actress described by the Presenter as having been 'suckled' on true dramatic art appears on the stage with a dummy in her mouth. Characters are literally 'painted' by a house-painter with a paint bucket and a brush.

Al-Maghut's savage attack on totalitarian government employing the methods of farce, has not lacked imitators in Syria. For instance, in *al-Shaykh Bahlūl fī Sūq al-Khayyāṭīn* (*Sheikh Bahlul in the Tailors' Market*), published in the Damascus periodical *al-Mawqif al-Adabī* in 1978, Khālid Muḥyī al-Dīn al-Barādiʿī made such an attempt; in it he produced an interesting variation on the theme of the Emperor's New Clothes.

Although there was no lack of dramatic writing in Lebanon, as we find in Saʿīd ʿAql's poetic but unactable dramas in the 1930s and the continued, albeit not very distinguished efforts of Saʿīd Taqiyy al-Dīn in the 1940s and 1950s since the 1960s, the Lebanese, unlike the Syrians, have been concentrating not on drama as a written text, but on the revival of the theatre as a living experience. This is best exemplified in the improvised theatre of *al-ḥakawātī* (story-teller) led by Roget ʿAssāf, in musical drama, translations, and adaptations of Western theatre, which benefit from the technique of the avant-garde, and address the local intellectual élite who could appreciate the subtleties of the political satire presented to them. A possible exception to this rule is ʿIṣām Maḥfūẓ (b. 1939), a poet who became interested in writing for the theatre. Among his plays are *al-Zanzalakht*, (*The China Tree*, 1968), *al-Qatl* (*The Assassination*, 1968), *al-Diktātūr* (*The Dictator*, 1970), and *Limādhā* (*Why*, 1971), the last of which he directed himself.

The best-known of his plays, *The China Tree*, written in 1963 but not produced and published until 1968, consists of a prologue and twelve scenes. The setting alternates between the outside of a palace gate and a courtroom by means of dimming parts of the stage, and when near the end of the play the entire stage is lit, the outside of the palace gate is shown to be a part of the courtroom.

In the prologue Saʿdūn, the 'hero' of the play, appears on an empty stage caning a chair, and tells the audience that he was originally a jeweller and that he is anxious to tell them his strange story, which he himself at times finds incredible, a story in which the main characters are the General, the Clerk, his own Godfather, and the Old Lady. Saʿdun is accused of murdering a young woman and brought to trial in a courtroom, full of spectators and, although his guilt is never proved by logical argument, he is sentenced to death. However, before the sentence is carried out, acting on the advice of a Mysterious Voice claiming to be a Tree, he stiffens his body by an act of will and manages to transform himself into a China Tree. He is carried out of the courtroom horizontally like a tree trunk by two enormous male nurses in white uniforms, to the satisfaction of the people in the courtroom. Immediately afterwards a Nun enters ringing a small bell announcing it is time to eat, at which everyone leaps towards the door, clamouring like school children at the end of classes; they are told by the Nun to wash their hands before eating.

Apart from Saʿdun's sudden change into a tree at the end very little happens in the play. In the courtroom Saʿdun responds after a fashion to the questions put to him and outside the palace gate he is engaged mainly in his desperate attempt to enter the palace, knocking patiently without avail. He engages in an 'absurdist' conversation with strange Beggars and behaves like one himself. In fact, as in the case of other characters, the exact identity of Saʿdun is never completely established. Is he a caner, a jeweller, a tramp *à la* Beckett, or is he Everyman? Equally, the General who tries him is at one and the same time the Judge in the courtroom, the authoritarian father, the military dictator, and the ruler of the State. Saʿdun's desperate attempt to get access to the inside of the palace, his bewildered helplessness as regards the murder charge levelled at him, as well as the wealth of sinister and haunting imagery of the play, make *The China Tree* a cross between a surrealist nightmarish variation on the Oedipal situation and a strikingly Kafkaesque brand of 'absurdist' drama. *The China Tree* has many remarkable features, such as its sinister and haunting atmosphere, its sophisticated technical devices, its stichomythia, its impressive verbal Ionesco-like style of dialogue, its rich political, psychological, and even metaphysical implications. But it is more the work of an élitist Arab intellectual thoroughly at home in the latest Western vogue than a truly Arab play that can appeal to the average Arab reader or audience.

With a few exceptions such as the Balalin Company, the collective authors of *al-ʿItma* (*Darkness*, 1973), and the recently publicized *al-hakawati* company of Jerusalem, the Palestinians have been primarily interested in drama as literature, and some of them wrote verse drama. For obvious reasons the Arab–Israeli conflict and the need for the struggle to liberate occupied Palestine figure largely in their plays, for example *Qaraqāsh* (1970) by the poet Samih al-Qasim (b. 1939) and *Thawrat al-Zanj* (*Al-Zanj's Revolution*, 1970) and *Shamshūn wa Dalīla* (*Samson and Delilah*, 1971) by another poet, Muʿin Basisu (1926–84). Though interesting as literary productions, these plays are generally not very successful as drama. A typical example is al-Qasim's *Qaraqash*, for which the 'time' is described in the stage directions as 'always' and the 'place' 'everywhere'. It opens with a chorus chanting 'Qaraqash is to be found anytime, anywhere'. This is followed by a pantomime showing processions first of tired ancient Greeks in chains crossing the stage slowly accompanied by strains of music, herded by a similarly dressed man with a whip, then of ancient Egyptians, and lastly modern Europeans, equally in chains, lashed by a whip, bearing a large photograph of Hitler, whose voice is heard delivering one of his speeches.

Then ensues a series of four tableaux. In the first Qaraqash, a one-eyed tyrant, addresses his disgruntled and starving subjects urging them to wage war on more fertile, richer land, and ordering the death of the revolutionary peasant who tries to incite his fellow citizens not to incur any more sacrifices. Tableau I ends with his execution. In tableau II Qaraqash, having achieved victory and enriched his followers with booty, goes on a hunting expedition, is annoyed to find simple folk singing and merrymaking after harvesting for fear that the noise might frighten the wild animals away, and orders them to stop at once. In the mean time the Prince, his son, falls in love with a peasant's daughter, and asks the Vizier to persuade Qaraqash to agree to this unequal marriage. In tableau III we see the tyrant Qaraqash sitting in judgement on several citizens with grievances all of whom receive only harsh sentences from him. In tableau IV the gallows are brought on the stage to hang those sentenced to death, including a man whose sole crime is that he could not beget a son to serve in Qaraqash's army. The Vizier tries to sound him out on the matter of a prince marrying a peasant girl, but Qaraqash's prompt reaction is that such a couple ought to be beheaded and he demands to see their heads at once, assuming that what the Vizier mentioned was not a hypothetical case, but something that has actually happened in his kingdom. The severed heads are brought before him and to his horror he discovers that one of them was his own son's. Controlling his grief, however, he proceeds to order his men to go to war. The peasants, however, having had enough of Qaraqash's reign of terror, rise against him and murder him and his Vizier. The play ends with the jubilant peasants being joined by the soldiers in a scene of dancing and singing.

The play is full of contemporary allusions; the one-eyed

Qaraqash obviously refers to General Moshe Dayan. Yet it is never really *dramatic*; the poetry remains lyrical or descriptive, but is never transmuted into drama. In *Qaraqash* there is neither real conflict, whether internal or external, nor real characterization for the author does not dwell long enough on his creations to render them psychologically plausible.

The same preoccupation with politics, with social injustice and corruption, and the call for revolutionary action, marks the work of Iraqi dramatists, of whom the most prominent is Yūsuf al-ʿĀnī (b. 1927). In his earlier work, which consisted largely of simple, naturalistic one-act plays, often more like sketches or scenes than properly structured drama, al-ʿAni dealt with issues such as the idleness of civil servants and the corruption of bureaucracy (*Ra'*s *al-Shullayla*, *The Gang Leader*, 1951), exorbitant prescription charges beyond the means of dying patients *(Fulūs al-Dawā'*, *Prescription Charges*, 1952), malpractices in private clinics *(Sittat Darāhim*, *Six Dirhams*, 1954), the persecution of political dissidents (*Anā Ummuk yā Shākir*, *I'm your Mother, Shakir*, 1955), the temptation to embezzle in order to provide medicine for a sick child *(al-Maṣyada*, *The Trap*, 1961), and the ill-treatment of a mentally retarded young man by his cruel stepmother (*Jamīl*, 1962). *Ahlan bi'l-Ḥayāh* (*Welcome, Life*, 1960) treats the abuse of the rights of citizens by a tyrannical regime and the restoration of these rights by the revolution, while *Ṣūra Jadīda* (*A New Image*, 1964), a longer play in seven tableaux, shows how a rich merchant who rose from poverty is saved from the folly of taking on a new wife, young enough to be his daughter, and of turning out his wife and children. Despite its sociological interest, the events in *A New Image* happen too fast and are presented merely externally, without any attempt to portray character in depth. Better known than these are al-ʿAni's later, longer works: *al-Miftāḥ* (*The Key*, 1967–8) and *al-Kharāba* (*The Waste Land*, 1970), in which he makes use of popular traditions and folklore and borrows the technique of the puppet-theatre and the documentary.

The Key is a dramatization of a nursery rhyme in a series of tableaux depicting the quest of a young couple for a baby and a life of security, interspersed with political commentary and folk-singing together with a Narrator filling in the gaps. It is a call for political action and the courage to face reality, dressed as a popular theatrical entertainment. *The Key* is more akin to musical drama with a simple unilinear structure, than to drama proper. It constitutes an attempt to make the theatre more accessible to the people. In the final analysis it is no more than a popular and entertaining dramatic spectacle with an obvious social message.

As for *al-Kharaba* (*The Waste Land*) it too is a didactic dramatic entertainment, but it presents a mixture of realism and fantasy, and is deliberately designed to break the dramatic illusion *à la* Brecht. The auditorium is dressed as an exhibition hall, showing photographs and documents, newspaper clippings illustrating the crimes committed by colonialism and world imperialism. The characters, who remain mostly nameless, are divided into two camps, the one representing the wicked supporters of imperialism and the other their victims, the good masses of humanity. The play offers no detailed characterizations, but a pageant of characters representing different aspects of ill-justice suffered or committed by different social groups or classes. It ends with a denunciation of American policy in Vietnam and the Middle East and a recital of quotations from poems by Palestinian poets. After the curtain falls one of the characters urges the audience to have another look at the exhibition before they leave the auditorium. *The Waste Land* may have been lively theatre, but as drama it has several shortcomings, not the least of which is its excessively large number of characters, which include figures from Babylonian mythology such as Astarte and Gilgamesh. To add to the confusion many parts are played by the same actors.

In North Africa dramatists, who are more deeply influenced by the contemporary French theatre, have been less obsessively political. ʿIzz al-Dīn al-Madanī (b. 1938) of Tunisia and al-Ṭayyib al-Ṣiddīqī (b. 1938) of Morocco are primarily interested in the search for a specifically Arab form of drama, the former deriving his themes from classical Arabic literary figures and works such as al-Hallaj and al-Maʿarri in *Riḥlat al-Ḥallāj* (*al-Hallaj's Journey*, 1973) and *al-Ghufrān* (*Forgiveness*), or from incidents from Arab history such as al-Zanj's revolution in *Dīwān al-Zanj* (1972). In these plays, al-Madani uses a loose form which mixes dramatic representation with narrative, and which he claims in the introduction to *al-Zanj* to be based upon a traditional structural principle in medieval Arabic writings, namely *istiṭrād* (digression). Applying a similar method, al-Siddiqi dramatized Hamadhānī's *maqamas* in an attempt to produce a truly popular theatre, for which he also wrote works that required audience participation. Younger writers such as the Moroccan ʿAbd al-Karīm Bū Rashīd followed their example. Yet, despite this hectic formal experimentation the content of their plays is seldom entirely free from a political component. For instance, in *al-Zanj* al-Madani uses the story of the revolution of the black slaves against the Abbasid Caliph in the ninth century to make a comment on the various revolutions and wars of liberation in Third-World countries, and how they ended in a new form of colonialism, economic servitude.

In fact, in much Arabic drama since the late 1950s and 1960s, particularly as the mood of anger and frustration deepened in the wake of the traumatic 1967 defeat, politics tended to assume enormous proportions. This has given Arabic drama a quality of seriousness and a sense of urgency which it might otherwise have lacked. More than any other literary form perhaps, even more than the novel and the short story, drama affords incontrovertible evidence that Arab writers have been the political conscience of the Arab nation. However, it must be admitted that at times politics have dominated Arabic drama to a suffocating degree. One is tempted to say that this obsessive interest in politics is perhaps one of the main features which distinguish modern Arabic drama, and perhaps drama produced in totalitarian states in general, from modern drama in the West, which on the whole tends to concentrate more on personal relations and on broad moral or philosophical issues. However, one is soon made aware of the dangers of hazarding such a generalization by the recent work of the British dramatists David Mercer, Tom Stoppard, and particularly Harold Pinter, whose studies of political torture in *One for the Road* (1984), and *Mountain Language* (1988) remind one of similar treatment of torture in, for instance, Mikha'il Ruman's *The Newcomer*, and ʿAli Salim's *The Buffet*.

SELECT BIBLIOGRAPHY

BOOKS IN EUROPEAN LANGUAGES MAINLY ENGLISH

1. *Background: Social, Political, and Intellectual*

ABDEL-MALEK, A., *La Pensée politique arabe contemporaine* (Paris, 1970).

ABU-LUGHOD, IBRAHIM, *Arab Rediscovery of Europe* (Princeton, NJ, 1963).

ADAMS, C. C., *Islam and Modernism in Egypt* (London, 1933).

AHMED, J. M., *The Intellectual Origins of Egyptian Nationalism* (London, 1960).

AMIN, AHMAD, *My Life* (tr. I. J. Boullata; Leiden, 1938).

ANTONIUS, G., *The Arab Awakening* (London, 1938).

BADRAN, MARGOT, and COOKE, MIRIAM, *Opening the Gates: A Century of Arab Feminist Writing* (Bloomington, Ind., 1990).

BERQUE, J. et al., *Bibliographie de la culture arabe contemporaine* (Paris, 1981).

GERSHONI, ISRAEL, and JANKOWSKI, JAMES R., *Egypt, Islam and the Arabs: The Search for Egyptian Nationhood, 1900–1930* (Oxford, 1986).

AL-HAKIM, TAWFIQ (Hakim, Tewfik), *The Return of Consciousness* (tr. R. Bayly Winder, London, 1984).

HEYWORTH-DUNNE, J., *Introduction to the History of Education in Modern Egypt* (London, 1938).

HOLT, P. M. (ed.), *Political and Social Change in Modern Egypt* (London, 1963).

HOPWOOD, D., *The Russian Presence in Syria and Palestine, 1843–1914* (Oxford, 1969).

HOURANI, A. H., *Arabic Thought in the Liberal Age, 1798–1939* (London, 1962).

HUSSEIN, TAHA, *The Future of Culture in Egypt* (tr. S. Glazer; London, 1982).

ISSAWI, CHARLES, *An Economic History of the Middle East and North Africa* (London, 1982).

AL-JABARTI, *Al-Jabarti's Chronicle of the First Seven Months of the French Occupation of Egypt* (tr. S. Moreh; Leiden, 1975).

KERR, M., *Islamic Reform: The Political and Legal Theories of Muhammad Abduh and Rashid Rida* (Berkeley, Calif., 1966).

LUTFI AL-SAYYID MARSOT, A., *Egypt's Liberal Experiment, 1922–1936* (Berkeley, Calif., 1977).

MANSFIELD, PETER, *The Arabs* (London, 1976; repr. with a Postscript, 1980).

MAZYAD, A. M. H., *Ahmad Amin 1886–1954: Advocate of Social and Literary Reform in Egypt* (Leiden, 1963).

MIKHAIL, MONA M., *Images of Arab Women* (Washington, DC, 1983).

MUSA, SALAMA, *The Education of Salama Musa* (tr. L. O. Schuman; Leiden, 1961).

OWEN, ROGER, *The Middle East in the World, 1800–1914* (London, 1981).

REID, D. M., *The Odyssey of Farah Antun: A Syrian Christian's Quest for Secularism* (Minneapolis, 1975).

SALIBI, K., *The Modern History of Lebanon* (London, 1965).

SCHÖLCH, A., *Egypt for the Egyptians* (London, 1981).

SHARABI, HISHAM B., *Arab Intellectuals and the West: The Formative Years 1875–1914* (Baltimore, 1970).

SMITH, CHARLES D., *Islam and the Search for Social Order in Modern Egypt* (New York, 1952).

AL-TAHTAWI, RIFAʿA RAFIʿ, *L'Or de Paris* (tr. Anouar Louca; Paris, 1989).

TIBAWI, A. L., *American Interests in Syria, 1800–1901* (London, 1966).

VATIKIOTIS, P. J., *The Modern History of Egypt* (4th edn., London, 1991).

WAHBA, MAGDI, *Cultural Policy in Egypt* (Paris, 1972).

WATERBURY, J., *The Egypt of Nasser and Sadat* (Princeton, NJ, 1983).

WENDELL, C., *The Evolution of the Egyptian National Image: From its Origins to Ahmad Lutfi al-Sayyid* (Berkeley, Calif., 1972).

WESSELS, ANTONIE, *A Modern Biography of Muhammad* (Beirut, 1972). [A critical study of Muhammad Husayn Ḥaykal's 'Hayāt Muhammad'.]

2. General Surveys, Literary Criticism, and Anthologies

ABDEL-MALEK, A., *Anthologie de la littérature arabe contemporaine:* ii. *Les essais* (Paris, 1965).

ALLEN, ROGER (ed.), *Modern Arabic Literature* (A Library of Literary Criticism; New York, 1987).

ALTOMA, SALIH, *Modern Arabic Literature: A Bibliography of Articles, Books, Dissertations and Translations in English* (Bloomington, Ind., 1975).

—— *Palestinian Themes in Modern Arabic Literature (1917–1970)* (Cairo, 1972).

ASHRAWI, HANAN MIKHAIL, *Contemporary Palestinian Literature Under Occupation* (Beir Zeit, 1976).

AWAD, LOUIS (ed.), *The Literature of Ideas in Egypt* (Atlanta, 1986).

BADAWI, M. M., *Modern Arabic Literature and the West* (London, 1985).

—— (ed.), *Modern Arabic Literature: The Cambridge History of Arabic Literature* (Cambridge, 1992).
BOULLATA, ISSA (ed.), *Critical Perspectives on Modern Arabic Literature* (Washington, DC, 1980).
BRINNER, W. M., and KHOURI, MOUNAH, *Readings in Modern Arabic Literature* (Leiden, 1971).
BROCKELMAN, C., *Geschichte der Arabischen Litteratur* (Supplementband III; Leiden, 1949).
BRUGMAN, J., *An Introduction to the History of Modern Arabic Literature in Egypt* (Leiden, 1984).
CACHIA, PIERRE, *An Overview of Modern Arabic Literature* (Edinburgh, 1990).
—— *Taha Husayn: His Place in the Modern Arab Literary Renaissance* (London, 1956).
COOKE, MIRIAM, *War's Other Voices: Women Writers on the Lebanese Civil War* (Cambridge, 1988).
FERNEA, ELIZABETH WARNOCK (ed.), *Women and the Family in the Middle East* (Austin, Tex., 1985).
FONTAINE, JEAN, *Aspects de la littérature tunisienne* (Tunis, 1985).
GIBB, H. A. R., 'Studies in Contemporary Arabic Literature' in S. J. Shaw and W. R. Polk (eds.), *Studies on the Civilization of Islam* (London, 1984).
HAFEZ, SABRY, 'The Modern Arabic Short Story' in M. M. Badawi (ed.), *Modern Arabic Literature: The Cambridge History of Arabic Literature* (Cambridge, 1992).
HAYWOOD, J. A., *Modern Arabic Literature 1800–1970* (London, 1971).
HAZO, SAMUEL (ed.), *Mundius Artium* 10:1, Special Arabic Issue (Texas, 1977).
JAYYUSI, SALMA KHADRA (ed.), *The Literature of Modern Arabia* (London, 1987).
KHEMIRI, TAHER, and KAMPFFMAYER, B., *Leaders in Contemporary Arabic Literature* (Berlin, 1930).
LAROUI, A., *La Crise des intellectuals arabes* (Paris, 1974).
LOUCA, ANOUAR, *Voyageurs et écrivains égyptiens en France au XIXème siècle* (Paris, 1970).
MEFTAH, TAHAR, *Taha Husain: sa critique littérature et ses sources françaises* (Tunis, 1976).
MONTEIL, VINCENT, *Anthologie bi-lingue de la littérature Arabe contemporaine* (Beirut, 1961).
MOOSA, MATTI, *The Origins of Modern Arabic Fiction* (Washington, DC, 1983).
MOREH, S., *Studies in Modern Arabic Prose and Poetry* (Leiden, 1988).
NAIMY, NADEEM, *The Lebanese Prophets of New York* (Beirut, 1985).
Nimrod 24:2 (Spring–Summer 1981).

OSTLE, ROBIN C. (ed.), *Modern Literature in the Near and Middle East* (London, 1991).
—— *Studies in Modern Arabic Literature* (Warminster, 1973).
PÉRÈS, HENRI, *Littérature arabe moderne: grands courants* (Algiers, 1940).
PHILIPP, T., *Gurgi Zaidan: His Life and Thought* (Beirut, 1979).
SEMAH, DAVID, *Four Egyptian Literary Critics* (Leiden, 1981).
SOUEID, P., *Ibrāhīm al-Yāzijī, l'homme et son oeuvre* (Beirut, 1969).
STETKEVYCH, J., *Modern Arabic Literary Language: Lexical and Stylistic Development* (Chicago, 1970).

3. Poetry

(A) STUDIES

ABDUL-HAI, MUHAMMAD, *Tradition and English and American Influence in Arabic Romantic Poetry* (London, 1982).
ASFOUR, JOHN MIKHAIL, *When the Words Burn: An Anthology of Modern Arabic Poetry, 1945–1987* (Ontario, 1988).
BADAWI, M. M., *An Anthology of Modern Arabic Verse* (Oxford, 1970).
—— *A Critical Introduction to Modern Arabic Poetry* (Cambridge, 1975).
BONDOT-LAMOTTE, ANTOINE, *Ahmad Shawqi: l'homme et l'oeuvre* (Damascus, 1977).
BUSHRUI, SUHEIL, *Gibran of Lebanon* (Gerrards Cross, 1987).
EDHAM, I. A., *Abushady the Poet* (Leipzig, 1936).
HAWI, KHALIL, *Kahlil Gibran: His Background, Character and Works* (Beirut, 1963).
JAYYUSI, SALMA KHADRA (ed.), *Modern Arabic Poetry: An Anthology* (New York, 1987).
—— *Trends and Movements in Modern Arabic Poetry* (2 vols.; Leiden, 1977).
KHOURI, MOUNAH, *Poetry and the Making of Modern Egypt* (Leiden, 1971).
MOREH, S., *Modern Arabic Poetry 1800–1970*, Leiden, (1976).
NAIMY, N., *Mikhail Naimy: An Introduction* (Beirut, 1967).
NIJLAND, C., *Mikha'il Nuʿayma: Promoter of Arabic Literary Revival* (Istanbul, 1975).
STEWART, DESMOND, *Poet of Iraq: Abdul Wahab al-Bayati: An Introductory Essay with Translations* (London, 1976).
SULEIMAN, KHALID A., *Palestine and Modern Arab Poetry* (London, 1984).

(B) TRANSLATIONS

ADUNIS (Adonis) [pseud. ʿAlī Aḥmad Saʿīd], *The Blood of Adonis* (tr. Samuel Hazo; Pittsburgh, 1971).
—— *Chants de Mihyar le Damascène* (tr. A. W. Minkowski; Paris, 1983).

—— *Livre de la migration* (tr. Martine Faideau; Paris, 1982).
—— *The Transformation of the Lover* (tr. S. Hazo; Athens, Oh., 1983).

ARBERRY, ARTHUR J., *Modern Arabic Poetry: An Anthology with English Verse Translation* (London, 1950).

ARURI, NASEER, and GHAREEB, EDMUND (eds.), *Enemy of the Sun: Poetry of Palestinian Resistance* (Washington, DC, 1970).

ASFOUR, JOHN MIKHAIL, *When the Words Burn: An Anthology of Modern Arabic Poetry 1945–1987* (Ontario, 1988).

AL-ASMAR, FAUZI, *Poems from an Israeli Prison* (tr. Jawad Buraq *et al.*; New York, 1973).

AL-BAYATI, ABD AL-WAHAB, *Eye of the Sun* (tr. Desmond Stewart *et al.*; Copenhagen, 1978).
—— *Lilies and Death* (tr. Mohamed Alwan; Baghdad, 1972).
—— *Love under the Rain* (tr. Desmond Stewart and George Masri; Madrid, 1985).

BENNANI, B. (ed. and tr.), *Bread, Hashish and Moon: Four Modern Arab Poets* (Greensboro, NC, 1982).

BOULLATA, ISSA (ed. and tr.) *Modern Arab Poets 1950–1975* (Washington, DC, 1976).

BOULLATA, KAMAL (ed.), *Women of the Fertile Crescent: Modern Poetry by Arab Women* (Washington, DC, 1978).

DARWISH, MAHMUD (Darwish, Mahmoud), *A Lover from Palestine and Other Poems* (ed. and tr. A. W. Elmessiri; Washington, 1970).
—— *The Music of Human Flesh* (tr. Denis Johnson-Davies; London, 1974).
—— *Sand and Other Poems* (tr. Rana Kabbani; London, 1986).
—— *Selected Poems* (tr. Ian Wedde and Fawwaz Tuqan; Cheshire, 1973).
—— *Splinters of Bone* (tr. B. M. Bennani; New York, 1974).

ELMESSIRI, A. W. (ed. and tr.), *The Palestinian Wedding* (Washington, DC, 1982).

ENANI, M. M., *An Anthology of New Arabic Poetry* (Cairo, 1986).

HAWI, KHALIL, *Naked in Exile, the Threshing Floors of Hunger* (tr. Adman Haydar and Michael Beard; Washington, DC, 1984).

AL-HAYDARI, BULAND, *Songs of the Tired Guard* (tr. Abdullah al-Udhari; London, 1977).

JAYYUSI, SALMA KHADRA (ed.), *Modern Arabic Poetry: An Anthology* (New York, 1987).

KHOURI, MOUNAH, and ALGAR, HAMID (eds.), *An Anthology of Modern Arabic Poetry* (Berkeley, Calif., 1975).

LU'LU'A, ABDUL-WAHID (tr.), *Modern Iraqi Poetry* (Baghdad, 1989).

MEGALLY, SHAFIK (tr.), *Arabic Poetry of Resistance: An Anthology* (Cairo, 1970).

NORIN, I., and TARABAY, F. (eds.), *Anthologie de la littérature Arabe contemporaine: La Poésie* (Paris, 1967).

AL-UDHARI, ABDULLAH (tr.), *A Mirror for Autumn: Modern Arab Poetry* (London, 1974).
—— (ed. and tr.), *Modern Poetry of the Arab World* (Harmondsworth, 1986).
—— *Victims of a Map* (London, 1984).

4. *The Novel and the Short Story*

(A) STUDIES

ABDEL MEGUID, ABDEL AZIZ, *The Modern Arabic Short Story* (Cairo, 1955).
ALLEN, ROGER, *The Arabic Novel: An Historical and Critical Introduction* (Syracuse, NY, 1982).
—— Hadith ʿIsa ibn Hisham, *Al-Muwaylihi's Study of Egypt During the British Occupation* (New York, 1974).
AMYUNI, MONA TAQIEDDINE (ed.), *Tayeb Salih's Season of Migration to the North: A Casebook* (Beirut, 1985).
AWAD, HANAN, *Arab Causes in the Fiction of Ghadah al-Samman* (Quebec, 1983).
BARAKAT, HALIM, *Visions of Social Reality in the Contemporary Arab Novel* (Georgetown, Va., 1977).
BEYERL, JAN, *The Style of the Modern Arabic Short Story* (Prague, 1971).
COOKE, MIRIAM, *The Anatomy of an Egyptian Intellectual: Yahya Haqqi* (Washington, DC, 1984).
EL-KHADEM, SAAD, *History of the Egyptian Novel: Its Rise and Early Beginnings* (New Brunswick, NJ, 1985).
FONTAINE, JEAN, *Mort-Resurrection: une lecture de Tawfiq al-Hakim* (Tunis, 1978).
FRANCIS, RAYMOND, *Taha Hussein Romancier* (Cairo, n.d.).
GHAZI, FERID, *Le Roman et la nouvelle en Tunisie* (Tunis, 1970).
HAFEZ, SABRY, 'The Modern Arabic Short Story' in M. M. Badawi (ed.), *The Cambridge History of Arabic Literature:, Modern Arabic Literature* (Cambridge, 1992).
—— and COBHAM, CATHERINE (eds.), *A Reader in Modern Arabic Short Stories* (London, 1988).
JAD, A. B., *Form and Technique in the Egyptian Novel: 1912–1971* (London, 1983).
KILPATRICK, HILARY, *The Modern Egyptian Novel: A Study in Social Criticism* (London, 1974).
KURPERSHOEK, P. M., *The Short Stories of Yusuf Idris* (Leiden, 1981).
MALTI-DOUGLAS, FEDWA, *Blindness and Autobiography: Al-Ayyām of Ṭāhā Husayn* (Princeton, NJ, 1988).

MOUSSA-MAHMOUD, FATMA, *The Arabic Novel in Egypt 1914–1970* (Cairo, 1973).

PELED, MATTITYAHU, *Religion, My Own—the Literary Works of Najīb Maḥfūẓ* (New Brunswick, NJ, 1983).

SAKKUT, HAMDY, *The Egyptian Novel and its Main Trends 1913–1952* (Cairo, 1971).

SHAHEEN, MUHAMMAD, *The Modern Arabic Short Story* (London, 1989).

SHERIF, NUR, *About Arabic Books* (Beirut, 1970).

SIDDIQ, MUHAMMAD, *Man is a Cause: Political Consciousness and the Fiction of Ghassan Kanafani* (Washington, DC, 1984).

SOMEKH, SASSON, *The Changing Rhythm—A Study of Najib Mahfuz's Novels* (Leiden, 1973).

STARKEY, PAUL, *From the Ivory Tower: A Critical Study of Tawfiq al-Hakim* (London, 1987).

TOMICHE, NADA, *Histoire de la littérature romanesque de l'Egypte moderne* (Paris, 1981).

VIDAL, CHARLES, *Le Personnage de la femme dans le roman et la nouvelle en Egypte de 1914 à 1960* (Damascus, 1979).

WILD, STEFAN, *Ghassan Kanafani: The Life of a Palestinian* (Wiesbaden, 1975).

(B) TRANSLATIONS

ABD AL-QUDDUS, IHSAN, *Le Voleur d'autobus et autres nouvelles* (tr. A. Mazouni; Algiers, 1970).

ABDULLAH, YAHYA TAHER, *The Mountain of Green Tea* (tr. Denys Johnson-Davies; London, 1984).

AQQAD, ABBAS MAHMUD (El Akkad, Abbas Mahmoud), *Sara* (tr. M. M. Badawi; Cairo, 1978).

ASLAN, IBRAHIM, *Evening Lake* (Cairo, 1990).

AWWAD, TAWFIQ YUSUF, *Death in Beirut* (tr. Leslie McLoughlin; London, 1976).

AZRAK, MICHEL G, and YOUNG, M. J. L., *Modern Syrian Short Stories* (Washington, DC, 1988).

BAʿALBAKI, LAYLA (Baalbaki, Laila), *Je vis* (tr. M. Barbot; Paris, 1958).

BARAKAT, HALIM, *Days of Dust* (tr. Trevor Le Gassick; Washington, DC, 1983).

—— *Six Days* (tr. Bassam Frangieh and Scott McGehee; Washington, DC, 1991).

EBEID, R. Y., and YOUNG, M. J. L., *Arab Stories—East and West* (Leeds, 1974).

EL-GABALAWI, SAAD, *Modern Egyptian Short Stories* (New Brunswick, NJ, 1977).

—— *Three Pioneering Egyptian Novels* (New Brunswick, NJ, 1986).

GHANIM, FATHI (Ghanem, Fathy), *The Man who Lost his Shadow* (tr. Desmond Stewart; London, 1966).

AL-GHITANI, JAMAL (al-Ghitani, Gamal), *Incidents in Zafrani Alley* (tr. Peter O'Daniel; Cairo, 1988).

—— *Zayni Barakat* (tr. Farouk Abdel Wahab; London, 1988).

HABIBY, EMILE, *The Secret Life of Saeed, the Ill-Fated Pessoptimist* (tr. S. K. Jayyusi and Trevor Le Gassick; New York, 1982).

AL-HAKIM, TAWFIQ (Hakim, Tewfik), *Bird of the East* (tr. R. Bayly Winder; Beirut, 1966).

—— *The Maze of Justice* (tr. A. S. Eban; London, 1947).

—— *Return of the Spirit* (tr. William Hutchins; Washington, DC, 1985).

HAQQI, YAHYA, *Un égyptien à Paris* (tr. A. Abul Naga; Algiers, 1973).

—— *Good Morning and Other Stories* (tr. Miriam Cooke; Washington, DC, 1987).

—— *The Saint's Lamp and Other Stories* (tr. M. M. Badawi; Leiden, 1973).

HUSAYN, MUHAMMAD KAMIL (Hussein, Kamil), *City of Wrong* (tr. K. Cragg; Amsterdam, 1959).

HUSAYN, TAHA (Hussein, Taha), *An Egyptian Childhood: The Autobiography of Taha Hussein* (vol. i of *al-Ayyām*; tr. E. H. Paxton; London, 1932, repr. 1981).

—— *The Stream of Days* (vol. ii of *al-Ayyām; tr.* Hilary Wayment; Cairo, 1943).

—— *A Passage to France*, (vol. iii of *al-Ayyām; tr. Kenneth Cragg; Leiden, 1976).*

—— *Adīb, ou l'aventure occidentale* (tr. A. and M. Taha Hussein; Cairo, 1960).

—— *L'Arbre de la misère* (tr. Gaston Wiet; Cairo, 1946).

—— *The Call of the Curlew* (tr. A. B. al-Safi, Leiden, 1980).

—— *The Dreams of Scheherezade* (tr. Magdi Wahba; Cairo, 1974).

HUTCHINS, W. M., *Egyptian Short Stories* (Cairo, 1986).

—— *Tales and Short Stories of the 1970s and 1980s* (Cairo, 1986).

IBRAHIM, JAMIL ATIYYA (Ibrahim, Gamil Atia), *Down to the Sea* (tr. Frances Liardet; London, 1991).

IBRAHIM, SUNALLAH (Ibrahim, Sonallah), *The Smell of It and Other Stories* (tr. D. Johnson-Davies; London, 1971).

IDRIS, YUSUF, *The Cheapest Nights and Other Stories* (tr. Wadida Wassef; London, 1978).

—— *In the Eye of the Beholder* (ed. Roger Allen; Minneapolis, 1978).

—— *Rings of Burnished Brass* (tr. Catherine Cobham; London, 1984).

—— *The Sinners* (tr. Kristin Peterson Ishak; Washington, DC, 1984).

JABRA, JABRA IBRAHIM, *The Ship* (tr. Adnan Haydar and Roger Allen; Washington, DC, 1985).

JIBRAN, JIBRAN KHALIL (Gibran, Kahlil), *The Broken Wings* (tr. A. R. Ferris; London, 1959).

—— *An Introduction to Kahlil Gibran* (ed. and sel. by Suheil B. Bushrui; Beirut, 1970).
—— *The Life of Gibran Khalil Gibran and His Procession* (ed. and tr. with a biographical sketch by J. Kheirallah; New York, 1958).
—— *Nymphs of the Valley* (tr. H. M. Nahmad; London, 1948, repr. London, 1972).
—— *The Parables of Kahlil Gibran* (tr. A. S. Otto; New York, 1963).
—— *Prose Poems* (tr. A. Ghareeb; London, 1964).
—— *Secrets of the Heart* (tr. A. R. Ferris; London, 1960).
—— *A Self Portrait* (tr. A. R. Ferris; New York, 1960).
—— *Spirits Rebellious* (tr. A. R. Ferris, New York; 1946).
—— *A Tear and a Smile* (tr. H. M. Nahmad; London, 1950, repr. 1972).
—— *Tears and Laughter* (tr. A. R. Ferris; New York, 1946).
—— *Thoughts and Meditations* (tr. A. R. Ferris; London, 1966).
—— *A Treasury of Kahlil Gibran,* (tr. A. R. Ferris; 2 vols.; New York, 1951).
—— *A Treasury of Kahlil Gibran,* (ed. M. L. Wolf, tr. A. R. Ferris; London, 1974).
—— *A Voice of the Master* (tr. A. R. Ferris; London, 1960, repr. 1973).
[The above list clearly does not include the works he wrote in English.]
JOHNSON-DAVIES, DENYS, *Arabic Short Stories* (London, 1983).
—— *Egyptian Short Stories* (London, 1978).
—— *Modern Arabic Short Stories* (Oxford, 1967).
KANAFANI, GHASSAN, *Men in the Sun* (tr. Hilary Kilpatrick; Washington, DC, 1978).
—— *Palestine's Children* (tr. Barbara Harlow; Washington, DC, 1985).
KASSEM, CEZA, and HASHEM, MALAK (eds.), *Flights of Fantasy* [Arabic short stories], (Cairo, 1985).
KHALIFA, SAHAR, *Wild Thorns* (tr. T. Le Gassick and Elizabeth Fernea; London, 1985).
AL-KHARRAT, EDWAR, *City of Saffron* (tr. Frances Liardet; London, 1989).
KHURI, ILYAS (Khoury, Elias), *Little Mountain* (tr. Maia Tabet; London, 1990).
LASHIN, MAHMUD Tahir, *Eve Without Adam* (in S. El-Gabalawi, *Three Pioneering Novels, see* above).
MAHFUZ, NAJIB (Mahfouz, Naguib), *Autumn Quail*, (tr. Roger Allen; New York, 1991).
—— *The Beggar* (tr. Kristin Walker Henry and Nariman Khales Naili al-Warraki; New York, 1991).
—— *The Beginning and the End* (tr. Ramses Awad; New York, 1989).
—— *Children of Gebelawi* (tr. Philip Stewart; London, 1981).
—— *The Day the Leader was Killed* (tr. Malak Hashem; Cairo, 1989).

MAHFUZ, NAJIB, *Fountain and Tomb* (tr. Soad Sobhy, Essam Fattouh, and James Kenneson; Washington, DC, 1988).
—— *God's World* [short stories], (tr. Akef Abadir and Roger Allen; Minneapolis, 1973).
—— *Midaq Alley* (tr. Trevor Le Gassick; London, 1981).
—— *Miramar* (tr. Fatma Moussa-Mahmoud; London, 1978).
—— *Mirrors* (tr. Roger Allen; Minneapolis, 1977).
—— *Palace Walk* (vol. i of the trilogy *al-Thulathiyya*; tr. William M. Hutchins and Olive E. Kenny; New York, 1990).
—— *Palace of Desire* (vol. ii of the trilogy *al-Thulathiyya*; tr. William M. Hutchins, Lorna M. Kenny, and Olive E. Kenny; New York, 1991).
—— *Sukkariah* (vol. iii of the trilogy *al-Thulathiyya*; tr. Angele Botros Samaan; forthcoming).
—— *Respected Sir*, (tr. Rasheed El-Enany; London, 1986).
—— *The Search* (tr. Mohamed Islam; Cairo, 1987).
—— *The Thief and the Dogs* (tr. M. M. Badawi and Trevor Le Gassick; New York, 1989).
—— *Wedding Song* (tr. Olive E. Kenny; New York, 1989).
MAHMUD, MUSTAFA (Mahmoud, Moustafa), *L'Impossible* (tr. Laila Enan; Cairo, 1965).
—— *The Rising from the Coffin* (tr. D. Bishai; Cairo, 1967).
MAKARIUS, R., and MAKARIUS, L. (eds.), *Anthologie de la littérature arabe moderne: le roman et la nouvelle* (Paris, 1964).
MANZALAOUI, MAHMOUD (ed.), *Arabic Writing Today—The Short Story* (Cairo, 1968).
AL-MAZINI, IRAHIM ʿABD AL-QADIR, *Al-Mazini's Egypt* [two novels and one short story], (tr. W. M. Hutchins; Washington, DC, 1983).
—— *Ibrahim the Writer* (tr. Magdi Wahba; Cairo, 1976).
MONTEIL, VINCENT, *Anthologie bilingue de la littérature arabe contemporaine* (Beirut, 1961).
MUNIF, ʿABD AL-RAHMAN (Abdelrahman), *Cities of Salt* (tr. Peter Theroux; London, 1988).
—— *Endings* (tr. Roger Allen; London, 1988).
MUSA, SABRI (Moussa), *The Incident* (tr. Hoda Ayyad; Cairo, 1987).
—— *Seeds of Corruption* (tr. Mona Mikhail; Boston, 1980).
MUWAYLIHI, MUHAMMAD *Hadith ʿIsa ibn Hisham* (tr. Roger Allen as *Al-Muwaylihi's Study of Egypt During the British Occupation* (*see* above)).
NUʿAYMA, MIKHA'IL, *The Memoirs of a Vagrant Soul or the Pitted Face* (New York, 1952).
—— *A New Year* (tr. J. R. Perry; Leiden, 1974).
AL-QAʿID, YUSUF (al-Qaid, Yusuf), *News from the Meneissi Farm* (tr. Marie-Thérèse Abdel-Messih; Cairo, 1987).
—— *War in the Land of Egypt* (tr. Olive O. Kenny and Christopher Tingley; London, 1986).

QASIM, ABD AL-HAKIM, *The Seven Days of Man* (Cairo, 1987).
RIFAAT, ALIFA *Distant View of a Minaret and Other Stories* (tr. D. Johnson-Davies; London, 1983).
AL-SAʿDAWI, NAWAL (El-Saadawi), *Death of an Ex-Minister* (tr. Shirley Eber; London, 1987).
—— *Ferdaous: une voix en enfer* (tr. Assia Trabelsi and Assia Djebar; Paris, 1982).
—— *God Dies by the Nile* (tr. Sherif Hetata; London, 1985).
—— *The Hidden Face of Eve* (tr. Sherif Hetata; London, 1980).
—— *Memoirs From the Women's Prison* (tr. Marilyn Booth; London, 1986).
—— *Two Women in One* (tr. Osman Nusairi and Jana Gough; London, 1985).
—— *Woman at Point Zero* (tr. Sherif Hetata; London, 1983).
SALIH, AL-TAYYIB (Salih, Tayeb), *Season of Migration to the North* (tr. Denys Johnson-Davies; London, 1969).
—— *The Wedding of Zein and Other Stories* (tr. Denys Johnson-Davies; London, 1968).
SHARQAWI, ʿABD AL-RAHMAN (Sharkawi, Abdul Rahman), *Egyptian Earth* (tr. D. Stewart; London, 1962).
SHARUNI, YUSUF, *Blood Feud* (tr. D. Johnson-Davies; London, 1987).
SIBAʿI, YUSUF, *The Cobbler and Other Stories* (Cairo, 1973).
TAMIR, ZAKARIYYA, *Tigers on the Tenth Day and Other Stories* (tr. Denys Johnson-Davies; London, 1985).
TAYMUR, MAHMUD, *The Call of the Unknown* (tr. H. Horan; Beirut, 1964).
—— *Nouvelles* (tr. Antoinette Tewfik; Cairo, 1975).
—— *Tales From Egyptian Life* (tr. Denys Johnson-Davies; Cairo, 1949).
TUBIYA, MAJID (Tobiya, Majid), *Nine Short Stories* (tr. Nadia Gohar; Cairo, 1988).

5. *Drama*

(A) STUDIES

ABDEL WAHAB, FAROUK (ed.), *Modern Egyptian Drama: An Anthology* (Minneapolis, 1974). [includes a long, informative introduction.]
ABUL NAGA, ATIA, *Les Sources françaises du théâtre égyptien (1870–1939)* (Algiers, 1972).
ANBAR, MOHAMED ʿABD AL-HAMID, *Le Théâtre en République Arabe Unie* (Cairo, 1969).
AZIZA, MOHAMED, *Regards sur le théâtre arabe contemporain* (Tunis, 1970).
BADAWI, M. M., *Early Arabic Drama* (Cambridge, 1988).
—— *Modern Arabic Drama in Egypt* (Cambridge, 1987).

BEN HALIMA, HAMADI, *Les Principaux Thèmes du théâtre arabe contemporain 1914–1960* (Tunis, 1969).

FONTAINE, JEAN, *Mort-Resurrection: une lecture de Tawfiq al-Hakim* (Tunis, 1973).

GENDZIER, IRENE L., *The Practical Visions of Ya ʿqub Sanuʿ* (Cambridge, Mass., 1966).

ISMAIL, ABD EL MONEM, *Drama and Society in Contemporary Egypt* (Cairo, 1967).

AL-KHOZAI, MOHAMED A., *The Development of Early Arabic Drama (1847–1900)* (London, 1984).

LANDAU, JACOB M., *Studies in the Arab Theater and Cinema* (Philadelphia, 1958).

LONG, RICHARD, *Tawfiq al-Hakim, Playwright of Egypt* (London, 1979).

MAZALAOUI, MAHMOUD (ed.), *Arabic Writing Today: The Drama* (Cairo, 1977). [Contains a long, critical introduction and a useful bibliography.]

MOOSA, MATTI, *The Origins of Modern Arabic Fiction* (Washington, DC, 1983).

REID, D. M., *The Odyssey of Faraḥ Anṭūn* (Minneapolis, 1975).

SALAMÉ, GHASSANE, *Le Théâtre politique en Liban (1968–1973)* (Beirut, 1974).

SOMEKH, SASSON, *Two Versions of Dialogue in Mahmud Taymur's Drama* (Princeton, NJ, 1975).

STARKEY, PAUL, *From the Ivory Tower: A Critical Study of Tawfīq al-Ḥakīm* (London, 1987)

TOMICHE, NADA, *Histoire de la littérature romanesque de l'Egypte moderne* (Paris, 1981).

—— *Le Théâtre arabe* (Paris, 1969)

(B) TRANSLATIONS

ABD AL-SABUR, SALAH. *A Journey at Night* (tr. Samar Attar; Cairo, 1970).

—— *Murder in Baghdad* (tr. Khalil I. Semaan; Leiden, 1972).

—— *Night Traveller: A Black Comedy* (tr. M. M. Enani; Cairo, 1980).

—— *Now the King is Dead* (tr. Nehad Selaiha; Cairo, 1986).

—— *The Princess Waits* (tr. Shafik Megally; Cairo, 1975).

ABDEL WAHAB, FAROUK, *Modern Egyptian Drama* (Minneapolis, 1974). [Contains: Tawfiq (Tewfik) al-Hakim, *The Sultan's Dilemma*; Mikhail Ruman (Roman), *The New Arrival*; Rashad Rushdi, *A Journey Outside the Wall*; Yusuf Idris, *The Farfours*.]

FARAJ, ALFRID (Farag, Alfred), *The Caravan* (tr. Rasheed El-Enani; Cairo, 1988).

AL-HAKIM, TAWFIQ (al-Hakim, Tewfik), *A Conversation with the Planet*

Earth, The World is a Comedy (tr. Riad Habib Yousef; Cairo, 1985).
—— *Fate of a Cockroach: Four Plays of Freedom* (tr. Denys Johnson-Davies; London, 1973). [Contains: *The Fate of a Cockroach, The Song of Death, The Sultan's Dilemma*, and *Not a Thing Out of Place.*]
—— *Isis* (tr. Edouard Gemayel; Cairo, 1975).
—— *Muhammad* (tr. I. H. El-Mougy; Cairo, 1964).
—— *Plays, Prefaces and Postscripts of Tawfīq al-Ḥakīm, i. Theater of the Mind* (tr. W. Hutchins; Washington, DC, 1981). [Contains: *The Wisdom of Solomon, King Oedipus, Shahrazad, Princess Sunshine*, and *Angel's Prayer.*]
—— *Plays, Prefaces and Postcripts of Tawfīq al-Hakīm, ii. Theater of Society* (tr. W. Hutchins; Washington, DC, 1984). [Contains: *Between War and Peace, Tender Hands, Food for the Millions, Poet on the Moon*, and *Voyage to Tomorrow.*]
—— *Schéhérazade* (tr. M. A. Khédry and M. Brin; Paris, 1936).
—— *Théâtre Arabe* (tr. M. A. Khédry and others; Paris, 1950). [Contains: *La caverne des songes, Schéhérazade, Salomon le sage, Oedipe roi, Pygmalion, Le Fleuve de folie, La Maison des fourmis, Le Metteur en scène, Le Joueur de flûte*, and *L'Art de mourir.*]
—— *Théâtre multicolore* (Paris, 1954). [Contains: *Madame politique, Satan en danger, Le Problème du pouvoir, Volte-Face, Je veux tuer, Un nid tranquille, Sorcière, Le Trésor, Le Chant de la mort, L'Heure a sonné*, and *Quand j'étais vieux.*]
—— *Théâtre de notre temps* (Paris, 1960). [Contains: *Demain, Mort ou amour*, and *j'ai choisi.*]
—— *The Tree Climber* (tr. D. Johnson-Davies; Oxford, 1966).
JOHNSON-DAVIES, DENYS, *Egyptian One-Act Plays* (London, 1981). [Contains: Farid Kamil, *The Interrogation*; Alfred Faraj (Alfred Farag), *The Trap*; ʿAbd al-Munʿim Salīm (Abdel Moneim Selim), *Marital Bliss*; ʿAlī Sālim (Salem), *The Wheat Well*; Tawfiq (Tewfik) al-Hakim, *The Donkey Market.*]
MAHFUZ, NAJIB (Mahfouz, Naguib), *One-Act Plays* (tr. Nehad Seleiha; Cairo, 1989). [Contains: *The Legacy, The Rescue, The Mountain*, and *Death and Resurrection.*]
MANZALAOUI, MAHMOUD (ed.), *Arabic Writing Today—The Drama* (Cairo, 1977). [Contains: Mahmoud Taymur, *The Court Rules* (tr. Medhat Shaheen); Tawfiq al-Hakim, *The Sultan's Dilemma* (tr. M. M. Badawi) and *Song of Death* (tr. M. M. Badawi); Mahmud Diyab, *The Storm* (tr. Wadida Wassef); Shawqi Abd al-Hakim, *Hassan and Naima* (tr. Medhat Shaheen); Yusuf Idris, *Flip-Flap and His Master* (tr. Trevor Le Gassick); Faruq Khurshid; *The Wines of Babylon* (tr. Wadida Wassef); Mikhail Ruman, *The Newcomer* (tr. Medhat Shaheen); Muhammad al-Maghut, *The Hunchback Sparrow* (tr. Mahmoud Manzalaoui).]
SALMAWY, MUHAMMAD, *Come Back Tomorrow and Other Plays* (tr. William Hutchins; Washington, DC, 1984).

SARHAN, SAMIR, *The Lady on the Throne* (tr. Mona Mikhail; Cairo, 1989).

SHAWQI, AHMAD, *Majnun Layla* (tr. A. J. Arbury; Cairo, 1932).

WAHBA, SA'D AL-DIN (Wahba, Sa'ad el-Din), *Mosquito Bridge* (tr. Charlotte Shabrawi; Cairo, 1987).

WOODMAN, DAVID, *Egyptian One-Act Plays* (Cairo, 1974). [Does not contain any work by a major writer.]

INDEX